AF477127

Multiphase Flows in Microfluidics: Fundamentals and Applications

Multiphase Flows in Microfluidics: Fundamentals and Applications

Editor

Jianzhong Lin

MDPI • Basel • Beijing • Wuhan • Barcelona • Belgrade • Manchester • Tokyo • Cluj • Tianjin

Editor
Jianzhong Lin
Ningbo University
Ningbo, China

Editorial Office
MDPI
St. Alban-Anlage 66
4052 Basel, Switzerland

This is a reprint of articles from the Special Issue published online in the open access journal *Applied Sciences* (ISSN 2076-3417) (available at: https://www.mdpi.com/journal/applsci/special_issues/Multiphase_Flows_Microfluidics).

For citation purposes, cite each article independently as indicated on the article page online and as indicated below:

LastName, A.A.; LastName, B.B.; LastName, C.C. Article Title. *Journal Name* **Year**, *Volume Number*, Page Range.

ISBN 978-3-0365-8334-1 (Hbk)
ISBN 978-3-0365-8335-8 (PDF)

Contents

About the Editor

Jianzhong Lin

Jianzhong Lin (PhD Science) is a professor in the Faculty of Mechanical Engineering & Mechanics, Ningbo University. He received his PhD degree from the Peking University in 1991. His scientific interests are multiphase fluid flows, nanofluids, micro fluid dynamics, turbulence and fluid machinery. His work has been funded by more than 40 research projects, including the National Natural Science Fund for Distinguished Young Scientists, and the Key Project of the National Science Foundation of China. To date, he has published more than 760 academic papers and won more than ten science and technology awards. He was the Associate Editor of *International Journal of Multiphase Flow*, and is currently serving as the Chief Editor of *Mechanics in Engineering*, Associate Editor of *Applied Mathematics and Mechanics*, Associate Editor of the *Journal of Drainage and Irrigation Machinery Engineering*, and Editorial Board Member of more than ten academic journals. He is now the member of the council of the Chinese society of mechanics.

 *applied sciences*

Editorial

Special Issue on Multiphase Flows in Microfluidics: Fundamentals and Applications

Jianzhong Lin [1,2]

1   Zhejiang Provincial Engineering Research Center for the Safety of Pressure Vessel and Pipeline, Ningbo University, Ningbo 315211, China; mecjzlin@public.zju.edu.cn
2   State Key Laboratory of Fluid Power Transmission and Control, Zhejiang University, Hangzhou 310027, China

Citation: Lin, J. Special Issue on Multiphase Flows in Microfluidics: Fundamentals and Applications. *Appl. Sci.* **2023**, *13*, 5907. https://doi.org/10.3390/app13105907

Received: 20 April 2023
Accepted: 6 May 2023
Published: 11 May 2023

1. Introduction

Microfluidics, a cutting-edge field involving various applications in advanced materials, new energy, single-cell/single-molecule studies, human health, biomedicine, and so forth, has advanced rapidly in the last two decades. Among the applications of microfluidics, multiphase flow is the fundamental element in various microfluidic subjects, such as those concerning emulsions, droplets, bubbles, micromixers/reactors, and microswimmers/robots. For example, microfluidic technology changes the motion of particles through varying the channel area of the diversion form, particle inertia, hydrophilicity, gravity characteristics, deterministic lateral displacement, viscoelastic separation, and zeta potential [1]. Controlling particle motion, the radial position, and the spacing between particles make them easier to capture, focus on, select, and separate, e.g., through cell separation and capture, bacterial selection, and DNA separation and focusing, to meet the needs of studies and fields such as biomedicine.

On the other hand, microfluidics (adding nanoparticles to the fluid) has been widely used to enhance heat transfer [2]. The impact of particle size, concentration, shape, and distribution on enhanced heat transfer has always been a research focus. When the particle size, concentration, and shape are fixed, the optimal distribution of particles can be obtained through controlled methods in order to achieve a better heat transfer effect. For instance, the magnetic particles in the fluid will form a chain-like structure under the action of a high-intensity magnetic field, which can enhance heat transfer. When the volume concentration of particles is 6.3%, the maximum enhancement value of thermal conductivity can be 300% [3]. Since multiphase flow in microfluidics is vital and common, it is necessary to research it.

2. Foundation and Application of Multiphase Flow in Microfluidics

In light of the above, this Special Issue aims to collect the latest original research and reviews on the fundamentals and applications of any functional multiphase flow in microfluidics. There were 24 papers submitted to this Special Issue, and 15 papers were accepted. They address numerous topics, mainly on the motion characteristics of particles with different scales and shapes.

The particles of multiphase flow in microfluidics are usually of a nanometer scale. Multiple papers in this Special Issue involve fundamentals and applications of nanofluids or nanoparticles in fluids. Li et al. [4] reviewed the heat transfer enhancement of nanofluids with non-spherical nanoparticles by dividing the particles into three categories according to the dimension of geometric particle structure. They evaluated the shape effect of particles on the thermal conductivity and convective heat transfer based on the measured data, and pointed out that no perfect model for predicting the thermal conductivity and convective heat transfer of nanofluids with non-spherical nanoparticles had been reported. Tu et al. [5] studied the effect of background particles on the nucleation of nanoparticles by solving the Reynolds-averaged Navier–Stokes equation with the Taylor-series expansion method of moments. They found that the nucleation of nanoparticles was inhibited with increasing background particle concentration by considering the effect of binary homogeneous nucleation, Brownian coagulation, condensation, and thermophoresis of nanoparticles. Lin et al. [6] numerically simulated the nanoparticle settlement and pressure drop in a gas-solid two-phase flow in a pipe by solving the momentum equation of the two-fluid model. They found that the pressure drop increased with increasing inlet velocity, particle volume concentration, and mass, but with decreasing particle diameter, and derived an expression of the settlement index and pressure drop as functions of inlet velocity, particle volume concentration, mass, and particle diameter based on the numerical data. Wang et al. [7] studied the collision rate of nanoparticle aggregations and aggregated structure with different particle volume fractions using the Langevin dynamics method, and showed that the self-preserving size distribution of particles broadened with increasing particle volume fraction; the radius of gyration was smaller with the same cluster size, i.e., the particle agglomerations were in a tighter coagulation when the particle volume fraction was higher. Yang et al. [8] explored experimentally the effects of tracer fluid flow velocity and porous medium permeability on the dispersion phenomenon using natural and sand-filled cores, respectively, and found that a higher volumetric flow rate and lower permeability caused a delay in the tracer breakthrough time and an increase in the dispersion coefficient; the combination of high velocity and low permeability yielded a large dispersion coefficient.

Most particles in the applications are non-spherical, and the transport and deposition of non-spherical particles are very complicated because particle rotation and orientation distribution are strongly coupled with the translation motion [9]. Some papers in this Special Issue are related to the motion characteristics of non-spherical particles. Lin et al. [10] numerically simulated the distribution and deposition of rod-like nanoparticles in a turbulent pipe flow by considering the Brownian and turbulent diffusion of nanoparticles. They showed that the penetration efficiency of particles decreased with increasing particle aspect ratio, Reynolds number, and pipe length-to-diameter ratio, and built a relationship between the penetration efficiency of particles and related synthetic parameters based on the numerical data. Kawaguchi et al. [11] studied the contribution of an elliptical particle flowing between parallel plates to the effective viscosity, focusing on the particle-wall distance and particle rotational motion, and found that the contribution of particle shape to the effective viscosity was enhanced when the particle flowed near the wall; the spatial variation of the local relative viscosity was larger than the temporal variation regardless of the aspect ratio and particle-wall distance. Wang et al. [12] numerically simulated the diffusion of non-spherical submicron particles in a converging–diverging micronozzle flow using the Euler–Lagrangian model, and showed how particle transportation with varying shape factors and densities resulted in different particle velocities, trajectories, and focusing; the particle with a larger shape factor or larger density exhibited a stronger aerodynamic focusing effect in a supersonic flow through the nozzle. Yang et al. [13] simulated the motion of rod-like particles in the turbulent contraction flow and indicated that the rod particles aligned with the streamline in the central region as the particle concentration increased, but tended to maintain the original orientation distribution in the boundary layer. Zhang et al. [14] studied the rising characteristics of shaped bubbles in near-wall static water using the volume of fluid method, and found that the wall surface and the distance between the bubble and the wall influenced the rising of the bubble; the effect of interaction between the bubbles was significantly greater than the effect of the wall surface.

There are also several papers on the motion of bi-disperse and self-driven particles, and the motion of particles in a non-Newtonian fluid. Chen et al. [15] numerically simulated the motion and distribution of bi-disperse particles in Poiseuille flow and showed that the particle spacing would increase and could not remain stable when the smaller particle was downstream; the particle spacing first increased and then decreased, and finally tended to be stable when the larger particle was downstream. Liu and Lin [16] reviewed multiphase flow with self-driven particles and focused on the interactions between self-propelled/self-rotary particles and passive particles, the aggregation, phase separation, and sedimentation of squirmers, the effect of rheological properties on its motion, and the kinematic characteristics of axisymmetric squirmers. Yang et al. [17] studied the trajectories and velocities of two side-by-side particles of different densities settling in a shear-thinning fluid with viscoelastic properties. They showed that the wake of the heavier particle could attract or rebound the light particle due to the shear-thinning or viscoelastic property of the fluid, and the sedimentation of the light particle could induce the distinguishable transverse migration of the heavy one.

There are also papers on specific engineering applications in the Special Issue. Yang et al. [18] proposed a three-phase foam (TPF) containing dispersed solid particles to improve foam stability under harsh reservoir conditions. They fabricated a novel TPF system, assessed the ability of the TPF to control steam channeling and enhance oil recovery, and observed a stronger foamability at a lower consolidation agent concentration. At the same time, there was a longer foam half-life period and solid particle settling time at a larger consolidation agent concentration. Lin et al. [19] studied the effect of velocity on particle behavior in membrane filtration. They gave the best working conditions to help suppress membrane pollution and indicated that particle deposition was weakest, resulting in better water productivity, when the inlet velocity was about 1 m/s.

3. Prospect

Although this Special Issue has been closed, more in-depth research on the multiphase flow in microfluidics is required. For example, more advanced computational fluid dynamics technology is expected to simulate micro flow and particle motion, more precise instruments and advanced experimental methods can be expected to test flow and capture particles, and more advanced manufacturing technology will improve microfluidic devices; as such, the technology of microfluidics is expected to be widely applied in more fields.

Funding: This work was supported by the National Natural Science Foundation of China (Grant No. 12132015).

Acknowledgments: Thanks are due to all the authors and reviewers for their valuable contributions to this Special Issue. Finally, I would like to express my gratitude to the editorial team of Applied Sciences.

Conflicts of Interest: The author declares no conflict of interest.

References

1. Wang, R.J.; Lin, J.Z.; Li, Z.H. Analysis of Electro-Osmotic Flow Characteristics at Joint of Capillaries with Step Change in Zeta-Potential and Dimension. *Biomed. Microdevices* **2005**, *7*, 131–135.
2. Bao, F.B.; Lin, J.Z. Burnett Simulation of Gas Flow and Heat Transfer in Nicro Poiseuille Flow. *Int. J. Heat Mass Transf.* **2008**, *51*, 4139–4144. [CrossRef]
3. Philip, J.; Shima, P.D.; Raj, B. Enhancement of Thermal Conductivity in Magnetite Based Nanofluid Due to Chainlike Structures. *Appl. Phys. Lett.* **2007**, *91*, 203108. [CrossRef]
4. Li, X.; Yuan, F.; Tian, W.; Dai, C.; Yang, X.; Wang, D.; Du, J.; Yu, W.; Yuan, H. Heat Transfer Enhancement of Nanofluids with Non-Spherical Nanoparticles: A Review. *Appl. Sci.* **2022**, *12*, 4767. [CrossRef]
5. Tu, C.; Liu, Y.; Wu, T.; Yu, M. Simulation of Aerosol Evolution within Background Pollution for Nucleated Vehicle Exhaust via TEMOM. *Appl. Sci.* **2021**, *11*, 4552. [CrossRef]
6. Lin, W.; Li, L.; Wang, Y. Pressure Drop and Particle Settlement of Gas–Solid Two-Phase Flow in a Pipe. *Appl. Sci.* **2022**, *12*, 1623. [CrossRef]
7. Wang, X.; Liu, Y.; Wu, T.; Yu, M. Polymerization and Collision in High Concentrations for Brownian Coagulation. *Appl. Sci.* **2021**, *11*, 6815. [CrossRef]
8. Yang, Y.; Liu, T.; Li, Y.; Li, Y.; You, Z.; Zuo, M.; Diwu, P.; Wang, R.; Zhang, X.; Liang, J. Effects of Velocity and Permeability on Tracer Dispersion in Porous Media. *Appl. Sci.* **2021**, *11*, 4411. [CrossRef]
9. Lin, J.Z.; Xia, Y.; Ku, X.K. Flow and Heat Transfer Characteristics of Nanofluids Containing Rod-like Particles in a Turbulent Pipe Flow. *Int. J. Heat Mass Transf.* **2016**, *93*, 57–66. [CrossRef]
10. Lin, W.; Shi, R.; Lin, J. Distribution and Deposition of Cylindrical Nanoparticles in a Turbulent Pipe Flow. *Appl. Sci.* **2021**, *11*, 962. [CrossRef]
11. Kawaguchi, M.; Fukui, T.; Morinishi, K. Contribution of Particle–Wall Distance and Rotational Motion of a Single Confined Elliptical Particle to the Effective Viscosity in Pressure-Driven Plane Poiseuille Flows. *Appl. Sci.* **2021**, *11*, 6727. [CrossRef]

12. Wang, Y.; Shen, J.; Yin, Z.; Bao, F. Numerical Simulation of Non-Spherical Submicron Particle Acceleration and Focusing in a Converging–Diverging Micronozzle. *Appl. Sci.* **2022**, *12*, 343. [CrossRef]
13. Yang, W.; Hu, P. Fibers Effects on Contract Turbulence Using a Coupling Euler Model. *Appl. Sci.* **2021**, *11*, 7126. [CrossRef]
14. Zhang, K.; Li, Y.; Chen, Q.; Lin, P. Numerical Study on the Rising Motion of Bubbles near the Wall. *Appl. Sci.* **2021**, *11*, 10918. [CrossRef]
15. Chen, D.; Lin, J.; Hu, X. Research on the Inertial Migration Characteristics of Bi-Disperse Particles in Channel Flow. *Appl. Sci.* **2021**, *11*, 8800. [CrossRef]
16. Liu, C.; Lin, J. A Review on the Some Issues of Multiphase Flow with Self-Driven Particles. *Appl. Sci.* **2021**, *11*, 7361. [CrossRef]
17. Yang, S.; Tu, C.; Dai, M.; Ge, X.; Xu, R.; Gao, X.; Bao, F. Sedimentation of Two Side-by-Side Heavy Particles of Different Density in a Shear-Thinning Fluid with Viscoelastic Properties. *Appl. Sci.* **2021**, *11*, 7113. [CrossRef]
18. Yang, Y.; Cheng, T.; You, Z.; Liang, T.; Hou, J. Profile Control Using Fly Ash Three-Phase Foam Assisted by Microspheres with an Adhesive Coating. *Appl. Sci.* **2021**, *11*, 3616. [CrossRef]
19. Lin, P.; Wang, Q.; Xu, X.; Zhu, Z.; Ding, Q.; Cai, B. Research on the Influence of Inlet Velocity on Micron Particles Aggregation during Membrane Filtration. *Appl. Sci.* **2022**, *12*, 7869. [CrossRef]

 *applied sciences*

Article

Distribution and Deposition of Cylindrical Nanoparticles in a Turbulent Pipe Flow

Wenqian Lin [1], Ruifang Shi [2] and Jianzhong Lin [2,*]

[1] School of Media and Design, Hangzhou Dianzi University, Hangzhou 310018, China; jiangnanshui253@126.com
[2] State Key Laboratory of Fluid Power Transmission and Control, Zhejiang University, Hangzhou 310027, China; yuquanhe20202@163.com
* Correspondence: mecjzlin@public.zju.edu.cn

Abstract: Distribution and deposition of cylindrical nanoparticles in a turbulent pipe flow are investigated numerically. The equations of turbulent flow including the effect of particles are solved together with the mean equations of the particle number density and the probability density function for particle orientation including the combined effect of Brownian and turbulent diffusion. The results show that the distribution of the particle concentration on the cross-section becomes non-uniform along the flow direction, and the non-uniformity is reduced with the increases of the particle aspect ratio and Reynolds number. More and more particles will align with their major axis near to the flow direction, and this phenomenon becomes more obvious with increasing the particle aspect ratio and with decreasing the Reynolds number. The particles in the near-wall region are aligned with the flow direction obviously, and only a slight preferential orientation is observed in the vicinity of pipe's center. The penetration efficiency of particle decreases with increasing the particle aspect ratio, Reynolds number and pipe length-to-diameter ratio. Finally, the relationship between the penetration efficiency of particle and related synthetic parameters is established based on the numerical data.

Keywords: cylindrical nanoparticles; distribution; deposition; turbulent pipe flow; numerical simulation

Citation: Lin, W.; Shi, R.; Lin, J. Distribution and Deposition of Cylindrical Nanoparticles in a Turbulent Pipe Flow. *Appl. Sci.* **2021**, *11*, 962. https://doi.org/10.3390/app11030962

Academic Editor: Artur Tyliszczak
Received: 6 January 2021
Accepted: 18 January 2021
Published: 21 January 2021

Publisher's Note: MDPI stays neutral with regard to jurisdictional clai-ms in published maps and institutio-nal affiliations.

1. Introduction

Transport of particles through pipes has the advantages of small space occupied, no backhaul, no pollution, flexible setting, long distance transport and so on. Therefore, the transport of particles has been widely used in various industries such as machinery manufacturing, metallurgy, power generation, material engineering, pharmaceutical and food production. The transport of particles is usually accompanied by the process of particle deposition upon the wall surface. It is crucial to reduce the particle deposition in order to improve the conveying efficiency of particles. The mechanism of nanoparticle deposition on a wall is complicated because it is related to the thermophoretic force [1], inertial force of particle, gravitational force [2], Brownian and turbulent diffusion [3].

In the past several decades the transport and deposition of particles in the pipe turbulent flow have been studied a lot for the spherical particles, but very few for non-spherical particles. Actually, the major amount of particles is non-spherical in shape, e.g., cylindrical particles. The transport and deposition of cylindrical particles are very complicated because particle rotation and its orientation distribution are strongly coupled with the translation motion [4]. Moreover, inhomogeneity in the spatial and orientational distribution of particles affects the turbulent flow properties. There are several published works in the literature discussing the transport and deposition of cylindrical particles. In the case of laminar flow with no turbulent diffusion, Guha [5] indicated that the deposition rate for the particles with an intermediate size was mainly dependent on the thermophoresis, turbophoresis and roughness. Tavakol et al. [6] developed a new model for predicting particle deposition and analyzed the impact of the particle aspect ratio on the deposition.

In the case of inertial cylindrical particle with no Brownian diffusion, Goldenberg et al. [7] measured the deposition velocity of particles with a diameter of 1–2 μm for different Reynolds numbers. They showed that the deposition velocity was mainly dependent on gravitation when Re ≤ 26,000, while dependent on the comprehensive effects of particle size, gravitation and turbulent fluctuations when Re > 26,000. Shapiro and Goldenberg [8] measured the deposition velocity of particles of 0.6–2.5 μm in diameter for different Reynolds numbers and particle aspect ratios, and found that the aspect ratios significantly affected the deposition velocity of particles. Podgorski et al. [9] studied the particle deposition from a gas stream. They found that the deposition rate of flexible particles was the lowest, while stiff particles had the highest deposition rate. Marchioli et al. [10] studied the dispersion and deposition of particles with considering the particle inertia and hydrodynamic forces. They found that particles tended to align with the flow direction near the wall, but such a state was unstable for particles with higher inertia. The deposition rate of particles with a larger aspect ratio was higher, but particle inertia had less effect on the particle deposition in the centerline. Tavakol et al. [11] showed that the deposition rate of particles was proportional to the particle aspect ratio, and the fluctuating velocity gradient had an insignificant effect on the deposition rate. Shachar-Berman et al. [12] indicated that oscillatory breathing had an important effect on the particle deposition in the lungs.

As is shown above, the transport and deposition of cylindrical particles are related to the inertial force of particle, gravitational force, thermophoretic force, Brownian diffusion and turbulent diffusion. For the transport of cylindrical nanoparticles in a turbulent flow with no temperature gradient, the deposition of a particle is mainly resulted from the Brownian and turbulent diffusion, while the thermophoretic force, inertial force of particle and gravitational force are negligible. However, there is a lack of study on the case of deposition of cylindrical nanoparticles under the combined effect of Brownian diffusion and turbulent diffusion. Such a case can be found in the transport of cylindrical nanoparticles at higher Reynolds number flows, for example, lung cancer caused by exposure to asbestos fibrous particles in inhalation toxicology. Besides, the deposition of cylindrical nanoparticles is related to the particle spatial and orientation distributions that affect the characteristics of the turbulent flow field, which has not been found in the literature. Besides, the existence of cylindrical particles would affect the turbulent flow. Lin et al. [13] derived the modified Reynolds averaged N–S equations and the probability distribution function for the mean orientation of cylindrical particles. Gillissen et al. [14] explored fiber-induced drag reduction using N–S equations supplemented with the fiber stress tensor. Lin et al. [15] solved numerically the Reynolds averaged N–S equations with the additional stress resulting from fibers in a contraction flow. Lin and Shen [16] developed a model by deriving the equations of modified Reynolds averaged N–S, turbulence kinetic energy and dissipation rate with additional terms of the fibers. In this study, therefore, the equations of mean momentum and turbulent kinetic energy and turbulent dissipation rate of fluid including the effect of cylindrical nanoparticles are solved numerically together with the mean equations of particle number density and the probability density function for particle orientation including the combined effect of Brownian diffusion and turbulent diffusion in a fully turbulent pipe flow at higher Reynolds numbers. Then the particle distributions on a cross-section and penetration efficiencies at outlet for different parameters are calculated. Based on the numerical data, the relationship between the penetration efficiency and related synthetic parameters is established.

2. Models and Equations

2.1. Flow Laden with Cylindrical Nanoparticles

In practical applications, there are many cases in which the fluid carries solid particles. At this time, to obtain the information of fluid flow and solid particle motion, it is necessary to establish the fluid equation containing solid particles. In the present study, the flow laden with cylindrical nanoparticles in a round pipe is shown in Figure 1. The flow is incompressible and fully developed turbulent. The modified Navier–Stokes with the additional term of cylindrical nanoparticles is:

$$\frac{\partial \overline{u}_i}{\partial t} + \overline{u}_j \frac{\partial \overline{u}_i}{\partial x_j} = -\frac{1}{\rho_m}\frac{\partial \overline{p}}{\partial x_i} + \frac{\mu}{\rho_m}\frac{\partial^2 \overline{u}_i}{\partial^2 x_j} - \frac{\partial \overline{u'_i u'_j}}{\partial x_j} + \frac{\mu_a}{\rho_m}\frac{\partial}{\partial x_j}[\overline{a}_{ijkl}\overline{\varepsilon}_{kl} - \frac{1}{3}(I_{ij}\overline{a}_{kl})\overline{\varepsilon}_{kl}] \tag{1}$$

in which $\overline{u}_i$ and $\overline{p}$ are the mean velocity and pressure, respectively; ρ_m is the mixing density (Equation (2)); μ is the fluid viscosity; $\overline{u'_i u'_j}$ is the Reynolds stress; additional viscosity μ_a is related to the particle concentration, aspect ratio and orientation distribution, and is given by extending Batchelor's theory to account for two-body interactions as shown in Equation (2) [17]; $\overline{\varepsilon}_{kl} = (\partial \overline{u}_k/\partial x_l + \partial \overline{u}_l/\partial x_k)/2$ is the mean rate-of-strain tensor and $\overline{a}_{kl}$ and $\overline{a}_{ijkl}$ are the mean second- and fourth-order tensors of particle orientation, respectively, as shown in Equation (3) [18]. The last term on the right hand side of Equation (1) represents the effect of cylindrical nanoparticles on the flow, and the cylindrical nanoparticles are non deformable.

$$\rho_m = (1 - \Phi)\rho + \Phi\rho_f; \ \mu_a = \frac{4\Phi\lambda^2\mu}{3\ln(1/\Phi)}\left\{1 - \frac{\ln[\ln(1/\Phi)]}{\ln(1/\Phi)} + \frac{0.6634}{\ln(1/\Phi)}\right\} \tag{2}$$

where ρ and ρ_f are the fluid and particle density, respectively; Φ is the particle volume fraction and λ is the particle aspect ratio.

$$\overline{a}_{ij} = \oint p_i p_j \overline{\psi(p)}\mathrm{d}p, \ \overline{a}_{ijkl} = \oint p_i p_j p_k p_l \overline{\psi(p)}\mathrm{d}p \tag{3}$$

where p is the particle orientation vector; p_i is the unit vector and $\overline{\psi(p)}$ is the mean probability density function for particle orientation.

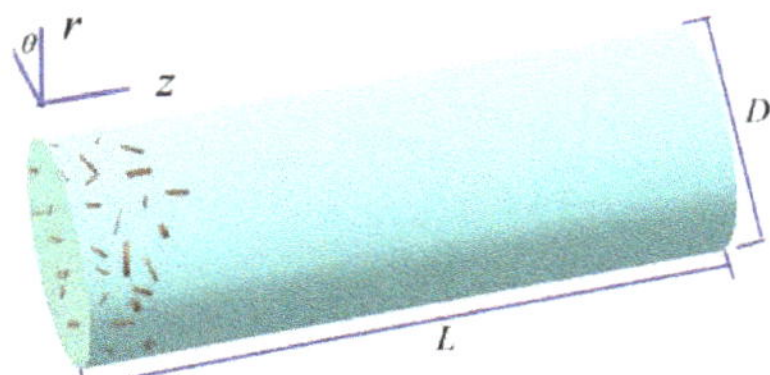

Figure 1. Flow laden with cylindrical particles in a pipe.

2.2. Reynolds Stress

The Reynolds stress in Equation (1) is given by:

$$-\rho_m \overline{u'_i u'_j} = 2\mu_T\left(\frac{\partial \overline{u}_i}{\partial x_j} + \frac{\partial \overline{u}_j}{\partial x_i}\right) - \frac{2}{3}\rho_m k\delta_{ij} \tag{4}$$

in which the eddy viscosity is $\mu_T = 0.09\,\rho_m\,k^2/\varepsilon$, where k and ε are the turbulent kinetic energy and dissipation rate, respectively.

In order to solve Equations (1) and (4), the equations of k and ε for turbulent flow with additional terms of cylindrical nanoparticles are given [16]:

$$\rho_m \overline{u}_j \frac{\partial k}{\partial x_j} = -\rho_m \overline{u'_i u'_j}\frac{\partial \overline{u}_i}{\partial x_j} - \rho_m\varepsilon + \frac{\partial}{\partial x_j}[(\mu_a + \mu_T)\frac{\partial k}{\partial x_j}] + \rho_m S_k \tag{5}$$

$$\rho_m \overline{u}_j \frac{\partial \varepsilon}{\partial x_j} = -1.44\frac{\varepsilon}{k}\rho_m \overline{u'_i u'_j}\frac{\partial \overline{u}_i}{\partial x_j} - 1.92\rho_m\frac{\varepsilon^2}{k} + \frac{\partial}{\partial x_j}[(\mu_a + \frac{\mu_T}{1.3})\frac{\partial \varepsilon}{\partial x_j}] + \rho_m S_\varepsilon \tag{6}$$

where S_k and S_ε are the contribution from the cylindrical nanoparticles.

2.3. Mean Probability Density Function for Orientation of Cylindrical Nanoparticles

The equation of probability density function $\psi(\boldsymbol{p})$ for the orientation of a cylindrical nanoparticle should be derived in advance in order to obtain the second- and fourth-order tensors of particle orientation in Equation (3). The equation of $\psi(\boldsymbol{p})$ is [19]:

$$\frac{d\psi}{dx_j} = D_{rB}\frac{\partial^2\psi}{\partial p_j^2} - \frac{\partial(\psi\Omega_j)}{\partial p_j}; \quad \Omega_j = -\omega_{ji}p_i + \eta\varepsilon_{ji}p_i - \eta\varepsilon_{kl}p_kp_lp_j - \frac{D_{rI}}{\psi}\frac{\partial\psi}{\partial p_j} \tag{7}$$

where $\partial/\partial p_j$ is the gradient operator projected onto the surface of the unit sphere; Ω_j is the angular velocity of particle; $\eta = (\lambda^2 - 1)/(\lambda^2 + 1)$; $\omega_{ij} = (\partial u_j/\partial x_i - \partial u_i/\partial x_j)/2$ is the vorticity tensor; D_{rI} is the rotary diffusion coefficient induced by the interaction between the particles [20] and D_{rB} is the Brownian rotary diffusion coefficient [21]:

$$D_{rB} = \frac{k_bT}{\sqrt{[3.84\pi\mu L_p^3(1+\frac{0.677}{\lambda}-\frac{0.183}{\lambda^2})/\lambda^2]^2+[\pi\mu L_p^3/3(\ln\lambda-0.662+\frac{0.917}{\lambda}-\frac{0.05}{\lambda^2})]^2}} \tag{8}$$

where T is the temperature; k_b is the Boltzmann constant and L_p is the particle length.

Averaging Equation (7) yields:

$$\frac{d\overline{\psi}}{dx_j} - D_{rB}\frac{\partial^2\overline{\psi}}{\partial p_j^2} - \overline{\omega}_{ji}p_i\frac{\partial\overline{\psi}}{\partial p_j} + \lambda\overline{\varepsilon}_{ji}p_i\frac{\partial\overline{\psi}}{\partial p_j} - \lambda\overline{\varepsilon}_{kl}p_kp_lp_j\frac{\partial\overline{\psi}}{\partial p_j} - \lambda\overline{\varepsilon}_{kl}\overline{\psi}p_kp_l - D_{rI}\frac{\partial^2\overline{\psi}}{\partial p_j^2} = \alpha_{\psi x}\frac{\partial^2\overline{\psi}}{\partial x_j^2} + \alpha_{\psi p}\frac{\partial^2\overline{\psi}}{\partial p_j^2} \tag{9}$$

where $\alpha_{\psi x} = 1.3(5\,k^2\mu/3\varepsilon\rho_m)^{1/2}$ and $\alpha_{\psi p} = 0.7(4\,\varepsilon\rho_m/15\,\mu)^{1/2}$ [22] are the particle dispersion coefficients of linear and angular displacement, respectively.

2.4. Volume Fraction Φ of Cylindrical Nanoparticles

In the past research, the particle volume fraction Φ in Equation (2) is usually assumed to be a constant and in a uniform distribution. In fact the distribution of Φ is non-uniform because of particle convection and diffusion. Therefore, in order to obtain the volume fraction Φ of cylindrical nanoparticles in Equation (2), the equation of the mean number density $\overline{n}$ for cylindrical nanoparticles should be solved. Considering the effect of convection and diffusion, the mean equation of mean number density $\overline{n}$ for cylindrical nanoparticles is [23]:

$$\frac{\partial\overline{n}(v)}{\partial t} + \overline{u}_j\frac{\partial\overline{n}(v)}{\partial x_j} - \frac{\partial}{\partial x_j}[(D_{tB} + v_t)\frac{\partial\overline{n}(v)}{\partial x_j}] = 0 \tag{10}$$

where v is the volume of particle; $v_t = 0.09\,k^2/\varepsilon$ is the turbulent diffusion coefficient and D_{tB} is the Brownian translational diffusion coefficient [21]:

$$D_{tB} = \frac{k_bT}{\sqrt{[2\pi\mu L_p/(\ln\lambda - 0.207 + \frac{0.980}{\lambda} - \frac{0.133}{\lambda^2})]^2 + [4\pi\mu L_p/(\ln\lambda + 0.839 + \frac{0.185}{\lambda} + \frac{0.233}{\lambda^2})]^2}} \tag{11}$$

$\overline{n}(v)$ can be transformed into the particle number N and volume V:

$$\int_0^\infty \overline{n}(v)dv = N, \quad \int_0^\infty v\overline{n}(v)dv = V \tag{12}$$

Then Φ can be calculated based on V.

2.5. Penetration Efficiency

Penetration efficiency (PE) of cylindrical nanoparticles though a pipe is inversely proportional to the deposition rate and can be defined as:

$$\text{PE} = \frac{V_{\text{out}}}{V_{\text{in}}} = \frac{V_{\text{in}} - V_{de}}{V_{\text{in}}} \tag{13}$$

in which V_{out} and V_{in} are the particle volume at the outlet and inlet of the pipe, respectively and V_{de} is the particle volume of deposition to the wall:

$$V_{de} = \sum_j A_j (D_{tB} + \nu_t) \left.\frac{\partial V}{\partial r}\right|_{\text{wall}, j} \tag{14}$$

where A_j is the area of the jth wall cell.

3. Numerical Method and Main Steps of Simulation

(1) Equations (1), (2), (4)–(6) with $\Phi = \mu_a = S_k = S_\varepsilon = 0$ are solved to get $\overline{u}_j$, k, ε and $\overline{u'_i u'_j}$.
(2) Equations (10)–(12) are solved to get $\overline{n}(v)$ and Φ.
(3) Substitute Φ into Equation (2) to get ρ_m and μ_a.
(4) Substitute $\overline{u}_j$, k, ε and Equation (8) into Equation (9) and solve it to get $\overline{\psi}$.
(5) Substitute $\overline{\psi}$ into Equation (3) to get $\overline{a}_{ij}$ and $\overline{a}_{ijkl}$.
(6) Substitute ρ_m, μ_a, $\overline{a}_{ij}$ and $\overline{a}_{ijkl}$ into Equations (1), (4)–(6) to get $\overline{u}_j$, k, ε and $\overline{u'_i u'_j}$.
(7) Turn to step (2) based on the new values of $\overline{u}_j$, k, ε and $\overline{u'_i u'_j}$ if necessary.
(8) Calculate the particle volume V with Equation (12).
(9) Calculate the deposited particle volume V_{de} with Equation (14) and penetration efficiency PE with Equation (13).

The equations in this paper are all partial differential equations and must be solved numerically. Equations (1), (4)–(6) and (10) are solved using the finite difference method. Equation (3) is integrated with the Simpson formula. The grid system consists of $70(r) \times 30(\theta) \times 240(z) = 504{,}000$ grid points. A grid independence test is performed by changing grid points from 60 to 80 in radial direction, 25 to 35 in circumferential and 230 to 250 in axial direction, respectively. The parameters used in the computation are: $\rho = 1.205\ \text{kg/m}^3$, $\mu = 1.808 \times 10^{-5}\ \text{Pa·s}$, $T = 293\ \text{K}$ and $k_b = 1.38 \times 10^{-23}\ \text{J/K}$.

4. Validation

In order to prove the validity of the model and numerical scheme, we compared the present numerical results of mean orientation of cylindrical particles with the experimental ones [24] in a turbulent pipe flow as shown in Figure 2 where ϕ is the angle between the particle axis and pipe's axis, and P is the probability. We also compared the penetration efficiency as a function of particle diameter as shown in Figure 3 where both numerical and experimental results [25] are given. In Figures 2 and 3, the parameters used in the numerical simulation were consistent with the experimental situation. The present numerical results could be seen to be qualitatively consistent with the experimental ones.

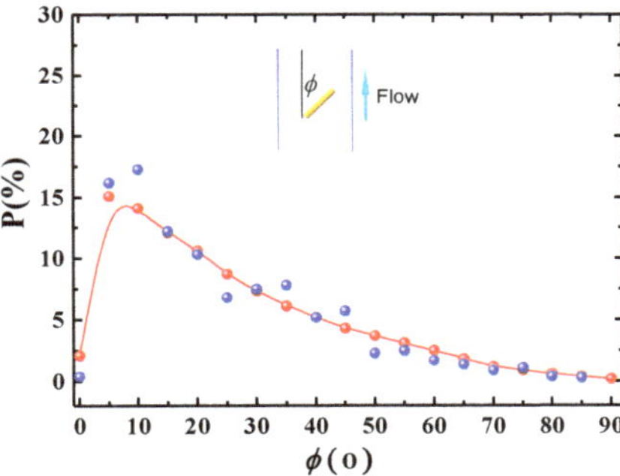

Figure 2. Probability distribution of mean cylindrical particle orientation ($\lambda = 8$, Re = 10,000). •: numerical results and •: experimental results [24].

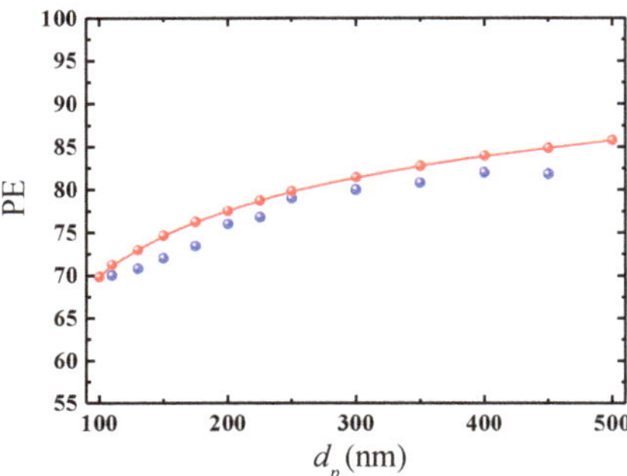

Figure 3. Penetration efficiency as a function of particle diameter ($\lambda = 1$, Re = 5120, $L/D = 375$). •: numerical results and •: experimental results [25].

5. Results and Discussion

In the following figures, only particle distributions on the half cross-section are shown because the distributions are symmetric about the centerline of the pipe.

5.1. Distribution of Particle Volume Concentration and Orientation at Different Axial Positions

When the particles enter the tube, the particles show different distributions of the concentration and orientation at different axial positions with the development of time. The distributions of particle concentration and orientation can be obtained by solving Equations (10) and (7). The distributions of particle volume concentration on the cross-section at different axial positions are shown in Figure 4a. The uniform distribution of volume concentration on the cross-section at inlet becomes non-uniform along the flow direction because the distribution of particle number density is affected by the shear-induced force caused by the mean shear rate of the fluid, Brownian diffusion and turbulent diffusion as shown in Equations (10) and (12). The non-uniformity becomes obvious with the increase in the axial distance from the inlet. The particle volume concentration first decreased and then increased from the pipe center to the wall, and there was a minimum around $r/R = 0.95$. As we know, Brownian diffusion makes particles move from a high concentration area to a low concentration one, resulting in a more uniform distribution of the particle volume concentration. So, it can be deduced that the non-uniform distributions of particle volume concentration were caused by the shear-induced force and turbulent diffusion. The particles in the region around $r/R \approx 0.95$ were subjected to the influence of larger shear-induced force and stronger turbulent diffusion because the mean shear rate and the turbulent diffusion coefficient v_t were large ($v_t = 0.09\, k^2/\varepsilon$, while turbulent kinetic energy k is large there), hence were diffused to the region near the centerline and the region close proximity to the wall where the turbulent diffusion diminished to zero and particles accumulated in the viscous sublayer with low fluid velocity.

The distributions of the mean orientation of a cylindrical nanoparticle at different axial positions are shown in Figure 4b where the mean orientation angle ϕ was obtained by averaging the orientation angles on the cross-section at a fixed axial position. The particles with uniform distribution of mean orientation angle on the cross-section at inlet will change their orientation angles along the flow direction. The distributions of orientation angle become non-uniform, more and more particles aligned with their major axis near to the flow direction. As shown in Equations (13)–(15), the mean probability density function for particle orientation was affected by the Brownian diffusion, turbulent diffusion and the shear-induced force, and the former two made the distribution of particle orientation become more uniform. The shear-induced force resulted from the mean shear rate of the fluid and the overall effect can be decomposed in two torques, one making a particle rotate around the vorticity axis (i.e., axis θ as shown in Figure 1), and another causing a particle spin around the flow direction, i.e., particles tended to align according to the mean shear of the flow. The particles flowing through the pipe were always subjected to the influence of the mean shear of the flow, so align with the flow direction.

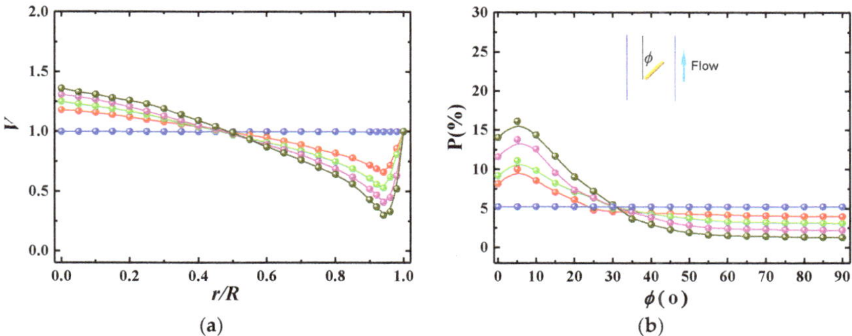

Figure 4. Distribution of (**a**) particle concentration and (**b**) particle orientation at different axial positions ($\lambda = 8$, Re = 20,000, $L/D = 200$). •: $z/D = 0$; •: $z/D = 50$; •: $z/D = 100$; •: $z/D = 150$; •: $z/D = 200$.

5.2. Distribution of Particle Number Concentration and Orientation at Outlet

5.2.1. Distribution of Particle Orientation

Distributions of mean particle orientation in different regions on the cross-section at outlet are shown in Figure 5 where the cross-section was divided into five regions and the mean particle orientation angle ϕ in different regions were obtained by averaging the orientation angles in the regions. We can see that more particles aligned with the flow direction by the interplay between the shear-induced force, Brownian diffusion and turbulent diffusion. The particles in the near-wall region were aligned with the flow direction obviously because the highest mean shear rate and even the largest shear-induced force appeared in the near-wall region, and only a slight preferential orientation was observed in the vicinity of pipe's center where the mean shear rate was low. So, it can be concluded that the mean shear rate of the fluid was dominant for affecting the orientation distribution of particles comparing with the Brownian diffusion and turbulent diffusion under the parameters involved in the paper.

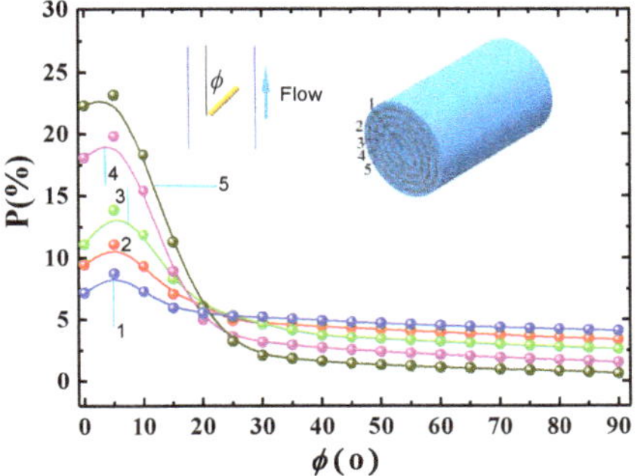

Figure 5. Distribution of mean particle orientation in different regions on the cross-section at outlet ($\lambda = 8$, Re = 20,000, $L/D = 200$). •: region 1; •: 2; •: 3; •: 4; •: 5.

5.2.2. Effect of the Particle Aspect Ratio

Figure 6 shows the distributions of particle volume concentration on the cross-section at the outlet for different particle aspect ratios. It can be seen that the distributions of particle volume concentration become more uniform with increasing the particle aspect ratio. The reason can be analyzed as follows. The evolution of particle number density

$\bar{n}(v)$ as shown in Equations (10) and (11) is determined by the mean shear rate of the fluid, Brownian translational diffusion coefficient D_{tB} and turbulent diffusion coefficient v_t. The existence of particles in the flow has an effect on the turbulent kinetic energy, which increases as the particle aspect ratio increases [16] because the particles with larger aspect ratio can make a stronger momentum transfer with providing a solid link between the adjacent fluid layers. In return, the increase of turbulent kinetic energy can promote particle diffusion. Besides, as shown in Equation (11), the Brownian diffusion coefficient D_{tB} is proportional to the particle aspect ratio, i.e., the particles are subjected to a larger Brownian diffusion when the aspect ratio is larger. Therefore, the larger the particle aspect ratio is, the stronger the Brownian diffusion and turbulent diffusion are, and the more uniform the distribution of particle volume concentration is.

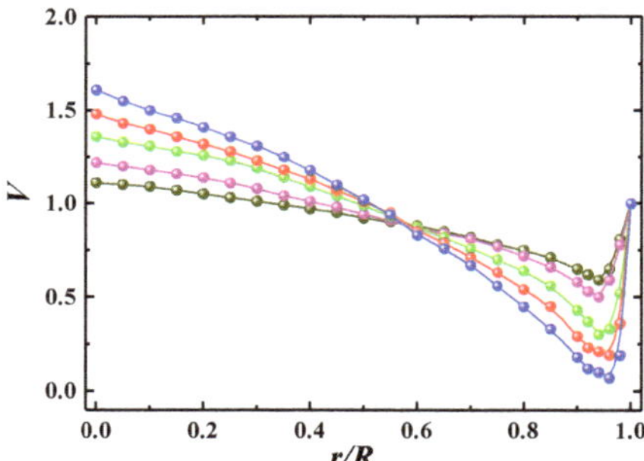

Figure 6. Distribution of particle volume concentration for different aspect ratio at outlet (Re = 20,000, L/D = 200). •: λ = 2; •: λ = 4; •: λ = 8; •: λ = 12; •: λ = 16.

Figure 7 shows the distributions of mean particle orientation in region 1 and 5 at outlet for different particle aspect ratios. The particles tended to align with the flow direction, and this preferential orientation is more obvious in the near-wall region and with increasing the particle aspect ratio. The mean probability density function for particle orientation is determined by the Brownian diffusion, turbulent diffusion and mean shear rate of the fluid. Firstly, the Brownian diffusion coefficient was inversely proportional to the particle aspect ratio as shown in Equation (8), so the distribution of mean particle orientation was more non-uniform for the case of a larger aspect ratio. Secondly, the turbulent dispersion coefficient $\alpha_{\psi p} = 0.7(4\varepsilon\rho_{nf}/15\mu)^{1/2}$ of angular displacement was proportional to the turbulent dissipation rate ε, which increased with increasing the particle aspect ratio [16], so the distribution of mean particle orientation was more uniform for the case of a larger aspect ratio. Thirdly, the shear-induced torque exerted on the particle was larger for the case with larger aspect ratio, which caused the particle to spin around the flow direction more effectively. The comprehensive effect of the above factors makes more particles aligned with the flow direction. As shown in Figure 7b, the difference in the distributions of mean particle orientation between the cases with a different aspect ratio was small for the large aspect ratio, which was consistent with the conclusion [26] that the orientation distribution was not sensitive to the aspect ratio for the inertial particles with an aspect ratio larger than 5.

5.2.3. Effect of the Reynolds Number

The distributions of the particle volume concentration on the cross-section for different Reynolds numbers are shown in Figure 8 where the concentration distributions become more uniform with increasing the Reynolds number, i.e., the larger the Reynolds number is, the smaller the difference in particle volume concentration between the near-wall region and near-center region is. The turbulent flow is characterized by some parameters among which the most important is the Reynolds number. As the Reynolds number increased, even though the mean velocity profile on the whole cross-section and the turbulent kinetic energy in the near-center region were almost unchanged [16], the turbulent kinetic energy and induced turbulent diffusion ($\nu_t = 0.09\,k^2/\varepsilon$) in the region around $r/R \approx 0.95$ increased obviously [16], resulting in a stronger particle diffusion and making the concentration distributions become more uniform.

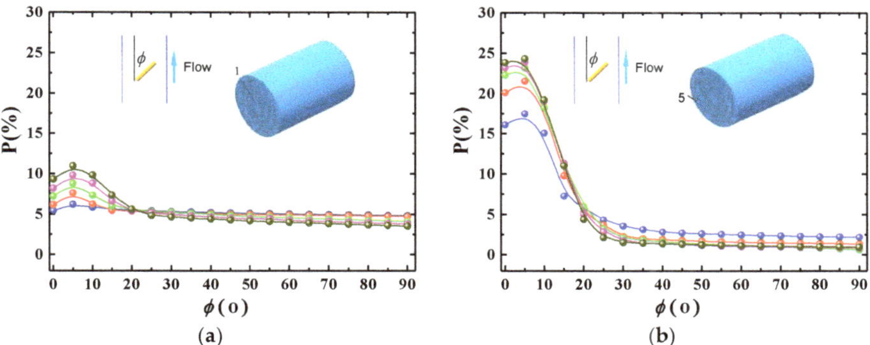

Figure 7. Distribution of mean particle orientation in region 1 and 5 for different particle aspect ratio (Re = 20,000, *L/D* = 200). (**a**) Region 1 and (**b**) region 5. •: $\lambda = 2$; •: $\lambda = 4$; •: $\lambda = 8$; •: $\lambda = 12$; •: $\lambda = 16$.

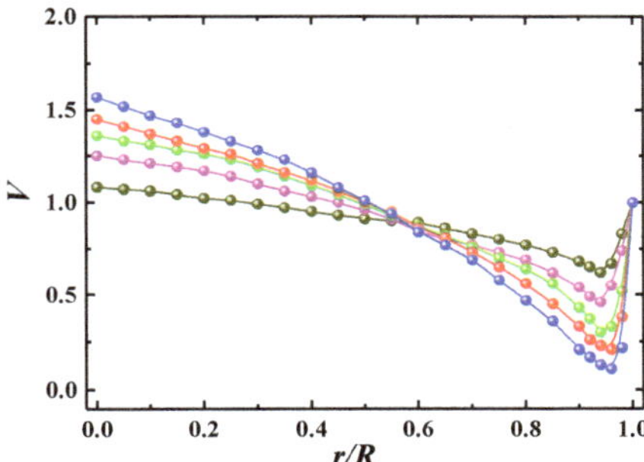

Figure 8. Distribution of particle concentration for different Reynolds numbers at outlet ($\lambda = 8$, *L/D* = 200). •: Re = 5000; •: Re = 10,000; •: Re = 20,000; •: Re = 30,000; •: Re = 40,000.

Figure 9 shows the distributions of mean particle orientation in region 1 and 5 at the outlet for different Reynolds numbers. As the Reynolds number decreased, the distributions of mean particle orientation become more non-uniform, i.e., more particles aligned with the flow direction. As we know, the larger the Reynolds number, the smaller the scale of minimum vortex, the wider the distribution of energy spectrum contained in the vortices of different scales, and less the energy contained in the large vortex related to the mean shear rate of the fluid are. Therefore, the shear-induced torque exerted on the particle by the mean shear rate of the fluid was smaller for the case with larger Reynolds number, resulting in not so many particles aligning with the flow direction.

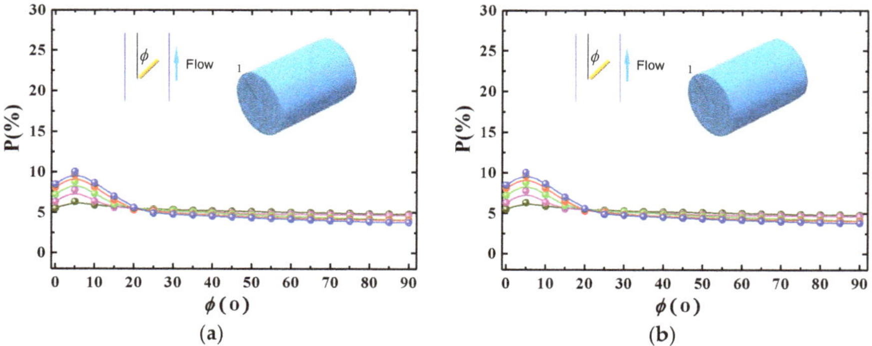

Figure 9. Distribution of mean particle orientation in region 1 and 5 for different Reynolds numbers ($\lambda = 8$, $L/D = 200$). (**a**) Region 1 and (**b**) region 5. •: Re = 5000; •: Re = 10,000; •: Re = 20,000; •: Re = 30,000; •: Re = 40,000.

5.3. Penetration Efficiency

The penetration efficiency is inversely proportional to the particle deposition velocity. In normal circumstances, the particle deposition velocity is mainly affected by the gravitational force, inertial force of particle, Brownian diffusion, turbulent diffusion and particle shape. In this paper, the gravitational force, and nanoparticles' inertial forces were negligible. The particles follow the fluid motion, which includes the mean motion and turbulence fluctuation, and the particles near the wall deposit on the wall due to Brownian diffusion and turbulent diffusion, resulting in the reduction of particle penetration efficiency. Therefore, the effects of Brownian diffusion, turbulent diffusion and particle shape on the deposition velocity and penetration efficiency should be explored. For the cylindrical nanoparticles, the shape was reflected by the aspect ratio.

In order to compare the numerical results of penetration efficiency with experimental ones, we calculated the penetration efficiency of cylindrical nanoparticles with aspect ratio $\lambda = 1$ and compared with the experimental result of spherical particles [27] as shown in Figure 10 where Sch is the Schmidt number and PE is the penetration efficiency. The experiment was performed in a tube of 1 m length and 4.8 mm inner diameter, and WOx particles with diameters from 3 to 17 nm were used. It can be seen that the penetration efficiency of particles with $\lambda = 1$ was lower than that of spherical particles, which indicates that the effect of particle shape was significant even for the aspect ratio close to unity.

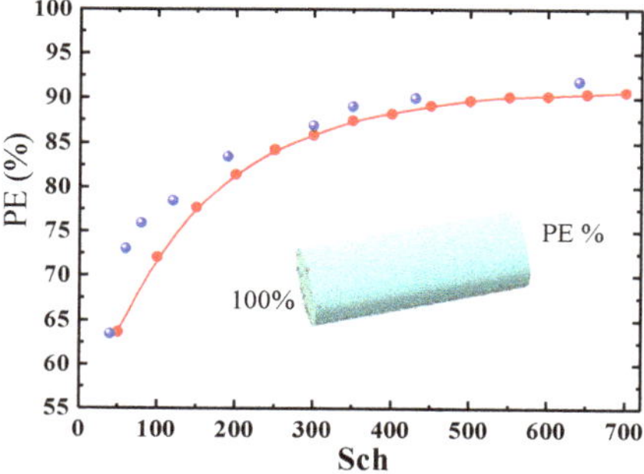

Figure 10. Penetration efficiency as a function of Sch (Re = 10,500, $L/D = 208$). •: numerical results (cylindrical particle, $\lambda = 1$) and •: experimental result (spherical particle) [27].

5.3.1. Effect of the Particle Aspect Ratio

The relationships between the penetration efficiency and the Reynolds number for different particle aspect ratios are shown in Figure 11 where the competitive effects of

Brownian diffusion, turbulent diffusion and particle aspect ratio upon the penetration efficiency are exhibited. It can be seen that the penetration efficiency was affected by the particles' shape, i.e., aspect ratio, the penetration efficiency decreased with increasing the particle aspect ratio. Firstly, the particle volume concentration in the near-wall region increased with increasing the particle aspect ratio as shown in Figure 6, which provides the condition for more particle deposition. Secondly, there was a viscous sublayer close to the wall where the particle Brownian diffusion plays a major role for the deposition velocity. As shown in Equation (11), the Brownian diffusion was proportional to the particle aspect ratio, i.e., the particles with large aspect ratio were subjected to a stronger Brownian diffusion and possessed a large deposition velocity, resulting in a low penetration efficiency. The result given above was consistent with the conclusion that longer particles tended to deposit at higher rates in the case of inertial particle with no Brownian diffusion [10], and high deposition efficiency corresponded to the spherical particles and even higher deposition efficiency for the stiff particles [9].

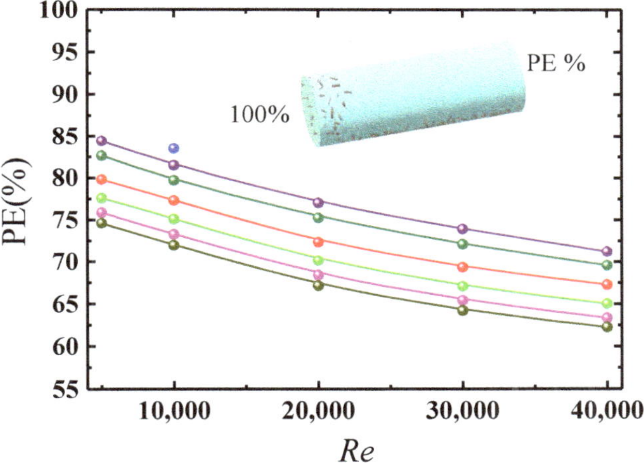

Figure 11. Penetration efficiency as a function of Re for different aspect ratios (*L/D* = 200). •:λ = 1; •: λ = 2; •: λ = 4; •: λ = 8;•: λ = 12;•: λ = 16; •: experimental result (spherical particle) [27].

5.3.2. Effect of the Particle Aspect Ratio

Figure 11 also shows that the penetration efficiency decreased as the Reynolds number increased, i.e., more particles deposited on the wall in the case with larger Reynolds number. As shown in Figure 8, the particle volume concentration in the viscous sublayer close to the wall increased with increasing the Reynolds number because the stronger turbulent diffusion associated with higher Reynolds number made more particles diffuse to the viscous sublayer, providing the condition for more particle deposition.

5.3.3. Effect of Pipe Length-to-Diameter Ratio

Figure 12 shows the penetration efficiency as a function of the pipe length-to-diameter ratio. It can be seen that the penetration efficiency decreased with increasing the pipe length-to-diameter ratio because the longer pipe was associated with the longer residence time of particles in the pipe. The longer residence time corresponded to a larger probability that particles will deposit on the wall with lower penetration efficiency.

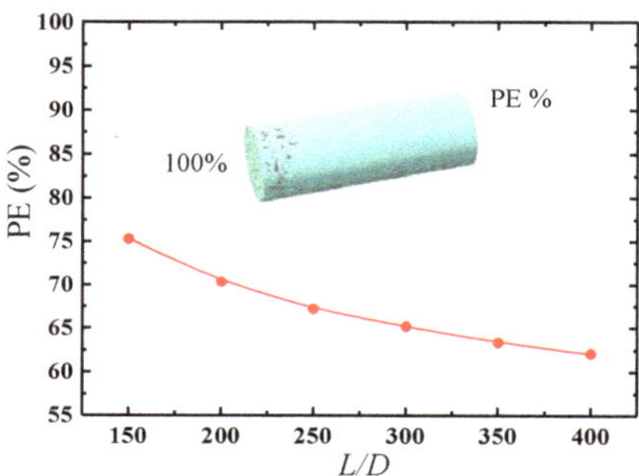

Figure 12. Penetration efficiency as a function of pipe length-to-diameter ratio (Re = 20,000, λ = 8).

5.3.4. Relationship of Penetration Efficiency and Related Parameters

It is necessary to build a relationship between the penetration efficiency and related parameters in order to effectively characterize the penetration efficiency. As shown in Figures 11 and 12, the penetration efficiency was inversely proportional to the particle aspect ratio λ, the ratio of pipe length to pipe diameter L/D and the Reynolds number ($Re = Q/vD$, where Q is the flow rate, v is the fluid viscosity and D is the pipe diameter). So, we combine λ, L/D and Re into a dimensionless synthetic parameter $\eta = D \times 10^9/\lambda LRe$. Based on the above numerical data, we could establish the following expression of penetration efficiency PE:

$$PE = 67.34105 + 4.43965 \ln(\eta - 2.65815) \tag{15}$$

Figure 13 shows the penetration efficiency as a function of the related synthetic parameter.

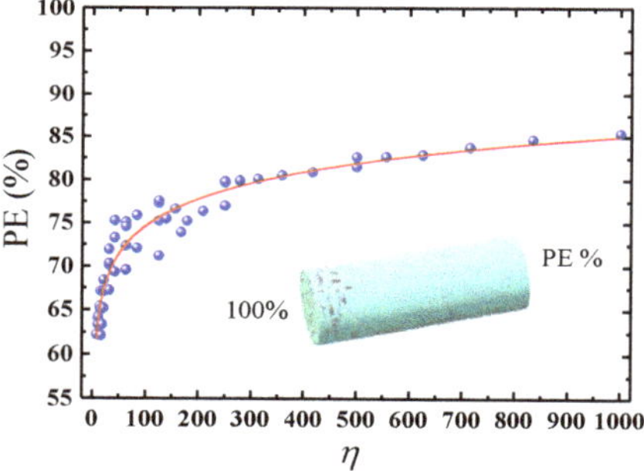

Figure 13. Penetration efficiency as a function of related synthetic parameter. •: numerical data and —: expression (15).

6. Conclusions

Transport and deposition of cylindrical nanoparticles in a turbulent pipe flow were studied. The equations of mean momentum and turbulent kinetic energy and turbulent dissipation rate of fluid including the effect of particles were solved together with the mean equations of particle number density and the probability density function for particle orientation including the combined effect of Brownian diffusion and turbulent diffusion. Distributions of particle volume concentration and particle orientation on the cross-section at different axial positions were given and analyzed. The penetration efficiencies for different parameters were calculated and discussed. The main conclusions were summarized as follows:

Distribution of the particle volume concentration on the cross-section becomes non-uniform along the flow direction. The particle volume concentration first decreased and then increased from the pipe center to the wall, and there was a minimum around $r/R \approx 0.95$.

The particles with uniform distribution of mean orientation angle on the cross-section at inlet will change their orientation angles along the flow direction. The distributions of orientation angle became non-uniform and more and more particles aligned with their major axis near to the flow direction. The particles in the near-wall region were aligned with the flow direction obviously, and only a slight preferential orientation was observed in the vicinity of the pipe's center.

Distribution of particle volume concentrations becomes more uniform on the cross-section with increasing the particle aspect ratio and Reynolds number. The particles tend to align in the flow direction and this phenomenon becomes more obvious with the increasing particle aspect ratio and with decreasing Reynolds number. The particle orientation distribution is not sensitive to the aspect ratio for the particles with an aspect ratio larger than 5.

The penetration efficiency of cylindrical particles decreased with an increasing particle aspect ratio, Reynolds number and pipe length-to-diameter ratio. Finally, the relationship between the penetration efficiency and related synthetic parameters was established based on the numerical data.

Author Contributions: Conceptualization, J.L. and W.L.; methodology, W.L. and R.S.; software, W.L. and R.S.; validation, R.S. and W.L.; writing, W.L. and R.S.; resources, W.L. and J.L.; review, J.L. All authors have read and agreed to the published version of the manuscript.

Funding: This work was supported by the National Natural Science Foundation of China (Grant no. 91852102).

Institutional Review Board Statement: Not applicable.

Informed Consent Statement: Not applicable.

Conflicts of Interest: There are no conflicts of interest regarding the publication of this paper.

References

1. Akshat, T.M.; Misra, S.; Gudiyawar, M.Y.; Salacova, J.; Petru, M. Effect of electrospun nano-particle deposition on ther-mo-physiology of functional clothing. *Part. Polym.* **2019**, *20*, 991–1002.
2. Tian, L.; Ahmadi, G.; Wang, Z.C.; Hopke, P.K. Transport and deposition of ellipsoidal particles in low Reynolds number flows. *J. Aerosol Sci.* **2012**, *45*, 1–18. [CrossRef]
3. Tu, C.; Yin, Z.; Lin, J.; Bao, F. A Review of Experimental Techniques for Measuring Micro- to Nano-Particle-Laden Gas Flows. *Appl. Sci.* **2017**, *7*, 120. [CrossRef]
4. Luo, Y.; Wu, T.-H.; Qi, D. Lattice-Boltzmann lattice-spring simulations of flexibility and inertial effects on deformation and cruising reversal of self-propelled flexible swimming bodies. *Comput. Fluids* **2017**, *155*, 89–102. [CrossRef]
5. Guha, A. A unified Eulerian theory of turbulent deposition to smooth and rough surfaces. *J. Aerosol Sci.* **1997**, *28*, 1517–1537. [CrossRef]
6. Tavakol, M.; Abouali, O.; Yaghoubi, M.; Ahmadi, G. Dispersion and deposition of ellipsoidal particles in a fully developed laminar pipe flow using non-creeping formulations for hydrodynamic forces and torques. *Int. J. Multiph. Flow* **2015**, *75*, 54–67. [CrossRef]
7. Goldenberg, M.; Gallily, I.; Shapiro, M. Deposition of nonspherical particles in turbulent air flows. *J. Aerosol Sci.* **1990**, *21*, S105–S108. [CrossRef]
8. Shapiro, M.; Goldenberg, M. Deposition of glass-particle particles from turbulent air-flow in a pipe. *J. Aerosol Sci.* **1993**, *2*, 65–87. [CrossRef]
9. Podgórski, A.; Gradoń, L.; Grzybowski, P. Theoretical study on deposition of flexible and stiff fibrous aerosol particles on a cylindrical collector. *Chem. Eng. J. Biochem. Eng. J.* **1995**, *58*, 109–121. [CrossRef]
10. Pitton, E.; Marchioli, C.; Lavezzo, V.; Soldati, A.; Toschi, F. Anisotropy in pair dispersion of inertial particles in turbulent channel flow. *Phys. Fluids* **2012**, *24*, 073305. [CrossRef]
11. Tavakol, M.M.; Abouali, O.; Yaghoubi, M.; Ahmadi, G. Stochastic dispersion of ellipsoidal particles in various turbulent fields. *J. Aerosol Sci.* **2015**, *80*, 27–44. [CrossRef]
12. Shachar-Berman, L.; Ostrovski, Y.; De Rosis, A.; Kassinos, S.; Sznitman, J. Transport of ellipsoid particles in oscillatory shear flows: Implications for aerosol deposition in deep airways. *Eur. J. Pharm. Sci.* **2018**, *113*, 145–151. [CrossRef] [PubMed]
13. Lin, J.Z.; Gao, Z.Y.; Zhou, K.; Chan, T.L. Mathematical modeling of turbulent fiber suspension and successive iteration solu-tion in the channel flow. *Appl. Math. Modeling* **2006**, *30*, 1010–1020. [CrossRef]
14. Gillissen, J.J.J.; Boersma, B.J.; Mortensen, P.H. On the performance of the moment approximation for the numerical com-putation of fiber stress in turbulent channel flow. *Phys. Fluids* **2007**, *19*, 035102. [CrossRef]

15. Lin, J.; Zhang, S.; Olson, J.A. Effect of fibers on the flow property of turbulent fiber suspensions in a contraction. *Fibers Polym.* **2007**, *8*, 60–65. [CrossRef]
16. Lin, J.; Shen, S. A theoretical model of turbulent fiber suspension and its application to the channel flow. *Sci. China Ser. G Phys. Mech. Astron.* **2010**, *53*, 1659–1670. [CrossRef]
17. Mackaplow, M.B.; Shaqfeh, E.S.G. A numerical study of the rheological properties of suspensions of rigid, non-Brownian fibres. *J. Fluid Mech.* **1996**, *329*, 155. [CrossRef]
18. Advani, S.G.; Tucker, C.L. The use of tensors to describe and predict particle orientation in short particle composites. *J. Rheol.* **1987**, *31*, 751–784. [CrossRef]
19. Cintra, J.S.; Tucker, C.L. Orthotropic closure approximations for flow-induced particle orientation. *J. Rheol.* **1995**, *39*, 1095–1122. [CrossRef]
20. Folgar, F.; Tucker, C.L., III. Orientation behaviour of fibres in concentrated suspensions. *J. Reinf. Plast. Compos.* **1984**, *3*, 98–119. [CrossRef]
21. Li, G.; Tang, J.X. Diffusion of actin filaments within a thin layer between two walls. *Phys. Rev. E* **2004**, *69*, 061921. [CrossRef] [PubMed]
22. Olson, J.A. The motion of fibres in turbulent flow, stochastic simulation of isotropic homogeneous turbulence. *Int. J. Multiph. Flow* **2001**, *27*, 2083–2103. [CrossRef]
23. Friedlander, S.K.; Marlow, W.H. Smoke, Dust and Haze: Fundamentals of Aerosol Behavior. *Phys. Today* **1977**, *30*, 58–59. [CrossRef]
24. Bernstein, O.; Shapiro, M. Direct determination of the orientation distribution function of cylindrical particles immersed in laminar and turbulent shear flows. *J. Aerosol Sci.* **1994**, *25*, 113–136. [CrossRef]
25. Lin, J.; Yin, Z.; Gan, F.; Yu, M. Penetration efficiency and distribution of aerosol particles in turbulent pipe flow undergoing coagulation and breakage. *Int. J. Multiph. Flow* **2014**, *61*, 28–36. [CrossRef]
26. Krushkal, E.M.; Gallily, I. On the orientation distribution function of non-spherical particles in a general shear flow-ii the turbulent case. *J. Aerosol Sci.* **1988**, *19*, 197–211. [CrossRef]
27. Ghaffarpasand, O.; Drewnick, F.; Hosseiniebalam, F.; Gallavardin, S.; Fachinger, J.; Hassanzadeh, S.; Borrmann, S. Penetra-tion efficiency of nanometer-sized particles in tubes under turbulent flow conditions. *J. Aerosol Sci.* **2012**, *50*, 11–25. [CrossRef]

Article

Profile Control Using Fly Ash Three-Phase Foam Assisted by Microspheres with an Adhesive Coating

Yulong Yang [1], Tingting Cheng [2,*], Zhenjiang You [3,*], Tuo Liang [1] and Jirui Hou [1]

[1] Unconventional Petroleum Research Institute, China University of Petroleum, Beijing 102200, China; yulong.yang@cup.edu.cn (Y.Y.); 2018310106@student.cup.edu.cn (T.L.); houjirui@126.com (J.H.)

[2] Key Laboratory of Complex Oil & Gas Fields Exploration and Development, Chongqing University of Science & Technology, Chongqing 401331, China

[3] School of Chemical Engineering, The University of Queensland, Brisbane, QLD 4072, Australia

** Correspondence: chengtingting@cqust.edu.cn (T.C.); z.you@uq.edu.au (Z.Y.)*

Abstract: Foam-assisted steam flooding is a promising technique to alleviate gas channeling and enhance sweep efficiency in heterogeneous heavy-oil reservoirs. However, long-term foam stabilization remains problematic at high temperatures. Three-phase foam (TPF), containing dispersed solid particles, has been proposed to improve foam stability under harsh reservoir conditions. We fabricated a novel TPF system by adding ultrafine fly ash particles, as well as high-temperature resistant microspheres with an adhesive coating layer. This work aims at assessing the ability of the generated TPF in controlling steam channeling and enhancing oil recovery. Static and core flood tests were performed to evaluate foam strength and stability. Our results suggested a stronger foamability at a lower consolidation agent concentration, while a longer half-life period of foam and settling time of solid particles at a larger consolidation agent concentration were observed. Bubbles suspended independently in the liquid phase, with sizes varying from 10 to 100 μm, smaller than that of the conventional foam, suggesting a significant enhancement of foam dispersity and stability. The plugging rate was close to 90% when the temperature was as high as 300 °C, demonstrating a well-accepted plugging effect under high temperatures. A larger pore volume injection of TPF yielded a higher EOR in parallel cores, which substantiated the effectiveness of the three-phase foam system in sealing high-permeability channels.

Keywords: three-phase foam; microspheres; adhesive coating layer; fly ash; enhanced oil recovery; profile control

---

Citation: Yang, Y.; Cheng, T.; You, Z.; Liang, T.; Hou, J. Profile Control Using Fly Ash Three-Phase Foam Assisted by Microspheres with an Adhesive Coating. *Appl. Sci.* **2021**, *11*, 3616. https://doi.org/10.3390/app11083616

Academic Editor: Jianzhong Lin

Received: 4 March 2021
Accepted: 15 April 2021
Published: 16 April 2021

Publisher's Note: MDPI stays neutral with regard to jurisdictional claims in published maps and institutional affiliations.

1. Introduction

Steam injection has been acknowledged as one of the most effective approaches for heavy-oil exploitation [1–3]. Nevertheless, due to the great density disparity, steam tends to flow in the upper reservoir (the so-called "gravity override"), which aggravates as the reservoir thickness increases [4,5]. Moreover, steam viscosity is much lower than that of the reservoir fluids, resulting in severe viscous fingering [6,7]. Steam channeling also emerges in heterogeneous reservoirs [8]. The abovementioned weaknesses lead to significant steam loss and low sweep efficiency.

Foam, marked by low density, small filtration loss and strong particle-carrying ability, preferentially enter high-permeability regions, block large pores or channels, and reduce the permeability of high-permeable layers [9–11]. Foam has been widely used to assist steam flooding in heavy-oil exploitation, enabling us to decrease vapor mobility, enlarge the swept volume and enhance oil recovery [12,13]. However, long-term foam stabilization remains challenging at high temperatures [14,15], concerning the effectiveness of profile control treatment by foam when injecting steam into heavy-oil reservoirs.

Solid particles, such as polymers and nanoparticles, have been commonly applied to enhance foam stability [16,17]. Dispersing solid particles into the conventional foam yields

---

the so-called three-phase foam (TPF) system [18]. The resultant high dispersity of bubbles and anomalous foam structure give rise to excellent foam stability, resulting in increased flow resistance, improved plugging efficiency and an extended swept volume [16,18].

Polymers are capable of generating a viscoelastic shell on the water-gas interface, which could mitigate liquid drainage between bubbles and hinder foam collapse, thereby improving foam stability [19–21]. Nevertheless, polymer-enhanced foam exhibits poor stability at reservoir conditions when contacting resident brines, crude oils, or minerals in porous media due to faster collapse of the thin liquid films at the gas-liquid interface [22,23]. Moreover, polymers may lose their viscosity-enhancing properties at a high-temperature and high-salinity condition [24]. Polymer concentrations can also increase by up to 10 to 15 times of their original value in formation water, causing pore blocking and the consequent formation damage [25]. Therefore, polymers might not be an appropriate candidate as the foam stabilizer in hydrocarbon reservoirs due to their short-term effectiveness and potential damage to a formation.

Hydrophilic nanoparticles can strongly adsorb onto the interface at harsh reservoir conditions and behave like surfactant molecules. The generated three-dimensional network structure allows slowing down thin liquid film drainage and improving foam stability [26,27]. In contrast, non-adsorbed nanoparticles in the intervening thin film could separate the dispersed phases [16,28]. It has been well documented that the synergetic effect of surfactant and certain types of nanoparticles is able to generate stronger foams and enhance foam stability against shrinkage and coalescence [29–31]. However, the aggregation of nanoparticles necessitates special chemical treatment in terms of their surface wettability, making them less cost-effective. As a result, using solid particles from widely available and commercially viable raw materials confers a distinguished economic superiority on particle-stabilized foam for enhanced oil recovery.

Fly ash is a coproduct of coal-fired power plants, serving as a source for the commercial foam stabilizers [32]. Using the abundantly available fly ash to generate the fly ash three-phase foam (FATPF) can significantly reduce the expense of the sealing system and lower the discharge of fly ash that could lead to waste pollution [33]. Lee et al. [34] acquired stable and dense CO_2 foam by adding fly ash nanoparticles (referred to "nanoash") combined with additives. Eftekhari et al. [35] demonstrated that nanoash could be utilized to stabilize nitrogen foam in the presence of crude oil at high temperatures and pressures. Guo et al. [36,37] showed that combining fly ash nanoparticles with a surfactant mixture of alpha-olefin sulfonate and lauramidopropyl betaine results in excellent foamability and stability and highly enhanced oil recovery in microfluidics. Singh et al. [38] generated nanoash-stabilized CO_2 foam for CO_2 mobility control in sandstone cores and sand packs. Their results suggested that the nanoash produced by the ball-milling method can greatly improve foam stability and the resistance factor. Lv et al. [39] found that the adsorption of fly ash at the CO_2-liquid interface may lead to a solid-like bubble film, and the viscosity of FATPF was thrice that of the pure surfactant foam. They further examined the micro-flow behavior and oil-displacement efficiency of the generated FATPF [40]. Given its practicability, fly ash is selected as the foam booster in our formula.

In addition to fly-ash particles, we developed a special micro-sized plugging material (MCL) that comprises a rigid internal core and an adhesive coating layer, which combines the merits of both organic and inorganic particles, including good injectivity, selective plugging, and high plugging intensity. The internal core is made of ultralight ceramsite, and the hot-molten adhesive layer coating out of the inner core is composed of cardanol-modified thermo-setting phenolic resin. When reaching a critical softening temperature, the coating layer starts to melt, and the particles tend to bond with each other under the interactions of these adhesive layers. The thickness of the adhesive outer layer is about 1.5 μm. A series of MCL with a broad range of bonding temperatures can be produced by modifying the ratio of cardanol and phenolic resin as well as the reaction temperature [41,42]. These MCL particles have been substantiated to be efficient in plugging high-permeability channels in porous media [43]. By adjusting the mixture ratio of MCL and fly ash, we can obtain TPF of various plugging rates.

In this study, modified starch gel, sodium dodecyl sulfate (SDS), and consolidation agents incorporating fly ash and MCL are used to generate a novel fly ash three-phase foam system assisted by high-temperature resistant MCL particles. Static evaluation tests are carried out to assess the foamability, stability and suspendability of the generated TPF. Single- and parallel-core floods are performed to test the plugging performance and oil-displacement efficiency.

2. Experimental Study

2.1. Materials and Preparation

2.1.1. Microsphere

The microsphere is composed of an internal core and a layer of coating materials (Figure 1). The internal core is made of ultralight ceramsite, with a bulk density between 1.06 g/cm^3 and 1.25 g/cm^3. A nominal breaking rate of the ceramsite varying from 3.5% to 18% under 52MPa is recorded by the manufacturer (Beijing Qisintal New Material Co., Ltd, Beijing, China). A hot molten layer with a critical softening temperature is made of cardanol modified thermosetting phenolic resin. When the surface temperature reaches a threshold, the exposed adhesive coating layer gradually melts and swells, and particles tend to bond with each other. The average size of MCL used in our experiments is about 100 μm. The critical molten temperature of the adhesive layer is 120 °C.

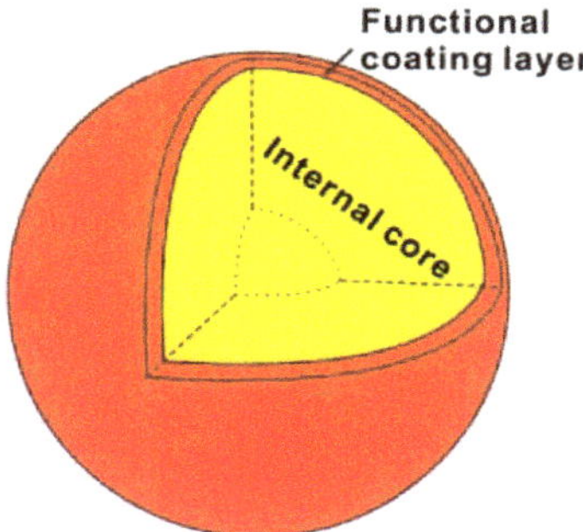

Figure 1. Schematic of MCL structure: the rigid internal core and the functional coating layer.

2.1.2. Three-Phase Foam

The compositions of the prepared three-phase foam contain sodium dodecyl sulfate (SDS), modified starch gel system, and consolidation agent (including fly ash and MCL, with a mass ratio of 1:4). The modified starch gel is the grafted copolymer of α-starch and acrylamide monomer, which has been successfully used to generate high tensile foam [44–46]. Fly ash with an average size smaller than 15 μm is provided by HX oil field company, China. The major components of the fly ash are SiO_2 and Al_2O_3, accounting for over 90 wt.% on the whole.

2.1.3. Quartz Sand

The main component of quartz sands used for core floods is SiO_2 (over 99%). Sands are first sieved to assist the reproducibility of core properties. The sand-washing procedures are delineated in [47].

2.1.4. Cores and Fluids

Single-phase plugging tests are performed in sand packs of various permeability ranging from 29 to 10,200 millidarcys (mD), filling with quartz sand of 10–40 mesh. The permeabilities of sand-filled pipes, consistent with the target reservoir in HX oil field,

China, can be regulated by changing the mixing ratio of quartz sands with different sizes and the degree of compaction. The diameter and length of the packed column are 2.5 cm and 50 cm, respectively. We use wet-packing procedures for quartz-sand compaction [47]. The porosity varies between 0.28 and 0.45. Oil-displacement tests are carried out in parallel heterogeneous artificial cores of different permeability ratios (defined as the ratio of the high permeability over the low permeability of the two parallel cores). The properties of the sand packs and artificial cores are given in Table 1.

Table 1. Parameters of parallel heterogeneous sand packs and artificial cores.

Core No.	Apparent Volume mL	Pore Volume mL	Porosity	Permeability mD	Permeability Ratio	Saturated Oil Volume mL	Saturation
SPS-1	493	217	0.44	2130	-	-	-
SPS-2	493	212	0.43	2065		-	-
SPS-3	493	221	0.45	2218	-	-	-
SPS-4	493	201	0.41	5830	-	-	-
SPS-5	493	219	0.45	8939	-	-	-
SPP-1	493	201	0.41	5520	190	-	-
		98	0.20	29		-	-
SPP-2	493	232	0.47	10,200	340	-	-
		103	0.21	30		-	-
AC-1	600	210	0.35	5000	5	295	0.78
		168	0.28	1000			
AC-2	605	200	0.33	5000	5	300	0.80
		175	0.29	1000			
AC-3	597	197	0.33	5000	10	266	0.77
		149	0.25	500			
AC-4	607	219	0.36	5000	10	292	0.80
		146	0.24	500			

Deionized water (Millipore Corporation, Burlington, MA, USA) is degassed and used for the preparation of artificial formation water (AFW) with the same ionic compositions as that in the studied reservoir. The major ionic components of AFW are given in Table 2. The degassed and dehydrated oil from the targeted reservoir in HX oil field is used for oil displacement tests. The oil viscosity is 7699 mPa·s at ambient conditions.

Table 2. Ionic compositions of AFW.

Ions	Ion Concentration, mg/L
Ca^{2+}	20.04
Mg^{2+}	9.24
Na^+	1012.00
HCO_3^-	2135.7
Cl^-	35.45
SO_4^{2-}	468.77

2.2. Laboratory Setup for Core Floods

A schematic diagram of the laboratory setup is illustrated in Figure 2.

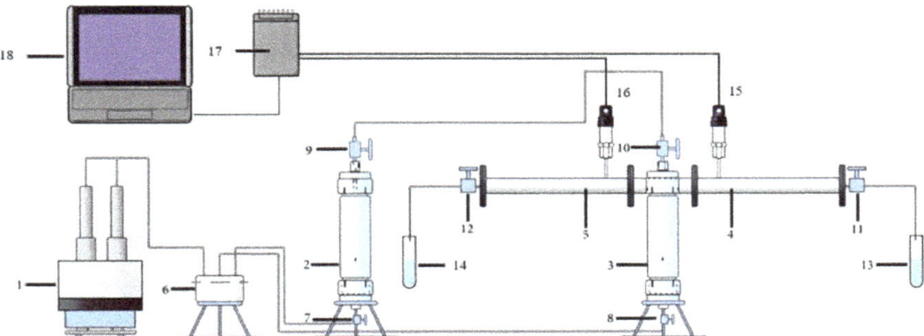

Figure 2. Experimental setup for core floods: 1—syringe pump, 2—AFW, 3—TPF, 4 and 5—sand packs, 6—six-way valves, 7–12—control valves, 13 and 14—test tubes, 15 and 16—pressure transducers, 17—data acquisition system, 18—PC with LabView.

Syringe pump 1 (100DX, Teledyne ISCO, Lincoln, NE, USA) equipped with two 90-mL stainless steel syringes is used for delivering AFW 2 or TPF 3 to parallel sand packs (or cores) 4 and 5, which allows us to emulate the co-existence of high- and low-permeability channels. A six-port valve 6 and six one-way valves 7–12 are used to connect the apparatus, ensuring continuous fluid injection into the sand pack. Valves 9–12 isolate the two sand packs (or cores) from other parts of the system, enabling one to eliminate fluid leakage during system assembly. Effluent fluids are collected at the outlets by test tubes 13 and 14. The injection pressure is measured by pressure transmitters 15 and 16. The acquired data are transmitted to the data collection system 17 and 18.

2.3. Methodology

2.3.1. Static Evaluation Tests

Foamability and Foam Stability

Foamability and stability are two essential indicators to assess the foam performance. Our foam system is fabricated following the Waring Blender method. A volume of 100 mL of solution containing the α-starch, methylene-bisacrylamide, potassium peroxodisulfate and sodium sulfite is first placed in a thermal chamber set at 80 °C. The solution viscosity is regularly recorded until it is gelatinized. Then, 100 mL of the prepared 80 °C dispersion containing lauryl sodium sulfate and consolidation agent is well mixed with the gelatinized starch gel system. The materials used for foam generation and their mass concentrations are shown in Table 3. It is followed by pouring the obtained mixture into a Warning blender and stirring for three minutes at 8000 rpm. The generated foam is then transferred into a 1000 mL measuring cylinder, and the initial volume of the foam is immediately recorded to evaluate the foaming capability. The measuring cylinder is placed into the thermal chamber to observe foam stability at 80 °C. When 50 mL solution is observed, the corresponding duration is regarded as the half-life period of the foam. The observation lasts for one week. Five tests are conducted to study the influence of consolidation agent concentrations (0.5%, 5%, 10%, 20% and 30%) on foaming capability and stability.

Suspendability Tests

The addition of MCL particles in the consolidation agent necessitates a good particle-carrying ability of the foam, so that the MCL can transport deeper in porous media and block high-permeability channels to achieve profile control. The prepared consolidation agents of various mass concentrations (0.5%, 5%, 10%, 20% and 30%) are well mixed with the generated foam. The obtained mixture stands in a measuring cylinder until approximately 10% of the MCL particles settle at the bottom. The sedimentation period is recorded to assess the foam's particle-carrying capability.

Table 3. List of experiments.

	Experiments	Materials for foam Generation	Temperature °C	Pressure MPa	Sand Packs
Static tests	Foamability	acrylamide (3%), α-starch (3%), methylene-bisacrylamide (0.1%), potassium peroxodisulfate (0.02%), sodium sulfite (0.2%), lauryl sodium sulfate (0.3%), consolidation agents (0.5%~30%)	80	ambient	-
	Foam stability		80	ambient	-
	Suspendability		80	ambient	-
Core floods	Thermal stability		80, 150, 300	ambient	SPS-1, SPS-2, SPS-3
	Permeability effects		80	ambient	SPS-4, SPS-5
	Permeability ratio effects		80	ambient	SPP-1, SPP-2
	Oil displacement		80	ambient	AC-1, AC-2, AC-3, AC-4

2.3.2. Single-Phase Plugging Tests

Thermal Stability

Dynamic foam stability under a high temperature signifies the transport and plugging properties of foam in hydrocarbon reservoirs. Therefore, core floods in the absence of oil are carried out at three temperatures to assess the dynamic thermal stability. Sand packs are first vacuumed and saturated with AFW, followed by injection of 0.3 PV starch-gel three-phase foam system containing 5% consolidation agent at a flow rate of 0.5 mL/min. The sand packs are then placed in a thermal chamber (80 °C, 150 °C, and 300 °C) for 24 h. In the last stage, the subsequent water is injected at 0.5 mL/min until the pressure reaches a plateau. The variation of injection pressure is regularly documented. The physical properties of the sand packs (SPS-1, SPS-2, and SPS-3) are given in rows 2–4, Table 1.

Permeability Influence

Permeability can significantly affect foam's plugging performance as it directly relates to the pore size distribution of porous media. Sand packs (SPS-4 and SPS-5) of permeabilities 5830 mD and 8939 mD are used to investigate permeability effect on the plugging performance of the generated three-phase foam. Following the procedure presented in 2.3.2.1, 0.3 PV starch-gel three-phase foam containing 5% consolidation agent is injected into the AFW saturated sand packs at a flow rate of 0.5 mL/min. The sand packs are then placed in a thermal chamber set at 80 °C for 24 h. The subsequent water is then injected with the same flow rate until the pressure is stable. The variation of injection pressure is regularly recorded.

Influences of Permeability Ratio

Heterogeneity is a critical factor that causes water/gas channeling during fluid injection. Permeability ratio is considered an indicator of the extent of reservoir heterogeneity. As a result, parallel heterogeneous sand packs with various permeability ratios (5520/30 and 10,200/30) are applied to study the influence of permeability ratio on foam plugging performance. Water is first injected into parallel cores at a flow rate of 0.5 mL/min until the fractional flow in each core becomes stable. It is followed by injecting 0.3 PV starch-gel three-phase foam. The mass concentration of the consolidation agent maintains the same as in previous tests, i.e., 5%. When foam injection terminates, the experimental system stands for 24 h to make the foam gelated. The subsequent water is then injected until the pressure reaches a steady state. The flow rate remains the same throughout the whole test. The fractional flow rates (defined as the ratio of the flow rate in each of the parallel cores over the total flow rate) are recorded.

The profile control efficiency is characterized by the profile improvement rate η, expressed by [48]

$$\eta = \left(1 - \frac{Q_{ha}/Q_{la}}{Q_{hb}/Q_{lb}}\right) \times 100\% \tag{1}$$

where Q_{ha} and Q_{la} are the flow rates in the high-permeability core and low-permeability core after foam injection, respectively, mL/min; Q_{hb} and Q_{lb} are the flow rates in the high-permeability core and low-permeability core before foam injection, respectively, mL/min.

After foam injection, the difference between the flow rates in high-permeability and low-permeability cores is narrowed down, yielding a higher profile control efficiency. Apparently, higher η indicates a better profile control efficiency.

2.3.3. Oil Displacement Tests

Parallel heterogeneous artificial cores (AC-1, AC-2, AC-3, and AC-4) of different permeability ratios (5000/1000 and 5000/500) are used for oil displacement tests. The dimension of the artificial cores is 30 cm × 4.5 cm × 4.5 cm. Cores are first vacuumed and saturated with AFW and then saturated with the degassed and dehydrated oil from the targeted reservoir, aging for 24 h. The primary water is injected at a constant flow rate of 0.5 mL/min until the water cut reaches 98%. A certain volume (0.2 PV and 0.3 PV) of three-phase foam is then injected, after which the system stands for 24 h. The subsequent water is injected until the water cut is as high as 98%. Water cut, oil recovery, and injection pressure are documented. Oil volumes produced from both of the parallel cores are counted for oil recovery.

3. Results and Discussion

This section presents the results and discussion on the experimental study described in Section 2. The experimental results of foamability, foam stability and particle-carrying capability are shown in Sections 3.1 and 3.2. The microstructure of the generated TPF is demonstrated in Section 3.3. Section 3.4 analyzes the influences of temperature, core permeability and permeability ratio on the plugging performance. Section 3.5 demonstrates oil-displacement efficiency.

3.1. Foamability and Foam Stability

Table 4 demonstrates the foaming volume and half-life period of the three-phase foam system containing various consolidation agents.

Table 4. Three-phase foam properties.

Consolidation Agent Concentration, wt%	Foaming Volume, mL	Half-Life Period, min	Gas-Liquid Ratio
0.5	580	110	19:10
5	520	1020	8:5
10	480	1370	7:5
20	320	Not observed	NA
30	250	Not observed	NA

Figure 3 shows the images of foam volume when it is just generated under various consolidation concentrations. It is observed that the foaming volume decreases as the consolidation agent concentration increases, indicating a weaker foamability at a higher consolidation agent concentration. This is ascribed to the less liquid proportion at a higher consolidation agent concentration, given that the base solution maintains the same volume. However, the half-life period of foam is highly increased with an increasing consolidation agent concentration, showing stronger stability. Fluid drainage does not show up when the consolidation agent concentration reaches 20%, and the system becomes solidified.

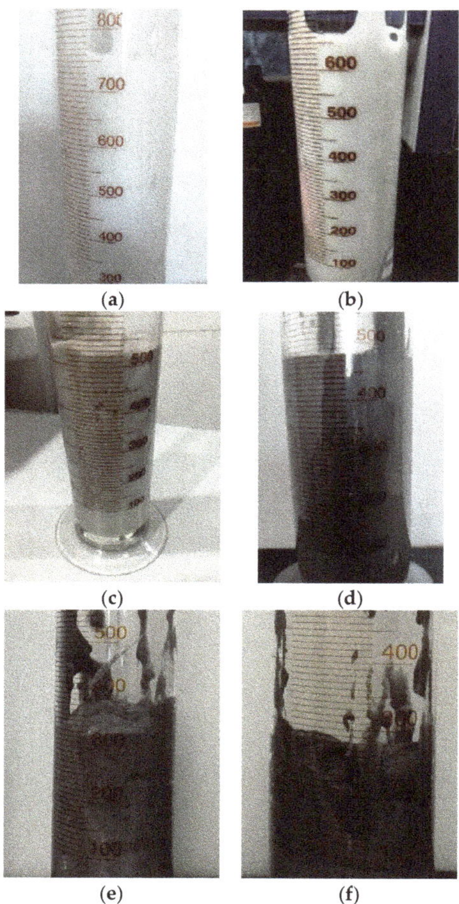

Figure 3. Images of the generated foam under various consolidation concentrations: (**a**) 0%; (**b**) 0.5%; (**c**) 5%; (**d**) 10%; (**e**) 20%; (**f**) 30%.

3.2. Suspendability

In the three-phase foam system, solid particles are suspended by the gaseous phase and squeezed by bubbles. When the bubbles supporting particles are deformed, particles might settle to the bottom. The consolidation agents used in our study cannot distort the bubbles due to their tiny sizes. As a result, those particles do not move or settle due to the existence of neighboring bubbles. Table 5 shows the influence of consolidation agent concentration on particle settling time. Increasing consolidation agent concentration yields a longer settling time. The three-phase foam system exhibits a splendid particle-carrying capability at all tested consolidation agent concentrations. It is worth noting that MCL settling is not observed in the foam containing 20% and 30% consolidation agents. As seen in Figure 3, the foam system becomes solidified due to the large proportion of solid particles at the consolidation agent concentrations of 20% and 30%. We conclude that consolidation agents ranged within 5% to 10% would be optimal for achieving a balance among foamability, stability, and suspendability. We select 5% as the solid particle concentration in the rest tests to lower the cost.

Table 5. Three-phase foam properties.

Consolidation Agent Concentration, wt%	Settling Time, min
0.5	1210
5	2180
10	2360
20	Not observed
30	Not observed

3.3. Foam Microstructure

Foam is a thermodynamically unstable system, and its stability is controlled by the process of liquid film thinning and bubble coalescence. During liquid film thinning, bubbles push against each other, while the total surface area is changeless. In comparison, bubble coalescence results in a larger bubble, leading to a decrease in the total surface area. The coalescence rate of bubbles is determined by the speed of liquid film thinning and rupture. The smaller is the bubble volume, the stronger is the pressure-resistant ability, and the harder is the liquid film rupture.

The fluid loss in a foam system arises from the mutual squeezing of bubbles and the effect of gravity. Bubble squeezing originates from the surface pressure of the so-called "Plateau border". As seen in Figure 4a, the conventional foam exhibits an unstable hexagonal structure that may lead to fast bubble fluid loss and rupture. However, in comparison, the bubbles of the three-phase foam exist in the liquid phase independently, showing high dispersity and a smaller size ranging from 10 to 100 µm if compared to the conventional foam (Figure 4b). Figure 4b demonstrates typical microstructure of aqueous foam stabilized by solid particles. Analogous figures have been reported in the literature [18,32,40]. The smaller bubble size of the three-phase foam might be attributed to the irreversible adsorption and aggregation of fly ash particles at the liquid-gas interface of the foam and plateau borders. The adsorbed particles can reduce the direct contact between the fluids to mitigate liquid drainage and decrease the rate of film rupture and bubble coarsening [32], thereby improve foam stability. Moreover, although the presence of fly ash particles cannot significantly affect the interfacial tension [27,40], the adsorbed solid particles can notably increase the dilatational interfacial viscoelasticity that characterizes bubbles' ability to resist external disturbances. At high viscoelasticity, the liquid film shows a solid-like behavior that is favorable to restrain the coalescence and rupture of bubbles [40]. Therefore, due to the protection of adsorbed particles, the tiny bubbles can survive longer than the conventional foam. The coagulation of MCL is anticipated to help the three-phase foam achieve better profile control, enhancing the plugging performance. Furthermore, the starch gel, serving as a suspending agent, increases liquid viscosity due to its reticulated texture and contributes positively to the mechanical strength of the liquid film surrounding a bubble.

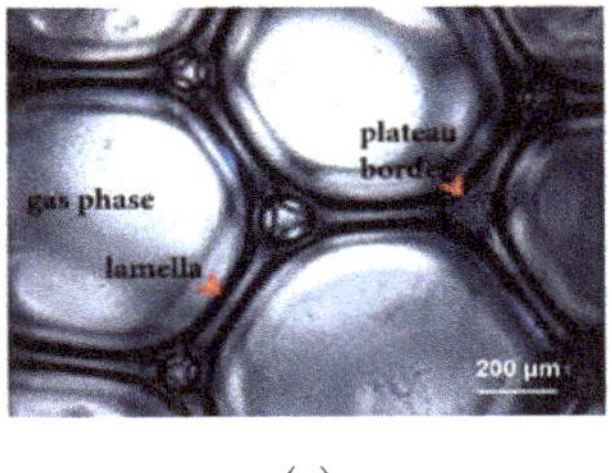

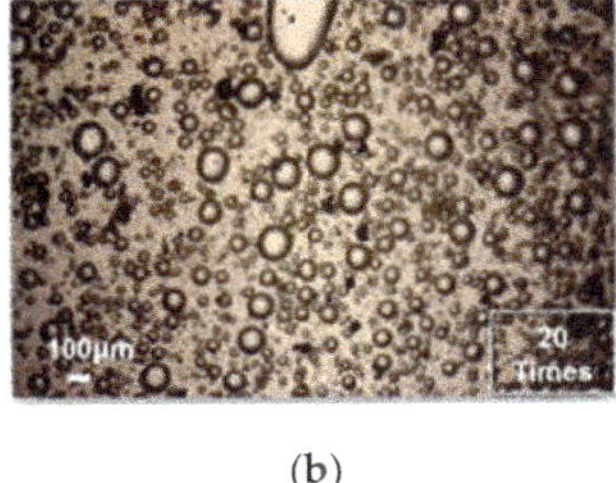

(**a**)   (**b**)

Figure 4. Images of the conventional foam system and the three-phase foam system: (**a**) conventional foam (adopted from [49]); (**b**) three-phase foam (magnified by 20 times).

3.4. Plugging Performance

3.4.1. Temperature Influence

Figure 5 shows the injection pressure of TPF under different temperatures. The injection pressure increases during TPF injection. The higher is the temperature, the weaker is the foam stability, and thus the lower is the injection pressure. When the subsequent water is injected, the injection pressure continues to increase until reaching a maximum value. The maximum value is referred to as the breakthrough pressure, after which the injection pressure drops dramatically due to foam destabilization. The breakthrough pressures are 6.7 MPa, 5.8 MPa, and 1.2 MPa at 80 °C, 150 °C, and 300 °C, respectively. The permeabilities after foam injection are 311 mD, 566 mD, and 309 mD, respectively. The corresponding plugging rates, defined as the ratio of the difference between the permeabilities before and after foam treatment over the initial permeability [50], are 85%, 73%, and 86%, respectively. The high values of plugging rates demonstrate a well-accepted plugging performance under high temperatures.

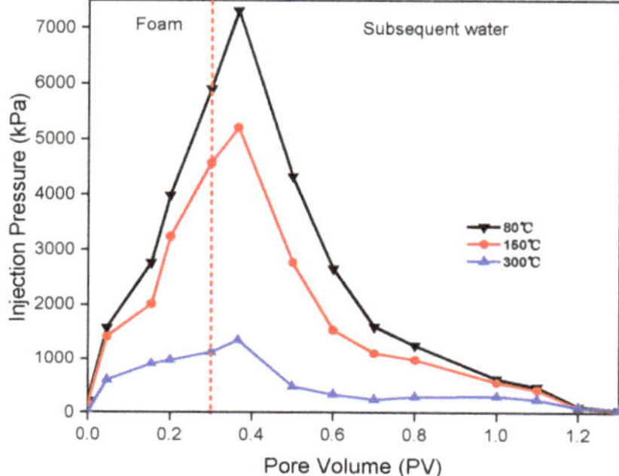

Figure 5. Influence of temperature on injection pressure.

3.4.2. Permeability Influence

As depicted in Figure 6, after 0.3 PV foam injection, the injection pressures rise to 2.1 MPa and 1.2 MPa for sand packs of permeability 5830 mD and 8939 mD, respectively. After the subsequent water injection, the pressure increases continuously. The corresponding breakthrough pressures are 4.5 MPa and 4.1 MPa for the low-permeability and high-permeability cores, respectively. Core permeabilities decrease to 711 mD and 1155 mD before the occurrence of water breakthrough, yielding corresponding plugging rates of 88% and 87%, respectively. The breakthrough pressure descends as permeability increases, resulting from the increasing pore size and decreasing capillary pressure. When the breakthrough occurs, the pressure shows a sharp decline due to a quick formation of water channeling.

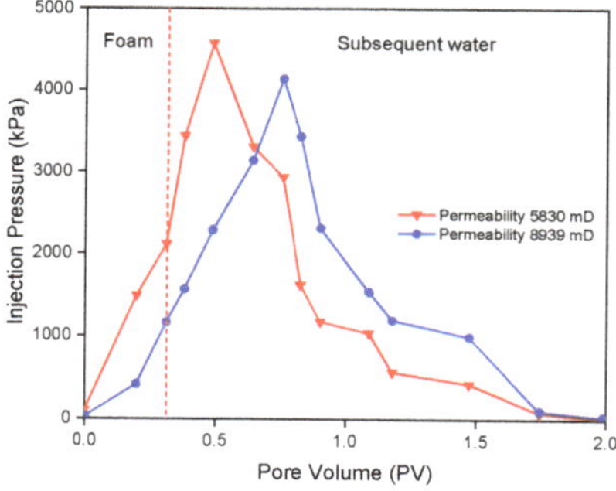

Figure 6. Influence of permeability on injection pressure.

3.4.3. Influence of Permeability Ratio

As shown in Figure 7, the three-phase foam can remarkably plug the high-permeability channel and achieve satisfactory profile control, while exhibiting indistinctive damage to the low-permeability zone. The profile control efficiencies are about 0.89 and 0.87 for the two tests, respectively. The larger the permeability ratio is, the greater the fractional flow difference is in the parallel heterogeneous sand packs, and the worse the profile control performance is.

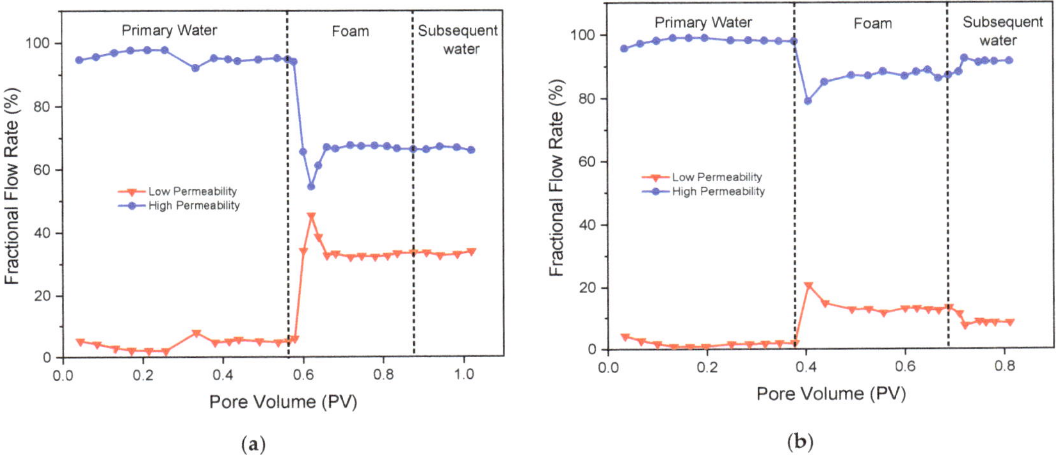

Figure 7. Influence of permeability ratio on fractional flow rates: (**a**) permeability ratio 5520/29; (**b**) permeability ratio 10,200/30.

3.5. Oil-Displacement Efficiency

As depicted in Figures 8 and 9, the oil recovery of parallel cores is improved to a certain extent after foam injection in all the performed experiments, demonstrating effective profile control by the three-phase foam.

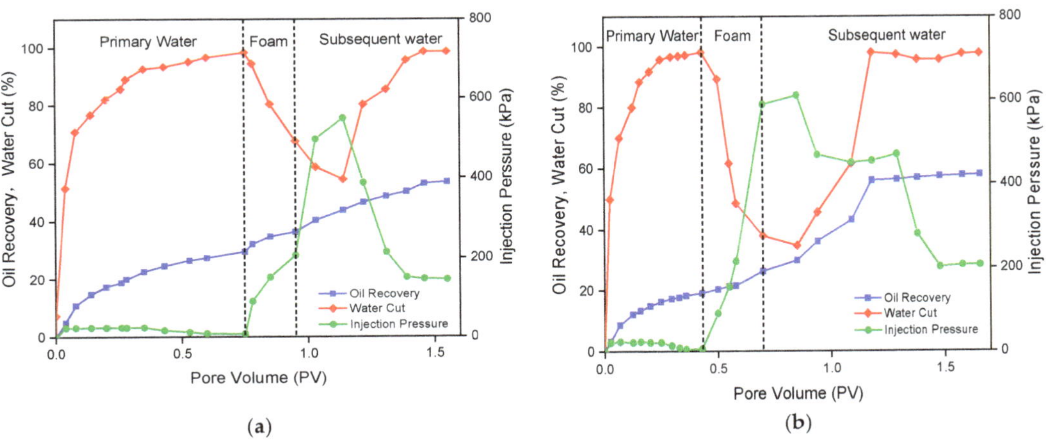

Figure 8. The influence of the three-phase foam slug size on oil displacement in parallel cores of permeability ratio 5: (**a**) 0.2 PV; (**b**) 0.3 PV.

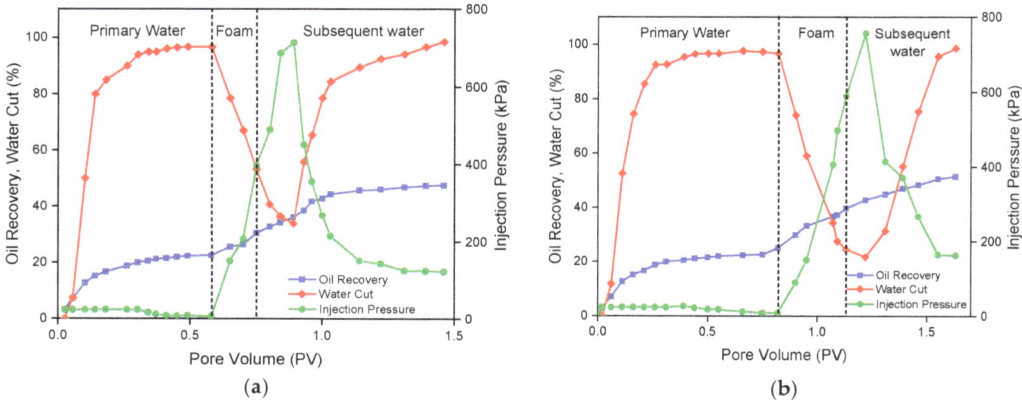

Figure 9. The influence of the three-phase foam slug size on oil displacement in parallel cores of permeability ratio 10: (**a**) 0.2 PV; (**b**) 0.3 PV.

During the primary water flooding, the injection pressure exhibits a slight decline, while the water cut surges. The decrease of the injection pressure and the increase of the water cut arise from the presence of a water breakthrough channel that reduces flow resistance. The oil recoveries after primary water injection into parallel cores of permeability ratio 5 are 29% and 20%, respectively. The difference might be ascribed to the variance of core heterogeneity, which causes different injection periods of the primary water floods. We cease the primary water flooding when the water cut reaches 98%. In comparison, the primary water flooding in parallel cores of permeability ratio 10 yields an oil recovery of 22% for both tests. The lower oil recovery originates from the higher permeability ratio that delivers a larger difference in the fractional flow rate, thereby less oil production in the low-permeability cores.

The notable increase of injection pressure during foam injection arises from the significant foam resistance. As continuously pumped into the parallel cores, the MCL assisted three-phase foam selectively enters the high-permeability zone, plugs the pore throats inside the water breakthrough channel, and thus significantly reduces water cut and expands the swept volume. Due to the growth in flow resistance, the difference between the fractional flow rates of the high- and low-permeability cores narrows down during the injection of the subsequent water. Thus, more oil is recovered from the low-permeable layer. The injection pressure presents a further remarkable growth in the early period of subsequent water injection, manifesting that the three-phase foam remains effective in pore plugging. It is worth mentioning that the injection pressure during the subsequent water flood declines to a level that is a bit higher than the initial injection pressure, which might be caused by the migration of MCL and its ability in profile control.

The enhanced oil recoveries in parallel cores of permeability ratio 5 are about 25% and 30% for 0.2 PV and 0.3 PV foam injection, respectively. In comparison, the enhanced oil recoveries in parallel cores of permeability ratio 10 are about 30% and 36% for 0.2 PV and 0.3 PV foam injection, respectively. As expected, the injection of 0.3 PV foam results in a higher EOR in parallel cores of various permeability ratios due to its better performance in pore blocking. This complies with the fact that 0.2 PV foam injection yields a lower breakthrough pressure than that of 0.3 PV foam injection. Furthermore, a higher permeability ratio leads to higher EOR, which substantiates the effectiveness of the three-phase foam system in sealing high-permeability channels. This conclusion is contradictory to the result presented in Section 3.4.3, where we conclude that a larger permeability ratio gives rise to worse profile control. The contradiction might originate from the wide difference in the permeability ratios of those cores used in our experiments. When the permeability ratio is small, a larger permeability ratio can lead to a more effective redistribution of the fractional flow. Nevertheless, when the permeability ratio is overlarge, the effectiveness of profile control is indistinctive and less fraction of fluid diverts to the low-permeability channels.

4. Conclusions

We present a novel fly ash three-phase foam system assisted by high-temperature resistant microspheres coated with an adhesive layer. This novel foam system allows mitigating gas channeling that occurs during steam injection into heterogeneous heavy-oil reservoirs. Therefore, it is a promising candidate for enhanced oil recovery via profile control. Our study allows drawing the following conclusions.

(1)   The foaming volume increases as the consolidation agent concentration decreases, suggesting a stronger foamability at a lower consolidation agent concentration. However, the half-life period of foam is remarkably declined with a descending consolidation agent concentration, showing weaker stability. Fluid drainage does not appear when the consolidation agent concentration reaches 20%. Additionally, increasing consolidation agent concentration yields a longer settling time of solid particles.

(2)   The presence of MCL in TPF enables an improvement in plugging performance under high temperature. The plugging rate is close to 90% when the temperature is as high as 300 °C, demonstrating a well-accepted plugging effect. The lower is the permeability, the higher is the breakthrough pressure.

(3)   As the permeability ratio increases, a more effective redistribution of the fractional flow is anticipated. Nevertheless, if the permeability ratio is overlarge, the effectiveness of profile control is indistinctive and less fraction of fluid diverts to the low-permeability channels.

(4)   A larger pore volume injection of TPF results in a higher EOR in parallel cores, which substantiates the effectiveness of the three-phase foam system in sealing high-permeability channels.

Author Contributions: Conceptualization, J.H.; methodology, Y.Y., T.C. and T.L.; validation, Y.Y. and Z.Y.; formal analysis, Y.Y. and T.C.; investigation, Y.Y. and T.C.; resources, J.H.; data curation, T.C.; writing—original draft preparation, Y.Y.; writing—review and editing, Z.Y.; supervision, J.H.; project administration, J.H.; funding acquisition, Y.Y. and J.H. All authors have read and agreed to the published version of the manuscript.

Funding: Financial supports from the National Natural Science Foundation of China (Grant No. 51804316, Grant No. 41702249, and Grant No. U1762211) and the Science Foundation of China University of Petroleum, Beijing (Grant No. 2462020XKBH013) are greatly acknowledged.

Data Availability Statement: Data is contained within this article.

Conflicts of Interest: The authors declare no conflict of interest.

References

1.   Li, S.; Li, Z.; Sun, X. Effect of flue gas and n-hexane on heavy oil properties in steam flooding process. *Fuel* **2017**, *187*, 84–93. [CrossRef]

2.   Zhao, D.W.; Wang, J.; Gates, I.D. Optimized solvent-aided steam-flooding strategy for recovery of thin heavy oil reservoirs. *Fuel* **2013**, *112*, 50–59. [CrossRef]

3.   Brame, S.D.; Li, L.; Mukherjee, B.; Patil, P.D.; Potisek, S.; Nguyen, Q.P. Organic bases as additives for steam-assisted gravity drainage. *Pet. Sci.* **2019**, *16*, 1332–1343. [CrossRef]

4.   Pang, Z.; Liu, H.; Zhu, L. A laboratory study of enhancing heavy oil recovery with steam flooding by adding nitrogen foams. *J. Pet. Sci. Eng.* **2015**, *128*, 184–193. [CrossRef]

5.   Lyu, X.; Liu, H.; Pang, Z.; Sun, Z. Visualized study of thermochemistry assisted steam flooding to improve oil recovery in heavy oil reservoir with glass micromodels. *Fuel* **2018**, *218*, 118–126. [CrossRef]

6.   Wang, Y.; Liu, H.; Pang, Z.; Gao, M. Visualization Study on Plugging Characteristics of Temperature-Resistant Gel during Steam Flooding. *Energy Fuels* **2016**, *30*, 6968–6976. [CrossRef]

7.   Norouzi, M.; Dorrani, S.; Shokri, H.; Bég, O.A. Effects of viscous dissipation on miscible thermo-viscous fingering instability in porous media. *Int. J. Heat Mass Transf.* **2019**, *129*, 212–223. [CrossRef]

8. Janssen, M.T.G.; Pilus, R.M.; Zitha, P.L.J. A Comparative Study of Gas Flooding and Foam-Assisted Chemical Flooding in Bentheimer Sandstones. *Transp. Porous Media* **2019**, *131*, 101–134. [CrossRef]

9. Farajzadeh, R.; Andrianov, A.; Krastev, R.; Hirasaki, G.; Rossen, W.R. Foam-Oil Interaction in Porous Media: Implications for Foam Assisted Enhanced Oil Recovery. *Adv. Colloid Interfac.* **2012**, *183*, 1–13. [CrossRef] [PubMed]

10. Hosseini-Nasab, S.M.; Zitha, P.L.J. Investigation of Chemical-Foam Design as a Novel Approach toward Immiscible Foam Flooding for Enhanced Oil Recovery. *Energy Fuels* **2017**, *31*, 10525–10534. [CrossRef]

11. Li, R.F.; Yan, W.; Liu, S.; Hirasaki, G.J.; Miller, C.A. Foam Mobility Control for Surfactant Enhanced Oil Recovery. *SPE J.* **2010**, *15*, 928–942. [CrossRef]

12. Guo, F.; Aryana, S.A. Improved sweep efficiency due to foam flooding in a heterogeneous microfluidic device. *J. Petrol. Sci. Eng.* **2018**, *164*, 155–163. [CrossRef]

13. Liu, P.; Li, W.; Shen, D. Experimental study and pilot test of urea- and urea-and-foam-assisted steam flooding in heavy oil reservoirs. *J. Pet. Sci. Eng.* **2015**, *135*, 291–298. [CrossRef]

14. Oetjen, K.; Bilke-Krause, C.; Madani, M.; Willers, T. Temperature effect on foamability, foam stability, and foam structure of milk. *Colloids Surf. A Physicochem. Eng. Asp.* **2014**, *460*, 280–285. [CrossRef]

15. Wang, H.; Guo, W.; Zheng, C.; Wang, D.; Zhan, H. Effect of Temperature on Foaming Ability and Foam Stability of Typical Surfactants Used for Foaming Agent. *J. Surfactants Deterg.* **2017**, *20*, 615–622. [CrossRef]

16. Zhao, G.; Dai, C.; Wen, D.; Fang, J. Stability mechanism of a novel three-Phase foam by adding dispersed particle gel. *Colloids Surf. A Physicochem. Eng. Asp.* **2016**, *497*, 214–224. [CrossRef]

17. Alargova, R.G.; Warhadpande, D.S.; Paunov, A.V.N.; Velev, O.D. Foam Superstabilization by Polymer Microrods. *Langmuir* **2004**, *20*, 10371–10374. [CrossRef]

18. Wang, T.; Fan, H.; Yang, W.; Meng, Z. Stabilization mechanism of fly ash three-phase foam and its sealing capacity on fractured reservoirs. *Fuel* **2020**, *264*, 116832. [CrossRef]

19. Zhou, W.; Xin, C.; Chen, S.; Yu, Q.; Wang, K. Polymer-Enhanced Foam Flooding for Improving Heavy Oil Recovery in Thin Reservoirs. *Energy Fuels* **2020**, *34*, 4116–4128. [CrossRef]

20. Zhao, G.; Dai, C.; Zhang, Y.; Chen, A.; Yan, Z.; Zhao, M. Enhanced foam stability by adding comb polymer gel for in-depth profile control in high temperature reservoirs. *Colloids Surf. A Physicochem. Eng. Asp.* **2015**, *482*, 115–124. [CrossRef]

21. Zhu, T.; Ogbe, D.O.; Khataniar, S. Improving the Foam Performance for Mobility Control and Improved Sweep Efficiency in Gas Flooding. *Ind. Eng. Chem. Res.* **2004**, *43*, 4413–4421. [CrossRef]

22. Yekeen, N.; Idris, A.K.; Manan, M.A.; Samin, A.M.; Risal, A.R.; Kun, T.X. Bulk and bubble-scale experimental studies of influence of nanoparticles on foam stability. *Chin. J. Chem. Eng.* **2017**, *25*, 347–357. [CrossRef]

23. Kutay, S.; Schramm, L. Structure/Performance Relationships for Surfactant and Polymer Stabilized Foams in Porous Media. *J. Can. Pet. Technol.* **2004**, *43*, 19–28. [CrossRef]

24. Emrani, A.S.; Nasr-El-Din, H.A. Stabilizing CO_2 Foam by Use of Nanoparticles. *SPE J.* **2017**, *22*, 494–504. [CrossRef]

25. Xu, X.; Saeedi, A.; Liu, K. An experimental study of combined foam/surfactant polymer (SP) flooding for carbone dioxide-enhanced oil recovery (CO_2-EOR). *J. Pet. Sci. Eng.* **2017**, *149*, 603–611. [CrossRef]

26. Risal, A.R.; Manan, M.A.; Yekeen, N.; Azli, N.B.; Samin, A.M.; Tan, X.K. Experimental investigation of enhancement of carbon dioxide foam stability, pore plugging, and oil recovery in the presence of silica nanoparticles. *Pet. Sci.* **2018**, *16*, 344–356. [CrossRef]

27. Alyousef, Z.; Almobarky, M.; Schechter, D. Enhancing the Stability of Foam by the Use of Nanoparticles. *Energy Fuels* **2017**, *31*, 10620–10627. [CrossRef]

28. Dong, X.; Xu, J.; Cao, C.; Sun, D.; Jiang, X. Aqueous foam stabilized by hydrophobically modified silica particles and liquid paraffin droplets. *Colloids Surf. A Physicochem. Eng. Asp.* **2010**, *353*, 181–188. [CrossRef]

29. Binks, B.P.; Kirkland, M.; Rodrigues, J.A. Origin of stabilisation of aqueous foams in nanoparticle-surfactant mixtures. *Soft Matter.* **2008**, *4*, 2373–2382. [CrossRef]

30. Bahraminejad, H.; Manshad, A.K.; Keshavarz, A. Characterization, Micellization Behavior, and Performance of a Novel Surfactant Derived from Gundelia tournefortii Plant during Chemical Enhanced Oil Recovery. *Energy Fuels* **2021**, *35*, 1259–1272. [CrossRef]

31. Singh, R.; Mohanty, K.K. Synergy between Nanoparticles and Surfactants in Stabilizing Foams for Oil Recovery. *Energy Fuels* **2015**, *29*, 467–479. [CrossRef]

32. Yekeen, N.; Manan, M.A.; Idris, A.K.; Padmanabhan, E.; Junin, R.; Samin, A.M.; Gbadamosi, A.O.; Oguamah, I. A comprehensive review of experimental studies of nanoparticles-stabilized foam for enhanced oil recovery. *J. Pet. Sci. Eng.* **2018**, *164*, 43–74. [CrossRef]

33. Phong, G.M.; Pilus, R.M.; Mustaffa, A.; Thangavel, L.; Mohamed, N.M. Relationship between fly ash nanoparticle-stabilized-foam and oil production in core displacement and simulation studies. *Fuel* **2020**, *266*, 117033. [CrossRef]

34. Lee, D.; Cho, H.; Lee, J.; Huh, C.; Mohanty, K. Fly ash nanoparticles as a CO_2 foam stabilizer. *Powder Technol.* **2015**, *283*, 77–84. [CrossRef]

35. Eftekhari, A.A.; Krastev, R.; Farajzadeh, R. Foam Stabilized by Fly Ash Nanoparticles for Enhancing Oil Recovery. *Ind. Eng. Chem. Res.* **2015**, *54*, 12482–12491. [CrossRef]

36. Guo, F.; Aryana, S. An experimental investigation of nanoparticle-stabilized CO_2 foam used in enhanced oil recovery. *Fuel* **2016**, *186*, 430–442. [CrossRef]

37. Guo, F.; He, J.; Johnson, P.A.; Aryana, S.A. Stabilization of CO_2 foam using by-product fly ash and recyclable iron oxide nanoparticles to improve carbon utilization in EOR processes. *Sustain. Energy Fuels* **2017**, *1*, 814–822. [CrossRef]
38. Singh, R.; Gupta, A.; Mohanty, K.K.; Huh, C.; Lee, D.; Cho, H. Fly Ash Nanoparticle-Stabilized CO_2-in-Water Foams for Gas Mobility Control Applications. In Proceedings of the SPE Annual Technical Conference and Exhibition, Houston, TX, USA, 28 September 2015; Society of Petroleum Engineers: Houston, TX, USA, 2015.
39. Lv, Q.; Li, Z.; Li, B.; Husein, M.M.; Li, S.; Shi, D.; Liu, W.; Bai, H.; Sheng, L. Synergistic Mechanism of Particulate Matter (PM) from Coal Combustion and Saponin from Camellia Seed Pomace in Stabilizing CO_2 Foam. *Energy Fuels* **2018**, *32*, 3733–3742. [CrossRef]
40. Lv, Q.; Zhou, T.; Zhang, X.; Zuo, B.; Dong, Z.; Zhang, J. Enhanced Oil Recovery Using Aqueous CO_2 Foam Stabilized by Particulate Matter from Coal Combustion. *Energy Fuels* **2020**, *34*, 2880–2892. [CrossRef]
41. Yang, Y.; Cheng, T.; Liu, H.; You, Z.; Hou, J. Oil Displacement Performance Using Bilayer-Coating Microspheres. *Ind. Eng. Chem. Res.* **2021**, *60*, 2300–2313. [CrossRef]
42. Cheng, T.; Hou, J.; Yang, Y.; You, Z.; Liu, Y.; Zhao, F.; Li, J. Study on the Plugging Performance of Bilayer-Coating Microspheres for In-Depth Conformance Control: Experimental Study and Mathematical Modeling. *Ind. Eng. Chem. Res.* **2019**, *58*, 6796–6810. [CrossRef]
43. Zhao, F.; Li, Z.; Wu, J.; Hou, J.; Qu, S. New type plugging particle system with high temperature & high salinity resistance. *J. Pet. Sci. Eng.* **2017**, *152*, 317–329. [CrossRef]
44. Barrufet, M.A.; Burnett, D.; Macauley, J. Screening and Evaluation of Modified Starches as Water Shutoff Agents in Fractures. In Proceedings of the SPE/DOE Improved Oil Recovery Symposium, Tulsa, OK, USA, 19–22 April 1998; Society of Petroleum Engineers: Tulsa, OK, USA, 1998.
45. Pledger, H., Jr.; Meister, J.J.; Hogen-Esch, T.E.; Butler, G.B. Starch-acrylamide graft copolymers for use in enhanced oil recovery. In Proceedings of the SPE Annual Technical Conference and Exhibition, Las Vegas, NV, USA, 23–26 September 1979; Society of Petroleum Engineers: Las Vegas, NV, USA, 1979.
46. Zhao, F.; Lv, C.; Hou, J.; Wang, Z. Formation adaptability of combining modified starch gel and nitrogen foam in profile modification and oil displacement. *J. Energy Inst.* **2016**, *89*, 536–543. [CrossRef]
47. Russell, T.; Pham, D.; Neishaboor, M.T.; Badalyan, A.; Behr, A.; Genolet, L.; Kowollik, P.; Zeinijahromi, A.; Bedrikovetsky, P. Effects of kaolinite in rocks on fines migration. *J. Nat. Gas. Sci. Eng.* **2017**, *45*, 243–255. [CrossRef]
48. Zhao, G.; You, Q.; Tao, J.; Gu, C.; Aziz, H.; Ma, L.; Dai, C. Preparation and application of a novel phenolic resin dispersed particle gel for in-depth profile control in low permeability reservoirs. *J. Pet. Sci. Eng.* **2018**, *161*, 703–714. [CrossRef]
49. Alimadadi, M. Foam-Formed Fiber Networks: Manufacturing, Characterization, and Numerical Modeling: With a Note on the Orientation Behavior of Rod-Like Particles in Newtonian Fluids. Ph.D. Thesis, Mid Sweden University, Östersund, Sweden, 2018.
50. Zhao, S.; Pu, W. Migration and plugging of polymer microspheres (PMs) in porous media for enhanced oil recovery: Experimental studies and empirical correlations. *Colloids Surf. A Physicochem. Eng. Asp.* **2020**, *597*, 124774. [CrossRef]

*applied
sciences*

Article

Effects of Velocity and Permeability on Tracer Dispersion in Porous Media

Yulong Yang [1], Tongjing Liu [1,*], Yanyue Li [2], Yuqi Li [1], Zhenjiang You [3,*], Mengting Zuo [4], Pengxiang Diwu [4], Rui Wang [5], Xing Zhang [6] and Jinhui Liang [7]

[1] Unconventional Oil and Gas Institute, China University of Petroleum, Beijing 102249, China; yulong.yang@cup.edu.cn (Y.Y.); lililiyuqi@163.com (Y.L.)
[2] CNOOC (China) Ltd., Tianjin 300452, China; liyy64@cnooc.com.cn
[3] School of Chemical Engineering, The University of Queensland, Brisbane, QLD 4072, Australia
[4] College of Science, China University of Petroleum, Beijing 102249, China; mmzfl@foxmail.com (M.Z.); diwupx@126.com (P.D.)
[5] Petroleum Exploration and Development Research Institute, Shengli Oilfield Company, SINOPEC, Dongying 257015, China; wangrui971.slyt@sinopec.com
[6] Research Institute of Petroleum Engineering, Shengli Oilfield Company, SINOPEC, Dongying 257001, China; zhangxing.slyt@sinopec.com
[7] Tianjin Dagang Oilfield Shengda Technology Co., Ltd., Tianjin 300280, China; eeceec@126.com
* Correspondence: ltjcup@cup.edu.cn (T.L.); z.you@uq.edu.au (Z.Y.)

Citation: Yang, Y.; Liu, T.; Li, Y.; Li, Y.; You, Z.; Zuo, M.; Diwu, P.; Wang, R.; Zhang, X.; Liang, J. Effects of Velocity and Permeability on Tracer Dispersion in Porous Media. *Appl. Sci.* **2021**, *11*, 4411. https://doi.org/10.3390/app11104411

Academic Editor: Jianzhong Lin

Received: 2 April 2021
Accepted: 5 May 2021
Published: 13 May 2021

Publisher's Note: MDPI stays neutral with regard to jurisdictional claims in published maps and institutional affiliations.

Abstract: During micro-scale tracer flow in porous media, the permeability and fluid velocity significantly affect the fluid dispersion properties of the media. However, the relationships between the dispersion coefficient, permeability, and fluid velocity in core samples are still not clearly understood. Two sets of experiments were designed to study the effects of tracer fluid flow velocity and porous medium permeability on the dispersion phenomenon in a core environment, using natural and sand-filled cores, respectively. From experimental data-fitting by a mathematical model, the relationship between the dispersion coefficient, flow velocity, and permeability was identified, allowing the analysis of the underlying mechanism behind this phenomenon. The results show that a higher volumetric flow rate and lower permeability cause a delay in the tracer breakthrough time and an increase in the dispersion coefficient. The core experimental results show that the dispersion coefficient is negatively correlated with the permeability and positively correlated with the superficial velocity. The corresponding regression equations indicate linear relations between the dispersion coefficient, core permeability, and fluid velocity, resulting from the micron scale of grain diameters in cores. The combination of high velocity and low permeability yields a large dispersion coefficient. The effects of latitudinal dispersion in porous media cannot be ignored in low-permeability cores or formations. These findings can help to improve the understanding of tracer flow in porous media, the design of injection parameters, and the interpretation of tracer concentration distribution in inter-well tracer tests.

Keywords: tracer dispersion; fluid velocity; core permeability; porous media; tracer concentration

1. Introduction

The inter-well tracer test is one of the most mature and advanced testing techniques in reservoir development at present [1]. Formation heterogeneity properties, such as waterflooding channel permeability and fracture network volume, can be obtained from tracer concentration interpretation [2]. Conservative tracers do not interact or alter during the transport, thus their concentration is not affected by processes other than dilution, dispersion, and partial redirection. Hydrodynamic dispersion, including mechanical dispersion and molecular diffusion, plays an important role in the tracer concentration distribution [3]. It is necessary to study the dispersion effect on tracer flow to improve formation heterogeneity characterization by inter-well tracer tests [4].

Hydrodynamic dispersion is one of the mixing effects that occur in laminar flow through a porous medium [5,6]. It is a macroscopic phenomenon determined by the interaction of molecular diffusion and advection processes, resulting in the development of a transition zone between miscible fluids with two different components [7]. This phenomenon, which was first discovered in groundwater, is now widely encountered in many fields, such as chemical engineering, materials science, hydrology, and petroleum engineering.

Hydrodynamic dispersion can be regarded as an attribute of the porous system, or as the spreading behavior of a solute during its transportation [8]. The dispersion process may be described with reference to a model system consisting of a cylindrical tube filled with homogeneous sand grains initially saturated with fresh water. At the start of the experiment—i.e., $t = 0$—water containing a type of tracer was injected into the porous medium. The produced tracer concentration was measured as a function of time t at a point located at a distance L downstream of the injection point, yielding the so-called breakthrough curve. Assuming that no dispersion occurs, the breakthrough curve should show a step change—i.e., a sharp front moving at the average velocity—which is determined by Darcy's law. However, due to the existence of hydrodynamic dispersion, the observed breakthrough curve is actually S-shaped, with a part of the tracer-containing water being ahead of the position where the average flow velocity is reached and a transition zone occurring between the tracer concentrations due to hydrodynamic dispersion.

Since the 1950s, many scholars have observed, analyzed, and summarized a large number of tracer dispersion experiments in the laboratory and proposed various models to describe the solute dispersion process in porous media. By the 1960s, a more systematic description of dispersion in porous media had been formulated. In theory, the hydrodynamic dispersion approximation follows Fick's law of material diffusion in free solutions. An advection-dispersion equation was established for solute transport based on this theory [3]. With increased research on miscible and chemical flooding, the effects of adsorption and other factors on solute transport have been incorporated, allowing the establishment of equations describing the dispersion phenomenon under different conditions [9,10], which can be solved using numerical techniques [11].

The main cause of the dispersion phenomenon is purely mechanical and is therefore different from that of molecular diffusion caused by concentration differences. The primary mechanism is the resistance caused by the friction between the fluid and the complex microstructure of the porous medium, which causes the fluid to pass through different pores at different velocities [12]. The dispersion coefficient is a parameter that characterizes the ability of a fluid to disperse in a porous medium at a certain flow rate [13]. It is significantly correlated with the parameters that describe the structure of a porous medium (such as porosity [14], pore size [15,16], pore uniformity [17], and tortuosity [18]) and the characteristics of particles (such as particle uniformity [19], shape (curvature) [20,21], and size [22,23]). Generally, dispersion is a phenomenon caused by differences in velocity due to the different structures in porous media, and the dispersion coefficient is considered to have a close relationship with the structures of the porous medium and the velocity of the fluid.

To further elucidate the relationship between the porous medium and the dispersion coefficient, Van der Meer et al. (1984) [24] proposed a correlation for a single solid phase considering the dispersion coefficient as a sole function of liquid superficial velocity. Galvin et al. (2006) [25] investigated the steady-state segregation and dispersion of a binary system of particles in a liquid-fluidized bed, illustrating that the dispersion coefficient exhibits a positive linear relationship with interstitial fluid velocity. Zhao (2007) [26] conducted core displacement experiments on sandstone, using a light volatile oil to displace crude oil. The results showed that the calculated dispersion coefficient was positively correlated with the core permeability on a semi-logarithmic scale. In 2010, Hua [27] conducted experiments on the relationship between the dispersion and flow conductivity in a horizontal fracture. The results showed that the dispersion in the Darcy flow was negatively correlated with the permeability coefficient. Qi et al. (2017) [28] used a particle tracking method based on a capillary network model, as well as the method of moments in conjunction with percolation theory to establish a three-dimensional percolation network model to determine the relationship between the dispersion coefficient and the permeability. The results showed that the dispersion coefficient was negatively correlated with the permeability if the hydraulic radii were constant and vice versa if they were variable. Khan et al. (2017) [29] utilized different dispersion correlations to describe the intermixing and segregation behavior for the binary particle species differing in density in terms of axial particle concentration profile. Moreover, Khan et al. (2020) [30] reported a model for dispersion coefficient along the line of definition for diffusion coefficient incorporating the mean free path of collision and interstitial fluid velocity as the characteristic velocity of collision. A summary of some of the main findings since the 1950s regarding the relationship between the dispersion coefficient and velocity is shown in Table 1.

Table 1. Main research findings on the relationship between the dispersion coefficient, structure of porous media, and fluid velocity.

Researchers	Research Method	Findings
Van der Meer et al. [24]	Single solid phase for dimensionless fractional liquid volume fraction distributed between 0.5 and 0.9, $0.002 < u < 0.3 \, \mathrm{m/s}$	Dispersion coefficient is a sole function of liquid superficial velocity $D = 0.25u^\beta$, exponential parameter β was fixed at 2.2
Taylor et al. [31–33]	Experiments on two glass spheres of different particle sizes in a one-dimensional vertical soil column	The dispersion coefficient varies linearly with the interstitial velocity, i.e., $D = \alpha u$
Galvin et al. [25]	Theoretical derivation and fluidization experiments verification in a Perspex tube, 50 mm in diameter	The dispersion coefficient varies linearly with the interstitial velocity—i.e., $D = \alpha du/\varphi$—adjustable parameter α was fixed at 0.7
Ebach and White [34]	Experiment in a packed bed	β is negatively correlated with the flow rate
Sahimi et al. [35]	Experiment in a two-dimensional porous medium	The longitudinal dispersion coefficient D_L does not vary linearly with water velocity
Pugliese and Poulsen [36]	Measuring the dispersion coefficient in a series of porous media with different grain sizes and shapes	The closer the particle is to a spherical shape, the more significant the nonlinear relationship between the dispersion coefficient and the velocity of water flow is—that is, β approaches 1.0 as the particle curvature increases
Kumar et al. [37,38]	Mathematical model on solute transport and dispersion in soil	In a certain range, the dynamic dispersion coefficient is linearly related to the square of the soil pore water velocity and the dispersion coefficient is positively related to the coefficient of variation of the velocity
Khan et al. [30]	Mathematical model and numerical model (CFD-DEM)	Dispersion coefficient incorporating the mean free path of collision and interstitial fluid velocity as the characteristic velocity of collision

The aforementioned research on the mechanism of dispersion phenomenon shows that there are different relationships between the dispersion coefficient, the structure of the particles (grains), and the fluid velocity. Moreover, there are few studies on the permeability–dispersion relationship, and they are all focused on soil or packed bed rather than porous media. Thus far, the relationships between the dispersion coefficient, permeability, and fluid velocity in core samples are not clearly understood.

To fill this gap, the present study applies two types of core samples to conduct experiments, exploring the influence of permeability and velocity on dispersion coefficients. Two sets of displacement experiments are conducted in natural and sand-filled cores, respectively, to obtain the tracer breakthrough concentrations. The experimental results will then be fitted using a correlation to ascertain the relationship between the dispersion coefficient and the fluid velocity and permeability. Finally, the underlying mechanisms behind these relations are discussed.

2. Materials and Method

2.1. Tracer Evaluation

The tracer thiocyanate ion (SCN^-) was selected for the experiments. Its traceability was evaluated as follows (Table 2): First, the background concentrations of the tracer in the rock samples and the formation water were measured to ensure that these materials were free of SCN^-. Second, the compatibility of SCN^- with the formation water was determined by placing the SCN^- solution in an incubator at the formation temperature (50 °C) for 10 days. The results of this observation showed that no precipitation occurred over the 10-day period, and the concentrations measured on days 3 and 10 were 49.5 and 49.0 mg/L, respectively, which represent rates of change in concentration of 1% and 2%, respectively. These results indicate that the SCN^- is compatible with the formation water.

Table 2. Tracer evaluation results.

Test Item	Test Results
Background concentration of SCN^- in formation water	0 mg/L
Compatibility test	No precipitation and lost concentration of 1% and 2% for days 3 and 10 in formation water, respectively
Static adsorption test	Adsorption ratio of 2.2%

Finally, a static adsorption test was performed. A total of 500 mL of 50 mg/L SCN^- solution was prepared, 150 mL of which was added to a triangle bottle along with 50 g of crushed rock sample. After stirring well, the bottle mouth was sealed and the bottle was shaken gently at the formation temperature for 48 h, before removing the supernatant and centrifuging. The concentration of the tracer was sampled and analyzed from the centrifuged solution. The result was 48.9 mg/L—i.e., an adsorption ratio of 2.2%. From these experimental measurements, it was concluded that SCN^- meets the requirements of the core flooding experiments under the selected experimental temperature.

2.2. Experimental Setup and Procedure

A schematic of the experimental setup for the tracer transport experiments is shown in Figure 1. The main experimental components included a constant flux pump, core holder, pressure gauge, tracer fluid tank, and formation water tank. The core sample (either natural or sand-filled) was placed in the core holder. The core was then saturated with water using a vacuum pump to ensure no air bubbles were present. A flask was used to collect the produced liquid. Finally, an oven was used to heat the core to determine its porosity.

Two sets of core displacement experiments were designed. The first set consisted of high-velocity (0.04 cm^3/s) and low-velocity (0.02 cm^3/s) displacement experiments performed on natural cores (Nos. 1–3) from the same formation and block. The second set consisted of four sand-filled cores (Nos. 4–7) with similar permeabilities subject to displacement experiments with different velocities (0.02, 0.03, 0.05, and 0.08 cm^3/s). The permeabilities of cores Nos. 1–3 were 1570, 610, and 230 mD, respectively. The permeabilities of cores Nos. 4–7 were between 574 and 699 mD, representing the typical permeability range of inter-well waterflooding channels in eastern oilfields in China. The fluid velocities in the experiments were selected based on the equivalent water injection velocities calculated from the injection rate.

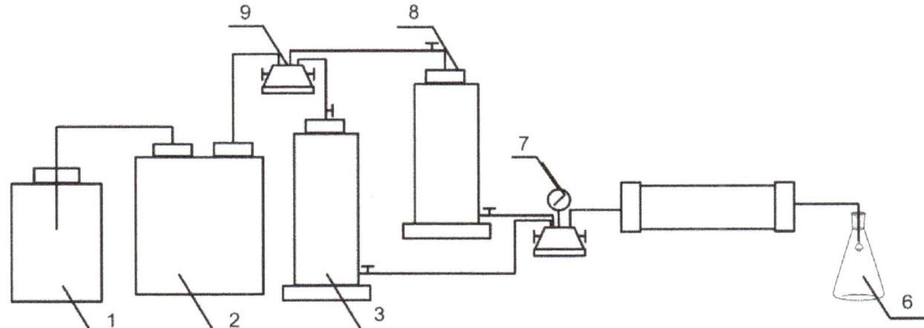

Figure 1. Schematic diagram of the experimental setup for tracer transport in cores: 1: Driving fluid pump; 2: constant flux pump; 3: tracer fluid tank; 4 and 9: six-way valves; 5: core holder; 6: collection flask; 7: pressure gauge; 8: formation water tank.

The experimental procedure for each group of experiments was as follows:

(1) A water displacement test was conducted to make sure there are no leaks in the system.

(2) A steady water displacement was carried out using a constant flux pump in order to calculate the absolute permeability of the core using the data from the pressure gauge and the injection flow rate.

(3) Once the absolute permeability was determined, the tracer, 50 mg/L SCN$^-$ solution, was injected at a constant flow rate. In total, two pore volumes (PV) of tracer were injected.

(4) Once the displacement experiments were completed, the core was heated in an oven and its porosity was determined.

3. Experimental Results and Discussion

3.1. Experimental Results

After the completion of the displacement experiment, the concentration of the produced tracer solution was measured. Figure 2 illustrates the tracer breakthrough concentrations from the natural cores (Nos. 1–3) for the high- and low-velocity displacement experiments. Figure 3 shows the tracer breakthrough concentration from the sand-filled cores (No. 4–7) at different displacement velocities.

3.2. Results Analysis

Based on the results obtained from the displacement experiments, the core dispersion coefficient was obtained by fitting the breakthrough concentration using the analytical solution Equation (A12) (see Appendix A) [3]. For the natural cores, Figures 4 and 5 show the fitting results for the low-velocity and high-velocity displacement experiments, respectively. For the sand-filled cores, Figure 6 shows the fitting results at different displacement velocities.

Tables 3 and 4 present the experimental parameters for the natural and sand-filled cores, respectively, including core porosity, length, permeability, flow rate, and velocity, as well as the dispersion coefficient values obtained by fitting.

As shown in Table 3, the interpreted dispersion coefficient increased slightly with the decrease in core permeability. As shown in Table 4, the interpreted dispersion coefficient increased from 0.004 to 0.023 cm^2/s with the increase in flow rate from 0.02 to 0.08 cm^3/s. Therefore, dispersion coefficient has a negative correlation with core permeability and a positive correlation with flow velocity. To examine whether the relationships are the same as for those with large particle sizes, including liquid-fluidized bed and Perspex tube, specific regression equations and the underlying mechanisms are studied in the next section.

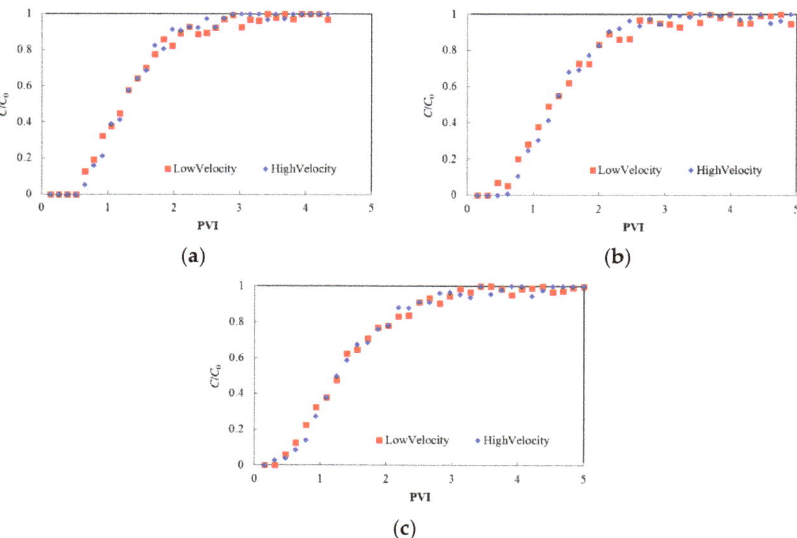

Figure 2. Tracer concentration ratio versus pore volume injected (PVI) at different flow rates in the natural cores (low rate = 0.02 cm^3/s; high rate = 0.04 cm^3/s): (**a**) core No. 1 (1570 mD), (**b**) core No. 2 (610 mD), and (**c**) core No. 3 (230 mD).

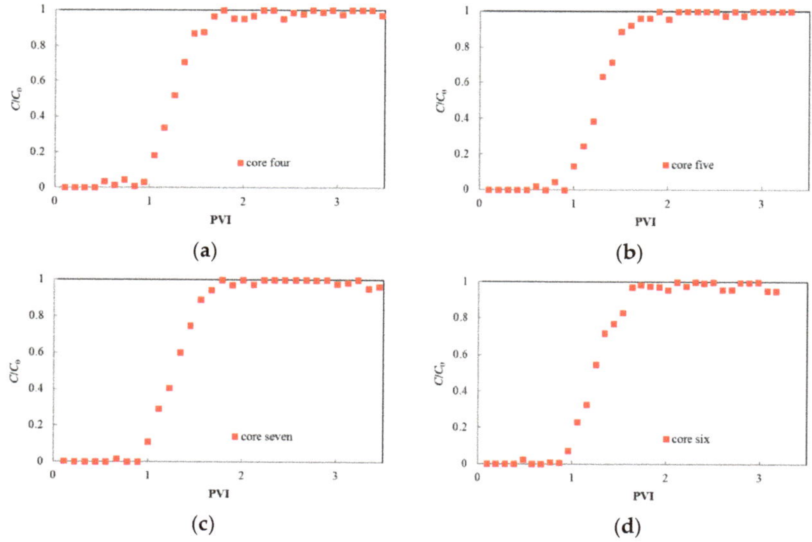

Figure 3. Tracer concentration ratio versus pore volume injected (PVI) at different flow rates in the sand-filled cores: (**a**) 0.02 cm^3/s; (**b**) 0.03 cm^3/s, (**c**) 0.05 cm^3/s, and (**d**) 0.08 cm^3/s.

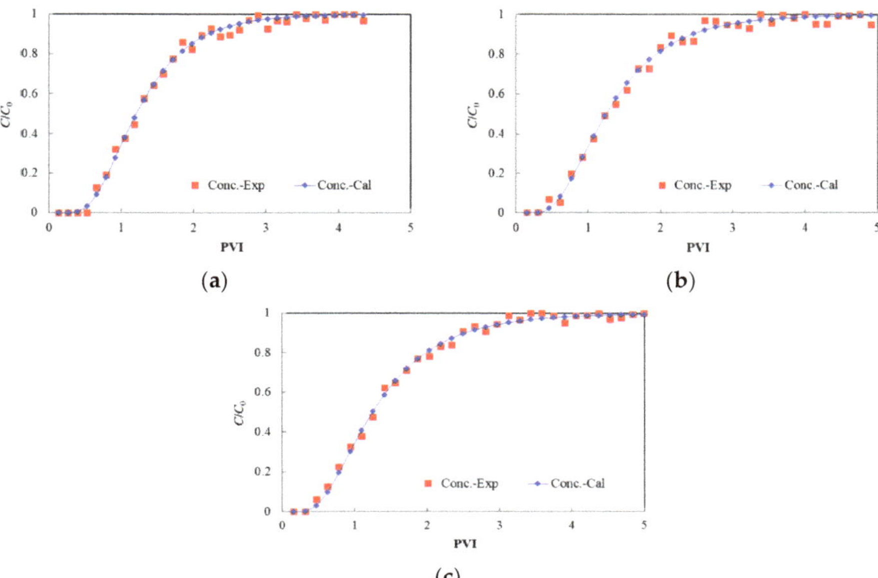

Figure 4. Data fitting for tracer concentration ratio versus pore volume injected (PVI) at low flow rate (0.02 cm^3/s) in natural cores: (**a**) core No. 1 (1570 mD), (**b**) core No. 2 (610 mD), and (**c**) core No. 3 (230 mD).

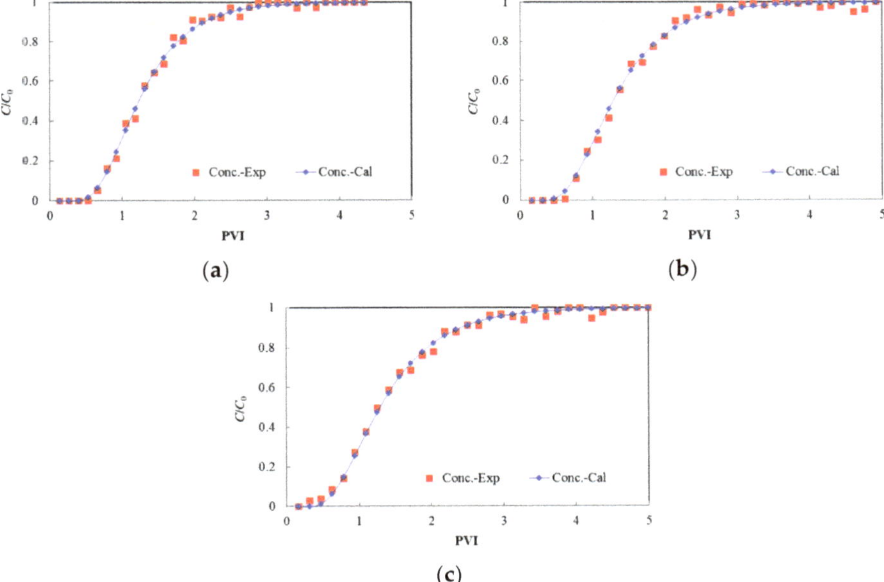

Figure 5. Data fitting for tracer concentration ratio versus pore volume injected (PVI) at high flow rate (0.04 cm^3/s) in natural cores: (**a**) core No. 1 (1570 mD), (**b**) core No. 2 (610 mD), and (**c**) core No. 3 (230 mD).

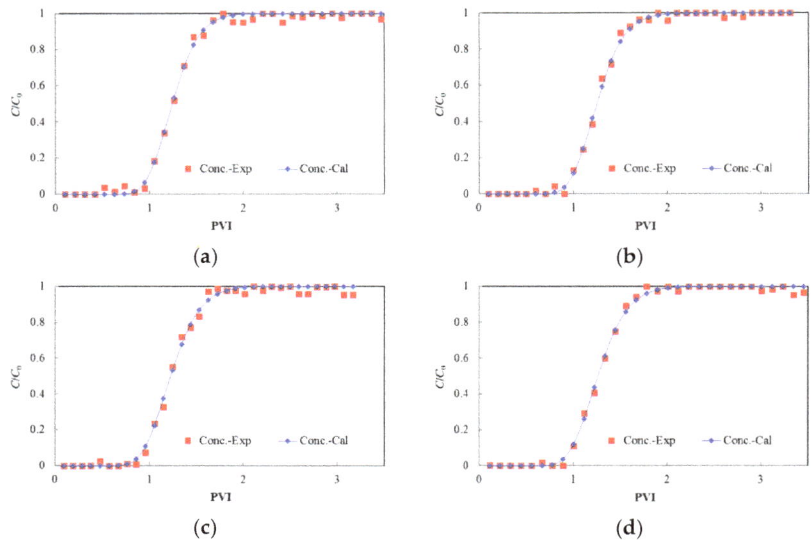

Figure 6. Data fitting for tracer concentration ratio versus pore volume injected (PVI) at different flow rates in sand-filled cores: (**a**) 0.02 cm^3/s; (**b**) 0.03 cm^3/s, (**c**) 0.05 cm^3/s, and (**d**) 0.08 cm^3/s.

Table 3. Experimental parameters and fitted dispersion coefficient for the natural cores.

Core No.	Factor	Porosity (%)	Length (cm)	Permeability (mD)	Flow Rate (cm^3/s)	Superficial Velocity (cm/s)	Dispersion Coefficient (cm^2/s)
1	Low velocity	0.31	24	1570	0.02	0.0131	0.037
	High velocity	0.31	24	1570	0.04	0.0263	0.060
2	Low velocity	0.27	23.6	610	0.02	0.0151	0.053
	High velocity	0.27	23.6	610	0.04	0.0302	0.077
3	Low velocity	0.26	24.1	230	0.02	0.0157	0.063
	High velocity	0.26	24.1	230	0.04	0.0314	0.096

Table 4. Experimental parameters and fitted dispersion coefficient for the sand-filled cores.

Core No.	Porosity (%)	Length (cm)	Permeability (mD)	Flow Rate (cm^3/s)	Superficial Velocity (cm/s)	Dispersion Coefficient (cm^2/s)
4	0.372	25	621	0.02	0.011	0.004
5	0.366	25	650	0.03	0.017	0.007
6	0.382	25	699	0.05	0.027	0.013
7	0.351	25	574	0.08	0.046	0.023

3.3. Discussion

3.3.1. Equations of Dispersion Coefficient in Cores

The dispersion coefficient values in Tables 3 and 4 demonstrate that the coefficient is positively correlated with superficial velocity, while it is negatively correlated with core permeability. Based on these results, the dispersion coefficient as functions of injection velocity for the natural and sand-filled cores are plotted in Figures 7 and 8, respectively. The linear relations between the dispersion coefficient, the velocity, and the permeability are obtained through calculation, as follows:

$$D_N = -1.2844 \times 10^{-5}K + 0.1040u + 0.0675 \tag{1}$$

$$D_A = -3.0807 \times 10^{-6}K + 0.5514u - 0.0041 \qquad (2)$$

where D_N and D_A are the dispersion coefficients of the natural and sand-filled cores, respectively (cm^2/s); K is the core permeability (mD); and u is the tracer superficial velocity. These figures confirm the trends observed in Tables 3 and 4.

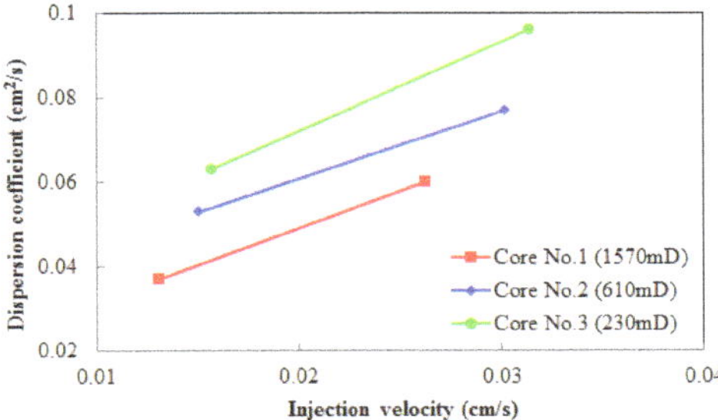

Figure 7. Dispersion coefficient versus injection (superficial) velocity in natural cores.

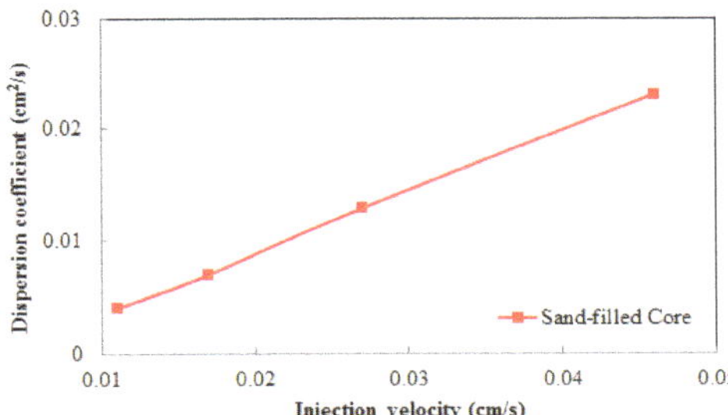

Figure 8. Dispersion coefficient versus injection (superficial) velocity in sand-filled cores.

The results of this work reveal a linear relationship between the dispersion coefficient and fluid velocity as shown in Equations (1) and (2), inconsistent with the previous findings of the nonlinear relationship [35–38]. The cause of this difference can be attributed to the grain shape and fluid velocity. As Pugliese and Poulsen [36] demonstrated, the closer a particle is to a spherical shape, the more significant the nonlinear relationship between the dispersion coefficient and the velocity of water flow. As the grain diameters in core samples are in the scale of micrometers and the grain shape is close to spherical, it is reasonable to approximate the grains as spheres and obtain a linear relationship.

3.3.2. Mechanisms of the Relations

To find the mechanisms of the relationships between the dispersion coefficient, permeability, and fluid velocity, two types of porous media were constructed as shown in Figure 9, which represent lower permeability (small pore sizes, Figure 9a) and higher permeability (large pore sizes, Figure 9b), respectively.

When tracers flow through the porous media, as shown in Figure 9, there are two main controlling factors, namely longitudinal and latitudinal dispersion [14,19]. Due to hydrodynamic retention, some of the tracers stay in the first layer while the rest continue on to the second layer, which is referred to as longitudinal dispersion. Additionally, due to the pore structure of the porous medium, the width of tracer liquid becomes twice that of the grain size in the second layer, resulting in dispersion in the latitudinal direction.

The relationship between dispersion coefficient and permeability can be explained using Figure 9. In the five-layer example illustrated here, at a given injection velocity, the width of tracer liquid becomes five times the grain size in the medium with small pore size (Figure 9a) but three times the grain size in the medium with a large pore size (Figure 9b) along the same flow distance. The difference in width is due to the difference in the average pore sizes at different permeabilities. Meanwhile, the pore structure of the lower-permeability core is more heterogeneous and small-scale breakthrough will occur, which results in an earlier breakthrough, slower rise in concentration, and larger dispersion coefficient.

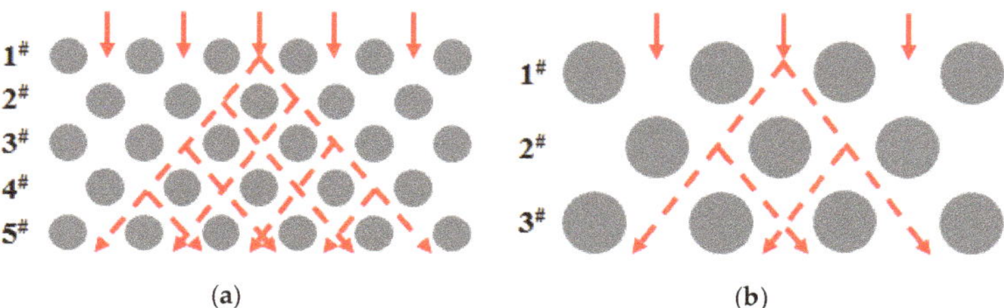

(a) (b)

Figure 9. Schematic diagram of structures of porous media: (**a**) small pore sizes, (**b**) large pore sizes.

The relationship between the dispersion coefficient and injection velocity can also be explained using Figure 9. When the permeability is fixed, the higher the superficial velocity, the greater the pressure gradient, and the smaller the fluid-activated pores—i.e., the fluid flows preferentially into the low-permeability pores. Along a given flow distance, the width of the tracer liquid becomes five times the grain size at high velocity (i.e., small pore size medium, Figure 9a) but three times the grain size at low velocity (i.e., large pore size medium, Figure 9b) due to the difference in the average size of flow pores at different velocities. Therefore, when a small volume of displacement fluid is injected, a tracer will be produced at the outlet, corresponding to the so-called "channeling effect" in the pore network. Meanwhile, as the injection rate increases, it may strengthen some of the microscopic heterogeneous features that actually exist inside the core, resulting in a small amount of intrusion and hence an earlier breakthrough, a slower concentration increase, and a larger dispersion coefficient. Therefore, in the core displacement experiments, the small sizes of flow pores at high velocities result in more complex flow paths within porous media and thereby experience stronger dispersion.

The work in this paper demonstrates that there are different dispersion coefficients resulting from different porous media size and tracer interstitial velocity. It can improve inter-well tracer test not only in injection parameters design, but also in tracer concentration interpretation. Firstly, the injection velocity in a project should be optimized, because the economic benefit can be reduced if the velocity is too low; on the other hand, the mixing effect can be amplified if the velocity is too high. Secondly, it is more suitable to use the dispersion coefficient of the high permeability layer, rather than that corresponding to the average reservoir permeability.

4. Conclusions

In this paper, the effects of velocity and permeability on the dispersion coefficient in cores were investigated. Two sets of core flooding experiments were conducted on natural and sand-filled cores, respectively. The relations between the dispersion coefficient, velocity, and permeability were obtained through fitting the experimental results with an analytical model. The main conclusions drawn from the results presented herein are as follows:

(1) The core experimental results show that the dispersion coefficient is negatively correlated with the permeability and positively correlated with the superficial velocity. Low permeability and high heterogeneity result in large latitudinal dispersion and high dispersion coefficient. If the superficial velocity is high, the pressure drop along the core is large. This causes the fluid to enter the small pores, resulting in large dispersion coefficient. The combination of high velocity and low permeability yields a large dispersion coefficient.

The effects of latitudinal dispersion in porous media cannot be ignored in low-permeability cores or formations.

(2) The interpretation results show that the dispersion coefficient increased from 0.063 to 0.037 cm^2/s with the decrease in core permeability from 230 to 1570 mD at the flow rate of 0.02 cm^3/s. The dispersion coefficient increased from 0.004 to 0.023 cm^2/s with the increase in flow rate from 0.02 to 0.08 cm^3/s. The corresponding regression equations indicate linear relations between the dispersion coefficient, core permeability, and fluid velocity, resulting from the micron scale of the grain diameters in the cores.

Author Contributions: Conceptualization, Y.Y., T.L.; Methodology, T.L.; Experiments, Y.L. (Yanyue Li), Y.L. (Yuqi Li); Mathematical modelling and solution, Z.Y., M.Z., P.D.; Analysis, Z.Y., P.D.; Writing—original draft preparation, Y.L. (Yanyue Li), Y.L. (Yuqi Li), R.W.; Writing—review and editing, Y.Y., Z.Y., X.Z., J.L. All authors have read and agreed to the published version of the manuscript.

Funding: This work was supported by National Key Research and Development Plan (No.2018YFB06 05500) and the Science Foundation of China University of Petroleum (2462019YJRC013, 2462020YXZZ 003 and 2462020XKJS02).

Institutional Review Board Statement: Not applicable.

Informed Consent Statement: Not applicable.

Data Availability Statement: Not applicable.

Conflicts of Interest: The authors declare no conflict of interest.

Nomenclature

C	tracer concentration in aqueous solution (mg/L)
C_0	tracer concentration in injected solution (mg/L)
D	dispersion coefficient (cm^2/s)
D_L	longitudinal dispersion coefficient (cm^2/s)
D_N	dispersion coefficients of the natural cores (cm^2/s)
D_A	dispersion coefficients of the sand-filled cores (cm^2/s)
u	tracer interstitial velocity (cm/s)
α	adjustable parameter in dispersion relationship
β	exponential parameter in dispersion relationship
x	flow distance (cm)
t	time (s)
t'	modified time
K	core permeability (mD)
Φ_f	flow porosity
Φ	porosity
ρ_r	rock density (g/cm^3)
S_o	oil saturation
S_{wc}	bound water saturation
a	Langmuir isothermal adsorption coefficient
s	Laplace variable

Appendix A. Mathematical Model and Analytical Solution of Tracer Flow in Porous Media

The governing equation of tracer flow at the pore level may be expressed as [3]:

$$D\frac{\partial^2 C}{\partial x^2} - u\frac{\partial C}{\partial x} = \frac{[\phi(1 - S_o) + a(1 - \phi)\rho_r]}{\phi_f(1 - S_o - S_{wc})}\frac{\partial C}{\partial t} \tag{A1}$$

where D is the dispersion coefficient (cm^2/s), C is tracer concentration in aqueous solution (mg/L), u is interstitial velocity (cm/s), x is flow distance (cm), Φ_f is flow porosity, Φ is porosity, S_o is oil saturation, S_{wc} is bound water saturation, a is the Langmuir isothermal adsorption coefficient, and ρ_r is the rock density (g/cm^3).

To obtain the analytical solution for the tracer flow equation at the pore scale, the modified time, t', is introduced as follows:

$$t' = \frac{\phi_f(1 - S_o - S_{wc})}{[\phi(1 - S_o) + a(1 - \phi)\rho_r]}t \tag{A2}$$

Consequently, the mathematical model for tracer flow at the pore level may be simplified as:

$$D\frac{\partial^2 C}{\partial x^2} - u\frac{\partial C}{\partial x} = \frac{\partial C}{\partial t'} \tag{A3}$$

$$C(x,0) = \begin{cases} C_0 & x \le 0 \\ 0 & x > 0 \end{cases} \tag{A4}$$

$$C(0,t) = C_0 \quad t > 0 \tag{A5}$$

$$C(\infty,t) = 0 \quad t > 0 \tag{A6}$$

where C_0 is the tracer concentration in injected solution (mg/L).

Using the method of Laplace transform allows the mathematical model for tracer flow at the pore scale to be expressed as follows:

$$\overline{C}(s) = L[C(t')] \tag{A7}$$

$$D\frac{d^2\overline{C}}{dx^2} - u\frac{d\overline{C}}{dx} - s\overline{C} = 0 \tag{A8}$$

$$\overline{C}(0) = \frac{C_0}{s} \tag{A9}$$

$$\overline{C}(\infty) = 0 \tag{A10}$$

where s is the Laplace variable.

Equation (A8) is an ordinary differential equation (ODE) with a general solution as follows:

$$\overline{C} = c_1 e^{\lambda_1 x} + c_2 e^{\lambda_2 x} \tag{A11}$$

where $\lambda_1 = \frac{u + \sqrt{u^2 + 4Ds}}{2D}$ and $\lambda_2 = \frac{u - \sqrt{u^2 + 4Ds}}{2D}$.

Considering the initial and boundary conditions (Equations (A9) and (A10)) allows the analytical solution to be obtained in Laplace space.

$$\frac{\overline{C}}{C_0} = e^{\frac{ux}{2D}}\frac{1}{s}e^{-a_1\sqrt{b_1^2 + s}} \tag{A12}$$

where $a_1 = \frac{x}{\sqrt{D}}$ and $b_1 = \sqrt{\frac{u^2}{4D}}$.

Through an inverse Laplace transform, the analytical solution in the time domain may be expressed as follows:

$$\frac{C}{C_0} = e^{\frac{ux}{2D}}L^{-1}\left[\frac{1}{s}e^{-a_1\sqrt{b_1^2 + s}}\right] = \frac{1}{2}erfc\left(\frac{x - ut'}{2\sqrt{Dt'}}\right) + \frac{1}{2}e^{\frac{ux}{D}}erfc\left(\frac{x + ut'}{2\sqrt{Dt'}}\right) \tag{A13}$$

References

1. Serres-Piole, C.; Preud'homme, H.; Moradi-Tehrani, N.; Allanic, C.; Jullia, H.; Lobinski, R. Water tracers in oilfield applications: Guidelines. *J. Pet. Sci. Eng.* **2012**, *98–99*, 22–39. [CrossRef]
2. Cao, V.; Schaffer, M.; Taherdangkoo, R.; Licha, T. Solute Reactive Tracers for Hydrogeological Applications: A Short Review and Future Prospects. *Water* **2020**, *12*, 653. [CrossRef]

3. Liu, T.J.; Liu, W.X.; Diwu, P.X.; Hu, G.X.; Xu, T.; Li, Y.Q.; You, Z.J.; Qiao, R.W.; Wang, J. Modeling Tracer Flow Characteristics in Different Types of Pores: Visualization and Mathematical Modelling. *Comp. Model. Eng. Sci.* **2020**, *123*, 1205–1222. [CrossRef]
4. Kamali, F.; Hussain, F. Field-scale simulation of CO_2 enhanced oil recovery and storage through SWAG injection using laboratory estimated relative permeabilities. *J. Pet. Sci. Eng.* **2017**, *156*, 396–407. [CrossRef]
5. Hussain, F.; Cinar, Y.; Bedrikovetsky, P. *Comparison of Methods for Drainage Relative Permeability Estimation from Displacement Tests*; SPE Improved Oil Recovery Symposium: Tulsa, OK, USA, 2010.
6. Zou, S.; Hussain, F.; Arns, J.; Guo, Z.; Arns, C.H. Computation of relative permeability from in-situ imaged fluid distributions at the pore scale. *SPE J.* **2018**, *23*, 737–749. [CrossRef]
7. Liu, T.J.; Jiang, B.Y.; Liu, R.; Zhang, X.H.; Xie, X.Q. Reservoir characteristics of chromatographic effect of tracer flow in porous medium. *J. Chongqing Univ.* **2013**, *36*, 58–63.
8. Tatomir, A.; McDermott, C.; Bensabat, J.; Class, H.; Edlmann, K.; Taherdangkoo, R.; Sauter, M. Conceptual model development using a generic Features, Events, and Processes (FEP) database for assessing the potential impact of hydraulic fracturing on groundwater aquifers. *Adv. Geosci.* **2018**, *45*, 185–192. [CrossRef]
9. Xu, J.P.; Wang, L.Z.; Zhu, K.Q. Concentration distribution and variation in a polymer-flooding reservoir. *J. Tsinghua Univ.* **2002**, *04*, 455–457.
10. Fan, Y.; Liu, C.Q. Two-dimensional Transport of solute in porous media and its numerical solution. *Acta Petrolei Sinica.* **1988**, *1*, 75–85.
11. Liu, T.J.; Diwu, P.X.; Liu, R.; Jiang, L.W.; Jiang, B.Y. Fast Algorithm of Numerical Solutions for Strong Nonlinear Partial Differential Equations. *Adv. Mech. Eng.* **2014**, *6*, 1–5. [CrossRef]
12. Zhang, P.Y. Penetration Migration of Suspended Particles in Porous Media: Pore Structure and Particle Scale Effects. Ph.D. Thesis, Beijing Jiaotong University, Beijing, China, 2016.
13. Yang, J.Z. Experimental study indoor of diffusion coefficient of dispersion coefficient. *Geotech. Investig. Survey* **1985**, *1*, 55–59.
14. Ma, X.Y.; Kang, X.B.; Wang, Z.M.; Wang, X.; Shi, X.D. Cl- Transport in Saturated Soils under Different Pore Conditions. *Res. Explor. Lab.* **2018**, *37*, 30–33+67.
15. Huang, K.L. Research on the Scale Effect of Hydrodynamic Dispersion in Porous Media-Current Status and Prospect. *Hydrogeol. Eng. Geo.* **1991**, *03*, 25–26+31.
16. Zou, L.Z.; Pan, J.; Yang, C.B.; Zhang, H.Y. Present situation on the study of scale effect of hydraulic parameter in aquifer. *J. Changchun Univ. Earth Sci.* **1994**, *1*, 66–69.
17. Wang, F. A Study on the Hydrodynamic Diffusion and Scale Effect of Loose Rock Mass Pore Media. Master's Thesis, Southwest Jiaotong University, Chengdu, China, 2015.
18. Xu, Y.L. Experimental Study of Contaminant Transport and the Velocity Dependence of Dispersion in Porous Media. Master's Thesis, Hefei University Technology, Hefei, China, 2017.
19. Rao, D.Y.; Bai, B. Study on the factors affecting dispersity of porous media by SPH simulation in solute transport. *J. Hydraul. Eng.* **2019**, *50*, 824–834.
20. Witt, K.J.; Brauns, J. Permeability allisotropy due to particle shape. *J. Waterw.* **1983**, *109*, 1181–1187.
21. Shinohara, K.; Oida, M.; Golman, B. Effect of particle shape on angle of internal friction by triaxle compression test. *Powder Technol.* **2000**, *107*, 131–136. [CrossRef]
22. Delgado, J.M.P.Q. A critical review of dispersion in packed beds. *Heat Mass Transf.* **2006**, *42*, 279–310. [CrossRef]
23. Rouse, P.C.; Fannin, R.J.; Shuttle, D.A. Influence of roundness on the void ratio and strength of uniform sand. *Geotechnique* **2008**, *58*, 227–231. [CrossRef]
24. Van der Meer, A.P.; Blanchard, C.M.R.J.P.; Wesselingh, J.A. Mixing of particles in liquid fluidized beds. *Chem. Eng. Res. Des.* **1984**, *62*, 214–222.
25. Galvin, K.F.; Swann, R.; Ramirez, W.F. Segregation and Dispersion of a Binary System of Particles in a Fluidized Bed. *AICHE J.* **2006**, *52*, 3401–3410. [CrossRef]
26. Zhao, G.J. Markov Process Describes Dispersion Phenomena in Porous Medium. Master's Thesis, Northeast Petrology University, Daqing, China, 2007.
27. Hua, F. Experimental Study of Dispersion Coefficient and Scale Effect in Single Horizontal Fracture. Master's Thesis, Hefei University Technology, Hefei, China, 2010.
28. Qi, T.; Li, M. Study of the relationship between dispersion coefficients and permeability by percolation network model. *Chin. J. Hydrodyn.* **2017**, *32*, 477–483.
29. Khan, M.S.; Mitra, S.; Ghatage, S.V.; Doroodchi, E.; Joshi, J.B.; Evans, G.M. Segregation and dispersion studies in binary solid-liquid fluidised beds: A theoretical and computational study. *Powder Technol.* **2017**, *314*, 400–411. [CrossRef]
30. Khan, M.S.; Evans, G.M.; Nguyen, A.V.; Mitra, S. Analysis of particle dispersion coefficient in solid-liquid fluidised beds. *Powder Technol.* **2020**, *365*, 60–73. [CrossRef]
31. Taylor, G.I. Dispersion of soluble matter in solvent flowing slowly through a tube. *Proc. R. Soc.* **1953**, *219*, 186–203.
32. Home, R.N.; Rodriguez, F. Dispersion in tracer flow in fractured geothermal systems. *Geophys. Res. Lett.* **1983**, *10*, 289–292.
33. Simpson, E.S. *Velocity and the Longitudinal Dispersion Coefficient in Flow through Porous Media*; Dewiest: San Diego, CA, USA, 1969; pp. 109–200.
34. Ebach, E.A.; White, R.R. Mixing of fluids flowing through beds of packed solids. *Am. Inst. Chem. Eng.* **1958**, *4*, 161–169. [CrossRef]

35. Sahimi, M.; Hughes, B.D.; Scfiven, L.E.; Davis, H.T. Dispersion in flow through porous media-One phase flow. *Chem. Eng. Sci.* **1986**, *41*, 2103–2122. [CrossRef]
36. Pugliese, L.; Poulsen, T.G. Estimating solute dispersion coefficients in porous media at low pore water velocities. *Soil Sci.* **2014**, *179*, 175–181. [CrossRef]
37. Kumar, A.; Kumar, D.J.; Kumar, N. Analytical solutions to one-dimensional advection–diffusion equation with variable coefficients in semi-infinite media. *J. Hydrol.* **2009**, *118*, 539–549. [CrossRef]
38. Kumar, D.J.; Kumar, A.; Kumar, A.; Yadav, R.R. Analytical solutions for temporally and spatially dependent solute dispersion of pulse type input concentration in one-dimensional semi-infinite media. *J. Hydro-Environ. Res.* **2009**, *2*, 254–263.

Article

Simulation of Aerosol Evolution within Background Pollution for Nucleated Vehicle Exhaust via TEMOM

Can Tu [1], Yueyan Liu [2,*], Taiquan Wu [2] and Mingzhou Yu [1]

[1] Laboratory of Areosol Science and Technology, China Jiliang University, Hangzhou 310018, China; s1701081110@cjlu.edu.cn (C.T.); mzyu@cjlu.edu.cn (M.Y.)

[2] College of Modern Science and Technology, China Jiliang University, Yiwu 322000, China; 07a0803079@cjlu.edu.cn

* Correspondence: 12a1803148@cjlu.edu.cn

Abstract: This work is intended to study the effect of background particles on vehicle emissions in representative realistic atmospheric environments. The coupling of Reynolds-Averaged Navier–Stokes equation (RANS) and Taylor-series Expansion Method Of Moments (TEMOM) is performed to track the emissions of the vehicle and simulating the evolution of the matters. The transport equation of mass, momentum, heat, and the first three orders of moments are taken into account with the effect of binary homogeneous nucleation, Brownian coagulation, condensation, and thermophoresis. The parameterization model is utilized for nucleation. The measured data for Beijing's particle size distribution under both polluted and nonpolluted conditions are utilized as background particles. The relationship between the macroscopic measurement results and the microscopic dynamic process is analyzed by comparing the variation trend of several physical quantities in the process of aerosol evolution. It is found with an increase of background particle concentration, the nucleation is inhibited, which is consistent with the existing studies.

Keywords: TEMOM; RANS; background aerosol; vehicle emissions

Citation: Tu, C.; Liu, Y.; Wu, T.; Yu, M. Simulation of Aerosol Evolution within Background Pollution for Nucleated Vehicle Exhaust via TEMOM. *Appl. Sci.* **2021**, *11*, 4552. https://dci.org/10.3390/app11104552

Academic Editor: Prashant Kumar

Received: 1 April 2021
Accepted: 4 May 2021
Published: 17 May 2021

Publisher's Note: MDPI stays neutral with regard to jurisdictional claims in published maps and institutional affiliations.

1. Introduction

The health effects of particulate matter (PM) air pollution have long been a matter of widespread concern [1–4]. Much of this work focuses on measurements of aerosols at different times of the day. This method can identify periods when particle concentrations are highest directly to judge the degree of its impact on health. However, this research method cannot analyze the factors affecting the evolution of aerosols and the origin of aerosols. The reason is that the pollution sources, temperature, humidity, etc., change with time during the day. All of these changes affect the evolution of aerosols as the aerosol evolves over the day. Therefore, the factors cannot be decoupled. Therefore, simulation plays an essential role in solving how physical quantities affect the evolution of aerosols. Simulation can keep irrelevant variables unchanged and only change the target variable.

The coupling of fine particles and macroscopic flow field belongs to multiphase flow in fluid mechanics. In this study, there are only two phases: air and particles. When dealing with the multiphase flow, the continuous phase is generally described by Navier–Stokes equation, and there are many options for the discrete phase. There are generally three choices. First, the discrete phase is equivalent to the continuous phase, which is the same as the continuous phase and is described by the NS equation. Second, use Lagrangian particles for tracking; third, use the PBE (Population Balance Equation) equation to describe the discrete phase. We are using the third method here.

Silva's work [5] has shown that these particulate matters, especially with diameters below 100 nm, have a more adverse influence on human health than ultrafine and coarse particles. The first study found the effect on background aerosol, including coagulation, condensation, and nucleation, coupled with Navier–Stokes equation. By comparing with the simulation data, the effect of background aerosol on the evolution process is investigated. We have set up six cases to evaluate the effect of background pollution on nucleation. The simulation method had been proved with a good agreement by Yu [6].

Many studies have reported aerosol's evolution under pollution conditions [7–9]. The background of pollution has a significant impact on the evolution of aerosols, which has reached a consensus. However, these studies are mainly based on experiments and measurements. They do not involve the quantitative analysis of the aerosol evolution process of the background physical quantities of the pollution background.

Kulmala [10] uses the thermodynamically consistent theory to treat the binary nucleation rate as a function of temperature, relative humidity, and acidity. Compared with the classical approach, they increased the computational efficiency of simulated nucleation by 25 times. Then, Vehkamaki [11] extended the applicable temperature range of the work to the high-temperature range, which led to applying this research to simulate vehicle emissions. The evolution of vehicle emissions will be diluted in three-dimensional space due to the consideration of the flow field. The temperature, concentration, etc. will change accordingly. This can lead to significant changes in particle size and its distribution. This is also the reason why the Euler–Euler model is challenging to track the particle phase. It is complicated to consider multiple processes at the same time. Thus, researchers have separately studied the influence of a single process on the single properties of particle population. For example, Kim [12,13] studied the effect of environmental dilution on the particle size distribution and concentration changes of the carrier by taking the particle size distribution as a function of time. Tat Leung Chan studied the influence of turbulent kinetic energy on coagulation [14], dilution on number concentration, and the relationship between internal combustion engine operating state and particle size [15].

The influence of the vehicle's shape on the flow field cannot be ignored during the driving process of the vehicle. The enrichment and desalination of the background particle concentration by the flow field will indirectly affect the evolution of aerosols. As Figure 2 shows, the figure uses log scale when mapping data to colors to observe the nucleation rate with a large span of magnitude. The vehicle's shape limits the spatial range of the evolution of particulate matter in the rear area of the car. This interference will increase turbulence and indirectly affect the coagulation process [16]. There are also related experiments to study the influence of the airflow angle of the exhaust tailpipe on the evolution of aerosols [17].

The study shows that the main source of urban pollution is automobile emission. However, the research on emission evolution focuses on the evolution of emission in a pure environment. In practice, a considerable degree of background particulate matter already exists in urban atmospheres. Moreover, the characteristics of background particulate matter under the condition of pollution are very different from those under the condition of no pollution. In practice, Seipenbusch [18] found that background particulate matter has its parameter characteristics. We believe that this has a significant impact on the evolution of emissions. To test this idea, Seipenbusch [18] analyzed fully evolved aerosols.

We plan to use simulation methods to predict the evolution of aerosols in the presence of background particles in order to find out the law of the control of urban air pollution and other occasions of aerosol physical property control.

2. Governing Equation

2.1. CFD Model

The one-way couple was used between the continuous and discrete phase considering that the particle has a minimum mass. Thus, we solved the fluid dynamic equation and moment transport equation separately. To obtain the information of fluid flow, the RANS equation coupled with Renormalized Group (RNG) $k \sim \omega$ turbulent model is utilized. The governing equations are described as follows:

$$\frac{\partial \overline{u_i}}{\partial x_i} = 0$$

$$\rho \frac{\partial \overline{u_i}}{\partial t} + \frac{\partial}{\partial x_j}(\rho \overline{u_i u_j}) = -\frac{\partial \overline{p}}{x_i} + \mu \frac{\partial^2 \overline{u_i}}{\partial x_j \partial x_i} - \frac{\partial R_{ij}}{\partial x_j} + \overline{f_i} \tag{1}$$

in which

$$R_{ij} = \mu_t \left(\frac{\partial \overline{u_i}}{\partial x_j} + \frac{\partial \overline{u_j}}{\partial x_i} \right) - \frac{2}{3}\rho k \delta_{ij} \tag{2}$$

where $\overline{u_i}$ and $\overline{u_j}$ are mean velocity in i th and jth direction coordinates, respectively; ρ is the fluid density; μ is the laminar viscosity; $\overline{f_i}$ is the body force in the ith direction coordinate, and μ_t is the turbulent dynamic viscosity. The enthalpy h is calculated by solving the following energy equation in this study:

$$\frac{\partial(\rho h)}{\partial t} + \frac{\partial}{\partial x_i}(\rho h \overline{u_i}) = \frac{\partial}{\partial x_i}\left(\frac{k_t}{C_p} \frac{\partial h}{\partial x_i} \right) \tag{3}$$

where k_t is the thermal conductivity and C_p is the specific heat at constant pressure. The temperature T is obtained by:

$$h = C_p T \tag{4}$$

the turbulence kinetic energy k_t and its rate of dissipation C_p are obtained by the equations below:

$$\frac{\partial(\rho k)}{\partial t} + \frac{\partial}{\partial x_i}(\rho k u_i) = \frac{\partial}{\partial x_j}\left[\left(\mu + \frac{\mu_\tau}{\delta_k} \right) \frac{\partial k}{\partial x_j} \right] + P_k + P_b - \rho \epsilon - Y_M \tag{5}$$

$$\frac{\partial(\rho \epsilon)}{\partial t} + \frac{\partial}{\partial x_i}(\rho \epsilon u_i) = \frac{\partial}{\partial x_j}\left[\left(\mu + \frac{\mu_\tau}{\delta_\epsilon} \right) \frac{\partial \epsilon}{\partial x_j} \right] + c_{\epsilon 1} \frac{\epsilon}{k}(P_k + c_{\epsilon 3}P_b) - c_{\epsilon 2}\rho \frac{\epsilon^2}{k} \tag{6}$$

where P_k represents the production of turbulence kinetic energy due to the mean velocity gradients. P_b represents the production of turbulence kinetic energy due to buoyancy. Y_M represents the partition of fluctuating dilatation incompressible turbulence to the overall dissipation rate. The turbulent Prandtl number for k, δ_k, is 1; the turbulent Prandtl number for ϵ, δ_ϵ, is 1.30; and $c_{\epsilon 1}$ is 1.44, $c_{\epsilon 2}$ is 1.92; the turbulent viscosity, μ_t, is obtained by:

$$\mu_t = c\rho \vartheta \ell = \rho c_\mu \frac{k^2}{\epsilon} \tag{7}$$

where c_μ is 0.09, $\vartheta = k^{1/2}$, $\ell = k^{3/2}/\epsilon$; and energy Prandtl number and Prandtl number are 0.85.

2.2. PBE Solution

Several studies has shown how the mechanism of PM evolution is established. It is only since Smoluchowski's work [19] that the study of coagulation kinetics has gained momentum. The work describes monodisperse systems of spherical particles. Systems are complex in most cases, in which particles are not the same size. Muller [20] expanded the Smoluchowski theory to polydisperse systems.

Population balance equation (PBE), as an extension of the Smoluchowski equation, is used to describe the time evolution of particle size distributions. To date, several numerical solutions for the PBE had been developed, including moment method (MM) [21], sectional method (SM) [22], and the Monte Carlo method (MC) [23]. The above three methods can be divided into sub-methods. We used TEMOM (Taylor-series Expansion Method Of Moments) [24] in this study, a type of method of moments. The present study concerns the new particle formation by binary homogeneous nucleation in a given aerosol situation and growth by coagulation and condensation. Thus, the three source terms are described in PBE as follows:

$$\frac{\partial n(v,t)}{\partial t} = \left\{ \frac{1}{2} \int_{v_{\min}}^{v_{\max}} \beta(v-u,u,t)n(v-u,t)n(u,t)\mathrm{d}u - n(v,t) \int_{v_{\min}}^{v_{\max}} \beta(v,u,t)n(u,t)\mathrm{d}u \right\}_{\text{coagulation}}$$

$$- \left\{ \frac{\partial(I(v,t)n(v,t))}{\partial v} \right\}_{\text{condensation}} + \{J(v,t)\delta(v_{\text{nul}},v)\}_{\text{nucleation}} \tag{8}$$

where $n(v,t)$ is number density function; $n(v,t)\mathrm{d}v$ is the number density of particles size between v and $v+\mathrm{d}v$ at the time t; $\beta(v,u,t)$ is the collision kernel for particles of volume v and u at the time t; $I(v,t)$ is the condensation kernel for particles of volume v at the time t; and $J(v,t)$ is the nucleation kernel for particles of volume v at the time t.

2.3. Coagulation Kernel

As summarized in the review [25], the vehicle nucleated particles are primarily between 32 nm and 90 nm. Thus, the collision kernel β in the present study is limited in the free molecular regime in the present study [21]:

$$\beta(v,u) = B_1 \left(\frac{1}{v} + \frac{1}{u} \right)^{1/2} (v^{1/3} + u^{1/3})^2 \tag{9}$$

in which

$$B_1 = \left(\frac{3\pi}{4} \right)^{1/6} \left(\frac{6k_bT}{\rho_p} \right)^{1/2} \tag{10}$$

where k_b is Boltzmann constant; and ρ_p is particles density. The kth moment of particle size distribution is defined as follows:

$$M_k(t) = \int_0^\infty v^k n(v,t)\mathrm{d}v \tag{11}$$

If only the first three moments are considered, the coagulation kernel moment equation is obtained by multiplying Equation (8) by v^k and then integrating it from 0 to ∞ [24]:

$$\left(\frac{\partial m_0}{\partial t} \right)_{\text{coa}} = \frac{\sqrt{2}B_2(65m_2^2 m_0^{23/6} - 1210m_2 m_1^2 m_0^{17/6} - 9223m_1^4 m_0^{11/6})}{5184m_1^{23/6}}$$

$$\left(\frac{\partial m_1}{\partial t} \right)_{\text{coa}} = 0 \tag{12}$$

$$\left(\frac{\partial m_2}{\partial t} \right)_{\text{coa}} = \frac{\sqrt{2}B_2(701m_2^2 m_0^{11/6} - 4210m_2 m_1^2 m_0^{5/6} - 6859m_1^4 m_0^{-1/6})}{2592m_1^{11/6}}$$

TEMOM is a general method for solving the PBE. The closure of the moment equations is approached by the Taylor-series expansion technique. This is why this method has no prior requirement for particle size distribution. As the study [24] shows, 3-order TEMOM is preferable when precision and efficiency are simultaneously considered in which the first three order moments are calculated. In other words, the most important indexes for describing aerosol, including particle number density, particle mass, and geometric standard deviation, are obtained.

2.4. Condensation Kernel

For particles smaller than the mean free path of the surrounding gas, the condensation models for sulfuric acid vapor molecules is [26]:

$$I(v,t)\mathrm{d}t = \frac{\pi d_p^2 v_m (p_1 - p_d)}{(2\pi mk_bT)^{1/2}} \tag{13}$$

where p_1 is the partial pressure of sulfuric acid vapor; p_d is the partial pressure of H_2SO_4 vapor at the particle surface, and v_m is the volume of one H_2SO_4 molecule.

Because the water vapor concentration is very high compared with sulfuric acid vapor and pre-existing particle concentration, the new solution particle is quickly in equilibrium with the surrounding water vapor [27]. Therefore, the molar fraction of sulfuric acid in particles is approximately equal to the molar fraction in gas phases. Taking into account the effect of water vapor and hydrate on condensation, the condensation size growth rate θ is:

$$\theta = \frac{dv_c}{dt}\alpha \tag{14}$$

where α is a coefficient that makes θ represent the volume growth rate of both sulfuric acid and water molecules by the volume growth rate of sulfuric acid molecules, in which $\alpha \times v_a$ can be interpreted as the average volume of molecules of sulfuric acid and molecules of water or the equivalent number of sulfuric acid molecules. Here, v_a is the volume of the sulfuric acid molecules. α is [6]:

$$\alpha = 1 + \frac{(1-\chi)v_w}{\chi v_a} \tag{15}$$

where χ is the mole fraction of sulfuric acid vapor; v_w is the volume of the water molecule. Substitute $p_1 = Y_1 k_b T$, $d_p = ((6v)/\pi)^{1/3}$ and Equation (13) into Equation (14). The condensation growth rate θ is:

$$\theta = B_2 v^{2/3} \eta \alpha \tag{16}$$

where $B_2 = (36\pi)^{1/3} n_s (k_b T/2\pi m_1)^{1/2} v_m$, $\eta = Y_1/n_s$ and n_s is the reference sulfuric acid concentration.

2.5. Thermophoresis and Particle Diffusion

In the present study, particle diameters are usually smaller than the mean free path of the gas. The velocity of thermophoresis u_{th} in Fredlander' work [28] is

$$u_{th} = \frac{-0.55\mu\nabla T}{\rho_g T} \tag{17}$$

The particle diffusion coefficient is the sum of Γ_t and Γ_B. Here, Γ_t is the turbulent diffusivity and Γ_B is the Brownian diffusivity [29].

$$\Gamma_B = k_b T \frac{C_c}{3\pi\mu d_a} \tag{18}$$

where C_c is the Cunningham correction factor [30], and d_a is the volume-averaged particle diameter.

2.6. Moment Transport Equation

The moment transport equation for the kth moment based on the TEMOM is [24]:

$$\frac{\partial m_k}{\partial t} = -\frac{\partial(u_j + u_{(th)j})m_k}{\partial x_j} + \frac{\partial}{\partial x_j}\left(\Gamma\frac{\partial m_k}{\partial x_j}\right) + kB_1\eta m_{k-1/3}\alpha + J(v^*)v^{*k} + \left(\frac{\partial m_k}{\partial t}\right)_{coa} \tag{19}$$

When three source terms can be considered at the same time, the Equation (19) expands to:

$$\frac{\partial m_0}{\partial t} = J^* + \frac{\sqrt{2}B_2\left(65m_2^2m_0^{23/6} - 1210m_2m_1^2m_0^{17/6} - 9223m_1^4m_0^{11/6}\right)}{5184m_1^{23/6}}$$

$$\frac{\partial m_1}{\partial t} = J^*\frac{v^*}{v} + m_{2/3}\eta\alpha \tag{20}$$

$$\frac{\partial m_2}{\partial t} = J^*\left(\frac{v^*}{v}\right)^2 + 2m_{5/3}\eta\alpha - \frac{\sqrt{2}B_2\left(701m_2^2m_0^{11/6} - 4210m_2m_1^2m_0^{5/6} - 6859m_1^4m_0^{-1/6}\right)}{2592m_1^{11/6}}$$

The dimensionless calculation equation is used in the process. The characteristic timescale for particle growth is calculated by $\tau = [n_s s_1 (k_b T/2\pi m_1)^{1/2}]^{-1}$. Dimensionless time is calculated by $\theta = t/\tau$. Kth moment is calculated by $m_k = M_k/n_s v_1^k$. Nucleation rate is calculated by $J^* = J/(n_s/\tau)$. Number concentration is calculated by $S = n_1/n_s$. Rate of gas to particle production is calculated by $R^* = R\tau/n_s$.

3. Simulation Configuration

3.1. Flow Field

It is necessary to pay special attention to the engine exhaust plume rather than the whole field where the engine truck is located because the time and space scales of nucleation and growth processes are tiny. The simulation flow field is shown in Figure 1. The two-dimensional space is a plane with a length of 10 m and a width of 3 m.

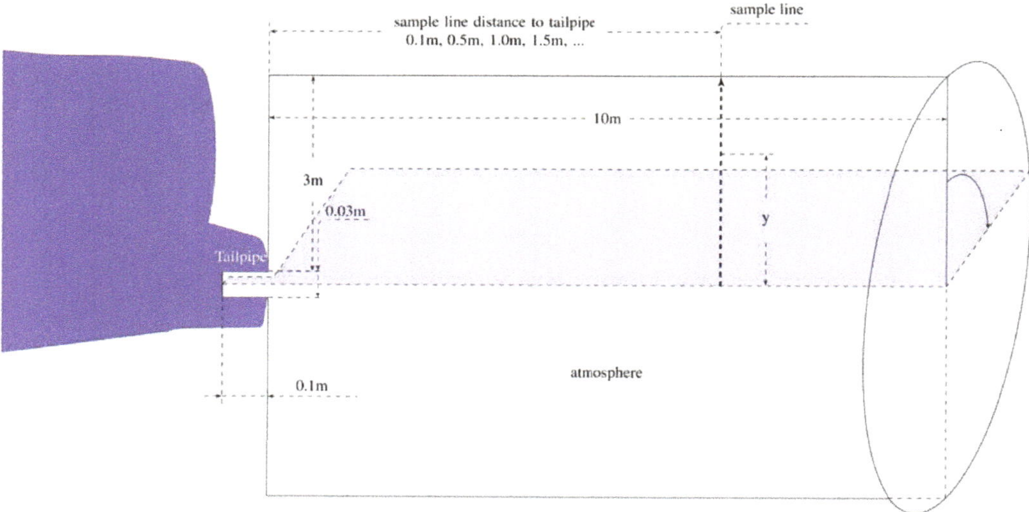

Figure 1. Flow field of simulation.

The mesh used in this paper is a square with a side length of 1 mm in the plume area (30 cm × 90 cm). In other regions, the edge length of the mesh increases by 1.01 times. The edge length of the farthest mesh is 20 mm. According to our calculation experience, the density of the mesh far exceeds the demand.

To study the details of the influence of various physical quantities on the evolution, we only consider the evolution of exhaust gas in the background pollution without involving experiments. In research similar to the present study [6], its simulation situation is similar to that of Ning's experiment [17]. The research proved the effectiveness of this method. The difference between this study and Yu's study lies in background pollutants and the absence of ground in the flow field. At the same time, this work applies to three-dimensional space.

Five scalars are defined in the flow field, representing water vapor, sulfuric acid vapor, and third-order moments, respectively. The flow, particle, and temperature are developed numerical code in SIMPLEC (Semi-Implicit Method for Pressure-linked Equations-Consistent).

3.2. Initial Conditions Calculation

The initial boundary condition numerical is calculated from research on the atmosphere of Beijing [31]. Table 1 is the atmospheric background aerosol data under pollution and non-pollution conditions in Beijing over three years.

Table 1. Average lognormal fit parameters of the particle number size distributions and meteorological factors on polluted and nonpolluted days in the summers of 2004, 2005, and 2006.

Mode	Nucleation			Aitken			Accumulation		
	Ni	GMD	δ	Ni	GMD	δ	Ni	GMD	δ
2004 nonpolluted	16	15.5	1.80	27	60.4	1.87	3	200	1.70
2004 polluted	14	17.0	1.90	19	80.9	1.93	7	245	1.58
2005 nonpolluted	7	14.4	2.00	20	58.9	2.00	5	174	1.71
2005 polluted	6	18.0	2.00	17	75.8	1.99	8	251	1.59
2006 nonpolluted	9	14.3	1.92	15	61.8	2.00	2	225	1.64
2006 polluted	5	18.7	1.89	15	84.6	1.96	6	246	1.54

Where Ni is mode particle number concentratio ($\times 10^3$ cm^{-3}); GMD is geometric mean diameter of the mode (nm); and δ is standard deviation of the mode.

The first three initial moments were calculated by Equation (21):

$$M_m = NV_g^m \exp\left(m^2 \frac{w_g^2}{2}\right) \tag{21}$$

where $w_g = 3\ln\delta_g$. The calculation results are Table 2.

Table 2. Initial moments of 2004, 2005, and 2006.

Condition		Nucleation	Aitken	Accumulation	Sum	Non-Dimensional
Nonpolluted 2004		1.60×10^{10}	2.70×10^{10}	3.00×10^{09}	4.60×10^{10}	3.07×10^{00}
Polluted 2004		1.40×10^{10}	1.90×10^{10}	7.00×10^{09}	4.00×10^{10}	2.67×10^{00}
Nonpolluted 2005	m_0	7.00×10^{09}	2.00×10^{10}	5.00×10^{09}	3.20×10^{10}	2.13×10^{00}
Polluted 2005		6.00×10^{09}	1.70×10^{10}	8.00×10^{09}	3.10×10^{10}	2.07×10^{00}
Nonpolluted 2006		9.00×10^{09}	1.50×10^{10}	2.00×10^{09}	2.60×10^{10}	1.73×10^{00}
Polluted 2006		5.00×10^{09}	1.50×10^{10}	6.00×10^{09}	2.60×10^{10}	1.73×10^{00}
Nonpolluted 2004		1.48×10^{-13}	1.82×10^{-11}	4.46×10^{-11}	6.29×10^{-11}	3.65×10^{00}
Polluted 2004		2.30×10^{-13}	3.69×10^{-11}	1.38×10^{-10}	1.75×10^{-10}	1.02×10^{01}
Nonpolluted 2005	m_1	9.51×10^{-14}	1.86×10^{-11}	5.04×10^{-11}	6.91×10^{-11}	4.00×10^{00}
Polluted 2005		1.59×10^{-13}	3.27×10^{-11}	1.74×10^{-10}	2.07×10^{-10}	1.20×10^{01}
Nonpolluted 2006		9.35×10^{-14}	1.61×10^{-11}	3.59×10^{-11}	5.21×10^{-11}	3.02×10^{00}
Polluted 2006		1.06×10^{-13}	3.65×10^{-11}	1.07×10^{-10}	1.44×10^{-10}	8.32×10^{00}
Nonpolluted 2004		3.05×10^{-35}	4.15×10^{-31}	8.36×10^{-30}	8.78×10^{-30}	4.42×10^{02}
Polluted 2004		1.54×10^{-34}	3.50×10^{-30}	1.79×10^{-29}	2.14×10^{-29}	1.08×10^{03}
Nonpolluted 2005	m_2	9.75×10^{-35}	1.30×10^{-30}	6.77×10^{-30}	8.07×10^{-30}	4.07×10^{02}
Polluted 2005		3.19×10^{-34}	4.45×10^{-30}	2.63×10^{-29}	3.08×10^{-29}	1.55×10^{03}
Nonpolluted 2006		4.47×10^{-35}	1.31×10^{-30}	5.82×10^{-30}	7.13×10^{-30}	3.59×10^{02}
Polluted 2006		8.63×10^{-35}	5.23×10^{-30}	1.02×10^{-29}	1.54×10^{-29}	7.77×10^{02}
Nonpolluted 2004		4.98×10^{-06}	1.40×10^{-04}	1.37×10^{-04}	3.39×10^{-04}	6.52×10^{-02}
Polluted 2004		5.99×10^{-06}	1.92×10^{-04}	4.15×10^{-04}	7.40×10^{-04}	1.42×10^{-01}
Nonpolluted 2005	$m_{2/3}$	2.46×10^{-06}	1.18×10^{-04}	1.75×10^{-04}	3.43×10^{-04}	6.60×10^{-02}
Polluted 2005		3.30×10^{-06}	1.64×10^{-04}	5.03×10^{-04}	7.79×10^{-04}	1.50×10^{-01}
Nonpolluted 2006		2.80×10^{-06}	9.73×10^{-05}	1.07×10^{-04}	2.58×10^{-04}	4.97×10^{-02}
Polluted 2006		2.55×10^{-06}	1.73×10^{-04}	1.02×10^{-29}	1.54×10^{-29}	7.77×10^{02}

There has been a dimensionless treatment in Section 2.6 Dimensionless processing is used to compare the calculation accuracy between different mathematical models without considering the influence of the number and volume of particles. In this study, in the simulation process, the particle size span is large. The effective number of digits is limited, and the rounding error in the calculation process, so the calculation also uses dimensionless processing.

3.3. Boundary Setting

The evolution of aerosols under six background particles with different size distributions was simulated using the data in Table 2 as the initial moment value, the evolution of aerosols under six background particles was simulated. The upper and lower boundaries are fixed values, meaning that the environment is maintained. When the moment value disappears during the simulation process, the environment can be supplemented; when the moment value increases sharply, the environment can be diluted. Only the inner wall of the exhaust pipe does not increase or decrease the moment—so zero flux. Table 3 is an example of the boundary conditions under the condition that there is no pollution in the simulation in 2004. S. means scalar.

Table 3. Example boundary setting of nonpolluted 2004.

Boundary	Temperature (K)	Velocity (m/s)	Boundary Type	Boundary Value				
				S.1	S.2	S.3	S.4	S.5
inlet	400	4.8	Fixed value	1	1000	0	0	0
inlet wall	350		Fixed flux	0	0	0	0	0
right	300		Fixed value	0.3	0	3.07×10^{00}	3.65×10^{00}	4.42×10^{02}
up (down)	300		Fixed value	0.3	0	3.07×10^{00}	3.65×10^{00}	4.42×10^{02}
left	300		Fixed value	0.3	0	3.07×10^{00}	3.65×10^{00}	4.42×10^{02}

4. Results and Discussion

The simulation results are shown through the sampling line shown in Figure 1. In the plane, the data are taken at a certain distance from the exhaust pipe, 0.1 m, 0.5 m, 2.0 m, 5.0 m. The nucleation rate has no value beyond the length greater than 1 m, so the sampling line distance of the nucleation rate is 0.1 m, 0.25 m, 0.5 m, 0.75 m. In the calculation process of nucleation rate, the upper and lower limits of nucleation rate are limited in order to ensure the correct value. The nucleation rate generally cannot break the upper limit. The lower limit can be considered to be approximately zero due to a difference of about 15 orders of magnitude from the normal value. The most detailed account of the process is to be found in the work of Binder and Stauffer [32].

Take the flow field without pollution in 2004 as an example, as shown in Figure 2, the speed of the flow field, m_0, m_1, and nucleation rate are shown in Figure 2. This study uses three years of data, and there are two situations each year. Six conditions need to be analyzed in one simulation. There are eight sampling lines in each situation, and each sampling line has five custom scalar quantities and eight custom physical quantities. There are 312 ($6 \times 4 \times 13$) cases of data that need to be classified and displayed. Quantitative analysis in two-dimensional figures is complicated. Other data will be organized and displayed according to conditions to facilitate the comparison of differences.

In the following figure, the blue dotted line represents the data under the condition of no pollution, and the solid red line represents the data under the condition of pollution. The horizontal y-axis represents the vertical distance from the exhaust pipe on the sampling line, and the maximum is 3.15 m.

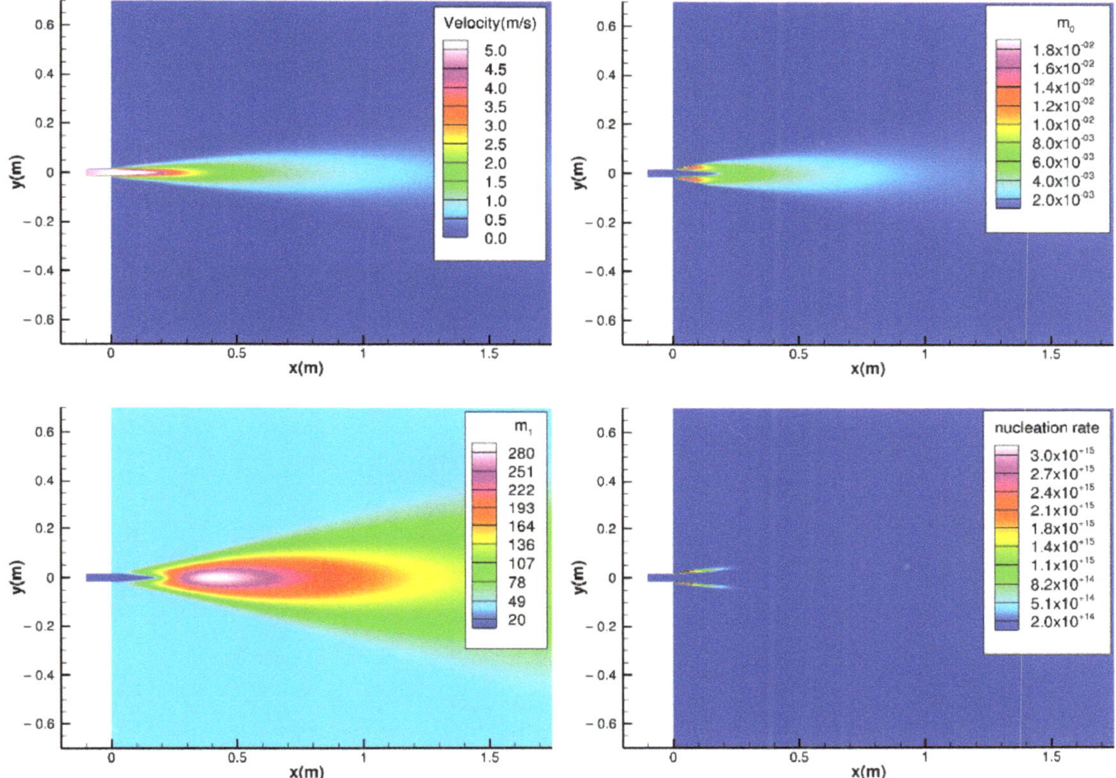

Figure 2. No polluted flow field data in 2004.

As Figure 3 shows, in three years, the m_0 under nonpolluted conditions on each sampling line is greater than the m_0 under polluted conditions. Seipenbusch and Yu once discovered this phenomenon and gave a qualitative explanation [18]. Seipenbusch's work focuses on measured data. The work only analyzes the result of quantity concentration but does not analyze how the various processes have an integrated effect.

The initial value in Table 2, m_0 under no polluted conditions is already more significant than that under polluted conditions. The right end of Figure 3 is the value at the boundary,that is, the environmental value. Except for the apparent difference in 2004, the two lines overlapped in the other two years. However, at the left end of the figure, this difference is significantly larger than the difference in the environment. Vehicle emissions will promote the difference in background aerosols. That is, the number concentration under non-polluting conditions is greater than the number concentration under pollution conditions.

In the process of aerosol evolution, nucleation and coagulation will affect the number concentration of particulate matter. Nucleation will increase the number concentration of particulate matter, and aggregation will reduce particulate matter concentration. As shown in Figure 4, on the sampling line, x = 0.1 m and x = 0.25 m, the nucleation rate under the nonpolluted condition is greater than the nucleation rate under the polluted condition. On the sampling line, x = 0.5 m and x = 0.75 m, the nucleation rate in the second half of the nonpolluted situation is greater than the nucleation rate in the polluted condition, and the opposite is the case in the first half. Since the ordinate axis is a logarithmic coordinate, at x = 0.1 m and x = 0.5 m, the part where no pollution exceeds the pollution is much larger than the difference between x = 0.5 m and x = 0.7 m. The situation has been the same for three years. The lower nucleation rate under the polluted condition is the direct cause of the lower m_0 under the polluted condition. As for why the nucleation rate is lower under polluted conditions, it needs to be analyzed by other physical quantities.

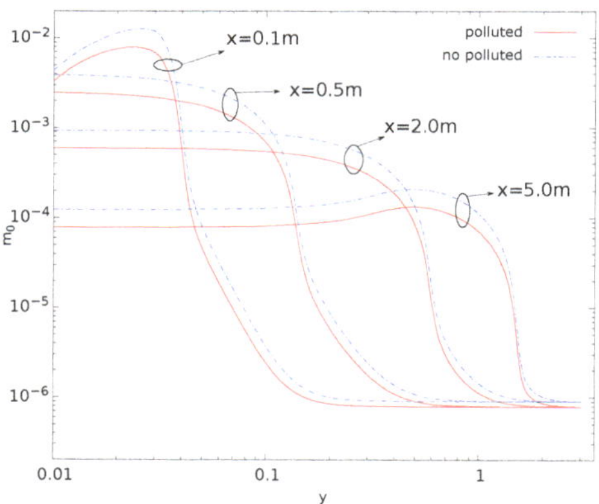

(**a**) 2004 every distance of polluted and nonpolluted m_0

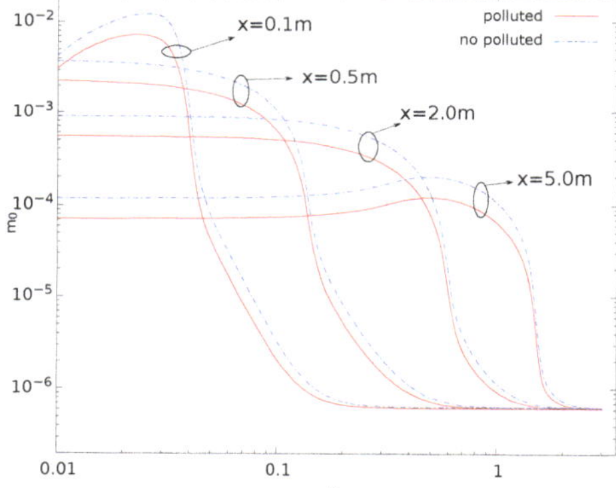

(**b**) 2005 every distance of polluted and nonpolluted m_0

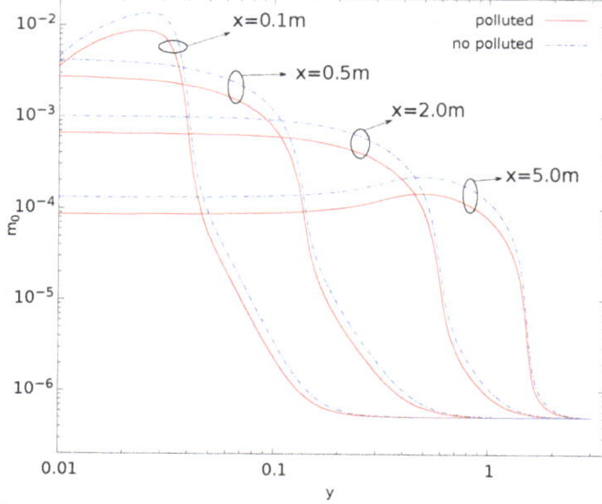

(**c**) 2006 every distance of polluted and nonpolluted m_0

Figure 3. Every distance of polluted and nonpolluted m_0 over three years.

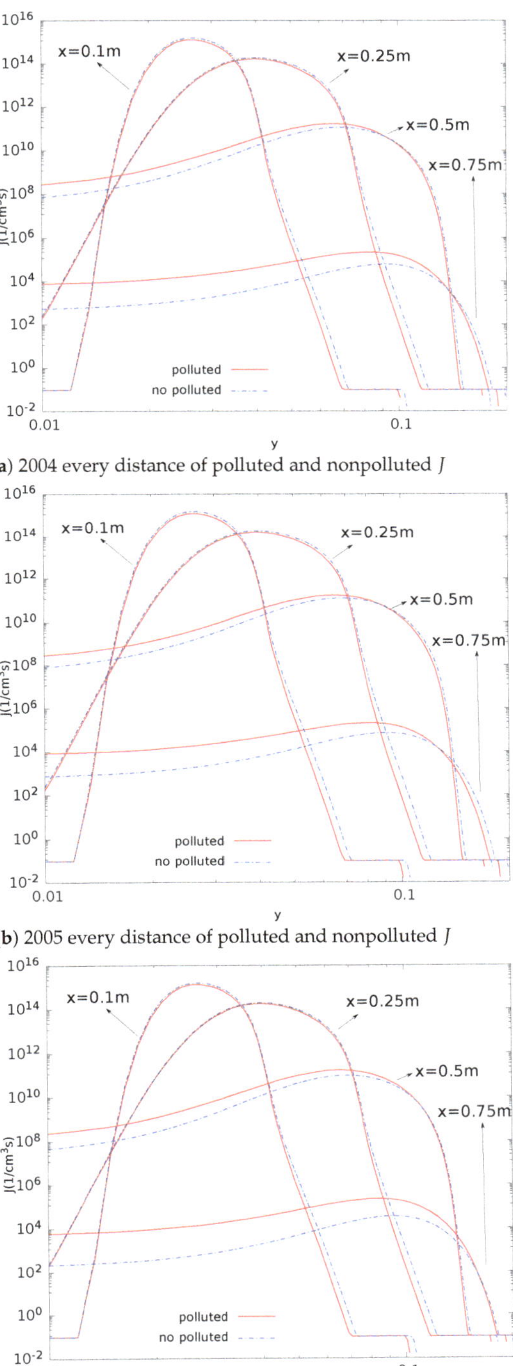

(**a**) 2004 every distance of polluted and nonpolluted *J*

(**b**) 2005 every distance of polluted and nonpolluted *J*

(**c**) 2006 every distance of polluted and nonpolluted *J*

Figure 4. Every distance of polluted and nonpolluted *J* in three years.

The value of each moment in the moment method contains the physical properties of the particles, such as surface area, volume, and diameter, and these physical quantities are not independent of each other. For the same volume of particle population, the smaller the particle size, the larger the total surface area of the particle population. For the particle population of the same volume, the larger the particle size, the fewer the particles. The correlation between these variables can be used to infer the mechanism of their evolution. As shown in Figure 5, it is the volume average particle diameter of the particles, defined as $(6m_1/\pi m_0)$. It can be seen that the particle size under the pollution condition in three years is always larger than the particle size under the no pollution condition. A large particle size means a larger surface area, which is suitable for condensation. Under polluted conditions, water molecules and sulfuric acid molecules are more involved in condensation, so the critical molecular clusters involved in nucleation are reduced, resulting in a lower nucleation rate.

This conclusion needs to be corroborated. First, introduce another physical quantity. In the log-normal theory, the geometric mean volume for particles is:

$$v_g = \frac{m_1^2}{m_0^{3/2} m_2^{1/2}} \tag{22}$$

From the area formula of the sphere, $s = \pi d^2$ and volume formula of the sphere, $v_g = (\pi/6)d^3$ the relationship between area and volume is:

$$S = (36\pi)^{1/3} v^{2/3} \tag{23}$$

Substituting Equation (22) into Equation (23) is the surface area of the particles, and multiplying by the number of particles, M_0, we can get the total particle surface area. Figure 6 compares the total particle surface area in the case of pollution and no pollution.

Under pollution conditions, the volume average diameter is larger, but the number concentration is minor. If the total volume of particulate matter under polluted and no polluted conditions is equal, then the smaller the number concentration, the smaller the particulate matters's total area. However, it can be seen from Figure 6 that the total area of particulate matter is larger under polluted conditions. This means that the total volume of particulate matter in a polluted condition is greater than the total volume of particulate matter in a no polluted condition. This is confirmed in the data of m_1 in Figure 7. At the same time, it should be noted that the nucleation rate is higher under no polluted conditions. The higher nucleation rate increases the total volume while increasing the total area. The total volume of particulate matter reflects the mass concentration of particulate matter, which is an index used to measure the degree of pollution. On this index, the total volume of particulate matter under no polluted conditions is always less than the total volume under polluted conditions.

In Figure 6, at the sampling line close to the exhaust tailpipe, such as x = 0.1 m, the total area of particulate matter under polluted conditions is more significant than that under no polluted conditions. This tendency diminishes as the sampling line moves away from the exhaust tailpipe. On the x = 5.0 m sampling line, the total area of particulate matter under no polluted condition exceeds that under polluted conditions. However, on the sampling line x = 0.5 m, the total area under polluted condition is still larger than that under no polluted conditions at the right end of the horizontal axis (that is, the amount in the environment).

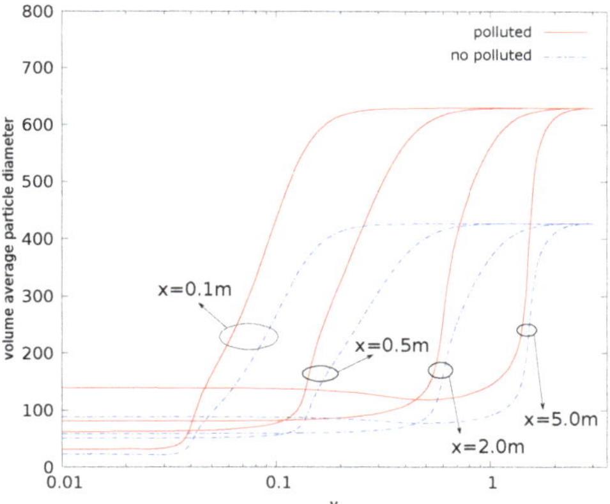

(**a**) 2004 every distance of polluted and nonpolluted volume average particle diameter

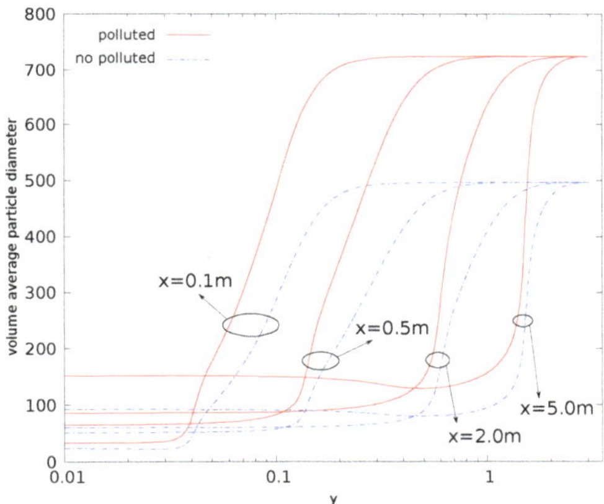

(**b**) 2005 every distance of polluted and nonpolluted volume average particle diameter

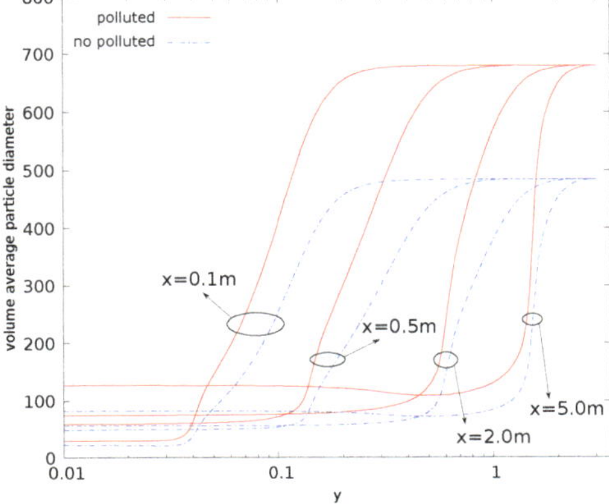

(**c**) 2006 every distance of polluted and nonpolluted volume average particle diameter

Figure 5. Status of volume average particle diameter over three different years.

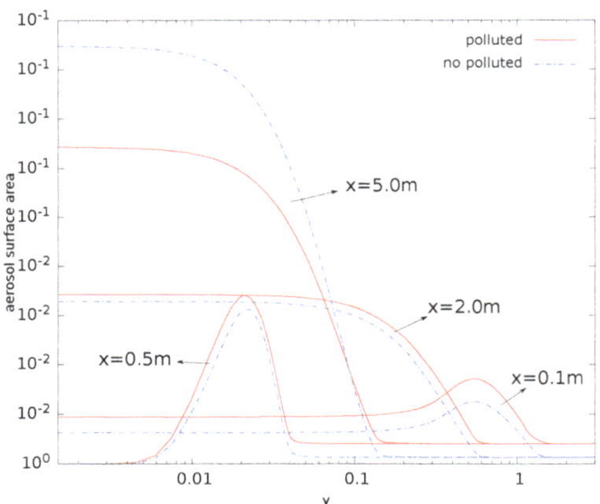

(**a**) 2004 every distance of polluted and nonpolluted aerosol surface area

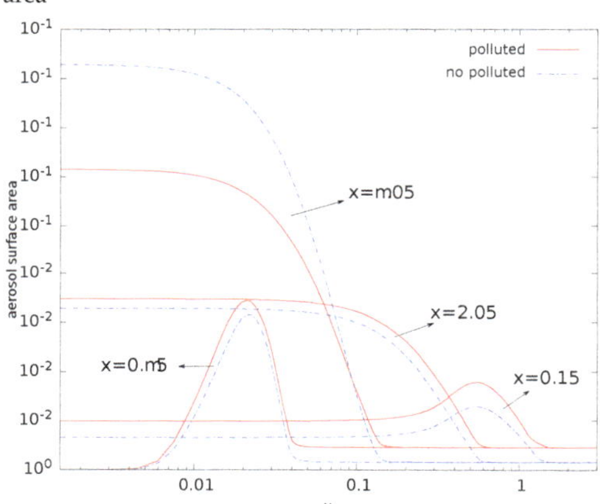

(**b**) 2005 every distance of polluted and nonpolluted aerosol surface area

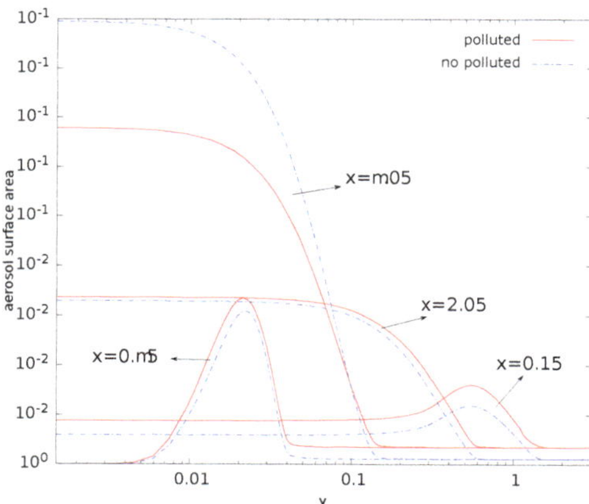

(**c**) 2006 every distance of polluted and nonpolluted aerosol surface area

Figure 6. Status of aerosol surface area over three different years.

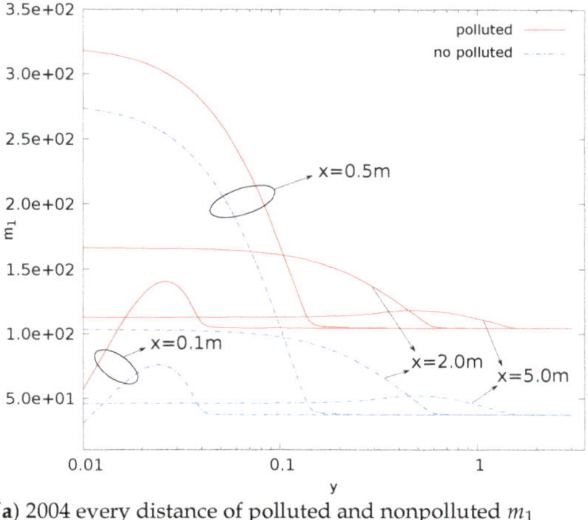

(**a**) 2004 every distance of polluted and nonpolluted m_1

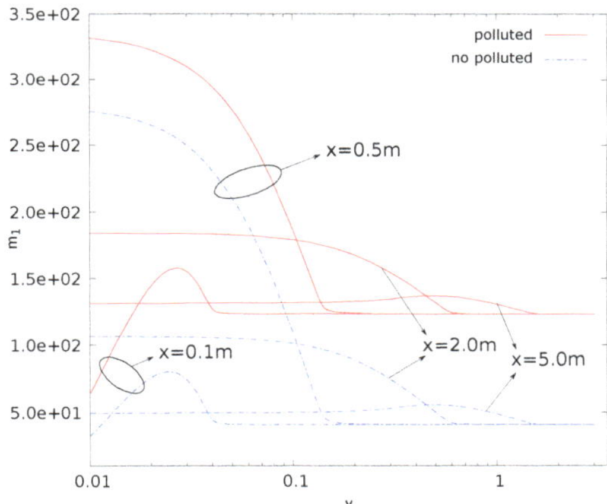

(**b**) 2005 every distance of polluted and nonpolluted m_1

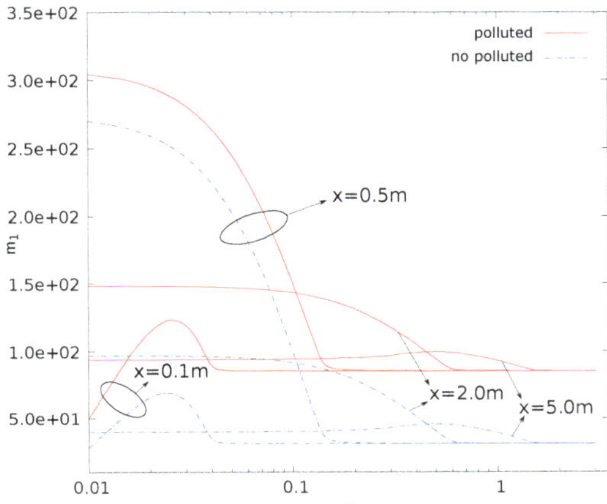

(**c**) 2006 every distance of polluted and nonpolluted m_1

Figure 7. Status of m_1 over three years.

Compared with the nucleation rate in Figure 4, it can be seen that the nucleation process is mainly near the sampling line x = 0.1 m and x = 0.25 m. The nucleation process results in a greater number concentration in no polluted condition. However, in this area, the total surface area of the particles under no polluted conditions is less than that under polluted conditions. When the sampling line is far away from the exhaust tailpipe, in Figure 6, the number concentration under no polluted condition is always greater than the concentration under the polluted condition. However, the difference between the total area of the particle population under the no polluted condition and the total area of the particle population under the polluted condition is reversed. This shows that the condensation process is mainly carried out in the area from x = 2.0 m to x = 5.0 m. The condensation process increases the surface area of the particles. This leads to an overshoot of the total particle area in no polluted conditions shown in Figure 6. Coagulation mainly occurs in the area after x = 5.0 m, which causes the total surface area of the particulate matter under no polluted conditions to be consistent with the environment and smaller than the total surface area of the particulate matter under the pollution conditions.

5. Conclusions

The coupling of the NS equation and the PBE is performed to study the effect of background aerosol on its evolution. The flow field simulation is implemented with SIMPLEC; PBE is solved by TEMOM. Coagulation, condensation, and nucleation are considered. Three years of data were used in the simulation to ensure the generality of the conclusions. According to the observed phenomenon, the number and concentration of particulate matter in the pollution condition are smaller. The reason and mechanism behind it are studied. The following conclusions can be drawn:

1. Compared with nonpolluted conditions (low concentration of background particles), the nucleation rate in polluted conditions will be reduced. In addition, the number concentration of particles will also be reduced. This phenomenon makes number concentration unable to reflect the degree of pollution. The decrease in nucleation rate makes the concentration of critical sulfuric acid molecular clusters higher in the flow field (this is limited to a relatively small area). This is a disadvantage in certain operations that remove contaminants;

2. The evolution of aerosols mainly depends on the nucleation rate. In addition, the nucleation rate has a strong regional distribution (that is, the spatial distribution of the nucleation rate is limited to a small range). Therefore, the source of controlling the pollutant is the key. Compared with the core area of nucleation, other regions have little impact on the generation and evolution of particulate matter;

3. The presence of background particulate matter will slow down the nucleation process of aerosol. The mass concentration of particulate matter in the polluted condition is higher than that in the nonpolluted condition. Therefore, the slowing effect of particulate matter on the nucleation process of aerosol will be more obvious in pollution conditions;

4. In the process of aerosol evolution, the independence of mass concentration and number concentration has guiding significance in various occasions involving the control of aerosol concentration. In this paper, the evolution mechanism behind this phenomenon is obtained by the simulation method. This is conducive to the use of this phenomenon. For example, it is necessary to confirm which factors effectively control the pollution situation; filtering to reduce the mass concentration of pollutants in order to reduce the number concentration is invalid;

5. The significant change regions of nucleation, condensation , and coagulation are different. The nucleation process is spatially closer to the source of pollution. The nucleation process also provides more particles for the condensation and coagulation processes. Condensation comes next, and coagulation comes last.

Author Contributions: Y.L. devised the project. M.Y. the main conceptual ideas and proof outline. C.T. worked out the technical details, and performed the numerical calculations for the suggested simulation. T.W. verified the numerical results. Conceptualization, Y.L.; methodology, M.Y.; software, C.T.; writing original draft, C.T.; writing review and editing, Y.L.; visualization, T.W. All authors have read and agreed to the published version of the manuscript.

Funding: This research received no external funding.

Institutional Review Board Statement: Not applicable.

Informed Consent Statement: Not applicable.

Data Availability Statement: Not applicable.

Conflicts of Interest: The authors declare no conflict of interest.

References

1. Brunekreef, B.; Holgate, S.T. Air Pollution and Health. *Lancet* **2002**, *360*, 1233–1242. [CrossRef]
2. Das, S.; Ghosh, S.; van Holten, J.W.; Pal, S. Generalized Particle Dynamics: Modifying the Motion of Particles and Branes. *J. High Energy Phys.* **2009**, *2009*, 115. [CrossRef]
3. Kumar, P.; Robins, A.; Vardoulakis, S.; Britter, R. A Review of the Characteristics of Nanoparticles in the Urban Atmosphere and the Prospects for Developing Regulatory Controls. *Atmos. Environ.* **2010**, *44*, 5035–5052. [CrossRef]
4. Zhang, R.; Khalizov, A.; Wang, L.; Hu, M.; Xu, W. Nucleation and Growth of Nanoparticles in the Atmosphere. *Chem. Rev.* **2012**, *112*, 1957–2011. [CrossRef]
5. Silva, L.; Lage, P. Development and Implementation of a Polydispersed Multiphase Flow Model in OpenFOAM. *Comput. Chem. Eng.* **2011**, *35*, 2653–2666. [CrossRef]
6. Yu, M.; Lin, J.; Chan, T. Numerical Simulation for Nucleated Vehicle Exhaust Particulate Matters Via the Temom/Les Method. *Int. J. Mod. Phys. C* **2009**, *20*, 399–421. [CrossRef]
7. Brines, M.; Dall'Osto, M.; Beddows, D.C.S.; Harrison, R.M.; Gómez-Moreno, F.; Núñez, L.; Artinano, B.; Costabile, F.; Gobbi, G.P.; Salimi, F. Traffic and Nucleation Events as Main Sources of Ultrafine Particles in High-Insolation Developed World Cities. *Atmos. Chem. Phys* **2015**, *15*, 5929–5945. [CrossRef]
8. Vaattovaara, P.; Petäjä, T.; Joutsensaari, J.; Miettinen, P.; Zaprudin, B.; Kortelainen, A.; Heijari, J.; Yli-Pirilä, P.; Aalto, P.; Worsnop, D.R. The Evolution of Nucleation-and Aitken-Mode Particle Compositions in a Boreal Forest Environment during Clean and Pollution-Affected New-Particle Formation Events. *Boreal Environ. Res.* **2009**, *14*, 662–682.
9. Rodríguez, S.; Van Dingenen, R.; Putaud, J.P.; Martins-Dos Santos, S.; Roselli, D. Nucleation and Growth of New Particles in the Rural Atmosphere of Northern Italy—Relationship to Air Quality Monitoring. *Atmos. Environ.* **2005**, *39*, 6734–6746. [CrossRef]
10. Kulmala, M.; Laaksonen, A.; Pirjola, L. Parameterizations for Sulfuric Acid/Water Nucleation Rates. *J. Geophys. Res. Atmos.* **1998**, *103*, 8301–8307. [CrossRef]
11. Vehkamäki, H.; Kulmala, M.; Lehtinen, K.E.J.; Noppel, M. Modelling Binary Homogeneous Nucleation of Water-Sulfuric Acid Vapours: Parameterisation for High Temperature Emissions. *Environ. Sci. Technol.* **2003**, *37*, 3392–3398. [CrossRef] [PubMed]
12. Kim, D.H.; Gautam, M.; Gera, D. Modeling Nucleation and Coagulation Modes in the Formation of Particulate Matter inside a Turbulent Exhaust Plume of a Diesel Engine. *J. Colloid Interface Sci.* **2002**, *249*, 96–103. [CrossRef] [PubMed]
13. Kim, D.; Gautam, M.; Gera, D. Parametric Studies on the Formation of Diesel Particulate Matter via Nucleation and Coagulation Modes. *J. Aerosol Sci.* **2002**, *33*, 1609–1621. [CrossRef]
14. Yang, H.; Lin, J.; Chan, T. Effect of Fluctuating Aerosol Concentrations on the Aerosol Distributions in a Turbulent Jet. *Aerosol Air Qual. Res.* **2020**, *20*, 1629–1639. [CrossRef]
15. Cheng, C.H.; Cheung, C.S.; Chan, T.L.; Lee, S.C.; Yao, C.D.; Tsang, K.S. Comparison of Emissions of a Direct Injection Diesel Engine Operating on Biodiesel with Emulsified and Fumigated Methanol. *Fuel* **2008**, *87*, 1870–1879. [CrossRef]
16. Ma, H.Y.; Yu, M.Z.; Jin, H.G. A Study of the Evolution of Nanoparticle Dynamics in a Homogeneous Isotropic Turbulence Flow via a DNS-TEMOM Method. *J. Hydrodyn.* **2020**. [CrossRef]
17. Ning, Z.; Cheung, C.; Lu, Y.; Liu, M.; Hung, W. Experimental and Numerical Study of the Dispersion of Motor Vehicle Pollutants under Idle Condition. *Atmos. Environ.* **2005**, *39*, 7880–7893. [CrossRef]
18. Seipenbusch, M.; Kasper, M.; Yu, M. *Interdependence of Particle Number Concentration and PM 2.5 in Highly Polluted Urban Atmospheres*; Karlsruhe Institute of Technology: Karlsruhe, Germany, 2003; p. 14.
19. Von Smoluchowski, M. Mathematical Theory of the Kinetics of the Coagulation of Colloidal Solutions. *Z. Phys. Chem.* **1917**, *92*, 129–168.
20. Müller, H. Zur allgemeinen Theorie der raschen Koagulation. *Kolloidchem. Beih.* **1928**, *27*, 223–250. [CrossRef]
21. Pratsinis, S.E. Simultaneous Nucleation, Condensation, and Coagulation in Aerosol Reactors. *J. Colloid Interface Sci.* **1988**, *124*, 416–427. [CrossRef]
22. Gelbard, F.; Tambour, Y.; Seinfeld, J.H. Sectional Representations for Simulating Aerosol Dynamics. *J. Colloid Interface Sci.* **1980**, *76*, 541–556. [CrossRef]

23. Balthasar, M.; Kraft, M. A Stochastic Approach to Calculate the Particle Size Distribution Function of Soot Particles in Laminar Premixed Flames. *Combust. Flame* **2003**, *133*, 289–298. [CrossRef]
24. Yu, M.; Lin, J.; Chan, T. A New Moment Method for Solving the Coagulation Equation for Particles in Brownian Motion. *Aerosol Sci. Technol.* **2008**, *42*, 705–713. [CrossRef]
25. Kittelson, D.B.; Arnold, M.; Watts, W.F. *Review of Diesel Particulate Matter Sampling Methods: Final Report*; University of Minnesota: Minneapolis, MN, USA, 1999; Volume 63.
26. Friedlander, S.K.; Marlow, W.H. Smoke, Dust and Haze: Fundamentals of Aerosol Behavior. *New York* **1977**, *30*, 58–59. [CrossRef]
27. Kulmala, M.; Laaksonen, A. Binary Nucleation of Water–Sulfuric Acid System: Comparison of Classical Theories with Different H_2SO_4 Saturation Vapor Pressures. *J. Chem. Phys.* **1990**, *93*, 696–701. [CrossRef]
28. Friedlander, S.K. Smoke, Dust, and Haze. Oxford University Press, New York, NY, USA, 2000; Volume 198.
29. Miller, S.E.; Garrick, S.C. Nanoparticle Coagulation in a Planar Jet. *Aerosol Sci. Technol.* **2004**, *38*, 79–89. [CrossRef]
30. Cunningham, E. On the Velocity of Steady Fall of Spherical Particles through Fluid Medium. *Proc. R. Soc. London. Ser. Contain. Pap. Math. Phys. Character* **1910**, *83*, 357–365.
31. Yue, D.; Hu, M.; Wu, Z.; Wang, Z.; Guo, S.; Wehner, B.; Nowak, A.; Achtert, P.; Wiedensohler, A.; Jung, J.; et al. Characteristics of Aerosol Size Distributions and New Particle Formation in the Summer in Beijing. *J. Geophys. Res. Atmos.* **2009**,*114*, D00G12. [CrossRef]
32. Binder, K.; Stauffer, D. Statistical Theory of Nucleation, Condensation and Coagulation. *Adv. Phys.* **1976**, *25*, 343–396. [CrossRef]

Article

Contribution of Particle–Wall Distance and Rotational Motion of a Single Confined Elliptical Particle to the Effective Viscosity in Pressure-Driven Plane Poiseuille Flows

Misa Kawaguchi, Tomohiro Fukui * and Koji Morinishi

Department of Mechanical Engineering, Kyoto Institute of Technology, Kyoto 606-8585, Japan; d9821001@edu.kit.ac.jp (M.K.); morinisi@kit.ac.jp (K.M.)
* Correspondence: fukui@kit.ac.jp

Abstract: Rheological properties of the suspension flow, especially effective viscosity, partly depend on spatial arrangement and motion of suspended particles. It is important to consider effective viscosity from the microscopic point of view. For elliptical particles, the equilibrium position of inertial migration in confined state is unclear, and there are few studies on the relationship between dynamics of suspended particles and induced local effective viscosity distribution. Contribution of a single circular or elliptical particle flowing between parallel plates to the effective viscosity was studied, focusing on the particle–wall distance and particle rotational motion using the two-dimensional regularized lattice Boltzmann method and virtual flux method. As a result, confinement effects of the elliptical particle on the equilibrium position of inertial migration were summarized using three definitions of confinement. In addition, the effects of particle shape (aspect ratio and confinement) on the effective viscosity were assessed focusing on the particle–wall distance. The contribution of particle shape to the effective viscosity was found to be enhanced when the particle flowed near the wall. Focusing on the spatial and temporal variation of relative viscosity evaluated from wall shear stress, it was found that the spatial variation of the local relative viscosity was larger than temporal variation regardless of the aspect ratio and particle–wall distance.

Keywords: inertial migration; rheology; effective viscosity; spatial and temporal variations; confinement effect; pressure-driven flow; lattice Boltzmann method

Citation: Kawaguchi, M.; Fukui, T.; Morinishi, K. Contribution of Particle–Wall Distance and Rotational Motion of a Single Confined Elliptical Particle to the Effective Viscosity in Pressure-Driven Plane Poiseuille Flows. *Appl. Sci.* **2021**, *11*, 6727. https://doi.org/10.3390/app11156727

Academic Editor: Jianzhong Lin

Received: 8 June 2021
Accepted: 20 July 2021
Published: 22 July 2021

Publisher's Note: MDPI stays neutral with regard to jurisdictional claims in published maps and institutional affiliations.

1. Introduction

Suspension flows are ubiquitous in industrial process such as filtration, cosmetics, and food processing and also in nature such as mud and blood flow. Rheological properties of a suspension flow partly depend on its microstructure, which refers to spatial arrangement and orientation of suspended particles [1]. Rheological properties of suspension play important roles in terms of product quality; therefore, it is important to reveal the relationship between macroscopic rheological properties of suspensions and their microstructures to handle suspension rheology effectively.

In a channel flow, suspended particles migrate transversal to the streamlines and converge at the equilibrium position due to inertial effects. This phenomenon is known as the "tubular pinch effect" or "Segré–Silberberg effect". Segré and Silberberg [2] found that rigid spheres in a Poiseuille flow through a tube accumulate at about 0.6 tube radii from the axis. After these findings, many attempts have been made to clarify the mechanism of inertial migration and to extend this phenomenon to broad applications. We have observed that the microstructure of a suspension changes in time mainly due to inertial effects of the suspended particles [3]. Such inertial effects might be significant in practical cases, such as industrial flow or blood flow; therefore, it is important to consider inertial migration.

Strictly speaking, suspended particles are commonly not always spherical in nature, i.e., non-spherical shapes should be considered. Chen et al. [4] investigated the motion of an elliptical particle in plane Poiseuille flow. The numerical results showed that the equilibrium position of the particle with higher aspect ratio is closer to the center of the channel. Wen et al. [5] also numerically investigated the inertial migration of the elliptical particle, and they showed that the equilibrium position of the elliptical particle changes with aspect ratio. However, in these previous studies, confinement, which is the ratio of particle size to the channel diameter (or width), or particle concentration was not kept constant with changing aspect ratio. It is important to take into account not only aspect ratio but also confinement when suspension rheology is considered because effective viscosity strongly depends on confinement as well as particle concentration.

Effective viscosity of a dilute suspension including spheres was firstly studied and summarized by Einstein [6]. According to his theory, the effective viscosity can be expressed as

$$\eta_{\text{eff}} = \eta_0 (1 + [\eta]\phi), \tag{1}$$

where η_{eff} is the effective viscosity, η_0 is the viscosity of the solvent, $[\eta]$ is the intrinsic viscosity, and ϕ is solid volume fraction in three-dimensional conditions or area fraction in two-dimensional conditions. Intrinsic viscosity $[\eta]$ is also called shape index because it depends on particle shape; for example, $[\eta] = 2$ [7] for a rigid circular particle and $[\eta] = 2.3$ [8] for an elliptical porous particle for Darcy number $Da = 10^{-12}$ with aspect ratio $AR = 2$ in two-dimensional conditions. Jeffery [9] extended Einstein's work to the case of ellipsoidal particles. He investigated the motion of a single ellipsoid in a shear flow and found that increase of viscosity can be represented by modifying the intrinsic viscosity. Huang et al. [10] numerically demonstrated that the intrinsic viscosity of spheroids depends on rotational mode such as tumbling or log rolling mode. They showed that the intrinsic viscosity agrees well with Jeffery's analytical solution for various aspect ratios. Doyeux et al. [11] studied the effects of confinement on the effective viscosity of two-dimensional suspensions. They found that intrinsic viscosity is also a function of confinement. As particle size becomes larger, intrinsic viscosity also increases. However, for the elliptical particle, the confinement effect is unclear due to ambiguity in the definition of confinement when comparing with different shapes.

It is important to consider rheological properties, especially effective viscosity, from the microscopic point of view in field of bioengineering. We have observed that suspension flow with homogeneously scattered rigid circular particles shows undulating wall shear stress (WSS) distribution due to existence of suspended particles [12,13]. Xiong and Zhang [14] simulated red blood cells flowing in microvessels to examine the induced WSS variation. They showed real dynamic features of WSS distributions. However, to the best of our knowledge, there are few studies on the relationship between dynamics of suspended particles, such as red blood cells, and induced local WSS distribution. Jou et al. [15] reported that ruptured aneurysms are more exposed to low WSS. It is important to investigate additional WSS distribution changes due to particle motion.

The aim of this study was to investigate the effects of particle–wall distance and rotational motion of elliptical particles on the effective viscosity considering confinement effects. Two-dimensional numerical simulations were conducted using the regularized lattice Boltzmann method and virtual flux method. The equilibrium position of inertial migration was investigated for various aspect ratios by introducing three definitions of confinement for elliptical particles. In addition, the spatial and temporal variations of relative viscosity were also evaluated.

2. Numerical Methods

2.1. Computational Models

We carried out two-dimensional numerical simulations of pressure-driven plane Poiseuille flow including a single circular or elliptical particle. Figure 1 shows the simulation model. The particle was initially located at the lower side and constrained in the y-directional motion (details in Section 2.5). The computational domain was set to width $D = 400$ μm and length $L = 4D = 1600$ μm with a periodic boundary condition with pressure difference in the flow direction [12] to reduce the computational costs. In Section 3.1, the effects of periodic length and grid resolution are assessed. The computational domain was filled with an orthogonal grid of equal spacing $\Delta x = \Delta y = 0.5$ μm. The Reynolds number was set to $Re = 32$ for all simulations to consider inertial effects.

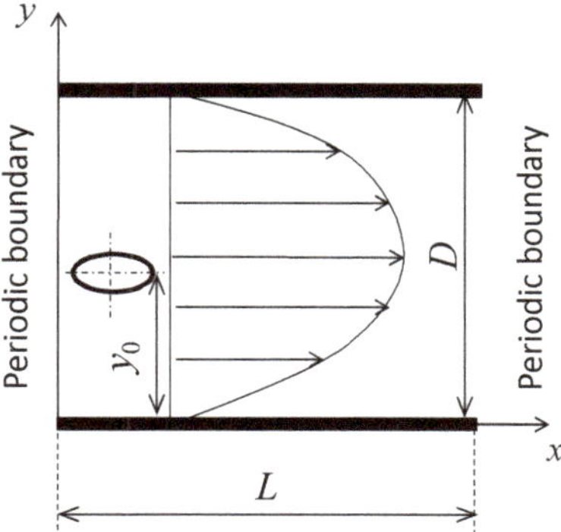

Figure 1. Simulation model including a single particle in pressure-driven plane Poiseuille flow. The center of the circular or elliptical particle was initially located at $y = y_0$ with particle angle to the flow direction $\theta_p = 0$. The computational domain was $L \times D$, and periodic boundary condition with pressure difference was applied in the flow direction.

The suspended particle was assumed to be rigid, neutrally buoyant, and non-Brownian. Aspect ratio was set to $AR = 1$, 2, and 4. Confinement is usually defined as the ratio of particle size to the channel width; however, when the particle is non-spherical, it is difficult to define it uniquely. Therefore, in this study, it was defined using three different characteristic lengths as follows: $C_1 = 2b/D$, $C_2 = 2a/D$, and $C_3 = 2r/D$, where a is semi-major axis, b is semi-minor axis, and r is equivalent radius of the circular particle with the same area as shown in Figure 2. Case 1 is for comparison of the same minor diameter. Case 2 is for comparison of the same major diameter. Case 3 is for comparison of the same area for different aspect ratios. The parameters of confinement were set to $C_3 = 0.05$, 0.1, and 0.2, which corresponds to the area fraction $\phi = 0.05\%$, 0.20%, 0.79%.

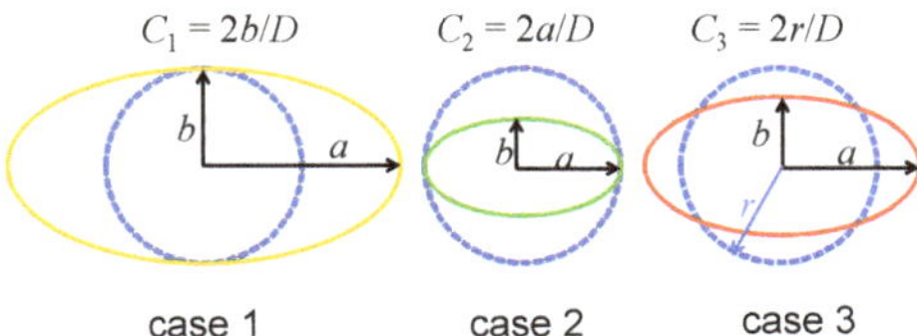

Figure 2. Schematic view of elliptical particles for comparison of three different definitions of confinement. The parameter of confinement C was chosen by the researchers, i.e., semi-major axis a, semi-minor axis b, and equivalent radius r of a circular particle with the same area.

In the studies on the inertial migration using numerical simulation, the comparison in case 2 (same major diameter) is often adopted [5,16]. Chen et al. [4] adopted the comparison similar to case 1 (the confinement increases as increasing aspect ratio). However, comparison in case 3 (with the same area fraction (particle concentration)) should be considered for rheological evaluation because the effective viscosity is predominantly dependent on particle concentration. Başağaoğlu et al. [17] adopted case 3 to compare the different geometrical shapes of particles in settling or flowing particle simulation. However, they investigated only trajectories of particles, and equilibrium positions of the inertial migration were not discussed. From the above background, these three definitions of confinement effects are discussed in this study.

2.2. Governing Equation for Fluid Part

The regularized lattice Boltzmann method (RLBM) [18] was used as a governing equation for the fluid part. This method is based on the lattice Boltzmann method (LBM). RLBM maintains simplicity, efficiency, and good scalability for parallel computing of LBM; in addition, it can reduce sufficient memory usage.

The distribution function f_α for the lattice Boltzmann equation can be written as

$$f_\alpha = w_\alpha \left(a_0 + b_i e_{\alpha i} + c_{ij} e_{\alpha i} e_{\alpha j} + d_{ijk} e_{\alpha i} e_{\alpha j} e_{\alpha k} + \cdots \right). \tag{2}$$

The expansion of the distribution function up to second-order moment is equivalent to incompressible Navier–Stokes equations; therefore, the distribution function is approximated as

$$f_\alpha \approx w_\alpha \left(a_0 + b_i e_{\alpha i} + c_{ijj} e_{\alpha i} e_{\alpha j} \right), \tag{3}$$

where e_α is the discrete velocity vector and subscript α represents velocity direction. The distribution functions propagate with velocities restricted to a finite set of discrete vectors, which is modeled in the DnQm model (m denotes discrete velocities in n dimensions). The D2Q9 model [19] was applied in our simulations. This model is one of the most common lattice speed models for two-dimensional lattice Boltzmann simulations and it has the following nine discrete lattice velocity vectors:

$$e_\alpha = \begin{cases} c(0,0) & (\alpha = 0) \\ c\left(\cos \frac{(\alpha-1)\pi}{2}, \ \sin \frac{(\alpha-1)\pi}{2} \right) & (\alpha = 1\text{–}4) \\ \sqrt{2}c \left(\cos \frac{(2\alpha-9)\pi}{4}, \ \sin \frac{(2\alpha-9)\pi}{4} \right) & (\alpha = 5\text{–}8) \end{cases} \tag{4}$$

In this model, weight coefficients w_α are defined as follows:

$$w_\alpha = \begin{cases} 4/9 & (\alpha = 0) \\ 1/9 & (\alpha = 1\text{–}4) \\ 1/36 & (\alpha = 5\text{–}8) \end{cases}, \tag{5}$$

The parameters a_0, b_i, and c_{ij} are determined to satisfy the following relationships:

$$\sum_\alpha f_\alpha = \rho, \tag{6}$$

$$\sum_\alpha f_\alpha e_{\alpha i} = \rho u_i, \tag{7}$$

$$\sum_\alpha e_{\alpha i} e_{\alpha j} f_\alpha = \frac{c^2}{3} \rho \delta_{ij} + \rho u_i u_j + \Pi_{ij}^{neq}, \tag{8}$$

where ρ is the fluid density, u is the fluid velocity vector, c is the lattice speed defined as $c = \delta x / \delta t$, δ_{ij} is the Kronecker delta, and Π_{ij}^{neq} is the non-equilibrium part of the stress tensor. The lattice units of $\delta x = 1$ and $\delta t = 1$ were used in this study. The parameters a_0, b_i, and c_{ij} are expressed by ρ, u, and Π_{ij}^{neq}. The distribution function f_α can therefore be written as

$$f_\alpha = w_\alpha \rho \left[1 + \frac{3(e_{\alpha i} u_i)}{c^2} + \frac{9(e_{\alpha i} u_i)^2}{2c^4} - \frac{3(u_i u_i)}{2c^2} \right]$$
$$+ \frac{9 w_\alpha}{2c^2} \left(\frac{e_{\alpha i} e_{\alpha j}}{c^2} - \frac{1}{3} \delta_{ij} \right) \Pi_{ij}^{neq}. \tag{9}$$

The first term on the right-hand side is equal to Maxwell equilibrium function f_α^{eq}. The second term on the right-hand side is described as f_α^1, and the distribution function f_α is expressed by

$$f_\alpha = f_\alpha^{eq} + f_\alpha^1. \tag{10}$$

The time evolution equation for the regularized lattice Boltzmann equation is then

$$f_\alpha(t + \delta t,\, x + e_\alpha \delta t) = f_\alpha^{eq}(t,\, x) + \left(1 - \frac{1}{\tau}\right) f_\alpha^1(t,\, x), \tag{11}$$

where τ is single relaxation time defined using kinetic viscosity of fluid ν as follows:

$$\tau = \frac{3\nu}{c\delta x} + \frac{1}{2}. \tag{12}$$

The single relaxation time τ was set to 0.88 for all simulations.

In addition, local pressure distribution function p_α introduced by He et al. [20] was applied to simulate incompressible flow. Local pressure distribution function p_α is

$$p_\alpha = c_s^2\, f_\alpha, \tag{13}$$

where c_s is the sound speed, and $c_s = c\,/\,\sqrt{3}$ in this model. Therefore, the time evolution equation for solving the fluid part is

$$p_\alpha(t + \delta t,\, x + e_\alpha \delta t) = p_\alpha^{eq}(t,\, x) + \left(1 - \frac{1}{\tau}\right) p_\alpha^1(t,\, x). \tag{14}$$

Accordingly, the pressure p, the velocity components u_i, and the non-equilibrium part of the stress tensor Π_{ij}^{neq} are given by

$$p = \sum_\alpha p_\alpha, \tag{15}$$

$$u_i = \frac{1}{\rho c_s^2} \sum_\alpha p_\alpha e_{\alpha i}, \tag{16}$$

$$\Pi_{ij}^{neq} = \frac{1}{c_s^2} \left(\sum_\alpha e_{\alpha i} e_{\alpha j} p_\alpha - \frac{c^2}{3} p \delta_{ij} - \frac{c^2}{3} \rho u_i u_j \right). \tag{17}$$

In the programming for the regularized lattice Boltzmann method, only pressure (Equation (15)), velocity components (Equation (16)), and non-equilibrium part of the stress tensor components (Equation (17)) need to be stored in the array to solve the time evolution equation (Equation (14)). The distribution function can be obtained from the parameters above, i.e., it does not need to be stored in the memory. Thus, this method is useful to reduce the computational memory usage compared to the original lattice Boltzmann method.

2.3. Governing Equation for Particles

The translational motion of a particle is determined by solving Newton's equation

$$m\frac{d^2 x_{\mathrm{p}}}{dt^2} = F_{\mathrm{p}}, \tag{18}$$

where m is mass of the suspended particle, x_{p} is the position vector, and F_{p} is the total force vector acting on the particle. The rotational motion of a particle is determined by the equation of angular motion

$$I\frac{d^2 \theta_{\mathrm{p}}}{dt^2} = T_{\mathrm{p}}, \tag{19}$$

where I is the moment of inertia, θ_p is the particle angle, and T_p is the torque exerted on the particle. The mass of the suspended particle m and moment of inertia I are $m = \rho_p \pi ab$ and $I = m(a^2+b^2)/4$, where ρ_p is the density of the particle. Both these two equations were discretized with the third-order Adams–Bashforth method and third-order Adams–Moulton method.

According to Mei et al. [21], the component of shear stress tensor $\tau_{i,j}$ in D dimension is given by

$$\tau_{i,j} = -\left(1 - \frac{1}{2\tau}\right) \sum_\alpha f_\alpha^{\text{neq}}(t,\,x) \left(e_{\alpha,\,i} e_{\alpha,\,j} - \frac{1}{D} e_\alpha \cdot e_\alpha \delta_{i,\,j}\right),\tag{20}$$

where f_α^{neq} is

$$f_\alpha^{\text{neq}}(t,\,x) = f_\alpha(t,\,x) - f_\alpha^{\text{eq}}(t,\,x).\tag{21}$$

The shear stress vector $\boldsymbol{\tau}_w = (\tau_x, \tau_y)$ is calculated using stress tensor T_w on the particle surface as follows:

$$\boldsymbol{\tau}_w = T_w \cdot \boldsymbol{n},\tag{22}$$

where $\boldsymbol{n}$ is the outward normal unit vector on the surface of the particle. The stress tensor T_w was extrapolated by stress tensor T_P and T_Q, on points P and Q (Figure 3), respectively. The components of the force $\boldsymbol{F}_p = (F_x, F_y)$ and the torque T_p on the solid particle are given by

$$F_x = -\int_C (p_P - p_0) n_x \mathrm{d}s + \int_C \tau_{w,\,x} \mathrm{d}s,\tag{23}$$

$$F_y = -\int_C (p_P - p_0) n_y \mathrm{d}s + \int_C \tau_{w,\,y} \mathrm{d}s,\tag{24}$$

$$T_p = |\,\boldsymbol{r} \times \boldsymbol{\tau}_w|_z,\tag{25}$$

where p_P is the pressure on the solid particle surface, p_0 is the reference pressure, and $\boldsymbol{r}$ is the vector on the particle surface from the particle center.

2.4. Virtual Flux Method

The virtual flux method [22,23] was applied to describe the curved boundary of particle shape on a Cartesian grid. Suspension flows including solid particle can be solved by reflecting the distribution functions calculated using the virtual flux method. One of the advantages of this method is simple algorism with no iterative calculations. The distribution function on the particle surface can be obtained by simply considering its hydrodynamic conditions. These procedures need no iterations. Compared to the immersed boundary method (IBM) [24], which is popularly coupled with LBM, the virtual flux method has superior spatial resolution without adding external force to the body surfaces to describe the arbitrary shape on the Cartesian grid.

Figure 3 shows the virtual boundary on the Cartesian grid. For example, the distribution function streams to nine directions in the D2Q9 model; however, the distribution function at grid point 3 cannot propagate to grid point 1 (described as direction α) because the virtual boundary point w exists at the position where $a{:}b$ divides the space between grid points 1 and 3.

A brief description of the calculation procedure to obtain the distribution function at grid point 1 $f_{\alpha,\,1}$ is as follows: First, the physical quantities on the virtual boundary (point w) were obtained by imposing both the no-slip boundary condition ($u_w = u_p$) and pressure boundary condition on the particle surface ($\partial p / \partial n = 0$). Pressure p_P and p_Q at point P and Q, which were located in the normal direction to the wall surface from the boundary point, were interpolated by using data neighboring four points. Pressure at grid point w p_w was obtained by extrapolating pressure p_P and p_Q as

$$p_w = \frac{h_2{}^2 p_P - h_1{}^2 p_Q}{h_2{}^2 - h_1^2},\tag{26}$$

where distances of h_1 and h_2 in this study were $\sqrt{2}$, and $2\sqrt{2}$, respectively. The equilibrium distribution function $f^{eq}_{\alpha,\,w}$ on the virtual boundary was then obtained, and the distribution function $f_{\alpha,\,w}$ was

$$f_{\alpha,\,w}= f^{eq}_{\alpha,\,w}(u_w,\,p_w)+\left(f_{\alpha,1} - f^{eq}_{\alpha,1}\right). \qquad (27)$$

Then, the virtual distribution function $f^{*}_{\alpha,\,3}$ and the equilibrium distribution function $f^{eq*}_{\alpha,\,3}$ at grid point 3 were obtained by extrapolation using these values at grid point 1 as follows:

$$f^{*}_{\alpha,\,3} = \frac{a+b}{a}f_{\alpha,\,w} - \frac{b}{a}f_{\alpha,\,1}, \qquad (28)$$

$$f^{eq*}_{\alpha,\,3} = \frac{a+b}{a}f^{eq}_{\alpha,\,w} - \frac{b}{a}f^{eq}_{\alpha,\,1}. \qquad (29)$$

Finally, the distribution function at grid point 1 for the next time step considering the virtual boundary using $f^{*}_{\alpha,\,3}$ and $f^{eq*}_{\alpha,\,3}$ can be obtained as

$$f_{\alpha,1}= f^{*}_{\alpha,\,3} + \frac{1}{\tau}\left(f^{eq*}_{\alpha,\,3} - f^{*}_{\alpha,\,3}\right). \qquad (30)$$

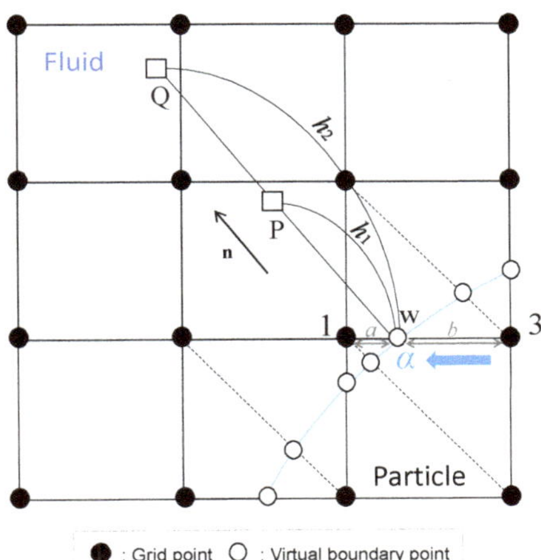

Figure 3. Schematic view of virtual boundary on a Cartesian grid.

2.5. Lift Coefficient

The equilibrium position of inertial migration in a pressure-driven flow can be obtained by the following two methods: the lift force profile of a particle constrained in lateral motion and the trajectory of a freely moving particle. In this study, the constraint method (the former method) was used to obtain the equilibrium position of inertial migration. This method has been previously used by many groups [25,26].

A brief description of the calculation procedure in this study is as follows: A single particle was released from five different initial positions (y/D = 0.2–0.4 with an interval of 0.05) between the lower wall and center line. The motion of the particle was restricted in the direction perpendicular to the flow direction, i.e., the particle was allowed to move only in the flow direction with rotation. The profiles of lift coefficient C_L were obtained using time averaged lift force acting on the particle. Note that the lift force at the center (y/D = 0.5) is assumed to be zero for the symmetry of the computational domain. The equilibrium position was then obtained as a position where the lift force is the closest to zero excluding $y/D = 0.5$ by using a cubic spline interpolation with a precision of the order of $y/D = 0.001$. The lift coefficient C_L was calculated by

$$C_L = \frac{F_y}{\rho U^2 r},$$ (31)

where U is a characteristic velocity.

2.6. Relative Viscosity

Relative viscosity η_{eff}/η_0 for pressure-driven flow [12] is given by

$$\frac{\eta_{\text{eff}}}{\eta_0} = \frac{\Delta p}{\Delta p_0} \approx \frac{\langle \tau_{ij} \rangle}{\tau_0},$$ (32)

where Δp is pressure drop over the channel length, Δp_0 is pressure drop for particle-free flow over the channel length, $\langle \tau_{ij} \rangle$ is the spatially averaged wall shear stress, and τ_0 is the wall shear stress for particle-free flow.

3. Results and Discussion

3.1. Periodic Length and Grid Resolution

The effects of periodic length, which refers to the length L of the parallel plates model, on the equilibrium position of inertial migration were assessed, and a grid independence study was conducted.

First of all, the effects of periodic length were investigated. This length should be sufficient to neglect the effect of the boundary condition. The lift coefficient profiles were compared to determine the periodic length. Figure 4 shows the profiles of lift coefficient of a single circular particle for four different periodic lengths $L/D = 1, 2, 4,$ and 6. On the lower wall side ($y/D = 0.2$), the lift force exerted on the particle was positive, which indicates that particle in this region is lifted up toward the center. On the other hand, when the lift force is negative, particle is lifted down from center region to the wall side. The profiles for $L/D = 4$ and 6 were almost the same. Table 1 shows equilibrium positions obtained from the lift coefficient profiles. The periodic length $L/D = 4$ was thus adopted in the simulation conditions.

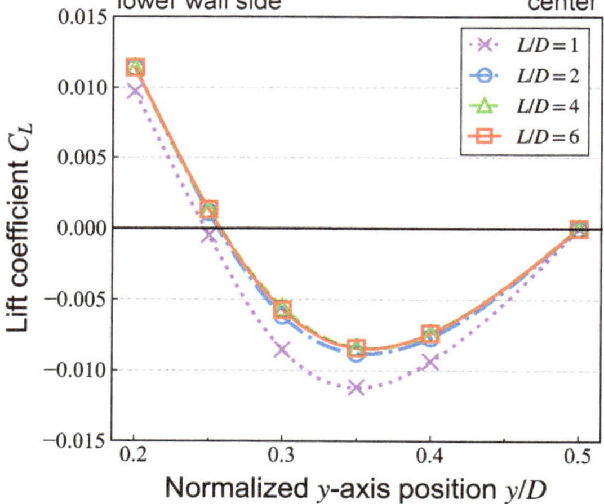

Figure 4. Lift coefficient profiles of a single circular particle with $C_3 = 0.05$ for four different periodic lengths $L/D = 1, 2, 4,$ and 6 (the number of cells for D was 600).

Table 1. Normalized equilibrium position y_{eq}/D of a single circular particle with $C_3 = 0.05$ for different periodic lengths $L/D = 1, 2, 4,$ and 6 (the number of cells for D was 600).

L/D [-]	y_{eq}/D [-]
1	0.248
2	0.256
4	0.258
6	0.258

Secondly, a grid independence study was performed. Figure 5 shows profiles of lift coefficient with three different grid resolutions. When the particle flowed near the lower wall, the lift coefficient became slightly larger with increasing grid resolutions as illustrated in Figure 5. The equilibrium position, where the lift force is zero, moved slightly toward the center for higher resolution. Table 2 shows equilibrium positions obtained from the lift coefficient profiles. The results show that the number of cells for channel width is required to be at least 600. Thus, the number of cells for channel width D was set to 800 in all simulations to take non-spherical particle shapes into account. At least 20 cells were used for the grid resolution of the minor axis of $AR = 4$ in case 3 for $C_3 = 0.05$.

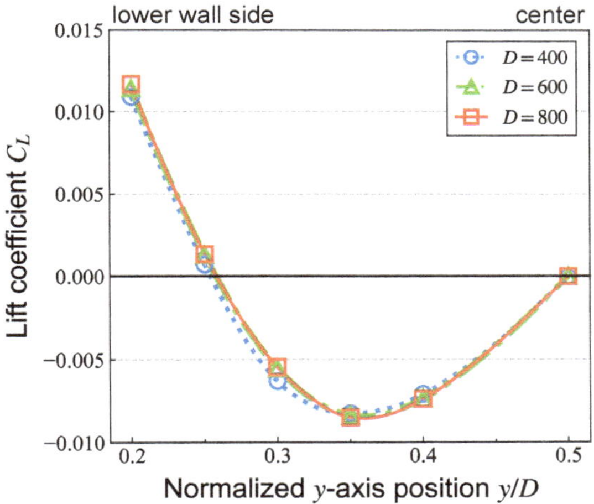

Figure 5. Lift coefficient profiles of a single circular particle with $C_3 = 0.05$ for different grid resolutions: 400, 600, and 800 cells for D in the condition of $L/D = 4$.

Table 2. Normalized equilibrium position y_{eq}/D of a single circular particle with $C_3 = 0.05$ for different grid resolutions. The parameters D and $2r$ denote the number of grids for channel width and particle diameter, respectively.

Number of Cells for D [Cells]	Number of Cells for $2r$ [Cells]	y_{eq}/D [-]
400	20	0.255
600	30	0.258
800	40	0.258

3.2. Effects of Aspect Ratio of Elliptical Particle on the Equilibrium Position Due to Inertial Migration

The effects of aspect ratio on the lift coefficient profiles and the equilibrium positions of the particles with the same area fraction (in case 3) are discussed. Figure 6 shows profiles of lift coefficient of an elliptical particle for different aspect ratios with various confinements. Note that the vertical axis scale depends on each figure for clarity. The lift coefficient profiles were similar between $AR = 1$ and $AR = 2$. On the contrary, those for $AR = 4$ were different from those for $AR = 1$ and 2. When the particle flowed on the lower wall side, the lift coefficient became larger with increasing aspect ratio, i.e., the repulsive force from the wall became larger with increasing aspect ratio. Table 3 shows equilibrium positions for different aspect ratios with various confinements. The equilibrium position shifted toward the center with the increase of aspect ratio, and it was enhanced with higher confinement (larger particle).

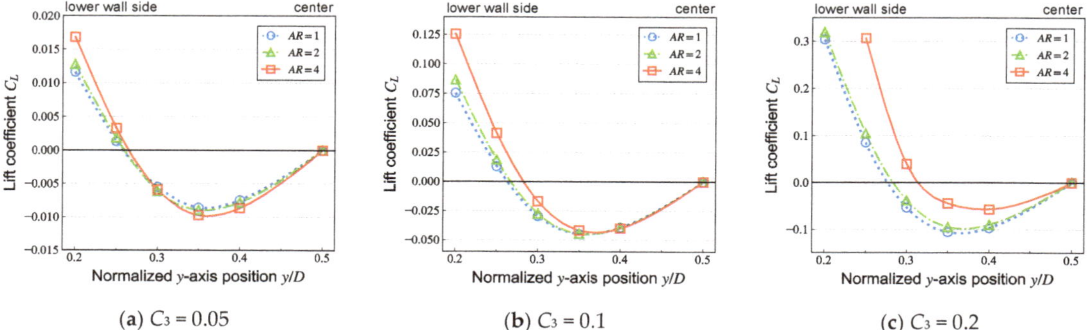

(a) $C_3 = 0.05$ (b) $C_3 = 0.1$ (c) $C_3 = 0.2$

Figure 6. Lift coefficient profiles of a single circular and elliptical particle with (**a**) $C_3 = 0.05$, (**b**) $C_3 = 0.1$, and (**c**) $C_3 = 0.2$ for different aspect ratios $AR = 1, 2$, and 4. Note that the vertical axis scale is different for each figure for clarity.

Table 3. Normalized equilibrium position y_{eq}/D of a single circular and elliptical particle with $C_3 = 0.05, 0.1$, and 0.2 for different aspect ratios.

AR [-]	y_{eq}/D [-]		
	$C_3 = 0.05$	$C_3 = 0.1$	$C_3 = 0.2$
1	0.258	0.263	0.277
2	0.260	0.267	0.284
4	0.260	0.282	0.314

The effects of aspect ratio on the equilibrium positions with the different confinement definitions are discussed. Figure 7 shows the comparison of equilibrium position as a function of confinement with three different definitions for $AR = 1$–4. For each confinement, changes in the equilibrium position with increasing AR are described. For comparison among C_1, which corresponds to the comparison with the same minor axis, the equilibrium position was shifted to the center with increasing AR. On the contrary, for comparison among C_2, which corresponds to the comparison with the same major axis, the equilibrium position was slightly shifted to the wall side ($AR = 2$), then shifted to the center ($AR = 4$) with increasing AR. For comparison among C_3, which corresponds to the comparison with the same area fraction, the equilibrium position was shifted to the center with increasing AR. These results showed that the effects of aspect ratio on the equilibrium position strongly depend on the confinement definition.

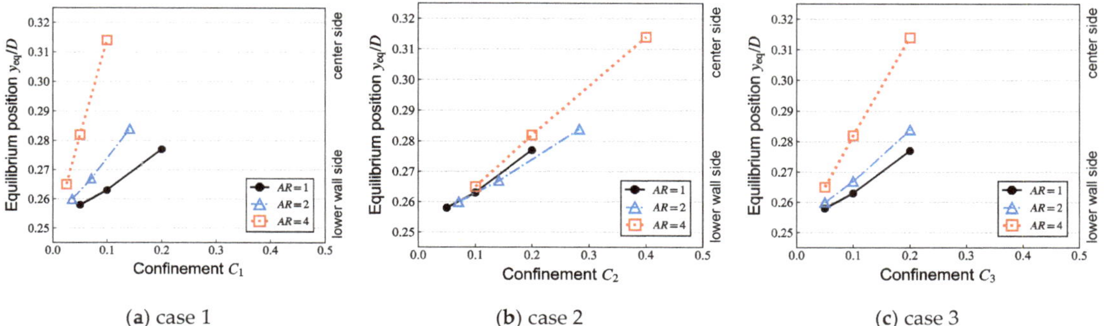

(a) case 1   (b) case 2   (c) case 3

Figure 7. Comparison of equilibrium position as a function of confinement with three different definitions.

Our results are qualitatively consistent with other results for case 1 and 2. Chen et al. [4], who discussed the effects of aspect ratio in a comparison similar to case 1, showed that the equilibrium position with higher AR is closer to the center. Hu et al. [16], who discussed the effects of aspect ratio with C_2 for non-Newtonian fluids, reported that the equilibrium position shifted toward the wall with increasing AR. Wen et al. [5] also discussed the effects of aspect ratio with C_2 on the equilibrium position. They reported that the equilibrium position changes from being closer to the wall to being closer to the center when a certain aspect ratio was exceeded. Our results are consistent with their results. The novel contribution of the present study is to determine the equilibrium positions in case 3 and to compare them among their definitions.

3.3. Effects of Aspect Ratio of Elliptical Particle on the Effective Viscosity

In this section, the relative viscosity contributed by a single particle with various aspect ratios and various distances from the walls is compared. Figure 8 shows the relative viscosity contributed by the elliptical particle with different aspect ratios for the various particle–wall distances. Note that the vertical axis scale is different for each figure for clarity.

For all cases, contribution of the particle to the viscosity increases when particle flows near the wall. Doyeux et al. [11] simulated the motion of confined circular particle in shear flow. They showed that the viscosity increases when the particle approaches the wall. Our results are consistent with their results. When the particle flows near the center line, the relative viscosity was almost independent of aspect ratio and confinement. For small particles, the relative viscosity was almost independent of aspect ratio. In a two-dimensional simulation, Liu et al. [8] reported that the intrinsic viscosity of the elliptical particle is higher than that of the circular particle. Although some factors such as flow field conditions and particle concentration are different from theirs, a significant contribution to the viscosity due to particle shape was not confirmed in this study. In order to validate our numerical results, the intrinsic viscosity in three-dimensional conditions was calculated, and the results were compared with those from Huang et al. [10]. Details of the simulation results are given in Appendix A.

On the contrary, for larger particles, when the particle flowed near the wall, effects of particle shape on the relative viscosity became significant. The contribution of particles with high aspect ratio to the viscosity is minor when the particle flows near the walls. One of the reasons is that particles are oriented in the flow direction for a long time. In previous research, Pozrikidis [27] investigated particle orientation under shear flow and reported that the effective viscosity decreases with higher aspect ratio. Our results are consistent with these results.

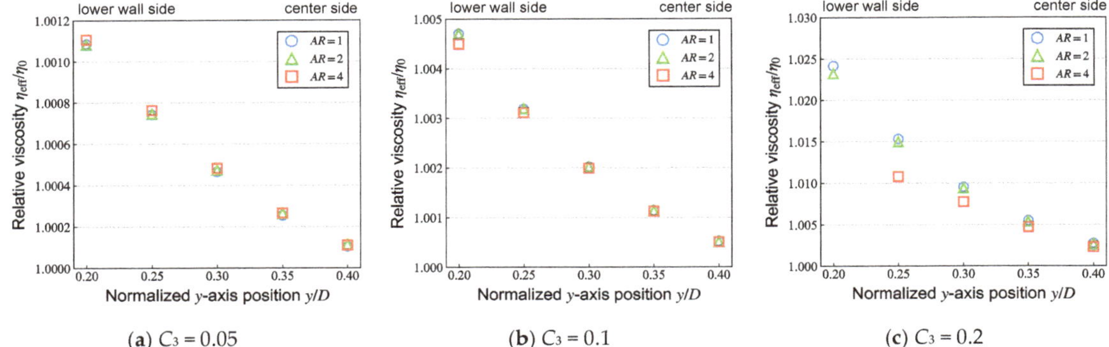

(**a**) $C_3 = 0.05$ (**b**) $C_3 = 0.1$ (**c**) $C_3 = 0.2$

Figure 8. Comparison of relative viscosity of different aspect ratios and confinement. Note that the vertical axis scale is different for each figure for clarity.

3.4. Spatial and Temporal Changes in the Effective Viscosity

The fluctuation of effective viscosity in time and space due to particle behavior was found to be quite significant [12,13]. In this section, the effects of the particle flow position and rotational motion on the spatial distribution of the relative viscosity are discussed, and the spatial and temporal changes in the viscosity are evaluated.

Figure 9 shows distributions of local WSS on the upper and lower wall for a circular particle flowing at $y/D = 0.2$ with various confinements $C_3 = 0.05$, 0.1, and 0.2. Figure 9b shows axial velocity distribution and particle position in connection with Figure 9a,c for $C_3 = 0.2$. Note that local WSS can also be interpreted as the local relative viscosity from Equation (32). The lowest local WSS lies on the lower wall in the region near the particle (Figure 9c). This is already reported by previous studies [12,14,28]. The higher regions of WSS on the lower wall were observed near the edge of the particle. The peak in front of the particle is denoted by τ_1, and that behind the particle is denoted by τ_2 (Figure 9c). In contrast, on the upper wall, the local relative viscosity near the particle becomes higher (Figure 9a). These characteristics are qualitatively consistent with the results from Inamuro et al. [28] who studied the inertial migration of a single circular particle flowing between the parallel plates using IBM-LBM.

In order to capture the characteristics of the variation of the spatial WSS distribution with rotational motions of the particle, we focused on the difference of peaks $\tau_1 - \tau_2$. Figure 10 shows the time history of angular acceleration and difference of peak $\tau_1 - \tau_2$. The elliptical particle rotates, accelerating and deaccelerating during the cycle. When the peak is positive, τ_1 is higher than τ_2, and vice versa. When the angular acceleration of the particle equals 0, the particle is oriented in the flow direction around non-dimensional time $t = 4.6$ and $t = 7$ in Figure 10, and the particle is perpendicular to the flow direction around non-dimensional time $t = 6$ and $t = 8$ in Figure 10. In addition, the negative difference of peak is dominant, which indicates that τ_2 is higher than τ_1 when the particle flows at $y/D = 0.2$, and this depends on the particle–wall distance.

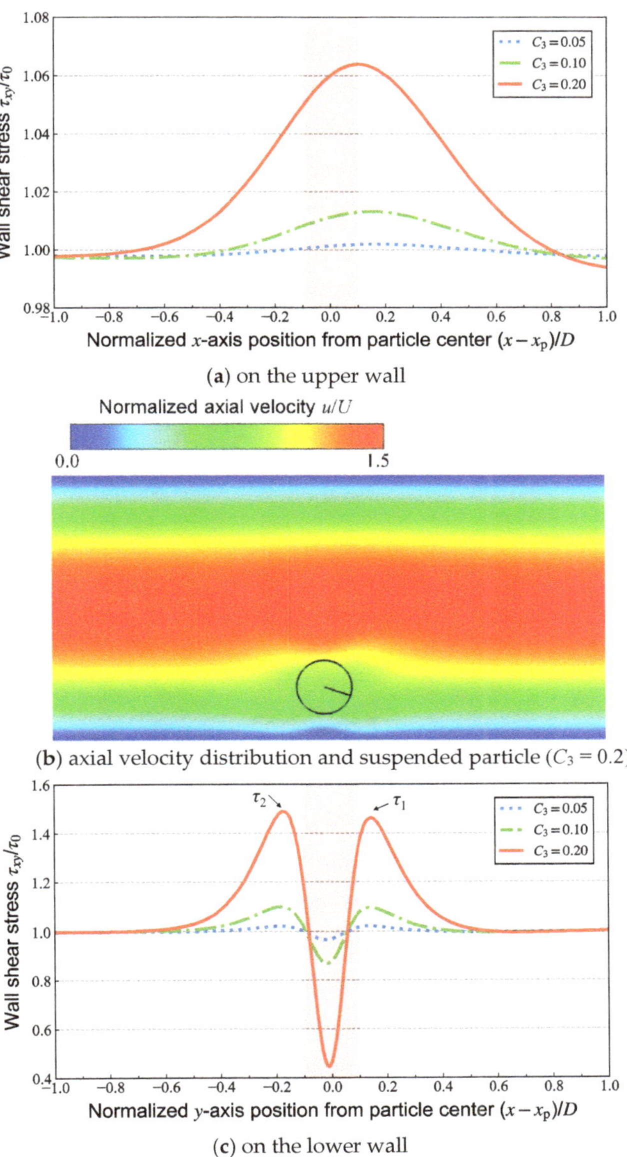

(**a**) on the upper wall

(**b**) axial velocity distribution and suspended particle ($C_3 = 0.2$)

(**c**) on the lower wall

Figure 9. Distributions of local relative viscosity determined by wall shear stress on the (**a**) upper and (**c**) lower wall for a circular particle flowing at $y/D = 0.2$ with various confinements $C_3 = 0.05$ (blue dashed line), 0.1 (green dot-dashed line), and 0.2 (red solid line). The red shadow indicates the region where the particle exists for $C_3 = 0.2$ as shown in (**b**) with axial velocity distribution. The forward and backward peaks of the local relative viscosity on the lower wall are denoted by τ_1 and τ_2, respectively.

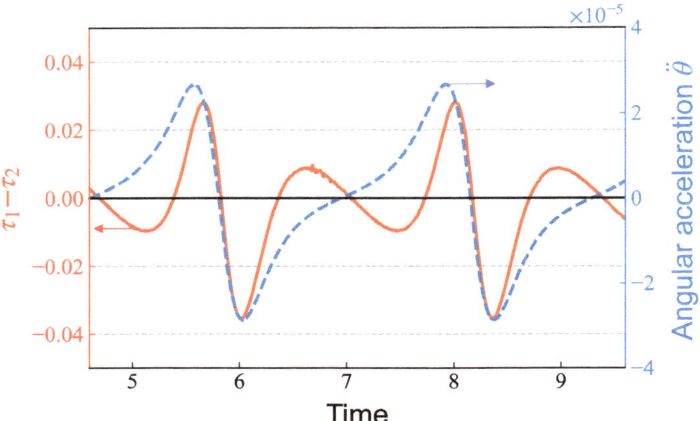

Figure 10. Time history of difference of peak relative viscosity on the lower wall (red solid line) and angular acceleration (blue dashed line) for $AR = 2$ and $C_3 = 0.1$.

Since the rotational motion of the non-circular particle is unsteady, the effective viscosity dramatically changes not only in space but also in time. The spatial and temporal changes in viscosity were evaluated, and these effects were compared. Figure 11 shows the comparison of spatial and temporal standard deviation (SD) of effective viscosity. The temporal and spatial SD was calculated by

$$\mathrm{SD}_{\mathrm{time}} = \sqrt{\frac{1}{n} \sum_{t=1}^{n} \left(\langle \tau(t) \rangle - \overline{\langle \tau(t) \rangle} \right)^2},$$ (33)

$$\mathrm{SD}_{\mathrm{space}}(t) = \sqrt{\frac{1}{2L} \sum_{i=1}^{2L} (\tau(t, i) - \langle \tau(t, i) \rangle)^2},$$ (34)

where $\langle \tau \rangle$ symbolizes the spatial average for τ, and $\overline{\tau}$ symbolizes time-average for τ. The spatial SD was evaluated as the one-cycle rotational averaged value of Equation (34).

The spatial SD of relative viscosity became large when the particle flowed near the wall, the same as the contribution of particle motion to the relative viscosity. The spatial SD of effective viscosity was larger than the temporal deviation, and these differences become larger with increasing confinement.

In the previous studies, Xiong and Zhang [14] observed peak-valley-peak structure of WSS induced by red blood cells, and τ_1 was larger than τ_2. Freund and Vermont [29] showed that blood cells led to WSS with fluctuations that may significantly exceed mean values. The present study extends their findings by focusing on the particle rotational motions, and it was found that the difference between the peaks on the lower wall around the particle was associated with the unsteady rotational motion of the elliptical particle. As Xiong and Zhang [14] mentioned, channel size is a major factor in the fluctuation of WSS. This change is expected to be important especially in microvessels where the particle surface is close to the wall.

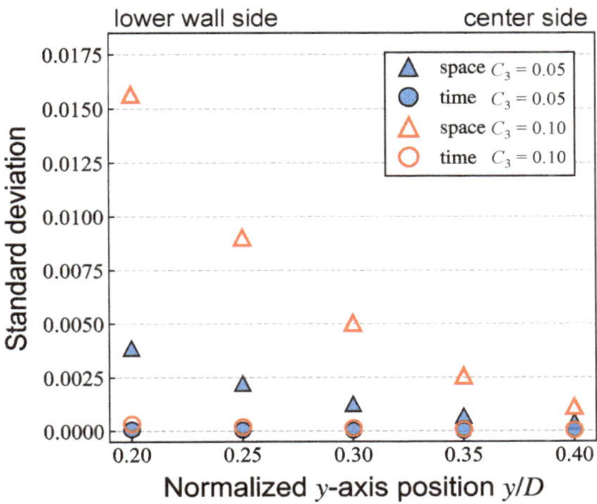

Figure 11. Comparison of temporal (circle) and spatial (triangle) standard deviation of effective viscosity for $AR = 2$ with confinement $C_3 = 0.05$ (filled in blue) and 0.1 (red).

4. Conclusions

The contribution of a single circular or elliptical particle motion, especially the particle–wall distance and rotational motion to the effective viscosity was studied using the regularized lattice Boltzmann method coupled with the virtual flux method. First, the effects of elliptical particle shape on the equilibrium position of inertial migration were summarized using three definitions of confinement. It was found that the effects of aspect ratio on the equilibrium position depend on the confinement definition. The effects of particle shape on the viscosity were also studied, and the contribution of particle shape to the effective viscosity was found to be enhanced when the particle flows near the wall. In terms of temporal and spatial variation of the relative viscosity, spatial variation is larger than temporal variation regardless of the aspect ratio and particle–wall distance.

Author Contributions: Conceptualization, M.K. and T.F.; methodology, M.K. and T.F.; software, M.K., T.F., and K.M.; validation, M.K.; investigation, M.K.; resources, T.F. and K.M.; writing—original draft preparation, M.K.; writing—review and editing, M.K., T.F., and K.M.; visualization, M.K.; supervision, T.F. and K.M.; project administration, T.F. and K.M.; funding acquisition, T.F. All authors have read and agreed to the published version of the manuscript.

Funding: This research was funded in part by JSPS KAKENHI Grant Number JP20K04266.

Institutional Review Board Statement: Not applicable.

Informed Consent Statement: Not applicable.

Data Availability Statement: Data sharing not applicable.

Conflicts of Interest: The authors declare no conflict of interest.

Nomenclature

AR	aspect ratio
a	semi-major axis
b	semi-minor axis
C (C_1, C_2, C_3)	confinement
c_s	sound speed

c	lattice speed
D	channel width (characteristic length)
D_p	diameter of sphere
e_α	discrete velocity vector
f_α	distribution function
f_α^{eq}	equilibrium distribution function
f_α^{neq}	non-equilibrium distribution function
f_α^*	virtual distribution function
f_α^{eq*}	virtual equilibrium distribution function
F_p	total force vector acting on the particle
I	moment of inertia
L	channel length
m	mass of the suspended particle
$\mathbf{n}$	normal unit vector
p_0	reference pressure
p_p	pressure on the solid particle surface
Δp_0	pressure drop for particle-free flow
Δp	pressure drop
p_α	pressure distribution function
Re	Reynolds number
Re_p	particle Reynolds number
r	radius of circular particle
t	time
T_p	torque for particle
T_w	stress tensor
U	characteristic velocity
$\mathbf{u}$	fluid velocity vector
$\Delta x, \Delta y$	grid resolution
x_p	position vector for particle
y_{eq}	equilibrium position of inertial migration
y_0	initial position of a particle in y-coordinate
w_α	weight coefficients
ε	ellipticity
η_{eff}	effective viscosity
η_0	viscosity of solvent
$[\eta]$	intrinsic viscosity
θ_p	particle angle
Π_{ij}^{neq}	non-equilibrium stress tensor
ρ	fluid density
τ	single relaxation time
τ_w	shear stress tensor
τ_0	wall shear stress for particle-free flow
ϕ	area fraction

Abbreviations

eq	equilibrium
neq	non-equilibrium
eff	effective

Appendix A

In order to validate the numerical results, a numerical simulation of shear flow with a tumbling plorate spheroid was carried out, and the intrinsic viscosity was calculated from Equations (1) and (32). The diameter of sphere D_p included 20 cells, and the computational domain was $20\,D_p \times 20\,D_p \times 20\,D_p$. The confinement was set to $C_3 = 0.05$, and each volume of the spheroids was the same. The particle Reynolds number was set to $Re_\mathrm{P} = 0.125$. To compare the geometry of the spheroid, ellipticity ε was defined as

$$\varepsilon = \frac{a - b}{a},\tag{A1}$$

by referring to Huang et al. [10]. The intrinsic viscosity was determined to be averaged for non-dimensional time $t = 15\text{--}20$ for $\varepsilon = 0$ and for one rotational period at $t > 20$ for $\varepsilon > 0$. The results are shown in Figure A1 with others.

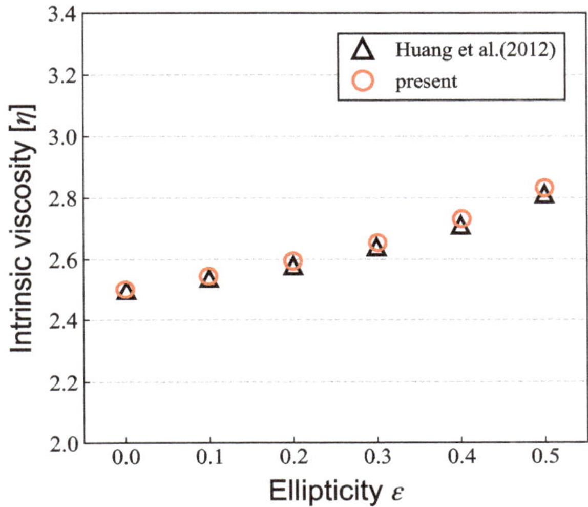

Figure A1. Intrinsic viscosities of a single prolate spheroid in the shear flow in three-dimensional condi-tions.

References

1. Stickel, J.; Powell, R.L. Fluid Mechanics and Rheology of Dense Suspensions. *Annu. Rev. Fluid Mech.* **2005**, *37*, 129–149. [CrossRef]
2. Segré, G.; Silberberg, A. Behaviour of macroscopic rigid spheres in Poiseuille flow: Part 2. Experimental results and interpretation. *J. Fluid Mech.* **1962**, *14*, 136–157. [CrossRef]
3. Fukui, T.; Kawaguchi, M.; Morinishi, K. Numerical Study of the Microstructure of a Dilute Suspension to Assess Its Thixotropic Behavior by a Two-Way Coupling Scheme. *Adv. Fluid Mech. XIII* **2020**, *128*, 47–58. [CrossRef]
4. Chen, S.-D.; Pan, T.-W.; Chang, C.-C. The motion of a single and multiple neutrally buoyant elliptical cylinders in plane Poiseuille flow. *Phys. Fluids* **2012**, *24*, 103302. [CrossRef]
5. Wen, B.; Chen, H.; Qin, Z.; He, B.; Zhang, C. Lateral migration and nonuniform rotation of suspended ellipse in Poiseuille flow. *Comput. Math. Appl.* **2019**, *78*, 1142–1153. [CrossRef]
6. Einstein, A. Eine neue bestimmung der molekuldimensionenm. *Ann. Phys.* **1906**, *19*, 289–306. [CrossRef]
7. Brady, J.F. The Einstein viscosity correction in n dimensions. *Int. J. Multiph. Flow* **1984**, *10*, 113–114. [CrossRef]
8. Liu, J.; Li, C.; Ye, M.; Liu, Z. On the shear viscosity of dilute suspension containing elliptical porous particles at low Reynolds number. *Powder Technol.* **2019**, *354*, 108–114. [CrossRef]
9. Jeffery, G.B. The motion of ellipsoidal particles immersed in a viscous fluid. *Proc. R. Soc. Lond. Ser. A Math. Phys. Sci.* **1922**, *102*, 161–179. [CrossRef]
10. Huang, H.; Wu, Y.; Lu, X. Shear viscosity of dilute suspensions of ellipsoidal particles with a lattice Boltzmann method. *Phys. Rev. E* **2012**, *86*, 046305. [CrossRef] [PubMed]
11. Doyeux, V.; Priem, S.; Jibuti, L.; Farutin, A.; Ismail, M.; Peyla, P. Effective viscosity of two-dimensional suspensions: Confinement effects. *Phys. Rev. Fluids* **2016**, *1*, 043301. [CrossRef]
12. Fukui, T.; Kawaguchi, M.; Morinishi, K. A two-way coupling scheme to model the effects of particle rotation on the rheological properties of a semidilute suspension. *Comput. Fluids* **2018**, *173*, 6–16. [CrossRef]
13. Fukui, T.; Kawaguchi, M.; Morinishi, K. Numerical study on the inertial effects of particles on the rheology of a suspension. *Adv. Mech. Eng.* **2019**, *11*, 1–10. [CrossRef]

14. Xiong, W.; Zhang, J. Shear Stress Variation Induced by Red Blood Cell Motion in Microvessel. *Ann. Biomed. Eng.* **2010**, *38*, 2649–2659. [CrossRef]
15. Jou, L.-D.; Lee, D.; Morsi, H.; Mawad, M. Wall Shear Stress on Ruptured and Unruptured Intracranial Aneurysms at the Internal Carotid Artery. *Am. J. Neuroradiol.* **2008**, *29*, 1761–1767. [CrossRef]
16. Hu, X.; Lin, J.; Guo, Y.; Ku, X. Motion and equilibrium position of elliptical and rectangular particles in a channel flow of a power-law fluid. *Powder Technol.* **2021**, *377*, 585–596. [CrossRef]
17. Başağaoğlu, H.; Succi, S.; Wyrick, D.; Blount, J. Particle Shape Influences Settling and Sorting Behavior in Microfluidic Domains. *Sci. Rep.* **2018**, *8*, 8583. [CrossRef] [PubMed]
18. Izham, M.; Fukui, T.; Morinishi, K. Application of Regularized Lattice Boltzmann Method for Incompressible Flow Simulation at High Reynolds Number and Flow with Curved Boundary. *J. Fluid Sci. Technol.* **2011**, *6*, 812–822. [CrossRef]
19. Qian, Y.H.; D'Humières, D.; Lallemand, P. Lattice BGK Models for Navier-Stokes Equation. *EPL Europhys. Lett.* **1992**, *17*, 479–484. [CrossRef]
20. He, X.; Luo, L.-S. Lattice Boltzmann Model for the Incompressible Navier–Stokes Equation. *J. Stat. Phys.* **1997**, *88*, 927–944. [CrossRef]
21. Mei, R.; Yu, D.; Shyy, W.; Luo, L.-S. Force evaluation in the lattice Boltzmann method involving curved geometry. *Phys. Rev. E* **2002**, *65*, 041203. [CrossRef]
22. Tanno, I.; Morinishi, K.; Matsuno, K.; Nishida, H. Validation of Virtual Flux Method for Forced Convection Flow. *JSME Int. J. Ser. B* **2006**, *49*, 1141–1148. [CrossRef]
23. Morinishi, K.; Fukui, T. An Eulerian approach for fluid–structure interaction problems. *Comput. Fluids* **2012**, *65*, 92–98. [CrossRef]
24. Peskin, C.S. Flow patterns around heart valves: A numerical method. *J. Comput. Phys.* **1972**, *10*, 252–271. [CrossRef]
25. Su, J.; Chen, X.; Hu, G. Inertial migrations of cylindrical particles in rectangular microchannels: Variations of equilibrium positions and equivalent diameters. *Phys. Fluids* **2018**, *30*, 032007. [CrossRef]
26. Udono, H.; Sakai, M. Numerical evaluation of lift forces acting on a solid particle in a microchannel. *J. Soc. Powder Technol. Japan* **2017**, *54*, 454–459. [CrossRef]
27. Pozrikidis, C. Orientation statistics and effective viscosity of suspensions of elongated particles in simple shear flow. *Eur. J. Mech. B/Fluids* **2005**, *24*, 125–136. [CrossRef]
28. Inamuro, T.; Maeba, K.; Ogino, F. Flow between parallel walls containing the lines of neutrally buoyant circular cylinders. *Int. J. Multiph. Flow* **2000**, *26*, 1981–2004. [CrossRef]
29. Freund, J.B.; Vermot, J. The Wall-stress Footprint of Blood Cells Flowing in Microvessels. *Biophys. J.* **2014**, *106*, 752–762. [CrossRef]

Article

Polymerization and Collision in High Concentrations for Brownian Coagulation

Xiaoyue Wang [1], **Yueyan Liu** [2,*], **Taiquan Wu** [2,*] **and Mingzhou Yu** [1]

[1] Laboratory of Aerosol Science and Technology, China Jiliang University, Hangzhou 310000, China; p1801085255@cjlu.edu.cn (X.W.); mzyu@cjlu.edu.cn (M.Y.)
[2] College of Modern Science and Technology, China Jiliang University, Yiwu 322000, China
* Correspondence: 12a1803148@cjlu.edu.cn (Y.L.); 07a0803079@cjlu.edu.cn (T.W.)

Abstract: Aggregation always occurs in industrial processes with fractal-like particles, especially in dense systems (the volume fraction, $\phi > 1\%$). However, the classic aggregation theory, established by Smoluchowski in 1917, cannot sufficiently simulate the particle dynamics in dense systems, particularly those of generat ed fractal-like particles. In this article, the Langevin dynamic was applied to study the collision rate of aggregations as well as the structure of aggregates affected by different volume fractions. It is shown that the collision rate of highly concentrated particles is progressively higher than that of a dilute concentration, and the SPSD (self-preserving size distribution) is approached ($\sigma_{g,n} \geq 1.5$). With the increase in volume fraction, ϕ, the SPSD broadens, and the geometric standard is 1.54, 1.98, and 2.73 at $\phi = 0.1$, 0.2, and 0.3. When the volume fraction, ϕ, is higher, the radius of gyration is smaller with the same cluster size (number-based), which means the particle agglomerations are in a tighter coagulation. The fractal-like property D_f is in the range of 1.60–2.0 in a high-concentration system. Knowing the details of the collision progress in a high-concentration system can be useful for calculating the dynamics of coagulating fractal-like particles in the industrial process.

Keywords: collision; Brownian motion; aggregation; molecular dynamics

Citation: Wang, X.; Liu, Y.; Wu, T.; Yu, M. Polymerization and Collision in High Concentrations for Brownian Coagulation. *Appl. Sci.* **2021**, *11*, 6815. https://doi.org/10.3390/app11156815

Academic Editor: Jianzhong Lin

Received: 15 May 2021
Accepted: 21 July 2021
Published: 24 July 2021

Publisher's Note: MDPI stays neutral with regard to jurisdictional claims in published maps and institutional affiliations.

1. Introduction

The coagulation of nanoparticles in the air or industrial processes is an inevitable outcome; in such a process, the total particle number decreases but the mean size of the particles increases [1–3]. In 1927, Smoluchowski established a governing equation for describing the coagulation process, which was later called the Smoluchowski equation (SE) or coagulation equation [4]. SE is suitable for a system where one spherical particle forms once two particles collide and the volume fraction of the system, ϕ, is limited ($\phi < 0.01$) [5]. The basis of this SE is Einstein's theory of particle diffusion in the flow field, which focuses on many assumptions and restrictive conditions in the process of Stokes's steady-state force on particles and Van't Hoff's calculation of osmotic pressure. However, when the multiphase system is far away from the dilute phase conditions ($\phi < 0.01$), the distance between adjacent particles will decrease accordingly. When the distance between particles reaches the magnitude of the particle-free path, the correlation between particles cannot be ignored—that is, the SE is no longer applicable [6].

The coagulation of nanoparticles in dense conditions happens in many industrial processes. For dealing with the ultrafine particles emitted from exhaust pipes [7], dust particle agglomerations formed of clusters [8], emulsions [9], and particle coagulations, the aerosol process has been described by the Smoluchowski theory of Brownian aggregation, which refers to the random motion in a fluid [10]. It is believed that the process of particle collision mostly depends on the grain size, the concentration of particles, and the transport coefficients in the mechanism.

Early examples of research into Brownian aggregation include research on the effect of bulk stress [11]; fluid shear involving polymerization [10]; the influence of transport on the coagulation rate, such as diffusion consistency [7] and fluid viscosity shear [12]; transition regime; and the mass transfer function of the Knudsen number [13]. Such approaches, however, have failed to address the dense particulate system (effect fraction $\phi > 0.01$). Simultaneously, a high solid concentration is common in industrial production—for instance, flame, plasma, and laser material synthetic technology works on high particle concentrations [14], the aerosol of aggregating clusters [15], and TiO_2 aerosol agglomerate at high solid concentrations [16].

The research results of Heine and Pratsinis [15] confirmed that the classical Smoluchowski theory is limited to cases where the particle volume concentration is less than 0.1%. When the particle volume concentration is higher than this value, the collision frequency between particles is higher than the predicted value given by the Smoluchowski theory, and the collision frequency of the particles in the system is a function of the volume rate of the particles in the system. The larger the particle volume ratio is, the higher the collision frequency of the system particles is and the greater the deviation between the real situation and the predicted value of the classical Smoluchowski theory is. Based on the numerical simulation results of Langevin dynamics (LD), Heine and Pratsinis [15] and Trzeciak et al. [6] give fitting expressions for the collision frequency between particles in the dense phase state. However, although the expressions they gave are quite different in form, they do not deviate from the framework of classical Smoluchowski theory. They are all modified expressions of the classical theory, and the fitting expressions cannot be interpreted in a strictly physical meaning. It should be pointed out that Trzeciak et al. (2006) studied monodisperse systems, while Heine and Pratsnis studied polydisperse systems, but the LD simulation gave very similar results. Both Heine and Pratsinis [15] and Trzeciak et al. [6] deal with spherical particles. While in real coagulation systems, particles are normally displayed as fractal-like agglomerates or aggregates, the collision rate and dynamics of aggregates are absolutely different from those of spherical particles. Thus, it is necessary to study collisions among particles due to coagulation when these particles appear in aggregate form.

Although several methods currently exist for the measurement of collision in an aggregation, numerical simulation is currently the most popular method for investigating the particle aggregation process [11]. The Monte Carlo method [17,18] and the Moment Method [19–24] are currently the most useful methods for investigating particle dynamics. Whilst it is quite complicated to predict the trajectory tracking in the motion process of every particle with the growth of particles for aggregation, the molecular dynamics method is calculated by following the movement of particles on the molecular scale [25]. The solvent molecules are not explicitly included in the simulation but contribute to the dynamics of Brownian particles collectively as a random force. This reduces the dimensionality of the problem, making the Langevin Dynamic (L-D) less computationally intensive than the corresponding numerical simulations [26].

Here, in this article, the collision of particles affected by the volume fraction is investigated. The evolution of the population of clusters is studied in different particle volume fractions ($\phi = 0.05, 0.1, 0.2, 0.3$). The nature of agglomerate particle dynamics is described using monomers in implicit solvent. Emphasis is placed on the attainment of self-preserving size distributions (SPSDs). The characterization of fractal-like structures dominated by Brownian coagulation is then discussed. The relationship of the radius of gyration and the fractal dimension (D_f) is investigated in the different volume fractions. Finally, a summary of the fractal aggregates distribution range and fractal-like structures in the nanoscales is given in detailed aggregates.

2. Materials and Methods

We consider particles as exclusively spheres; sphere–sphere collisions have occurred in the random motion. The force of particle j acting on particle i is defined by the Langevin Dynamic equation.

$$\vec{F}_i = \left(F_c + F_f + F_r \right) F_{ij},\tag{1}$$

where $\vec{F}_i$ is the conservative force of atom i given by atom j computed; F_f is the friction term proportional to the particle's velocity; F_r is the force due to implicit solvent atoms bumping into the particle, which represents the randomicity of Brownian motion; F_{ij} is the unit vector of direction of r_i to r_j. Equation (1) is the motion of the particles in the simulating procedure and the MD simulation.

$$F_f = -fv_i,\tag{2}$$

$$f = -m\gamma,\tag{3}$$

$$F_r = \alpha\sqrt{\frac{2k_B T\gamma}{\Delta t}},\tag{4}$$

where v_i is the velocity of particle i; m is the mass of the particle; k_B is the Boltzmann constant; T is the temperature; Δt is the timestep size; α is a Gaussian random number; γ is the friction rate between nanoparticles and implicit solvent fluid; f is the friction constant, which equals the mass of the particle multiplied by the friction rate [26].

The force corresponding to the potential function is:

$$F_c = -\nabla u\left(a_{ij} \right),\tag{5}$$

$$u\left(a_{ij} \right) = 4\epsilon \left[\left(\frac{\sigma}{a_{ij}} \right)^{12} - \left(\frac{\sigma}{a_{ij}} \right)^6 \right] a_{ij} < r_c.\tag{6}$$

The Lennard-Jones (L-J) potential equation describes both the attractive force and repulsive force [27,28], where the former part of Equation (6) expresses the repulsive effect while the latter expresses the attraction.

The aggregation in the L-D simulation is completed with the collision of pair particles (or multiple), occurring once two (or multiple) particles contact or overlap (Figure 1). In the initial state, all nanoparticles in the fluid environment are in a simple cubic distribution, and the distances between the particles are equal. It is not necessary to consider the effects of gravity coagulation and shear coagulation due to the small size of the nanoparticles [29]. In order to facilitate the calculation, all particles in the simulation system are divided into neighbor lists. A concentric circle in the cutoff distance, r_c, is constructed to calculate the interaction force between particles.

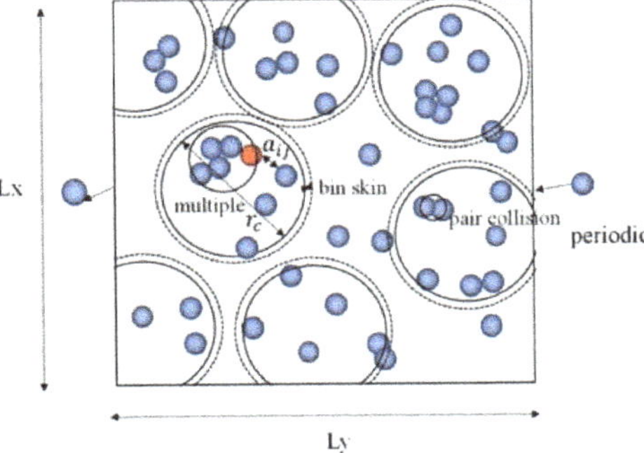

Figure 1. Neighbor list and collision progress.

The simulation boundary condition is periodic and the neighbor list store with r_c. The statistic of collision in unit time Δt of particle I could be described by:

$$\beta_c(Collision) \Longleftrightarrow a_{ij} \leq r_{min},$$

(7)

where a_{ij} is the collision diameter with particle i and particle j; $r_{min} = d_p$. The particles were sampled under the steady state. In order to make the list effective in continuous time steps and increase the fault tolerance rate, bin skin is added out of the cutoff distance, which is generally set to 0.3 or 0.4. All particles in the neighbor list should be calculated at collision (Figure 1). Each particle is regarded as the center particle, i, and the surrounding particles are regarded as the collision particle, j. It is supposed that each particle has an effective cross-section when the collision particle contacts with the center particle, which is determined by the effect diameter $a_{ij} = d_p$ (Figure 1). For analysis, the number of aggregations is counted once particles, excepting the center particle, are in the effective cross-section. The center particle is also in the flow state. As depicted in Figure 1, the random movement of particle j with radius r_j enters the range of influencing spheres.

In this article, the definition for dilution and dense condition from the reference [2] is accepted, such that the volume fraction $\phi < 0.01$ is a dilute concentration while $\phi > 0.01$ is a high concentration. The volume fraction at the dilute concentration in classic coagulation theory is:

$$\phi = \frac{\pi \sum_{i=1}^{n} d_i^{\,3}}{6 L_x L_y L_z},$$

(8)

where $L_x L_y L_z$ is the domain volume. The primary particles turn into the new cluster with the center of mass, radius of gyration, and velocity due to the collision and growth of particles. The fractal agglomerates are formed when agglomerates account for more than 15% of the system concentration. Because of the sharp decrease in the concentration of the number of particles, the probability of Brownian collisions is very low, which is consistent with the self-preserving size distributions [16].

With the collision of Brownian motion, the monomers polymerize into aggregation with short living for the hard model. The clusters, composed of monomers, are identified by the position statistics of each primary particle (Figure 2). Accounting for the size of non-spherical aggregates on a long time length, the diameter of the aggregate is shown in Figure 2, in which particle rotation during collision is neglected. The cluster consists of many monomers with different degrees of overlap, and the circle of the clusters could roughly indicate the size of it (Figure 2). The growth of the aggregate structure via particle–particle collisions is formed by the coagulation of primary diameter d_p. In particular, fractal aggregates are investigated by the radius of gyration [30–33]:

$$n_p = k_g \left(\frac{d_g}{d_p}\right)^{D_f}.$$

(9)

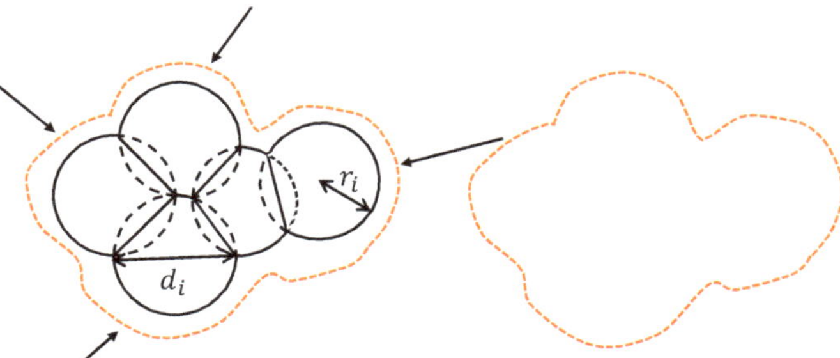

Figure 2. The aggregates composed of monomers and the circle of the cluster.

Here, for fractal-like aggregates, n_p is the number of particles in the aggregates; the k_g is the fractal per factor (also described as the structure coefficient), which is always roughly 1.5 for $n_g > 10$, and this increases with the overlapping of primary monomers; D_f is the fractal dimension, which is typically assumed to be $D_f \approx 1.8$ [28]. The ability to track the individual particle position is permitted to calculate the radius of gyration without assuming the values k_g and D_f. The d_g is the diameter of gyration, which consists of n_i primary particles at the position of $(x_1, \cdots\cdots, x_n)$, and is given by:

$$d_g^2 = \frac{4}{\sum_i m_i} \sum_i m_i \left(|x_i - o|^2 + R_{g,i}{}^2 \right),$$

(10)

$$R_g = \sqrt{\frac{1}{n} \sum_{i=1}^{n} \|x_i - o\|^2},$$

(11)

where o denotes the center of mass. One monomer acting on another only in a single point is assumed, while several aggregates have a certain degree of overlapping. Additionally, the fractal dimension could be described among the radius of gyration:

$$n_p = k_g \left(\frac{R_g}{a_p} \right)^{D_f},$$

(12)

where a_p is the initial radius of particles.

3. Results and Discussion

In all cases, particles are placed by sample cubic unit cell in the periodic boundary conditions. Note that the employed box size $L_x L_y L_z$ changes to accommodate different volume fractions ϕ, as in Equation (7), whilst keeping a constant number of particles ($n = 1$). In particular, the domain box size is 2.79641e + 07 nm^3, 1.39919e + 07 nm^3, 6.99583e + 06 nm^3, or 4.66159e + 06 nm^3 when the volume fraction ϕ is equal to 0.05, 0.1, 0.2, or 0.3, respectively. The particles are initially monodispersed, $d_p = 3$ nm in diameter, with a density of 2.2 g/cm^3. The particles are randomly placed in a box without overlapping and touching. They will grow by Brownian motion and aggregate in the implicit solvent at T = 300 K. The temperature of LD simulation is modified by modifying the force without performing time integration. Therefore, specific time integration (NVE ensemble) must be used to fix the velocity and position of particles.

3.1. Splitting Time Step

The length of the operator splitting time step size affects the accuracy and stability of the coupling between the gas phase and particle population balance [34]. If the running step is too long, the balance of the system could be broken and lead to a sinking term in the particle phase [35]. Due to the principle of molecular dynamics simulation, fs(10^{-12} s) is generally selected as the timestep scale and it is converted to units of ns(10^{-9} s) to fit the overall scale of nanoparticles. The small timestep could increase the calculation cost; moreover, the timestep should be small enough so that the force on a particle can be assumed to be constant during the timestep [36]. Thus, choosing an appropriate time step is necessary to investigate convergence behavior.

In order to ensure the practical significance of the sampling results, a sufficiently substantial number of particles was used to operate with multi-running for convergence. The number of particles before collision (n) is 100,000 and the total time length (L) is 60 ns. The cluster is in a self-preserving distribution based on Brownian collision, while the particle population is balanced [37], which is reasonably used as an examination standard for the convergence of the system in different timestep sizes.

Figure 3 describes the cluster concentration based on the different time step sizes in the same simulation range (L = 60 ns). It can be seen that the convergence is finally completed within 45 ns in addition to the disturbance of the end acquisition time, which is the error of the acquisition method for molecular dynamics. When the timestep size Δt is 0.001, the growth trend of the curve line is smoother, and it takes longer for it to reach convergence. Compared to the stable stage with other timesteps, the smaller the timestep size is, the less disturbance there is with the sampling.

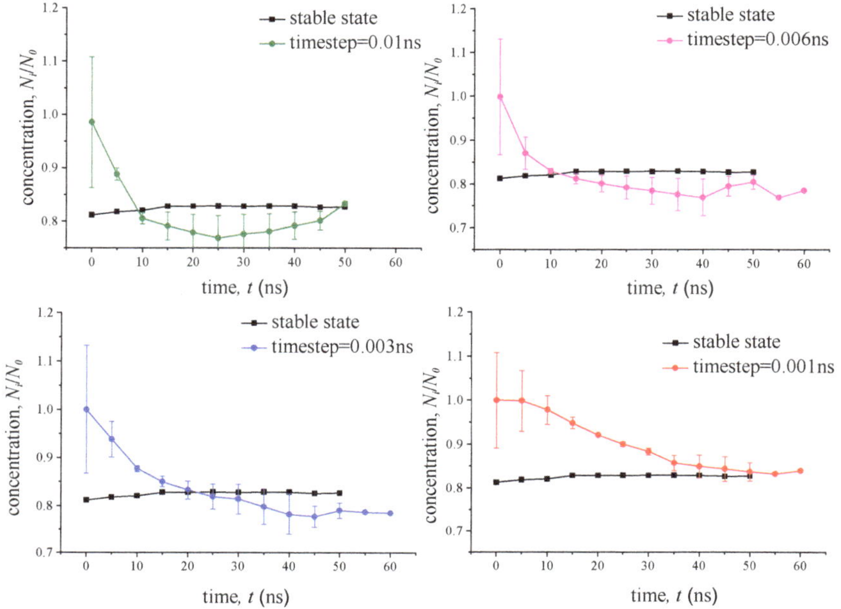

Figure 3. Aggregates concentration with time range (L = 60 ns).

The average value of the cluster distribution with different timesteps is taken as a stable value $\xi(t)$ to solve the error $e_r(t)$ of random operation with different timesteps:

$$e_r(t) = \frac{|u(t) - \xi(t)|}{\xi(t)}, \tag{13}$$

where $u(t)$ represents the cluster distribution at each timestep. The results of errors are shown in Figure 3. It is found that the convergence of different timesteps is roughly the same under the long range of simulation time. The smaller timestep has been tending to lower error in the stable range. Figure 4 is the CPU calculating time with various timestep scales, which indicates more simulation time in a smaller timestep. The CPU total running time is in the controllable range even if the timestep is 0.001 ns. As discussed above, it is a better choice if the timestep of simulation is 0.001 ns and the whole time range L is 60 ns.

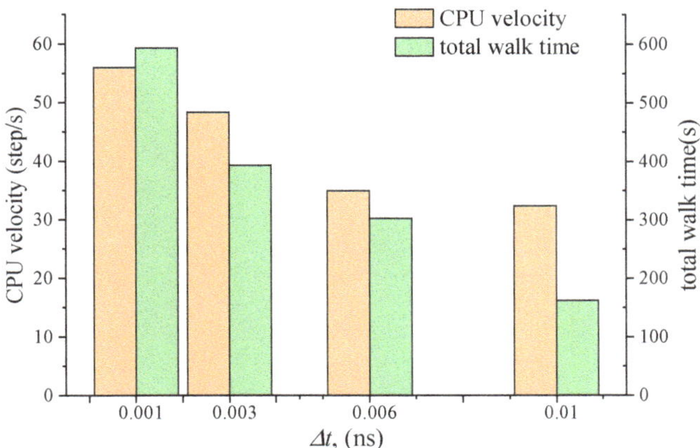

Figure 4. The CPU velocity and total walk time in the same running range.

3.2. Particle Collisions at Different Volume Fractions

The number of particle clusters with the occurrence of collisions is shown in Figure 5. N_0 is the initial number of particles (N_0 = 100,000); N_i represents the population of particle clusters, and the initial monomers are regarded as one cluster ($N_i \leq N_0$). In addition, highly concentrated fractal-like aggregates undergoing coagulation develops SPSDs only temporarily, and they approach gelation at an effective agglomerate concentration of about 0.15 [10]. All the clusters are monomers before the collision. In Figure 5a, the scaled number concentration of clusters is $N_i / N_0 = 1$ when the time is at 0 ns. The number of clusters decreases rapidly in an earlier period, but finally it stabilizes with the evolution of time. Figure 5a also shows the larger volume fraction in the initial condition, the faster decay rate of the aggregate number. In the figure, the evolution of particle numbers with time is also displayed by implementing classical steady-state Smoluchowski model using Brownian Dynamics Simulations (BDS) in the volume fraction, ϕ = 0.005, 0.0005 [36]. It is clear that the decay of particle numbers in the BDS is much slower than that in the present simulation, which indicates that the collision rate in dense conditions is much larger than that in the dilute condition. Figure 5b shows all the aggregates concentrations in the cases that are more than 15% so that all the systems can be developed into SPSDs.

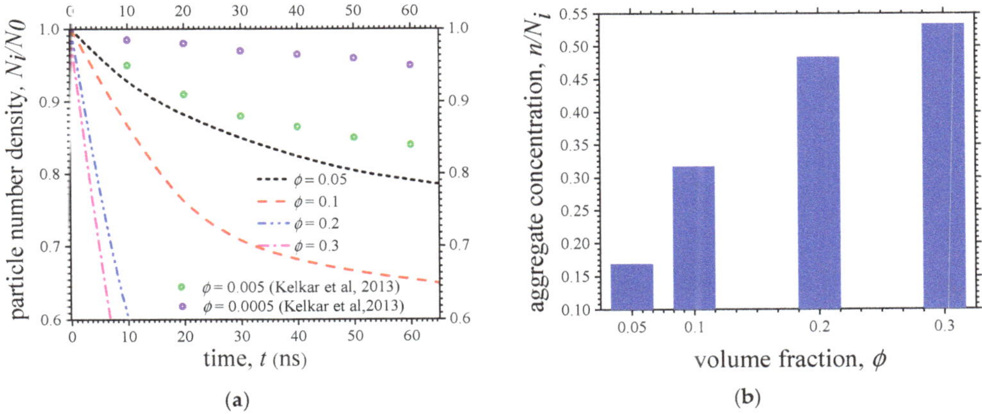

Figure 5. Agglomeration concentration with the change in particle numbers: (**a**) the evolution of particle numbers with time; (**b**) the effective agglomerate concentration in the system.

Figure 6 shows the static structural "snapshot" of aggregate systems at the same time point, t = 100 ns, from the different volume fractions (ϕ = 0.05, 0.1, 0.2, 0.3). For the convenience of the visualization and analysis of the simulation data, the calculated data in the present study are rendered according to cluster size (number based) by OVITO [38]. In order to note the form of aggregates clearly, the clusters with only one monomer are restricted to transparent states. Among all the investigated cases, the system with initial volume fraction ϕ = 0.05, has the least probability of occurrence of aggregates; in contrast, the system with the initial volume fraction ϕ = 0.3 has the greatest probability. From the static structural "snapshot" shown in Figure 6, it can also be found that at the larger volume fractions, the aggregates are composed of more monomers and the fractal-like form is more obvious. This is consistent with the finding that the coagulation kinetic in the dense condition is faster than those at dilute concentrations [10].

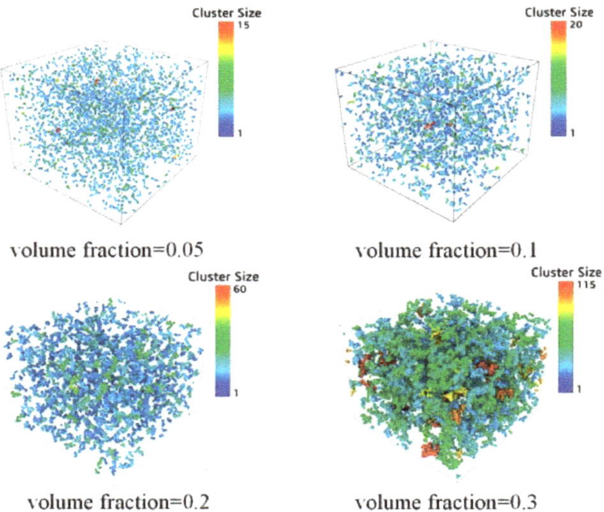

Figure 6. Collision results of primary particles from different volume fraction.

Figure 7a is the normalized particle number size distributions at the same time t = 100 ns, generated from various solid volume fractions. In the figure, d_i represents the number-based size of aggregates i, and the monomer seems as d_i = 1; d_{ave} is the number based geometric mean diameter. The distribution is closer to dilute concentration when the volume fraction is 0.05. As compared to the dilute particle system, the system with a higher volume fraction shows a wider distribution of numbers. It implies that under dense conditions, particles have more probability to collide, as shown in Equation (7).

Figure 7b is the number-based average geometric standard deviations as the function of different volume fractions, σ_g as the function of different volume fractions, ϕ. As a comparison, the calculation data from Heine and Pratsinis [10] is displayed. When $\phi < 0.1$, the present LD simulation and Heine and Pratsinis's work match for the geometric standard deviations (σ_n = 1.52). The present LD simulation agrees well with Heine and Pratsinis' data under the dilute condition; with an increase in the volume fraction, the deviation between the two works increases. This is because in Heine and Pratsinis's work [10], the complete coalescence process for spherical particles is considered, while in the present work the aggregate process for fractal-like particles is considered. By comparing the two works, it can be concluded that the number distribution for the aggregate process has a broader distribution than that for spherical particle coagulation.

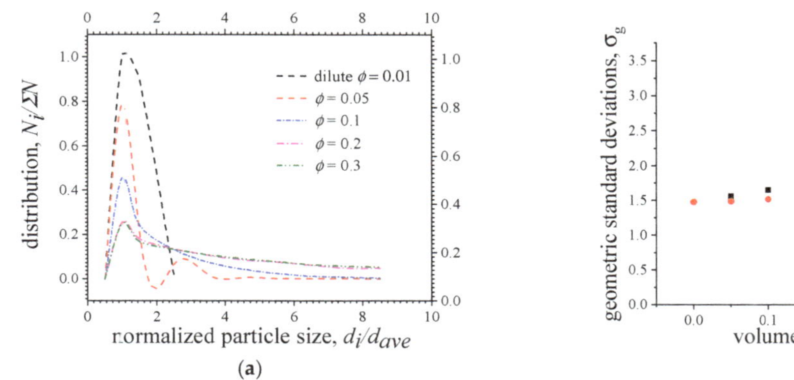
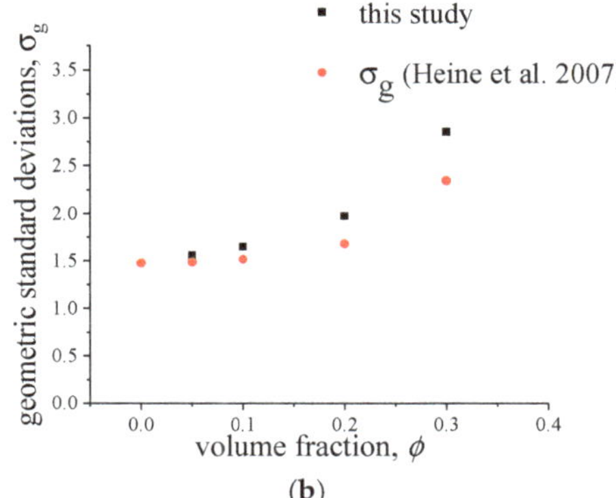

Figure 7. (**a**) Normalized particle size distributions; (**b**) geometric standard deviations with different volume fractions.

3.3. Cluster Analysis of Collision Particles

The relationship between the radius of gyration and the cluster size of aggregates at different volume fractions is studied (Figure 8). When the volume fraction, ϕ, is higher, the radius of gyration is smaller with the same cluster size (number-based), which means the aggregates are in a tighter structure. When the monomers in aggregations are less than two, the radius of gyration of clusters is less than the initial radius ($r_p = 1.5$) in all the volume fractions. An increasing particle concentration results in clusters with larger collision diameters and a higher degree of aggregate, which is consistent with Grass [39]. Assuming the $k_g = 1$, with fractal dimensions $D_f = 1.8$ and $D_f = 3$ according to Equation (12), the radius of gyration as the function of cluster sizes is displayed in the green and purple scatters. The results of different volume fractions are between 1.8 to 2.0 when the agglomerations appear in a fractal-like structure. Agglomerates containing about 10 to 30 primary particles on average attain their asymptotic fractal dimension, D_f, of 1.91 or 1.78 by ballistic or diffusion-limited cluster–cluster agglomeration, corresponding to coagulation in the free molecular or continuum regimes, respectively [40]. The transition of D_f from three (initial monomers) to its asymptotic 1.78 or 1.91 occurs as particle coalescence upon collision slows down by increasing particle size. The aggregates have not rigorously attained a fractal-like structure when the volume fraction $\phi = 0.05$ because such structures have not reached sufficiently large sizes.

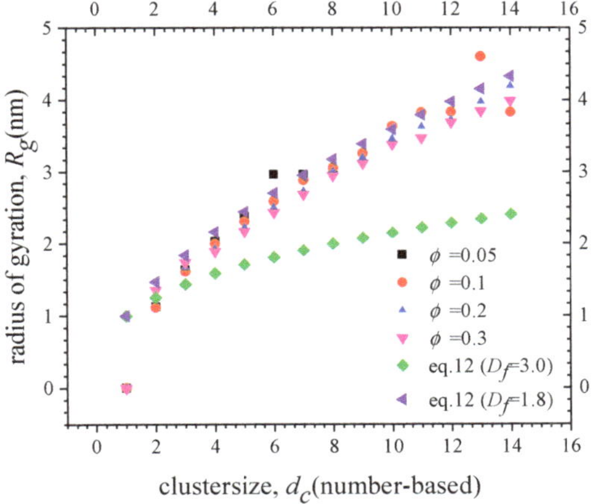

Figure 8. Agglomeration compactness under different initial particle sizes.

The particle j coordination number in the range of d_{ij} of particle i with different volume fractions is shown in Figure 9. Here, $Z(x)$ indicates the average number of contacts per monomer, and N_d is the count that indicates the number of monomers whose coordination number is $Z(x)$. When the volume fractions are more than 0.1, the distributions of coordination numbers are similar, but the coordination numbers are more aggregated with single connected particles (value 1). The aggregation of monomers formed with a larger geometric diameter and wider distribution as the increase in the volume fraction, which means that the polydisperse of coagulation is higher with the denser system. Teichmann and Van also found that the coordination number (i.e., the average number of contacts per monomer) increases with the compression of aggregates [41].

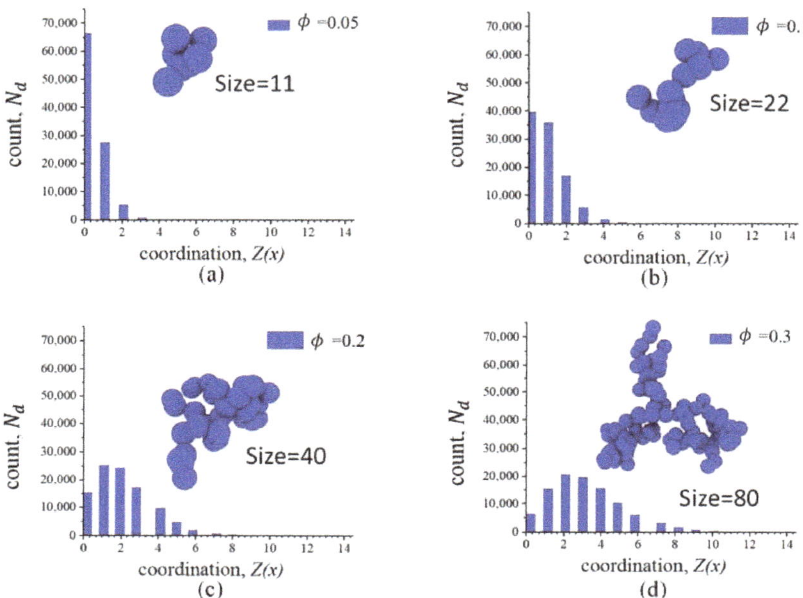

Figure 9. Coordination number analysis with different volume fractions: (**a**) $\phi = 0.05$; (**b**) $\phi = 0.1$; (**c**) $\phi = 0.2$; (**d**) $\phi = 0.3$.

Figure 10 shows the power-law relationship between the radius of gyrations and the number of monomers in each aggregate under stable conditions. The slope of the straight line is the fractal dimension of the cluster, and the length of the straight line is the size distribution width of the cluster [40]. With an increase in the volume fraction, the aggregates cluster tends to be a fractal-like structure and the fractal dimension in the range of 1.614–2.060. The aggregate structure and D_f both depend on the ratio of collision time. Under the restrictive condition, $t_c > \Delta t$, monomers evolve into fractal-like aggregates immediately upon collision. Lower D_f exhibits an increased cross surface area, which leads to a faster collision among aggregates and monomers. Hence, the aggregate system achieves its SPSD faster with a decreasing D_f [42]. For agglomerates, the primary particles stick upon inter-particle collision, forming fractal-like agglomerates with $D_f = 1.9$ [42–44]. When the volume fractions are higher, the D_f of aggregates formed by collision is closer to 1.9.

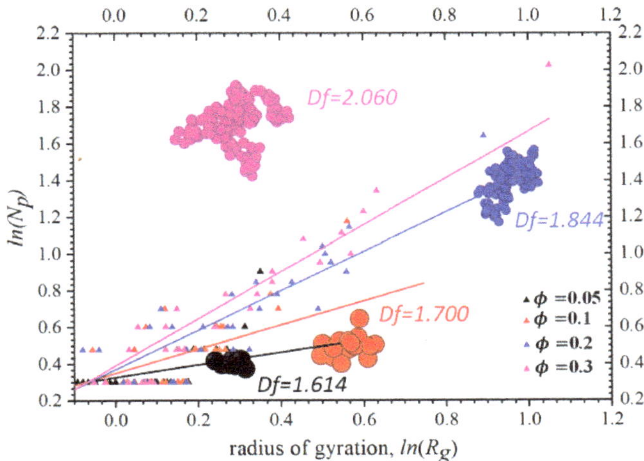

Figure 10. The fractal dimension and monomers number in the aggregates with different volume fractions.

4. Conclusions

The effect of the particle volume fraction on particle collision and growth by Brownian coalescence in the dense system was investigated using LD simulation. Self-preserving particle size distributions (SPSDs) were obtained at all investigated particle volume fractions ϕ from 0.05 to 0.3. With the increase in ϕ, the SPSD broadens, and the geometric standard deviation becomes 1.54, 1.98, and 2.73 at $\phi = 0.1, 0.2, 0.3$.

Aggregates formed by particle collision have significant differences for the volume fraction $\phi = 0.05, 0.1, 0.2, 0.3$ with the same initial particle size $d_p = 3$ nm. When the volume fraction ϕ is higher, the radius of gyration is smaller with the same cluster size (number-based), which means that the particle agglomerations are in a tighter coagulation. With the increase in the volume fraction, the aggerates tend to be fractal agglomeration and the fractal dimension in the range of 1.614–2.060. When the volume fraction is high, the agglomeration from the collision develops fractal-like structures.

A summary of the fractal aggregate distribution range and fractal-like structures in the nanoscales is given, which could be applied to progress design for multi-collision nanoclusters. Finally, the detailed size distributions can be readily used with the dynamics of industrial progress design, air pollution, and meteorology.

Author Contributions: Conceptualization, M.Y.; methodology, M.Y.; software, X.W.; validation, X.W. and Y.L.; formal analysis, T.W.; investigation, M.Y.; resources, T.W.; data curation, X.W.; writing-original draft preparation, X.W.; writing-review and editing, Y.L.; visualization, X.W. All authors have read and agreed to the published version of the manuscript.

Funding: This research was funded by National Natural Science Foundation of China (11872353, 91852102).

Institutional Review Board Statement: Not applicable.

Informed Consent Statement: Not applicable.

Data Availability Statement: Raw data are available on request.

Acknowledgments: The authors thank the National Natural Science Foundation of China (11872353, 91852102) for their support.

Conflicts of Interest: The authors declare no conflict of interest.

References

1. Yu, M.; Lin, J. Nanoparticle-laden flows via moment method: A review. *Int. J. Multiph. Flow* **2010**, *36*, 144–151. [CrossRef]
2. Liu, S.; Lin, J.-Z. Numerical Simulation of Nanoparticle Coagulation in a Poiseuille Flow Via a Moment Method. *J. Hydrodyn.* **2008**, *20*, 1–9. [CrossRef]
3. Lin, J.-Z.; Yu, M.-Z.; Nie, D.-M. On the nanoparticulate flow. *J. Hydrodyn.* **2016**, *28*, 961–970. [CrossRef]
4. Pratsinis, S.E. Flame aerosol synthesis of ceramic powders. *Prog. Energy Combust. Sci.* **1998**, *24*, 197–219. [CrossRef]
5. Heine, M.C.; Pratsinis, S.E. High Concentration Agglomerate Dynamics at High Temperatures. *Langmuir* **2006**, *22*, 10238–10245. [CrossRef] [PubMed]
6. Trzeciak, T.M.; Podgórski, A.; Marijnissen, J.C. Brownian coagulation in dense systems: Thermal non-equilibrium effects. *J. Aerosol Sci.* **2014**, *69*, 1–12. [CrossRef]
7. Thajudeen, T.; Gopalakrishnan, R., Jr.; Christopher, J.H., Jr. The Collision Rate of Nonspherical Particles and Aggregates for all Diffusive Knudsen Numbers. *Aerosol Sci. Technol.* **2012**, *46*, 1174–1186. [CrossRef]
8. Blatz, P.J.; Tobolsky, A.V. Note on the Kinetics of Systems Manifesting Simultaneous Polymerization-Depolymerization Phenomena. *J. Phys. Chem.* **1945**, *49*, 77–80. [CrossRef]
9. Batchelor, G.K. The effect of Brownian motion on the bulk stress in a suspension of spherical particles. *J. Fluid Mech.* **1977**, *83*, 97–117. [CrossRef]
10. Heine, M.C.; Pratsinis, S.E. Brownian Coagulation at High Concentration. *Langmuir* **2007**, *23*, 9882–9890. [CrossRef] [PubMed]
11. Sheldon, K.F. Smoke, Dust, and Haze: Fundamentals of Aerosol Dynamics. *Physics Today* **1977**, *30*, 58–59.
12. Ketzel, M.; Berkowicz, R. Modelling the fate of ultrafine particles from exhaust pipe to rural background: An analysis of time scales for dilution, coagulation and deposition. *Atmos. Environ.* **2004**, *38*, 2639–2652. [CrossRef]
13. Ringl, C.; Urbassek, H.M. A LAMMPS implementation of granular mechanics: Inclusion of adhesive and microscopic friction forces. *Comput. Phys. Commun.* **2012**, *183*, 986–992. [CrossRef]
14. Buesser, B.; Heine, M.; Pratsinis, S. Coagulation of highly concentrated aerosols. *J. Aerosol Sci.* **2009**, *40*, 89–100. [CrossRef]
15. Sorensen, C.; Hageman, W.B.; Rush, T.J.; Huang, H.; Oh, C. Aerogelation in a Flame Soot Aerosol. *J. Aerosol Sci.* **1998**, *29*, S623–S624. [CrossRef]
16. Heine, M.C.; Pratsinis, S.E. Agglomerate TiO$_2$ Aerosol Dynamics at High Concentrations. *Part. Part. Syst. Charact.* **2007**, *24*, 56–65. [CrossRef]
17. Fry, D.; Sintes, T.; Chakrabarti, A.; Sorensen, C.M. Enhanced Kinetics and Free-Volume Universality in Dense Aggregating Systems. *Phys. Rev. Lett.* **2002**, *89*, 148301. [CrossRef]
18. Gimel, C.J.; Durand, D.; Nicola, T.I. Transition between flocculation and percolation of a diffusion-limited clus-ter-cluster aggregation process using three-dimensional Monte Carlo simulation. *Phys. Rev. B Condens. Matter* **1995**, *51*, 11348–11357. [CrossRef] [PubMed]
19. Arias-Zugasti, M. Adaptive orthogonal collocation for aerosol dynamics under coagulation. *J. Aerosol Sci.* **2012**, *50*, 57–74. [CrossRef]
20. Liu, S.; Chan, T.L.; Liu, H. Numerical simulation of particle formation and evolution in a vehicle exhaust plume using the bimodal Taylor expansion method of moments. *Particuology* **2019**, *43*, 46–55. [CrossRef]
21. Yu, M.; Lin, J.; Chan, T.L. A New Moment Method for Solving the Coagulation Equation for Particles in Brownian Motion. *Aerosol Sci. Technol.* **2008**, *42*, 705–713. [CrossRef]
22. Yu, M.; Lin, J. Solution of the agglomerate Brownian coagulation using Taylor-expansion moment method. *J. Colloid Interface Sci.* **2009**, *336*, 142–149. [CrossRef]
23. Yu, M.; Lin, J. Taylor-expansion moment method for agglomerate coagulation due to Brownian motion in the entire size regime. *J. Aerosol Sci.* **2009**, *40*, 549–562. [CrossRef]
24. Yu, M.; Liu, Y.; Lin, J.; Seipenbusch, M. Generalized TEMOM Scheme for Solving the Population Balance Equation. *Aerosol Sci. Technol.* **2015**, *49*, 1021–1036. [CrossRef]
25. Drew, M.G. The art of molecular dynamics simulation. *Comput. Biol. Chem.* **1996**, *20*, 489. [CrossRef]
26. Erban, R. From Molecular Dynamics to Brownian Dynamics. *Proc. Math. Phys. Eng. Sci.* **2014**, *470*, 20140036. [CrossRef]
27. Tahery, R.; Modarress, H. Lennard-Jones Energy Parameter for Pure Fluids from Scaled Particle Theory. *Iran. J. Chem. Chem. Eng. Int. Engl. Ed.* **2007**, *26*, 1–9.
28. Maitland, G.; Rigby, M.; Smith, E.; Wakeham, W.; Henderson, D. Intermolecular Forces: Their Origin and Determination. *Phys. Today* **1983**, *36*, 57–58. [CrossRef]
29. Wang, K.; Yu, S.; Peng, W. An analytical solution of the population balance equation for simultaneous Brownian and shear coagulation in the continuum regime. *Adv. Powder Technol.* **2020**, *31*, 2128–2135. [CrossRef]
30. Poulin, P.; Stark, H.; Lubensky, T.C.; Weitz, D.A. Novel Colloidal Interactions in Anisotropic Fluids. *Science* **1997**, *275*, 1770–1773. [CrossRef]
31. Brasil, A.M.; Farias, T.L.; Carvalho, M.D.G.; Koylu, U.O. Numerical characterization of the morphology of aggregated particles. *J. Aerosol Sci.* **2001**, *32*, 489–508. [CrossRef]
32. Schneider, T.; Stoll, E. Molecular-dynamics study of a three-dimensional one-component model for distortive phase transitions. *Phys. Rev. B* **1978**, *17*, 1302–1322. [CrossRef]
33. Xiong, C.; Friedlander, S.K. Morphological properties of atmospheric aerosol aggregates. *Proc. Natl. Acad. Sci. USA* **2001**, *98*, 11851–11856. [CrossRef]

34. Lindberg, C.S.; Manuputty, M.Y.; Yapp, E.K.; Akroyd, J.; Xu, R.; Kraft, M. A detailed particle model for polydisperse aggregate particles. *J. Comput. Phys.* **2019**, *397*, 108799. [CrossRef]

35. Vemury, S.; Pratsinis, S.E. Self-preserving size distributions of agglomerates. *J. Aerosol Sci.* **1995**, *26*, 175–185. [CrossRef]

36. Kelkar, A.V.; Dong, J.; Franses, E.I.; Corti, D.S. New models and predictions for Brownian coagulation of non-interacting spheres. *J. Colloid Interface Sci.* **2013**, *389*, 188–198. [CrossRef] [PubMed]

37. Lister, J.D.; Smit, D.J.; Hounslow, M. Adjustable discretized population balance for growth and aggregation. *AIChE J.* **1995**, *41*, 591–603. [CrossRef]

38. Stukowski, A. Visualization and analysis of atomistic simulation data with OVITO–the Open Visualization Tool. *Model. Simul. Mater. Sci. Eng.* **2010**, *18*, 2154–2162. [CrossRef]

39. Grass, R.N.; Tsantilis, S.; Pratsinis, S.E. Design of high-temperature, gas-phase synthesis of hard or soft TiO_2 agglomerates. *AIChE J.* **2006**, *52*, 1318–1325. [CrossRef]

40. Goudeli, E.; Eggersdorfer, M.L.; Pratsinis, S.E. Coagulation–Agglomeration of Fractal-like Particles: Structure and Self-Preserving Size Distribution. *Langmuir* **2015**, *31*, 1320–1327. [CrossRef]

41. Arakawa, S.; Tatsuuma, M.; Sakatani, N.; Nakamoto, T. Thermal conductivity and coordination number of compressed dust aggregates. *Icarus* **2019**, *324*, 8–14. [CrossRef]

42. Teichmann, J.; Van, D. Cluster models for random particle aggregates—Morphological statistics and collision distance. *Spat. Stat.* **2015**, *12*, 65–80. [CrossRef]

43. Koch, W. The effect of particle coalescence on the surface area of a coagulating aerosol. *J. Colloid Interface Sci.* **1990**, *20*, 891–894. [CrossRef]

44. Eggersdorfer, M.L.; Pratsinis, S.E. Agglomerates and aggregates of nanoparticles made in the gas phase. *Adv. Powder Technol.* **2014**, *25*, 71–90. [CrossRef]

applied sciences

MDPI

Article

Sedimentation of Two Side-by-Side Heavy Particles of Different Density in a Shear-Thinning Fluid with Viscoelastic Properties

Sensen Yang [1], Chengxu Tu [1,2,3,*], Minglu Dai [1], Xianfu Ge [4], Rongjun Xu [1], Xiaoyan Gao [1] and Fubing Bao [1,*]

[1] Zhejiang Provincial Key Laboratory of Flow Measurement Technology, China Jiliang University, Hangzhou 310018, China; s1902080446@cjlu.edu.cn (S.Y.); s20020804009@cjlu.edu.cn (M.D.); xurongjun628@163.com (R.X.); gaoxy_star@cjlu.edu.cn (X.G.)
[2] College of Control Science and Engineering, Zhejiang University, Hangzhou 310027, China
[3] LEO Group Co., Ltd., Wenling 317500, China
[4] Zhejiang Machinery & Electrical Group Co., Ltd., Hangzhou 310002, China; gexf@zj926.com
[*] Correspondence: tuchengxu@cjlu.edu.cn (C.T.); dingobao@cjlu.edu.cn (F.B.)

Abstract: Particle sedimentation has widely existed in nature and engineering fields, and most carrier fluids are non-Newtonian. Recently, the manipulation of a settling particle in liquid has been a topic of high interest to those involved in engineered processes such as composite materials, pharmaceutical manufacture, chemistry and the petroleum industry. Compared with Newtonian fluid, the viscosity of non-Newtonian fluid is closely related to the shear rate, leading to a single settling particle having different dynamic behaviors. In this article, the trajectories and velocities of two side-by-side particles of different densities (heavy and light) settling in a shear-thinning fluid with viscoelastic property were studied, as well as that for the corresponding single settling particle. Regardless of the difference in the particle density, the results show the two-way coupling interaction between the two side-by-side settling particles. As opposed to a single settling particle, the wake of the heavier particle can clearly attract or rebound the light particle due to the shear-thinning or viscoelastic property of the fluid. Regarding the trajectories of the light particle, three basic path types were found: (i) the light particle is first attracted and then repelled by the wake of the heavy one; (ii) the light particle approaches and then largely traces within the path of the heavy one in the limited field of view; (iii) the light particle is first slightly shifted away from its original position and then returns to this initial position. In addition to this, due to the existence of a corridor of reduced viscosity and negative wake generated by the viscoelastic property, the settling velocity of a light particle can exceed the terminal velocity of a single particle of the same density. On the other hand, the sedimentation of the light particle can induce the distinguishable transverse migration of the heavy one.

Keywords: particle sedimentation; two side-by-side particles; viscoelastic fluid; shear-thinning fluid

Citation: Yang, S.; Tu, C.; Dai, M.; Ge, X.; Xu, R.; Gao, X.; Bao, F. Sedimentation of Two Side-by-Side Heavy Particles of Different Density in a Shear-Thinning Fluid with Viscoelastic Properties. *Appl. Sci.* **2021**, *11*, 7113. https://doi.org/10.3390/app11157113

Academic Editor: Francesca Scargiali

Received: 1 July 2021
Accepted: 29 July 2021
Published: 31 July 2021

1. Introduction

Particle sedimentation can be found in a wide range of natural and industrial processes, such as river flows, blood flows, microfluidic chips and fluidization etc. [1–5]. The settling particle is strongly affected by the rheological properties of surrounding fluid as well as the physical properties of the particle. Knowledge on particle behaviors in Newtonian liquids is relatively extensive. Magnaudet [6] summarized the forces that act on spherical particles, which usually include steady drag, history force, added mass effects and lift force. In addition, it is possible to predict interactions between dispersed particles moving in Newtonian fluids [7]. Clift proposed that when the particle Reynolds number is large $(750 < Re < 2 \times 10^5)$, the viscous resistance of the particle is negligible compared with the inertial force [5]. Considering the relationship between the Reynolds number (Re) and the mass ratio (m^*), three typical sedimentation trajectories of a single particle settling in glycerin-water mixture were found: vertical, oblique and zigzag [8], where (m^*) is the relative density of the particle compared to the fluid, a map of regimes of the particle trajectories is presented for $Re = 100$–$12{,}000$ and $m^* = 0$–1.5. Five types of trajectories of a free-settling particle in Newtonian fluids have been found: steady and oblique, oblique and oscillating regime with low frequency, oblique and oscillation regime with high frequency, zigzagging periodic regime and three-dimensional chaotic regime [9]. The settling velocities of dual particles would be larger than a single particle at small Reynolds numbers [10]. It has been widely confirmed that the drag coefficient of a particle settling in Newtonian fluids only depends on Re. In the case of two particles, based on a numerical study using the three-dimensional lattice Boltzmann method, Nie and Lin [11] identified six sedimentation patterns for two side-by-side particles of different densities settling in a Newtonian fluid. They also simulated two particles of different densities released in tandem [12]. As for the theoretical analysis, the asymptotic forms of the far-field and near-field for the particle velocities were given by Wacholder and Sather [13]. In this work, the two particles were unequal in size and density, and both the inertia of the particles and the fluid can be neglected, as opposed to with the viscous forces.

Since many processes involving particle settling occur in non-Newtonian fluids [14,15], such as hydraulic fracture for oil exploration [16], sedimentation velocity analytical ultra-centrifugation in biopharmaceuticals [17], the behavior of particles in the human respiratory tract [18] and the transport of the particles in microfluidic chips [19], understanding particle settling behavior in non-Newtonian fluids is of significant importance to the above applications. However, this is much more complex for particles moving in non-Newtonian fluids. Specifically, the viscosity of the fluid around the particle changes with the variation of the distribution of shear stress caused by the settling particle, which finally results in a change in the drag coefficient [7]. Thus, the conclusions drawn from the investigation of Newtonian fluid are not appropriate for non-Newtonian fluids. Various experimental and numerical studies have been carried out on the sedimentation of particles in different non-Newtonian fluids, such as power-law fluids [20], Carreau fluids [21], and Boger fluids [22,23]. Particles can behave in completely different ways in non-Newtonian fluids due to the coupling effects of viscoelasticity and shear-dependent viscosity. For example, obvious negative wakes would occur when particle settling in different viscoelastic fluids. The increase in the elasticity would cause the negative wakes to move closer to the particle [24]. The pioneering studies on the two particles settling in viscoelastic fluids were performed by Riddle et al. [25], Joseph et al. [26], and Bot et al. [27]. A critical distance which distinguishes between the attraction and repulsion of a pair of particles settling in water-glycerin mixture of polyacrylamide was revealed by Riddle et al. [25]. A particular range of the initial particle–particle distance, within which inter-particle attraction of two side-by-side settling particles was observed, was given by Joseph et al. [26]. They considered the first normal stress difference to be the explanation for particle–particle attraction. As particles settled in a shear-thinning fluid with a thixotropic and viscoelastic effect, three types of particle interaction, strong particle–particle attraction, weak particle–particle attraction and repulsion were observed [28]. For two identical particles released in tandem in viscoelastic fluid, two settling modes were observed numerically: (i) a dipole would emerged as the trailing particle approaching the leading one; (ii) a stable terminal distance between the particles was established [29]. The two settling modes have also been recently confirmed by the experimental results reported by Freire et al. [30], in which shear thinning fluid with a viscoelastic effect was adopted, and which modes occurred depended on the initial distance and the fluid viscosity.

In this paper, the sedimentation of a single particle in a shear-thinning viscoelastic fluid was first examined for comparison. Then, we investigated the settling behavior of two side-by-side particles with different densities and focused on the effect of the initial particle–particle distance and the density difference on their interaction.

2. Experimental Method

The experimental setup was mainly composed of a transparent tank, a particle releasing system and a shadowgraph setup, as shown in Figure 1. The tank is an open acrylic container with a height of 1000 mm with a squared cross-section with a 500-mm width, and is filled with polyacrylamide solution. The two side-by-side particles arranged horizontally can be released simultaneously with a specified distance as required by the particle releasing system, which uses an ejector to generate the vacuum pressure in the two particle pipettes. We used two high-speed cameras (FASTCAM Mini UX, Photron, Yonezawa, Japan), two LED arrays and a computer linked to the cameras to facilitate high-speed shadowgraph binocular-imaging. Thus, the particle trajectories can be tracked on both x-z and y-z planes through this binocular imaging system. Meanwhile, we used the particle image velocimetry (PIV) system to investigate the flow field in the wake of the particle (Figure 2). The PIV system includes a high-speed camera (FASTCAM Mini UX, Photron, Yonezawa, Japan), a continuum laser (SN: CL007, Beijing SMHY Technology Co. Ltd., Beijing, China), a computer linked to the camera and the fluorescent tracer particles (W-TG1, Beijing HSKT Technology Co. Ltd., Beijing, China). Three types of spherical particles (with less than a 0.25 μm diameter variation and spherical error and 0.02 μm of the surface roughness) were used in our experiments (Table 1), and 0.5 wt% polyacrylamide (PAAm, supplied by Shanghai Macklin Biochemical Co., Shanghai, China) solution was used. The density of PAAm solution is 1005 kg/m^3, which is very close to that of water. The rheological properties of the PAAm solution were examined at 20 °C by a rheometer (MCR 702 Multidrive, Anton Paar Co., Graz, Austria). Figure 3 show the rheological curves of the shear stress τ to the shear rate γ with steady state in the PAAm solution and pure water, where the slope of the curves represents the fluid viscosity η. Figure 4 shows the rheological curves of the fluid viscosity η to the shear rate γ in the PAAm solution and pure water. It can be seen that the shear stress τ and shear rate γ of pure water have a linear relationship, while PAAm solution exhibits a very high viscosity value at a low shear rate γ. With the increase of the shear rate γ, the viscosity of PAAm solution decreases and becomes stable. This indicates that the PAAm solution has a strong shear thinning property [31].

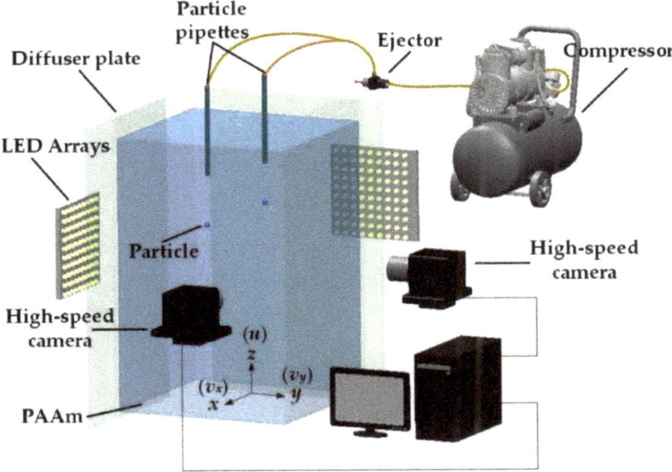

Figure 1. Schematic of the experimental setup for two side-by-side particles settling.

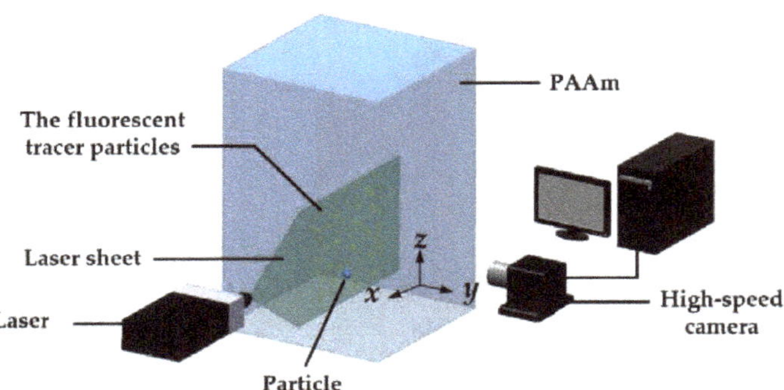

Figure 2. Schematic of the PIV system for investigating the flow field of the wake behind the particle.

Table 1. Properties of spherical particles.

Material	Density (kg/m^3)	Diameter (mm)
Silicon nitride ceramics (Si$_3$N$_4$)	3200	9.525
Zirconia ceramics (ZrO$_2$)	6000	9.525
Stainless steel	7930	9.525

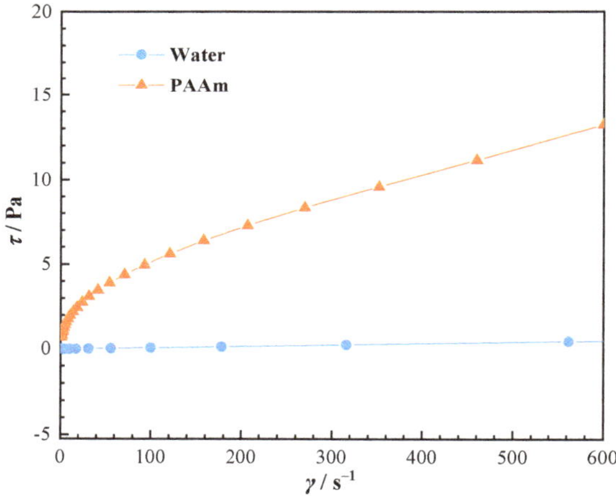

Figure 3. Rheogram of 0.5 wt% PAAm solution.

In order to verify whether the PAAm solution has viscoelasticity, the frequency sweep response was performed through the MCR rheometer at a shear strain = 1%. The data (Figure 5) indicate that the storage modulus G′ and loss modulus G″ increased with the increasing frequency, which indicates the yield behavior of the test solution. This demonstrates that the PAAm solution in this study is a viscoelastic fluid by Liu et al. [32]. Apart from this, the negative wake (the instantaneous profile) was confirmed by our results using PIV (Figure 6). In the previous work, the negative wake was considered a large strain phenomenon associated with viscoelasticity [33,34] and the reason for this formation was proven to derive from the shear and extensional motion of the particle wake in the viscoelastic fluid. Under the complex shear and extensional motion, the viscoelastic fluid exhibits rapid elastic recoil, similar to an elastic thread, which seems to be the cause of the negative wake [33,34]. Thus, it can be concluded that the PAAm solution in this study is a viscoelastic fluid.

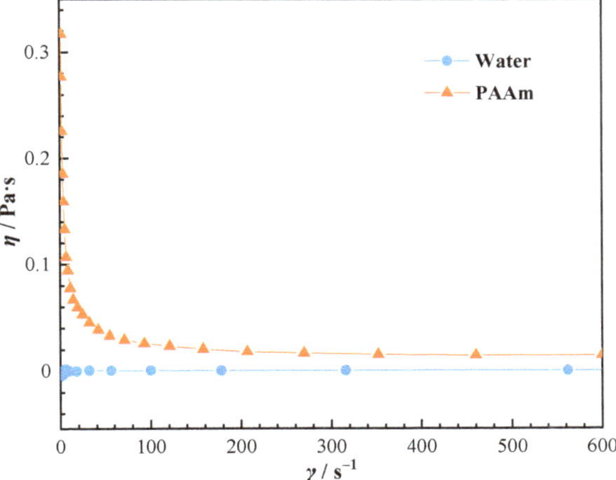

Figure 4. Dynamic viscosity for the 0.5 wt% PAAm solution as a function of the shear rate.

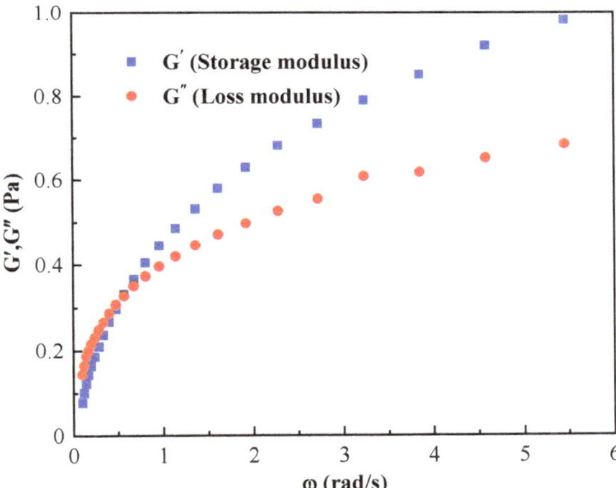

Figure 5. Viscoelastic modulus of PAAm solution as a function of frequency.

For comparison, the settling behavior of a single particle and two particles were both detected using the binocular imaging system at a frame rate of 1000 fps. In order to prevent the gas film or bubbles from adhering on the particle surface during particle sedimentation, the particles were immersed in PAAm solution preliminarily several times.

In our experiments, both the initial particle–particle distance and the density difference between the two particles were varied, but the particle size remained similar. The dimensionless distance, L^*, was adopted to describe the initial horizontal distance between the two particles (Figure 7), given as

$$L^* = L/d \tag{1}$$

where L is the initial center distance between the two particles, and d is the particle diameter ($d = 9.525$ mm).

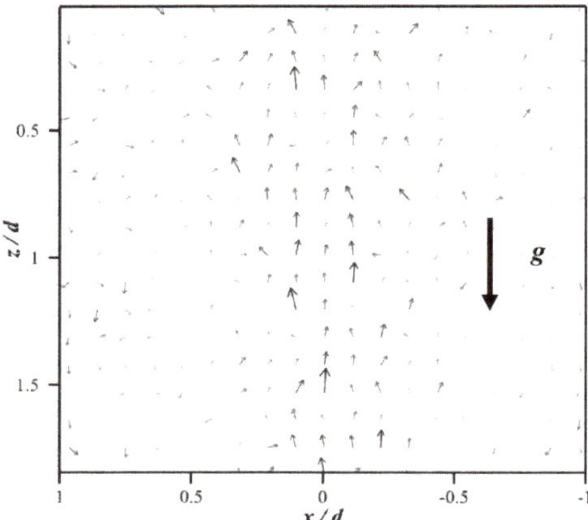

Figure 6. The negative wake at 7*d* downstream from the particle center.

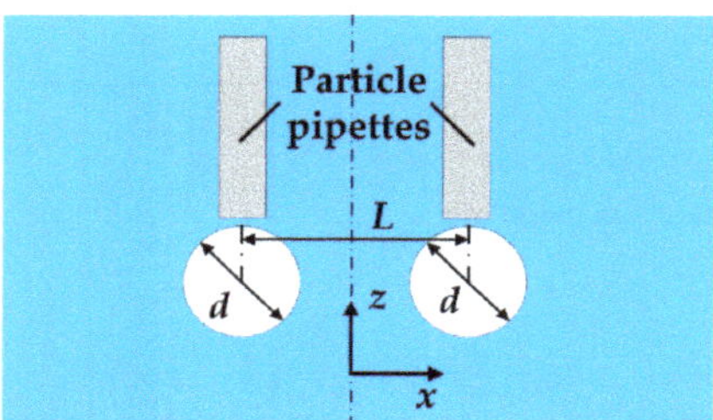

Figure 7. Schematic of the sedimentation of two side-by-side particles.

Additionally, parameter α is introduced to denote the density difference between the two particles and is given by [35]

$$\alpha = \frac{\rho_{pH} - \rho_{pL}}{\rho_l} \tag{2}$$

where ρ_{pL}, ρ_{pH} are the densities of light particle and heavy particle, respectively; ρ_l is the density of fluid. The different α values used in our experiments are listed, i.e., $\alpha = 1.92$ (ZrO_2 and Stainless steel), 2.79 (Si_3N_4 and ZrO_2) and 4.71 (Si_3N_4 and Stainless steel).

In our experiments, there were several sources of experimental error of the spherical particles such as the diameter variation, spherical error and the surface roughness. Three types of spherical particles with a diameter variation less than 0.25 μm and spherical error and a surface roughness 0.02 μm were used in our experiments. Compared with the *d* (9.525 mm), the errors of the spherical particles can be ignored.

Meanwhile, in order to improve the sensitivity and synchronization of the control particles in the experiment, we designed a new synchronous particle release device, which uses the vacuum suction principle of the ejector (Figure 1). This device can precisely control the release timing and spatial location of the particles and ensure the simultaneous release and of the two side-by-side particles at the same horizontal level. The particles settling experiments under each condition are performed at least 4~10 times to ensure the recurrence. The particle settling path in the PAAm solution was remarkably stable and the experimental results have good repeatability. After each set of test experiment, an interval period of 1 h was required to restore fluid stability.

3. Results and Discussion

3.1. Force Analysis

The forces acting on the moving particles in a quiescent fluid have been widely studied [5,7,36]. When the moving particles reach the terminal velocity, the particles are in a force equilibrium. During sedimentation, the particles are mainly subject to gravity G, and buoyancy F_B, and the total drag force F_D (Figure 8).

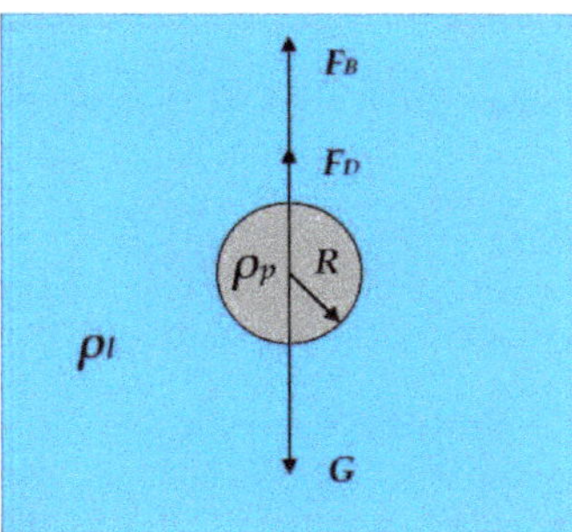

Figure 8. Schematic of the forces acting on the particle.

The forces acting on the particle in Figure 8 can be expressed as

$$G = F_B + F_D \tag{3}$$

The gravity on the particles can be expressed as

$$G = mg = \frac{1}{6}\pi d^3 \rho_p g \tag{4}$$

And the buoyancy of the particles during settling:

$$F_B = V\rho_l g = \frac{1}{6}\pi d^3 \rho_l g \tag{5}$$

where d is the particle diameter, ρ_p is the particle density, and ρ_l is the fluid density.

In non-Newtonian fluids, the power law model, which has been used widely in previous work to describe the fluids' rheology, has the following form [37]:

$$\tau = k\gamma^n \tag{6}$$

where k is the consistency index and n is the power law index.

Meanwhile, n and k are the power law constants in a power law fluid. For a Rheogram of 0.5 wt% PAAm solution (Figure 3), we can determine that the value of n is 0.484 and the value of k is 0.572 (Goodness of fit = 0.997) by the curve fitting equation (Equation (6)).

A modified particle Reynolds number was defined for the settling particle in the shear thinning fluid [38]:

$$Re^* = \frac{d^n u_p{}^{2-n} \rho_l}{k} \tag{7}$$

where u_p is the sedimentation velocity of particles.

The total drag force of the particle settling in a power law fluid was given by [39]

$$F_D = 3\pi k d^2 \left(\frac{u_p}{d}\right)^n f(n) \tag{8}$$

where $f(n)$ is a function of the power law constant.

From the above equation, we can obtain the following:

$$f(n) = \frac{d^{n+1}g(\rho_p - \rho_l)}{18ku_p{}^n} \tag{9}$$

In our experiments, the terminal velocities of single particle settling in the PAAm solution are 1.44 m/s (for stainless steel), 1.24 m/s (for ZrO_2), and 0.77 m/s (for Si_3N_4), respectively.

Therefore, the values of $f(n)$ are 5.539 (for stainless steel), 4.295 (for ZrO_2), and 2.377 (for Si_3N_4), respectively.

Apart from this, the values of Re^* are 321 (for stainless steel), 256 (for ZrO_2), and 124 (for Si_3N_4), respectively.

3.2. Sedimentation of a Single Particle

In this section, the behavior of a single settling solid spherical particle in the PAAm solution is presented, which was used to compare with that of two side-by-side particles in Section 3.3.

In the previous work, we obtained the settling velocity of the corresponding particles in water [40]. The results show that the sedimentation velocity in the initial acceleration stage is basically proportional to the time for $t < 0.2$ s, regardless of the particle density. After this linear acceleration stage, all the particles in water achieved their terminal velocities at $t \approx 0.4$ s.

Figure 9 shows the settling behaviors of a single particle in the PAAm solution with different particle densities. It is clear that for all cases the particle motion in both x-z and y-z planes is almost straight and the transverse motion can be neglected. In other words, the particle settling path can be regarded as a vertical line in the PAAm solution. This phenomenon can be caused by the viscoelastic property of PAAm solution, the fluidization boundary between the settling particles and the viscoelastic fluid acts as a cylinder wall [24,28]. Therefore, the friction generated by the fluidization boundary position in relation to the settling particle surface results in a sharp decline in the transverse velocity of the particle settling [41]. Thus, the transverse migration for a single particle can be neglected and the settling path can be regarded as a vertical line. In contrast, particles settling in water usually exhibit a three-dimensional unstable path [36,40] due to the unsteady trajectory and the wake turning to three-dimensional and unsteady behind the settling particle.

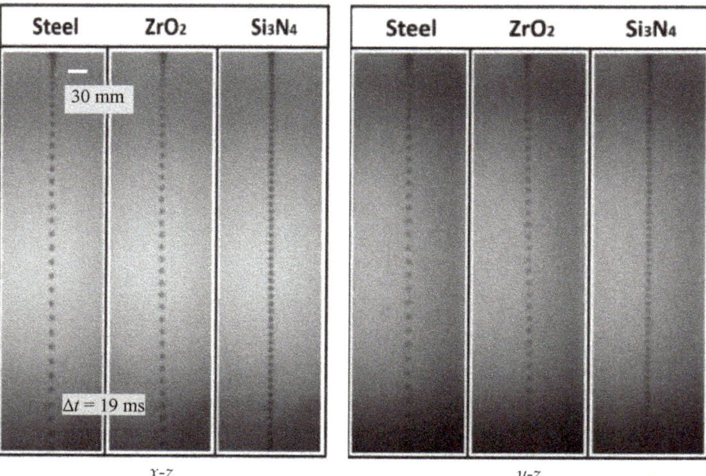

Figure 9. Settling behaviors of single particle. The time interval between adjacent particles is 19 ms.

In addition, Figure 10 shows the variation of the particle velocity and the normalized trajectory in PAAm solution for different particles. The migration velocity is decomposed into the transverse velocities v_x in x-z plane, v_y in y-z plane and the vertical velocity u. The transverse migration is normalized by the particle diameter and denoted as s^*, which is also plotted as a function of time in Figure 10. The very small s^* quantitatively reflects that there is no obvious transverse motion of the settling particles. This can also be confirmed from the near-zero transverse velocities during the whole testing process.

In our experiments, before reaching the terminal velocity, the particle would experience a short acceleration leading to an increase in the vertical velocity, while this acceleration hardly changes the transverse velocity in the viscoelastic fluid.

In PAAm solution, although the difference in particle density leads to a difference in the terminal settling velocity, the particles almost achieved their terminal velocities at $t \approx 0.4$ s. As shown in the Figure 11, the terminal settling velocity of the particle (Si_3N_4) in PAAm solution is lower than that in water. Apart from this, the terminal velocities of other particles (stainless steel and ZrO_2) are higher than that in water, and the deviation of terminal velocity from that of the particle settling in water increases with the particle density. Based on this, we speculate that there is a critical value of Re^*, i.e., another particle with a different density, and its terminal settling velocity in the PAAm solution is consistent with that in water. The reason why the terminal settling velocity of the particle (Si_3N_4) in the PAAm solution is lower in water but not the other two particles is the relatively weak shear thinning effect. The modified particle Reynolds number (321 (for stainless steel), 256 (for ZrO_2), and 124 (for Si_3N_4)) was mentioned for the settling particle in the PAAm solution. Moreover, it has been confirmed that the terminal settling velocity increases with the increasing Re^* in the shear thinning fluids in the previous work [36], which can also be observed in Figure 11. We can find that the Re^* (Si_3N_4) is smaller than that in the other two particles, which indicates that the viscous resistance occupies a more dominant role than the initial resistance in the particle (Si_3N_4) sedimentation [36]. Thus, the terminal settling velocity of the particle (Si_3N_4) in the PAAm solution is slower and the shear thinning effect is relatively weak. As shown in the Figure 11, the error bar of the u in the PAAm solution represents the standard error of a set of the parallel experiments. Notably, the u of Si_3N_4 particle settling in water fluctuates at $t = 0.2$ s, which is probably caused by the unsteady trajectory and the wake becoming three-dimensional and unsteady behind the settling particle [5,7], but this phenomenon disappeared due to the obvious viscoelastic property of the PAAm solution.

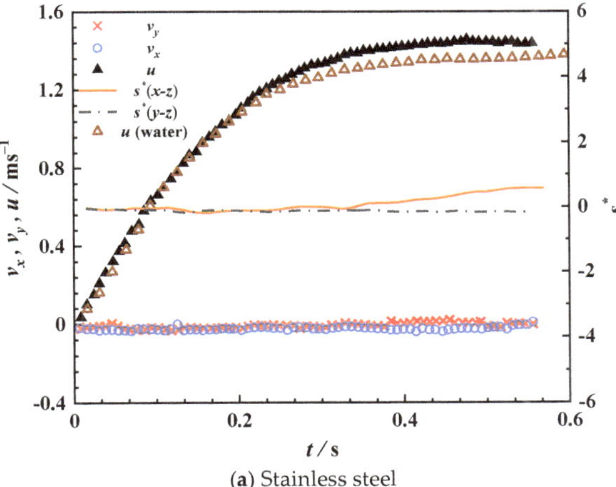

(a) Stainless steel

Figure 10. *Cont.*

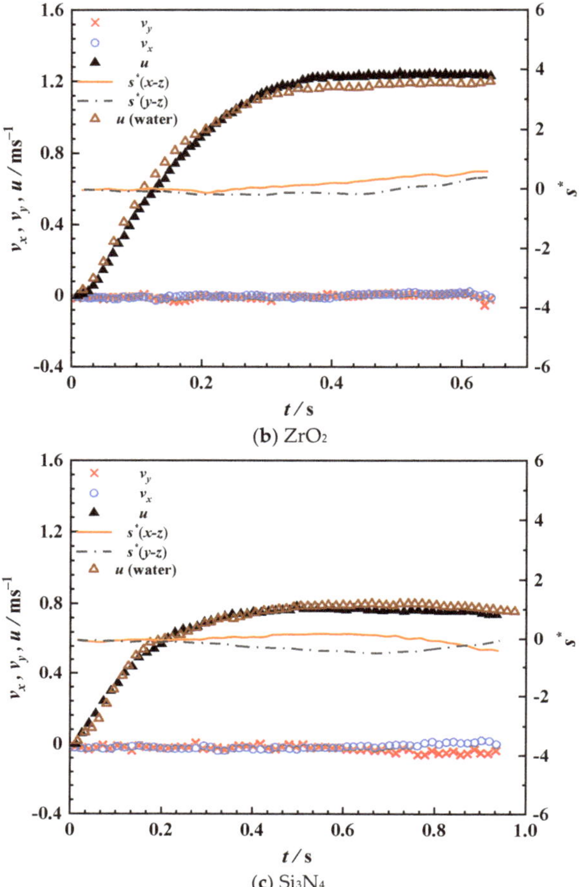

(**b**) ZrO₂

(**c**) Si₃N₄

Figure 10. Variations in the trajectories and velocity of a single particle settling in PAAm solution. v_x is the transverse velocity in x-z plane, v_y is the transverse velocity in y-z plane, u is the vertical velocity.

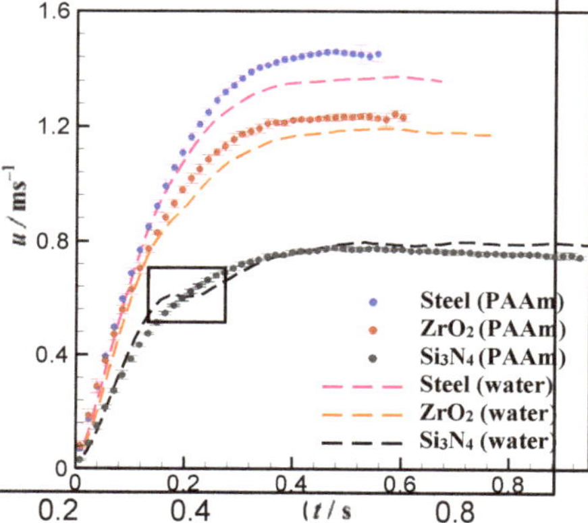

Figure 11. Variation in vertical velocity u of a single particle with different densities in PAAm solution and water.

3.3. Trajectory of Side-by-Side Particles of Different Densities

As discussed above, the path of a single particle settling in PAAm solution can be approximately regarded as a vertical line. In comparison, for the sedimentation of two similar side-by-side particles, a particle–particle interaction would occur and cause the particles to deviate from the vertical path at small L^* [7]. This interaction and deviation from the case of a single particle can be enhanced by the identical particle terminal velocity, which results in a highly similar elevation of the two particles. Therefore, within the critical distance L^*, the drafting-kissing-tumbling phenomenon (DKT) had been widely observed for this initial particle configuration [7,28].

In our study, we found that the difference of particles' density leads to great difference in settling velocity (Figure 12), and then the vertical distance between the particles is enlarged with time. Nevertheless, the wake of the heavy particle, in a leading position, can still affect the light particle settling into a non-linear path. The particle–particle interaction can also cause the transverse migration of the heavy particle, and the smaller the α, the greater the transverse migration. Notably, at the low value of α, the path of the heavy particle settling can be approximately regarded as a vertical line at $L^* < 3$. The clear transverse migration of the heavy particle occurred at $3 < L^* < 6.1$ and disappeared at $L^* > 7.1$.

Compared to the trajectory of heavy particles, the particle–particle interaction has a stronger impact on the light particle. There are three basic types of trajectories of light particles in the x-z plane as the light particle traces the heavy one:

Type (i) in the horizontal direction (x), the light particle first is strongly attracted and then is repelled by the rectilinear path of the heavy one (for $L^* = 1.2$ and $\alpha = 1.92, 2.79$ and 4.71).

Type (ii) the light particle approaches the heavy one in the x direction, and then travel a certain distance within the path of the heavy one (for $L^* = 2.0$ and $\alpha = 1.92$ and 2.79) without bouncing from the wake of the heavy particle in the limited field of view of the camera.

Type (iii) the light particle is slightly away from the path of the heavy one at first in the horizontal direction, and then the light particle moves back to its original position in the x direction (for $L^* = 3$ and $\alpha = 1.92, 2.79$ and 4.71)

Figure 13 shows three basic types of settling trajectories of the side-by-side particles. The line connecting the particles illustrates the instantaneous position of this pair of particles at a certain moment.

In the cases of type (i), two particles settle vertically at first, and the heavy particle travels faster due to its larger density, causing the appearance of a corridor with reduced viscosity (CRV) due to the shear-thinning property of the fluid. Then, the light particle deviated from its initial position and was attracted by this corridor in the x direction. This phenomenon is similar to the drafting stage of the DKT pattern in the settling of two particle with different densities in a Newtonian fluid [11] and the attracting behavior reported in two particles settling in viscoelastic fluids [7,20,28]. In Newtonian fluids, the approach of two particle is mostly due to the lower pressure caused by the wake of the leading particle [42]. While in viscoelastic fluids (such as PAAm solution), a widely accepted explanation for particle–particle attraction is that the first normal stress difference of the viscoelastic fluid modifies the pressure distribution on the particle surface [7]. Hence in the current experiments, the viscoelasticity of the PAAm solution could have caused the light particle to approach the heavy one in the x direction. Further, the light particle would be sucked into the corridor with a reduced viscosity behind the heavy particle. The particle–particle collision that has been reported in the settling of two identical particles in shear thinning liquids [20,28] was not observed in our experiments as a result of the different sedimentation velocities caused by the different densities. The heavier particle's settling velocity is larger than the lighter one; thus the lighter particle is only attracted to the CRV. Interestingly, after a certain distance following the heavy particle's wake, the light particle would rebound from the CRV and the horizontal distance between the particles increases gradually. Since the PAAm solution is a shearing thinning viscoelastic fluid, the fluid will deform under stress due to the particle motion and partial recovery to the undeformed state once the stress disappears [7]. Inspired by this, the negative wake behind the settling particles was successfully captured in our experiments, as shown in Figure 6. The negative wake probably induced the downstream fluid and the particle to move upwards. Therefore, the combined effect of the shear-thinning property of the PAAm solution and the negative wake could be responsible for the type (i) path of the light particle.

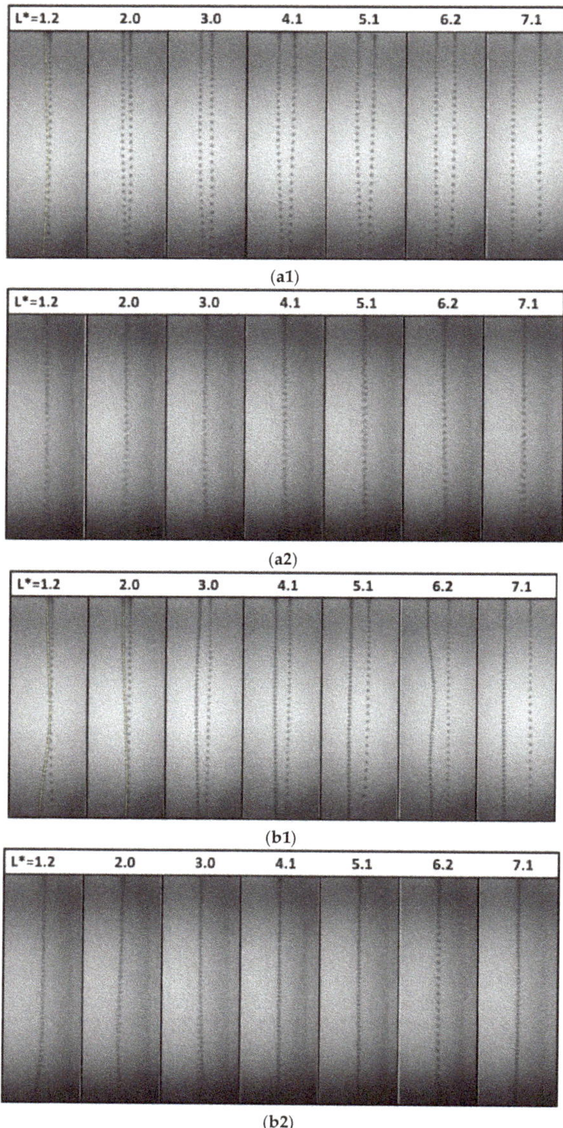

Figure 12. *Cont.*

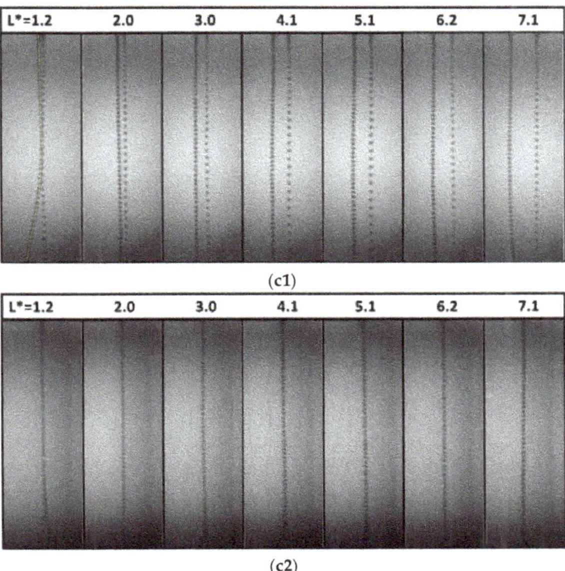

Figure 12. The settling process of two side-by-side particles at different initial separation distance under binocular vision; (**a1**) *x-z* plane, Left particle: ZrO_2, right particle: Stainless steel; (**a2**) *y-z* plane, Particle: ZrO_2, Stainless steel; (**b1**) *x-z* plane; Left particle: Si_3N_4; right particle: ZrO_2; (**b2**) *y-z* plane, Particle: Si_3N_4, ZrO_2; (**c1**) *x-z* plane; Left particle: Si_3N_4; right particle: Stainless steel; (**c2**) *y-z* plane, Particle: Si_3N_4, Stainless steel.

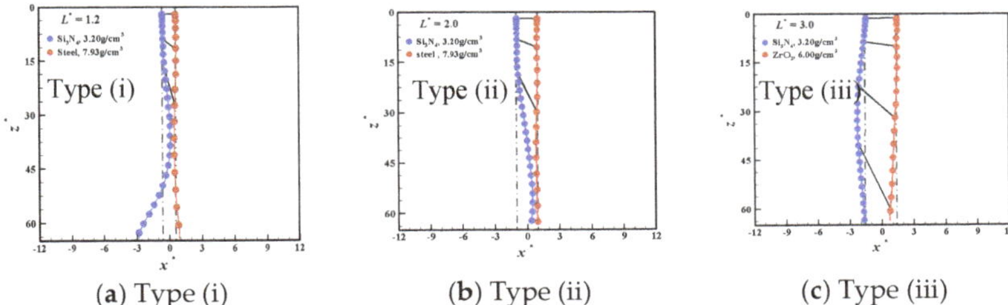

(**a**) Type (i)   (**b**) Type (ii)   (**c**) Type (iii)

Figure 13. Typical settling trajectories of two particle settling side by side, with an example for each type.

In the cases of type (ii), after a time period of vertical settling of the two particles, the light particle was attracted by CRV, which is similar to the early attractive stage of type (i). The trajectories of the two particles obtained from type (ii) also exhibit a similarity to the work in which the particles tended to attract [28]. In this previous study [28], two identical stainless steel particles were released side by side; however, the two particles gradually converge until they touch each other, and then settle (one up and one down) at the same velocity. In our experiments, the density difference always causes the heavy particle to settle ahead of the light one without collision when the two particles were released side by side. Although obvious tendency of the light particle to approach the heavy one can be seen in the test section, the rebounding stage in the type (i) is not observed in type (ii), which is probably caused by our limited field of the view of the camera.

In the cases of type (iii), the light particle first slightly shifted away from its original position in the horizontal direction, and then returned to this initial position. A similar repulsive effect had been reported in the settling of two side-by-side particles of identical densities when the initial separation distance was larger than a critical value [26,28].

According to a previous deduction [28], the particle–particle repulsion can be attributed to the fluid inertia. This is a different phenomenon from the settling behaviors of two identical particles in different non-Newtonian fluids [20]. As explained above, the particle–particle attraction is mainly caused by the effects of the shear-thinning viscoelasticity properties of the fluid, hence, the first normal stress difference of the PAAm solution and the lower pressure of the CRV can drive the light particle back to its original lateral-position. It is worth mentioning that the particle–particle interaction decreased with increasing α or L^*, as shown in Figure 12. Particularly, when $\alpha = 4.71$ and $L^* = 7.1$, the light particle hardly affects the heavy particle, which falls as a single particle, but the disturbance of the heavy particle is still present.

3.4. Settling Velocity

Corresponding to the three types of settling paths in Figure 13, the snapshot of the settling velocities of a single particle and two side-by-side particles are shown in Figure 14. For path type (i), after the discharge of the particles, the settling velocities u increased and the transverse velocities v_x in x-z plane remain around 0 m/s. As the light particle was dragged toward the CRV, at around 0.2 s, the v_x of light particle (v_{xL}) started to increase and reached a maximal positive transverse-velocity of 0.031 m/s at $t = 0.422$ s. Meanwhile, the u of light particle (u_L) became higher than the terminal velocity of a single particle (0.77 m/s for Si_3N_4), and continued to increase to the maximum value 0.866 m/s at $t = 0.641$ s. Then, the light particle rebounding from the CRV resulted in an obvious increase in the negative traverse velocity, while u_L would fall back.

The variation of the particles settling velocities can be explained by the energy transfer. The sedimentation of a particle in a stagnant fluid can be regard as the transport between potential energy and kinetic energy accompanied by energy dissipation. For two particles settling side by side in PAAm solution, the energy dissipation due to the viscosity decreases when the light particle settles into the CRV, and more potential energy is transferred into the kinetic energy of the light particle and the fluid around it. Thus, the settling velocity of a light particle during above process will be larger than the terminal settling velocity when it settles as an isolated particle in the same fluid, as discussed above. Then the kinetic energy is transformed from the vertical direction into the horizontal direction once the lateral migration occurs, which is possibly due to the shear-thinning property of PAAm solution or the appearance of negative wake (Figure 6).

In the cases of type (ii), the u_L can always exceed the terminal settling velocity for a single settling particle of the same density. This is possibly due to the combined effect of the lower amount of energy dissipated and the dragging of the fluid in the CRV. Moreover, as shown in Figure 14b, for mediate L^*, the particle–particle interaction tends to cause a slight fluctuation in the v_{xL}, which corresponds to the lateral migration of the light particle in path type (ii). With the separation distance increasing, the effects caused by the shear-thinning property of PAAm solution and the negative wake act on the light particle became continuously weaker.

As for path type (iii), no significant difference in the settling velocities between the single particle and the two side-by-side particles shown in Figure 14c was found.

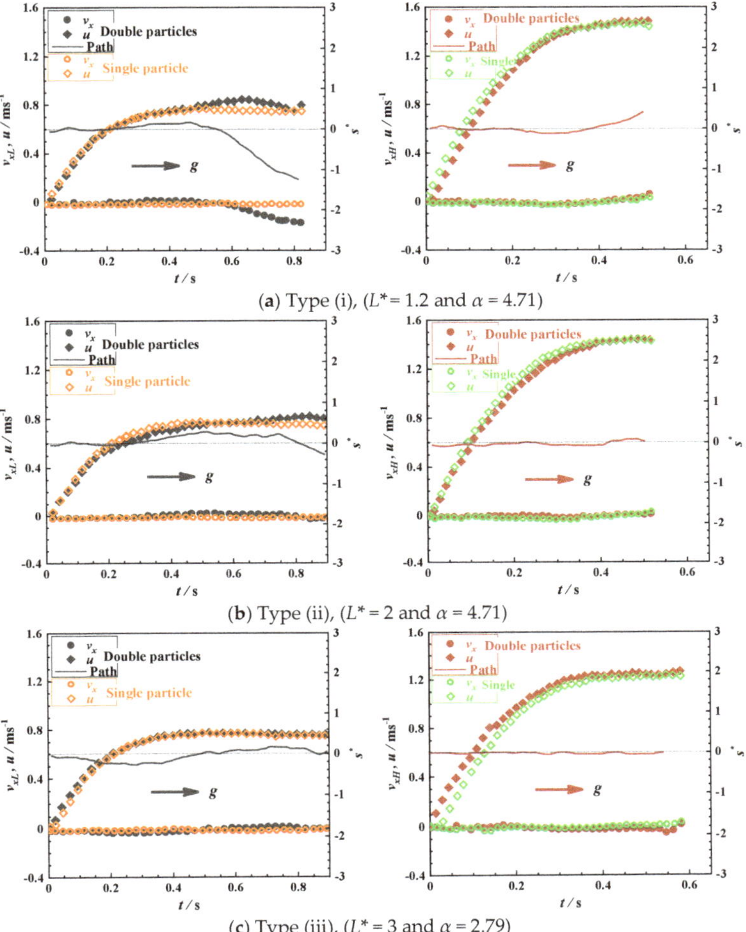

(a) Type (i), ($L^* = 1.2$ and $\alpha = 4.71$)

(b) Type (ii), ($L^* = 2$ and $\alpha = 4.71$)

(c) Type (iii), ($L^* = 3$ and $\alpha = 2.79$)

Figure 14. The velocities and the trajectories of the two side-by-side settling particles at different separation distance L^*; Left: the light particle; Right: the heavy particle.

4. Conclusions

In this work, we studied the trajectories and velocities of two side-by-side particles of different density settling in a non-Newtonian fluid with shear thinning viscoelastic properties, as well as that for the corresponding single settling particle.

In contrast to from the three-dimensional unstable path of a single particle settling in water, the particle settling path can be regarded as a vertical line in the PAAm solution. The terminal settling velocity of the particle (Si_3N_4) in PAAm solution is lower than that in water. Apart from this, the terminal velocities of other particles (stainless steel and ZrO_2) are higher than that in water, and the deviation of terminal velocity from that of the particle settling in water increases with the particle density. The reason may be that there is a critical value of Re^*, i.e., another particle with a different density, and its terminal settling velocity in the PAAm solution is consistent with that in water.

In addition to this, an experimental study on the effect of the initial separation distance on settling side-by-side particles motion at different density ratios was conducted in PAAm solution. The results show that the wake of the heavy particle, in a leading position, can affect the light particle settling into a non-linear path. For the heavy particle, the particle–particle interaction can also cause the transverse migration of the heavy one, and the smaller the density ratio, the greater the transverse migration. For the light particle, three basic path types were found: (i) the light particle is first attracted and then repelled by the wake of the heavy one; (ii) the light particle approaches and then largely traces within the path of the heavy one in the limited field of view; (iii) the light particle is first slightly shifted away from its original position and then returns to this initial position. In these, the light particle can be attracted or rebounded by the CRV behind the heavy particle. Meanwhile, we conclude that the u of light particle became higher than the terminal velocity of a single particle, due to the existence of a corridor with a reduced viscosity and the negative wake generated by the viscoelastic property. As explained above, particle–particle attraction is mainly caused by the effects of the shear-thinning viscoelasticity properties of the PAAm solution. As discussed throughout this study, the trajectory and velocity of particle sedimentation in PAAm solution are affected by the density difference and initial spacing of the two particles and fluid properties. These findings will make contributions to the future studies and applications in this area.

Author Contributions: Conceptualization, C.T., F.B.; methodology, S.Y., M.D., R.X. and C.T.; formal analysis, X.G. (Xiaoyan Gao) and S.Y.; investigation, S.Y., M.D. and X.G. (Xianfu Ge), and R.X.; writing—original draft preparation, S.Y., C.T., X.G. (Xiaoyan Gao), and M.D.; and writing—review and editing, C.T., and F.B.; All authors have read and agreed to the published version of the manuscript.

Funding: This research received no external funding.

Acknowledgments: This work was supported by the National Natural Science Foundation of China (Grants No. 11632016, No. 11972336, No. 11872217, and No. 11972334).

References

1. Haddadi, H.; Naghsh-Nilchi, H.; Di Carlo, D. Separation of cancer cells using vortical microfluidic flows. *Biomicrofluidics* **2018**, *12*, 014112. [CrossRef] [PubMed]
2. Whitesides, G.M. The origins and the future of microfluidics. *Nature* **2006**, *442*, 368–373. [CrossRef]
3. Xuan, X.; Zhu, J.; Church, C. Particle focusing in microfluidic devices. *Microfluid. Nanofluidics* **2010**, *9*, 1–16. [CrossRef]
4. Fernando, H.; Lee, S.; Anderson, J.; Princevac, M.; Pardyjak, E.; Grossman-Clarke, S. Urban fluid mechanics: Air circulation and contaminant dispersion in cities. *Environ. Fluid Mech.* **2001**, *1*, 107–164. [CrossRef]
5. Clift, R.; Grace, J.R.; Weber, M.E. *Bubbles, Drops, and Particles*; Dover Publications, Inc.: Mineola, NY, USA, 2005.
6. Magnaudet, J.J. The forces acting on bubbles and rigid particles. In Proceedings of the ASME Fluids Engineering Division Summer Meeting, FEDSM, Vancouver, BC, Canada, 22–26 June 1997; pp. 22–26.
7. Zenit, R.; Feng, J. Hydrodynamic interactions among bubbles, drops, and particles in non-Newtonian liquids. *Annu. Rev. Fluid* **2018**, *50*, 505–534. [CrossRef]
8. Horowitz, M.; Williamson, C. The effect of Reynolds number on the dynamics and wakes of freely rising and falling spheres. *J. Fluid Mech.* **2010**, *651*, 251. [CrossRef]
9. Jenny, M.; Dusek, J.; Bouchet, G. Instabilities and transition of a sphere falling or ascending freely in a Newtonian fluid. *J. Fluid Mech.* **2004**, *508*, 201. [CrossRef]
10. Wu, J.; Manasseh, R. Dynamics of dual-particles settling under gravity. *Int. J. Multiph. Flow* **1998**, *24*, 1343–1358. [CrossRef]
11. Nie, D.; Lin, J. Simulation of sedimentation of two spheres with different densities in a square tube. *J. Fluid Mech.* **2020**, *896*. [CrossRef]
12. Apte, S.V.; Martin, M.; Patankar, N.A. A numerical method for fully resolved simulation (FRS) of rigid particle–flow interactions in complex flows. *J. Comput. Phys.* **2009**, *228*, 2712–2738. [CrossRef]
13. Wacholder, E.; Sather, N. The hydrodynamic interaction of two unequal spheres moving under gravity through quiescent viscous fluid. *J. Fluid Mech.* **1974**, *65*, 417–437. [CrossRef]
14. D'Avino, G.; Maffettone, P.L. Particle dynamics in viscoelastic liquids. *J. Non Newton. Fluid Mech.* **2015**, *215*, 80–104. [CrossRef]
15. Kumar, G.; Natale, G. Settling dynamics of two spheres in a suspension of Brownian rods. *Phys. Fluids* **2019**, *31*, 073104. [CrossRef]
16. Malhotra, S.; Sharma, M.M. Settling of spherical particles in unbounded and confined surfactant-based shear thinning viscoelastic fluids: An experimental study. *Chem. Eng. Sci.* **2012**, *84*, 646–655. [CrossRef]
17. Uchiyama, S.; Noda, M.; Krayukhina, E. Sedimentation velocity analytical ultracentrifugation for characterization of therapeutic antibodies. *Biophys. Rev.* **2018**, *10*, 259–269. [CrossRef] [PubMed]

18. Heyder, J. Deposition of inhaled particles in the human respiratory tract and consequences for regional targeting in respiratory drug delivery. *Proc. Am. Thorac. Soc.* **2004**, *1*, 315–320. [CrossRef] [PubMed]
19. Hu, X.; Lin, J.; Chen, D.; Ku, X. Influence of non-Newtonian power law rheology on inertial migration of particles in channel flow. *Biomicrofluidics* **2020**, *14*, 014105. [CrossRef]
20. Sulaymon, A.-H.; Wilson, C.A.; Alwared, A.I. An experimental investigation of the settling behavior of two spheres in a power law fluid. *J. Non Newton. Fluid Mech.* **2013**, *192*, 29–36. [CrossRef]
21. Hsu, J.-P.; Shie, C.-F.; Tseng, S. Sedimentation of a cylindrical particle in a Carreau fluid. *J. Colloid Interface Sci.* **2005**, *286*, 392–399. [CrossRef] [PubMed]
22. Gheissary, G.; Van Den Brule, B. Unexpected phenomena observed in particle settling in non-Newtonian media. *J. Non Newton. Fluid Mech.* **1996**, *67*, 1–18. [CrossRef]
23. Solomon, M.; Muller, S. Flow past a sphere in polystyrene-based Boger fluids: The effect on the drag coefficient of finite extensibility, solvent quality and polymer molecular weight. *J. Non Newton. Fluid Mech.* **1996**, *62*, 81–94. [CrossRef]
24. Goyal, N.; Derksen, J. Direct simulations of spherical particles sedimenting in viscoelastic fluids. *J. Non Newton. Fluid Mech.* **2012**, *183*, 1–13. [CrossRef]
25. Riddle, M.J.; Narvaez, C.; Bird, R.B. Interactions between two spheres falling along their line of centers in a viscoelastic fluid. *J. Non Newton. Fluid Mech.* **1977**, *2*, 23–35. [CrossRef]
26. Joseph, D.; Liu, Y.; Poletto, M.; Feng, J. Aggregation and dispersion of spheres falling in viscoelastic liquids. *J. Non Newton. Fluid Mech.* **1994**, *54*, 45–86. [CrossRef]
27. Bot, E.; Hulsen, M.; Van den Brule, B. The motion of two spheres falling along their line of centres in a Boger fluid. *J. Non Newton. Fluid Mech.* **1998**, *79*, 191–212. [CrossRef]
28. Gumulya, M.; Horsley, R.; Pareek, V.; Lichti, D. The effects of fluid viscoelasticity on the settling behaviour of horizontally aligned spheres. *Chem. Eng. Sci.* **2011**, *66*, 5822–5831. [CrossRef]
29. Pan, T.-W.; Chiu, S.-H.; Glowinski, R. Numerical study of two balls settling in viscoelastic fluids from an initial vertical configuration. *Phys. Fluids* **2019**, *31*, 123104.
30. Freire, D.; Sarasúa, L.; Vernet, A.; Varela, S.; Usera, G.; Cabeza, C.; Martí, A. Separation regimes of two spheres falling in shear-thinning viscoelastic fluids. *Phys. Rev. Fluids* **2019**, *4*, 023302. [CrossRef]
31. Eisenberg, D.; Klink, I.; Phillips, R. Axisymmetric sedimentation of spherical particles in a viscoelastic fluid: Sphere–wall and sphere–sphere interactions. *J. Rheol.* **2013**, *57*, 857–880. [CrossRef]
32. Liu, C.; Shao, H.; Chen, F.; Zheng, H. Rheological properties of concentrated aqueous injectable calcium phosphate cement slurry. *Biomaterials* **2006**, *27*, 5003–5013. [CrossRef]
33. Arigo, M.T.; McKinley, G.H. An experimental investigation of negative wakes behind spheres settling in a shear-thinning viscoelastic fluid. *Rheol. Acta* **1998**, *37*, 307–327. [CrossRef]
34. Harlen, O.G. The negative wake behind a sphere sedimenting through a viscoelastic fluid. *J. Non Newton. Fluid Mech.* **2002**, *108*, 411–430. [CrossRef]
35. Nie, D.; Lin, J.; Gao, Q. Settling behavior of two particles with different densities in a vertical channel. *Comput. Fluids* **2017**, *156*, 353–367. [CrossRef]
36. Chhabra, R.P. *Bubbles, Drops, and Particles in Non-Newtonian Fluids*; CRC Press: Boca Raton, FL, USA, 2006.
37. Reynolds, P.; Jones, T. An experimental study of the settling velocities of single particles in non-Newtonian fluids. *Int. J. Mineral. Process.* **1989**, *25*, 47–77. [CrossRef]
38. Acharya, A.; Mashelkar, R.; Ulbrecht, J. Flow of inelastic and viscoelastic fluids past a sphere. *Rheol. Acta* **1976**, *15*, 454–470. [CrossRef]
39. Lockyer, M.; Davies, J.; Jones, T. The importance of rheology in the determination of the carrying capacity of oil-drilling fluids. In *Rheology*; Springer: Berlin, Germany, 1980; pp. 127–132.
40. Xu, R.; Tu, C.; Bao, F.; Yin, Z. Study on the dynamic characteristics of two side-by-side particles of different density settling in water. *J. China Univ. Metrol.* **2020**, *31*, 168–176.
41. Fraggedakis, D.; Dimakopoulos, Y.; Tsamopoulos, J. Yielding the yield-stress analysis: A study focused on the effects of elasticity on the settling of a single spherical particle in simple yield-stress fluids. *Soft Matter* **2016**, *12*, 5378–5401. [CrossRef] [PubMed]
42. Liu, M.-l. Numerical simulation of particle sedimentation in 3D rectangular channel. *Appl. Math. Mech.* **2011**, *32*, 1147. [CrossRef]

applied sciences

MDPI

Article

Fibers Effects on Contract Turbulence Using a Coupling Euler Model

Wei Yang [1,*] and Pei Hu [2]

[1] College of Science & Technology, Ningbo University, Ningbo 315300, China
[2] College of Mechanical and Mechanics, Ningbo University, Ningbo 315211, China; hup93@outlook.com
* Correspondence: yangwei1@nbu.edu.cn

Abstract: Fiber additive will induce the rheological behavior of suspension, resulting in variation in velocity profile and fiber orientation especially for the non-dilute case. Based on the fluid-solid coupling dynamics simulation, it shows that the fiber orientation aligns along the streamline more and more quickly in the central turbulent region as the fiber concentration increases, especially contract ratio Cx > 4. However, fibers tend to maintain the original uniform orientation and are rarely affected by the contract ratio in the boundary layer. The fibers orientation in the near semi-dilute phase is lower than that in the dilute phase near the outlet, which may be the result of the hydrodynamic contact lubrication between fibers. The orientation distribution and concentration of the fibers change the viscous flow mechanism of the suspension microscopically, which makes a velocity profile vary with the phase concentration. The velocity profile of the approaching semi-dilute phase sublayer is higher than that of the dilute and semi-dilute phases on the central streamline and in the viscous bottom layer, showing weak drag reduction while the situation is opposite on the logarithmic layer of the boundary layer. The relevant research can provide a process strategy for fiber orientation optimization and rheological control in the industrial applications of suspension.

Keywords: fibers orientation; velocity profile; coupling simulation; contract turbulence

Citation: Yang, W.; Hu, P. Fibers Effects on Contract Turbulence Using a Coupling Euler Model. *Appl. Sci.* **2021**, *11*, 7126. https://doi.org/10.3390/app11157126

Academic Editor: Jianzhong Lin

Received: 29 June 2021
Accepted: 27 July 2021
Published: 2 August 2021

Publisher's Note: MDPI stays neutral with regard to jurisdictional claims in published maps and institutional affiliations.

1. Introduction

Fiber suspensions are widely used in many fields, such as wood pulp used in the modern papermaking industry. Main components of the mixture are water and the fibers. Previous studies have indicated that the addition of fibers can change the transport properties of the flow field, and in turn influence the fibers orientation and distribution, which will ultimately affect the quality of finished products. Related studies focus on the pipe and channel flow more than the contraction.

Contract flow is mainly used to accelerate the flow rate, such as jet nozzle and the headbox. The headbox is the key part of the modern paper machine, which can produce high intensity micro-turbulence to effectively disperse the fibers and determine their distribution along the horizontal and longitudinal direction of paper. Thus, it can prevent the fiber from settling and flocculating to improve the strength of the paper sheet. The internal flow field in the headbox is similar to the turbulent contraction. The contraction ratio C_x is an important parameter of the contract field, which is the ratio of the local average velocity to the inlet average velocity. In view of the complexity of the fluid-solid coupling mechanism between the carrier fluid and the fibers, some simulations have been made in many researches. Harris et al. [1], Ullmar et al. [2,3] and Zhang [4] studied the fiber orientation distribution in the dilute turbulent contraction. It is found that the anisotropy of fibers orientation is mainly determined by the contraction ratio rather than the Reynolds number. Increasing contraction ratio would increase fiber alignment significantly and vice versa. Because the turbulent effect is not taken into account in their studies, the relationship between the orientation anisotropy of the fibers and the turbulence pulsation of the flow field is not known clearly.

Olson et al. [5] thought that fibers orientation depends on the combined effect of fibers motion and turbulence. Ignoring the influence of the latter is the reason why the theoretical prediction of fiber orientation alignment is higher than the experimental measurements. Then Olson et al. [6] used the Euler model to predict the fiber orientation distribution. When the contraction ratio grew from 5 to 50, the fiber alignment increases obviously. The fibers orientation distribution changed slightly with inlet velocity. Parsheh et al. [7,8] analyzed the effects of four kinds of wall shapes on the anisotropy of fiber orientation by ignoring the interaction between fibers and fluids. It was shown that the anisotropy of fibers orientation varied with the contract shape and was dominated by the rotating Peclet number. When the contract ratio and Peclet number are both large, the turbulence effect can be ignored. Otherwise, turbulence has a great influence on fiber orientation. Lin et al. [9] used slender body theory to simulate fiber orientation distribution. Then Lin et al. [10] obtained the orientation angle of a single fiber by the analytical and numerical method and concluded that contraction ratio had an important effect on fiber orientation distribution. Yang [11] gave the optimal contract wall for desired fibers orientation in dilute suspension by the one-way coupling RSM method.

The existing methods mainly consider the effect of the carrier fluid on the fibers (e.g., Olson [5,6,12], Gillissen [13] and Johnson etc. [14]). In fact, the effect of additive on the turbulence varies with its concentration and scale (e.g., Lin etc. [10,15–17] and Yang etc. [18]). Therefore, the coupling numerical simulation will contribute to a further research about the orientation characteristics of the fiber under the different additive concentration. It'll also achieve a better control over flow behaviors during the fiber-reinforced materials production.

2. Coupling Models and Methods

In order to understand the interaction mechanism between the fluid-solid phases of fibers suspension, the variation of fiber orientation and flow velocity profile with the additive concentration nL^3 and the contract ratio Cx is mainly studied in the contract turbulence.

2.1. Models

Based on Parsheh's experiment [7] the two-dimensional model of axisymmetric contraction is shown in Figure 1. The coordinate origin is located at the inlet of the flow field. The contraction length l is 550 mm, inlet height h_0 is 179.2 mm, outlet height h_e is 16 mm and the maximum contraction ratio C_{max} is about 11.2. The angle between the projection of the fiber orientation P on the x-y plane and the X-axis is ϕ. The angle between fiber orientation P and Z-axis is θ. X-axis is along the flow direction; Y-axis is vertical to the flow direction and Z-axis is the span direction of the flow.

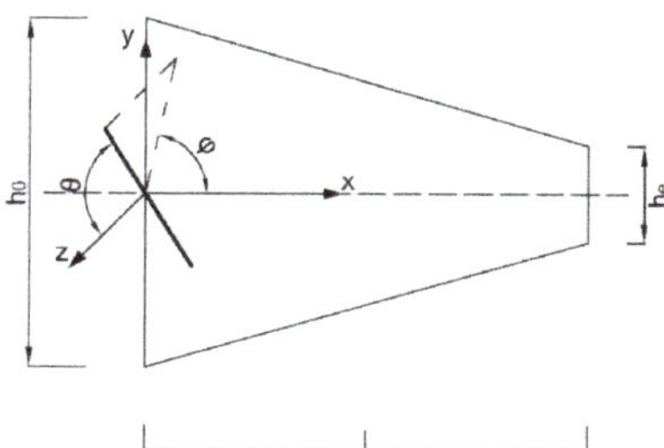

Figure 1. Two-dimension model of contraction.

2.2. Mathematical Description of Fibers Orientation Distribution

There are two premises to assure that the suspension flow can be regarded as a single continuum medium: (1) The size of the added particles would be much smaller than the characteristic scale of the flow field and the suspension is quasi-uniform; (2) The Reynolds number of the particles, characterized by the relative velocity of the particles in the flow field, should be small enough to satisfy the quasi-Newtonian fluid.

Therefore, the flow behavior of the fiber suspension can be described by using Euler method. The orientation state of abundant suspended fibers in the dilute flow is described by a Fokker-Plank type function $f(t, x, \phi)$, which is the probability of a fiber orienting p occurring at time t and placement x. Considering the turbulent effect according to the Reynolds average idea, Equation (1) is given for a 2D steady incompressible flow and its detailed derivation is shown in the literature [18].

$$\frac{\partial^2 \overline{f}}{\partial^2 \phi} = H\frac{\partial \overline{f}}{\partial \phi} + R\overline{f} + B\frac{\partial \overline{f}}{\partial x} + G\frac{\partial \overline{f}}{\partial y} \tag{1}$$

where the coefficients in the Equation (1) can see Equations (2)~(5):

$$B = \frac{\sin^2(2\phi)}{4D_r}\overline{u}, \tag{2}$$

$$G = \frac{\sin^2(2\phi)}{4D_r}\overline{v} \tag{3}$$

$$H = -\frac{\sin^2(2\phi)}{2D_r}\left(\frac{\partial \overline{u}}{\partial x}\sin(2\phi) + \frac{\partial \overline{v}}{\partial x}\sin^2\phi - \frac{\partial \overline{u}}{\partial y}\cos^2\phi\right) \tag{4}$$

$$R = -\frac{\sin^2(2\phi)}{4D_r}\left(\frac{\partial \overline{u}}{\partial x}\cos(2\phi) + \frac{1}{2}(\frac{\partial \overline{u}}{\partial y} + \frac{\partial \overline{v}}{\partial x})\sin(2\phi)\right) \tag{5}$$

Here p is a fiber's unit orientation vector along the coordinate axes (see Figure 1), i.e., $p = (\cos\phi, \sin\phi)^T$. ϕ is an orientation angle of fibers; $D_r = \left[a(v/\varepsilon)^{1/2} + bL(v\varepsilon)^{-1/4}\right]^{-1}$, is the rotational diffusion rate of fibers; v is the kinematic viscosity; ε is the turbulent dissipation rate. u, v are the x-component and y-component of flow velocity V respectively.

2.3. Numerical Solution

Equation (1) is similar to the conventional convection-diffusion equation with the convection terms just for the position space and the diffusion terms for the orientation angle space. A difference scheme is adopted like $f_k^{i,j} = f(x_{ij}, \phi_k)$.

For the convenience of numerical calculation, the variables in the calculation region, such as $0 \leq x \leq M, 0 \leq y \leq N, -\pi/2 \leq \phi \leq \pi/2$, are firstly discretized, like $x_0 = 0, x_i = x_{i-1} + \Delta x_i, i = 1, 2, \ldots, I, I+1; y_0 = 0, y_j = y_{j-1} + \Delta y_j, j = 1, 2, \ldots, J, J+1; \phi_0 = -\pi/2, \phi_k = k\Delta\phi, k = 1, 2, \ldots, K, K+1$. If a discrete method with high order accuracy is used for the derivative of orientation angle ϕ, it'll introduce too many angle quantities and make the solution harder. Hence the semi-discrete approximation form is adopted for Equation (1) here and the original partial differential equation can be transformed into an ordinary differential equation with respect to ϕ. Moreover, the fourth-order Runge-Kutta method is suitable for ordinary differential equations, which can improve the accuracy of orientation derivative approximation.

To do this, set $F = \partial \overline{f}/\partial \phi$ and the original equation can be written as:

$$f' = F, f(x_i, y_j, \phi_0) = 1/\pi \tag{6}$$

$$F' = Z(x, y, \phi, f, F) = R_k^{i,j} f_k^{i,j} + H_k^{i,j} F_k^{i,j} + B_k^{i,j}\frac{\overline{f}_{k-1/2}^{i,j} - \overline{f}_{k-1/2}^{i-1,j}}{\Delta x_i} + G_k^{i,j}\frac{\overline{f}_{k-1/2}^{i,j} - \overline{f}_{k-1/2}^{i,j-1}}{\Delta y_j} \tag{7}$$

Based on the fourth-order Runge-Kutta format, we have:

$$f_{k+1}^{x,y} = f_k^{x,y} + \frac{\Delta\phi}{6}(K_1 + 2K_2 + 2K_3 + K_4) \tag{8}$$

$$F_{k+1}^{x,y} = F_k^{x,y} + \frac{\Delta\phi}{6}(L_1 + 2L_2 + 2L_3 + L_4) \tag{9}$$

where

$$K_1 = F_k^{i,j}, \qquad L_1 = Z(x_i, y_j, f_k^{i,j}, F_k^{i,j}) \tag{10}$$

$$K_2 = F_k^{i,j} + \frac{\Delta\phi}{2}L_1 \qquad L_2 = Z(x_{i+1/2}, y_{j+1/2}, f_k^{i,j} + \frac{\Delta\phi}{2}K_1, F_k^{i,j} + \frac{\Delta\phi}{2}L_1) \tag{11}$$

$$K_3 = F_k^{i,j} + \frac{\Delta\phi}{2}L_2 \qquad L_3 = Z(x_{i+1/2}, y_{j+1/2}, f_k^{i,j} + \frac{\Delta\phi}{2}K_2, F_k^{i,j} + \frac{\Delta\phi}{2}L_2) \tag{12}$$

$$K_4 = F_k^{i,j} + \Delta\phi L_3 \qquad L_4 = Z(x_{i+1}, y_{j+1}, f_k^{i,j} + \Delta\phi K_3, F_k^{i,j} + \Delta\phi L_3) \tag{13}$$

The solution of equations f satisfies the condition $\oint f(x,p)dp = 1$ and the periodic condition $\overline{f}(\phi) = \overline{f}(\phi + \pi)$.

2.4. Coupling Equations of Fiber Suspension Flow

According to the volume concentration nL^3 or volume fraction Φ_c of the additive, the suspension flow may be divided into a dilute phase, a semi-dilute phase and a dense phase. It is generally believed that the distance D between fibers is much larger than the fiber length L to meet the condition of $nL^3 << 1$ or $\Phi_c << a_r^{-2}$ and there is almost no contact between the fibers in the dilute phase. In a semi-dilute phase, the distance D between the fibers is less than L but is much larger than fiber diameter d, that is, $D \leq L \,\&\, D >> d$. Although there are little physical contacts among fibers to meet $nL^3 >> 1$ and $nL^2 d < 1$ or $a_r^{-2} << \Phi_c << a_r^{-1}$, the fibers are mainly affected by the hydraulic action within a range of fiber length. In the case of a dense phase, the distance D between fibers is a multiple of the fiber diameter d to meet $nL^2 d > 1$ or $\Phi_c >> a_r^{-1}$. Here $a_r = L/d$, is the aspect ratio of fibers. n is the number density of fibers.

A coupling Reynolds stress model is needed to reflect the interaction mechanism between the fluid-solid phase of dilute as Equation (14) [19]. Thus compared with Newtonian fluid, the Reynolds average series equation for the suspension will produce the fiber additional stress terms. The concrete forms of the terms are given in detail by Yang etc. [18] and can be found in the Equations (15)–(25). Then the effects of fiber concentration on the carrier fluid were investigated by solving these equations.

$$\tau_f = \mu_f(<pppp> - \frac{I}{3}<pp>) : E \tag{14}$$

$$\frac{\partial \overline{V}_i}{\partial t} + \overline{V}_j \frac{\partial \overline{V}_i}{\partial x_j} = (\cdots) + Q_i^V \tag{15}$$

$$Q_i^V = \frac{\mu_f}{\rho}\frac{\partial}{\partial x_j}\left((\overline{a_{ijmn}} - \frac{I_{ij}}{3}\overline{a_{mn}})\frac{\partial \overline{V}_m}{\partial x_n} \right) \tag{16}$$

$$\frac{D\overline{(V'_i V'_j)}}{Dt} = (\cdots) + Q_{ij}^R + S_{ij}^R \tag{17}$$

$$Q_{ij}^R = \frac{\mu_f}{2\mu}\left\{ \frac{\partial}{\partial x_k}\left((\overline{a_{jkmn}} - \frac{I_{jk}}{3}\overline{a_{mn}})v\frac{\partial \overline{V'_i V'_m}}{\partial x_n} \right) + \frac{\partial}{\partial x_k}\left((\overline{a_{ikmn}} - \frac{I_{ik}}{3}\overline{a_{mn}})v\frac{\partial \overline{V'_j V'_m}}{\partial x_n} \right) \right\} \tag{18}$$

$$S_{ij}^R = -\frac{\mu_f}{\mu}\left(\sum_k (\overline{a_{ikmn}} - \frac{I_{ik}}{3}\overline{a_{mn}})\frac{2\varepsilon}{3}\delta_{im}\delta_{nk}\delta_{ij} \right) \tag{19}$$

$$\frac{\partial k}{\partial t} + \overline{V}_k\frac{\partial k}{\partial x_k} = (\cdots) + Q^k + S^k \tag{20}$$

$$Q^k = \frac{\mu_f}{2\mu}\frac{\partial}{\partial x_k}\left((\overline{a_{ikmn}} - \frac{I_{ik}}{3}\overline{a_{mn}})v\frac{\partial \overline{V'_i V'_m}}{\partial x_n} \right) \tag{21}$$

$$S^k = -\frac{\mu_f}{\mu}\left(\sum_{i,k}\left(\overline{a_{ikmn}} - \frac{I_{ik}}{3}\overline{a_{mn}}\right)\frac{\varepsilon}{3}\delta_{im}\delta_{nk}\right) \tag{22}$$

$$\frac{D\varepsilon}{Dt} = (\cdots) + \frac{\mu_f}{\mu}\left(Q^S + S^S\right) \tag{23}$$

$$Q^S = 2v\frac{\partial^2}{\partial x_j \partial x_k}\left(\sum_{i,n}\left(\overline{a_{ijmn}} - \frac{I_{ij}}{3}\overline{a_{mn}}\right)\frac{\varepsilon}{3}\delta_{im}\delta_{nk}\right) - v\frac{\partial}{\partial x_j}\left(\sum_{i,n}\left(\overline{a_{ijmn}} - \frac{I_{ij}}{3}\overline{a_{mn}}\right)\frac{\partial}{\partial x_k}\left(\frac{\varepsilon}{3}\right)\delta_{im}\delta_{nk}\right)$$
$$-v\sum_{i,n}\frac{\partial\left(\overline{a_{ijmn}} - \frac{I_{ij}}{3}\overline{a_{mn}}\right)}{\partial x_k}\frac{\partial}{\partial x_k}\left(\frac{\varepsilon}{3}\right)\delta_{im}\delta_{nj} \tag{24}$$

$$S^S = -\sum_{i,n}\left(\overline{a_{ijmn}} - \frac{I_{ij}}{3}\overline{a_{mn}}\right)\frac{\varepsilon^2}{3k}C_{2\varepsilon}\rho\delta_{im}\delta_{nj} \tag{25}$$

where: <pppp> and <pp> are the fourth order and second order tensor of averaged fibers orientation respectively $\langle pp \rangle = \int ppf(p,t)dp$, $\langle pppp \rangle = \int ppppf(p,t)dp$; a_{ijmn} and a_{ij} are the compents of <pppp> and <pp> respectively. ρ is the density of carrier fluid; τ_f is the fibers additional stress; Here μ is the dynamic viscosity, $v = \mu/\rho$; μ_f is the additive dynamic viscosity coefficient, $\mu_f = \pi n L^3 \mu \zeta g(\xi)/6$; $\zeta = [\ln(2a_r)]^{-1}$; $g(\xi) = (1 + 0.64\xi)/(1 - 1.5\xi) + 1.659\xi^2$. E is the strain rate of carrier fluid; V_i is the velocity component of flow field; I_{ij} is the compent of identity matrix I; $\overline{A}$ is a mean part of the physical quantity A; A' is a fluctuating part of A; $(\cdots)$ denotes the terms of original Reynolds equation; k is the turbulent kinetic energy; ε is the turbulent dissipation rate; $C_{2\varepsilon} = 1.92$.

2.5. Main Numerical Step for Coupling Simulation

The fluid-solid coupling Euler model with fiber additional stress terms can achieve the numerical solutions of the whole computational domain by using the turbulence solver of Fluent. The main calculation steps are as follows:

(1) Equations (15), (17), (20) and (23) with $Q_i^V = Q_{ij}^R = S_{ij}^R = Q^k = S^k = Q^S = S^S = 0$, are solved to get $\overline{V}_i$, $\overline{V'_i V'_j}$, k and ε of Newtonian fluid.
(2) Equation (1) is solved by Equations (6)~(13) to get $f(x,\varphi)$.
(3) Substitute $f(x,\varphi)$ into $a_{ijmn} = \int p_i p_j p_m p_n f(x,\varphi)d\varphi$, $a_{ij} = \int p_i p_j f(x,\varphi)d\varphi$ to get a_{ijmn} and a_{ij}.
(4) Calculate μ_f with the fiber geometry and concentration parameters.
(5) Substitute μ_f, a_{ijmn}, a_{ij}, $\overline{V}_i$, $\overline{V'_i V'_j}$, k ε etc. to Equations (15), (17), (20) and (23) with Equations (16), (18), (19), (21), (22), (24) and (25) and update $\overline{V}_i$, $\overline{V'_i V'_j}$, k and ε of suspension flow after iterative calculation.
(6) Iteration ends if convergence, otherwise return to step (2) through (5).

3. Validation

The fibers has a nominal length of 3.2 mm, a diameter of 57 um and a volume concentration nL^3 of 0.0053 here by Parsheh's experimental data [7], which is a dilute suspension. It is assumed that the initial condition of fiber distribution is uniform. a_{1111} is the component of the fourth order tensor <pppp> of averaged fibers orientation and it is an index of fiber orientation alignment. The data of the mean flow field is calculated from the Reynolds Stress Model (RSM) on the inlet conditions as Table 1, and the parameter subscript "0" represents the inlet conditions.

Table 1. Parameters of carrier fluid.

ε_0 (m²/s³)	k_0 (m²/s²)	u_0 (m/s)	a	b
3.05×10^{-3}	1.034×10^{-3}	0.4375	8.0	1.2

Under the same flow conditions, the one-way coupling and the two-way coupling model are used respectively and then simulation results of mean velocity in the x direction and the orientation distribution a_{1111} are compared with those of Parsheh et al. [8] in Figure 2.

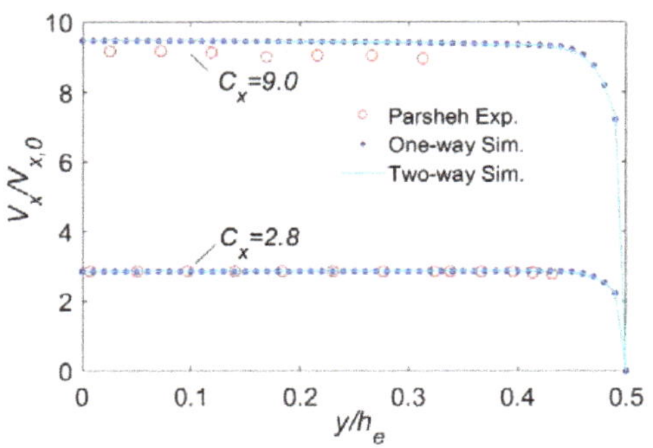

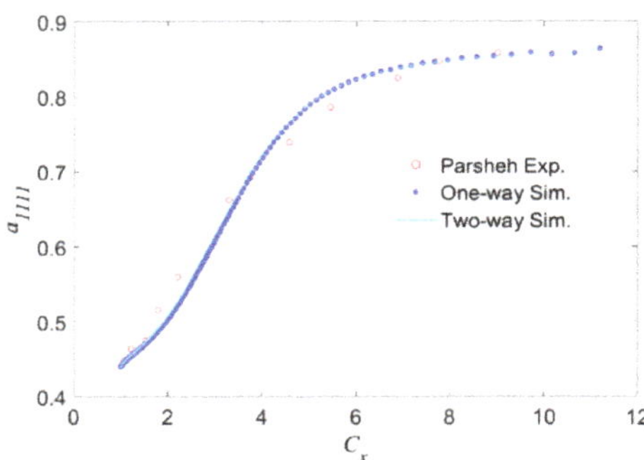

(**a**) Mean velocity profile relative to the inlet at Cx = 2.8, 9.0   (**b**) Evolution of a_{1111} with the contract ratio Cx

Figure 2. Comparison of consequences at the center streamline by Parsheh's experiments, one-way and two-way simulation.

The simulation results are almost consistent with Parsheh's. The mean flow is approximately one-dimensional potential one at the central area of the contraction in Figure 2a. When C_x is 2.8, the relative velocity profile is in good agreement with the experimental measured value. When the contraction ratio is 9.0, the simulated data is slightly higher than the experimental value. That's because the velocity calculation is more easily affected by the grid difference precision when the contraction ratio C_x is large. The overall error between them is no more than 5%, which meets the calculation accuracy.

As shown in Figure 2a,b, the fiber orientation tends to be consistent rapidly with the increase of contraction ratio C, especially above $C_x > 2$. When $C_x < 2$, fibers present a local random distribution. This is mainly because the suspended fibers are orientated by turbulent effect and tensile effect in the contraction flow. When the effect of the former is higher than or equal to that of the latter in the flow field, the fiber orientation distribution will be more uniform. On the contrary it will show obvious alignment.

At the same time, simulation shows that there is no significant difference in fiber orientation distribution between one-way coupling and two-way coupling calculation, which indicates that the influence of additional fiber stress term can be ignored for extremely dilute fiber suspended flow, and the unidirectional coupling method can satisfy the calculation accuracy.

4. Results and Discussion

As is known above, the orientation distribution of suspended fibers is easily affected by the local flow in the field with a large contact ratio. The concentration of fibers would affect the distributions of fibers orientation as illustrated in the figures below.

4.1. Effect of Fibers Concentrations on Fibers Orientation

The orientation alignment index a_{1111} is simulated for the suspension of Table 1 by using the coupling RSM model. Six groups of volume concentration parameters including dilute phase ($nL^3 \ll 1$) and semi dilute phase ($nL^3 \gg 1$ and $nL^2d < 1$) were used. The impact of fibers concentration on fibers orientation is illustrated as Figures 3 and 4 below.

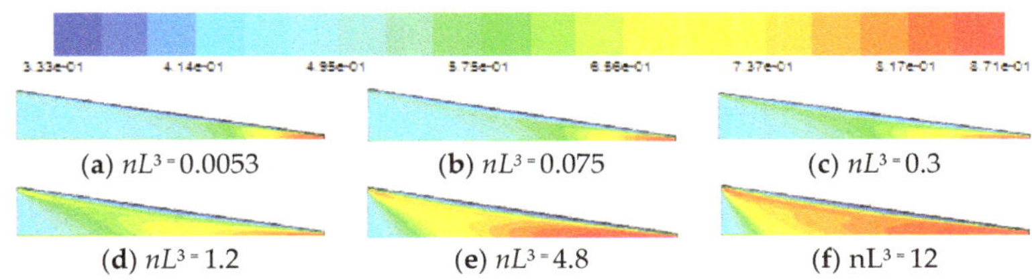

Figure 3. a_{1111} distribution in the contract flow at different nL^3.

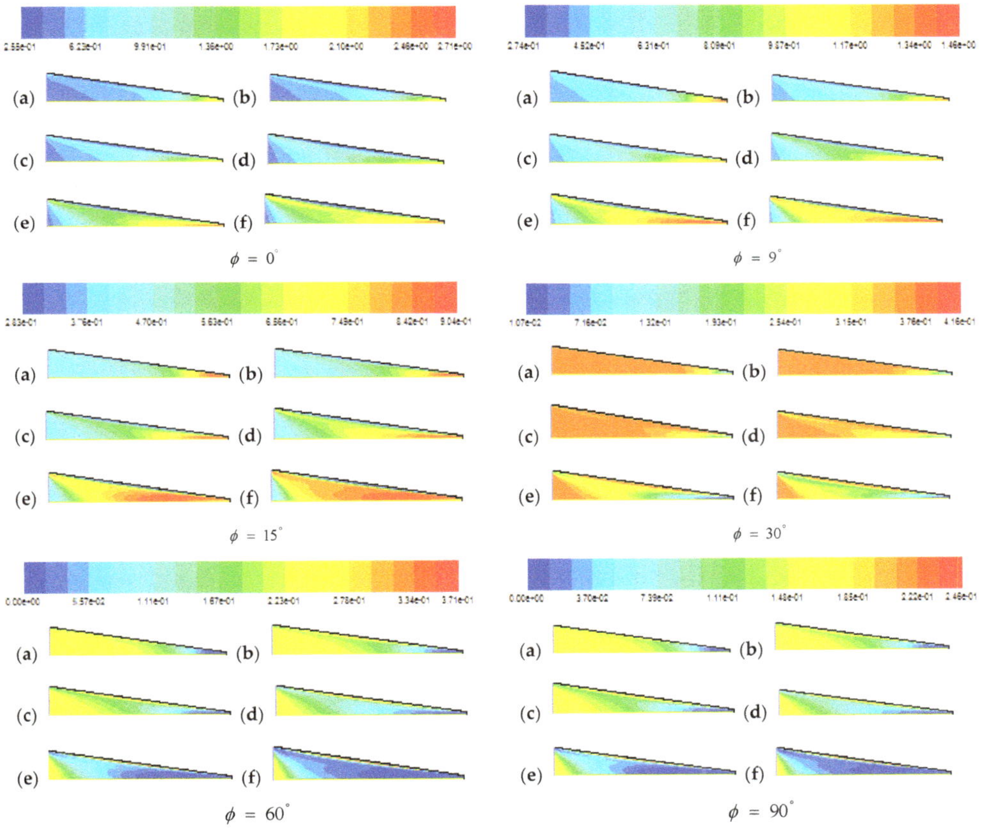

Figure 4. *Probability distribution $f(\varphi)$ of fibers orientation angle φ varying with nL^3 in the contraction where* (**a**) $nL^3 = 0.0053$, (**b**) $nL^3 = 0.075$, (**c**) $nL^3 = 0.3$, (**d**) $nL^3 = 1.2$, (**e**) $nL^3 = 4.8$, (**f**) $nL^3 = 12$.

It is showed from the Figure 3 that the fiber orientation aligns along the streamline more and more quickly with the increasing fiber concentration though almost all of the fibers at different concentration have a higher aligning orientation at the outlet. One of the more interesting findings is that the fibers orientations of $nL^3 = 0.3$ and $nL^3 = 1.2$ are not only slightly lower than that of the semi dilute phase $nL^3 = 4.8$ and $nL^3 = 12$ but also slightly lower than that of the dilute phase $nL^3 = 0.0053$ and $nL^3 = 0.075$ near the center streamline. However, the fibers orientations are all close to the even distribution near the wall in Figure 3. It may be inferred that whether the orientation of the suspended fibers is uniform or aligned depends largely on the local flow structure. Moreover, the probability distribution of fiber orientation in a dilute phase is more dependent on the velocity gradient structure of the flow field than that in a semi-dilute phase. With the increase of the contraction ratio, its distribution in the semi-dilute phase shows a certain degree of viscous hysteresis, whose pattern is obviously different from that of velocity field.

From Figure 4, there is little difference between the probability density distribution $f(\varphi)$ of the orientation angle $\varphi = 0°$ and $\varphi = 90°$ near the inlet no matter the fibers concentration. However, with the increase of contract ratio, the higher the concentration is, the more obviously $\varphi = 0°$ is dominant. At the same time, the probability $f(\varphi)$ of fibers orientation $\varphi = 60°$ and $\varphi = 90°$ decreases sharply in the semi dilute phase, which indicates that the fibers tend to be oriented along the flow direction due to the tensile effect of local flow in the field with large contract ratio.

Based on the near wall velocity, the boundary layer thickness of the case is estimated to be about 1.38 mm. Then the boundary layer grid is divided accordingly. The rest area is a turbulence central region. In the turbulent boundary layer, the fiber orientation alignment index a_{1111} is shown in the Figure 5.

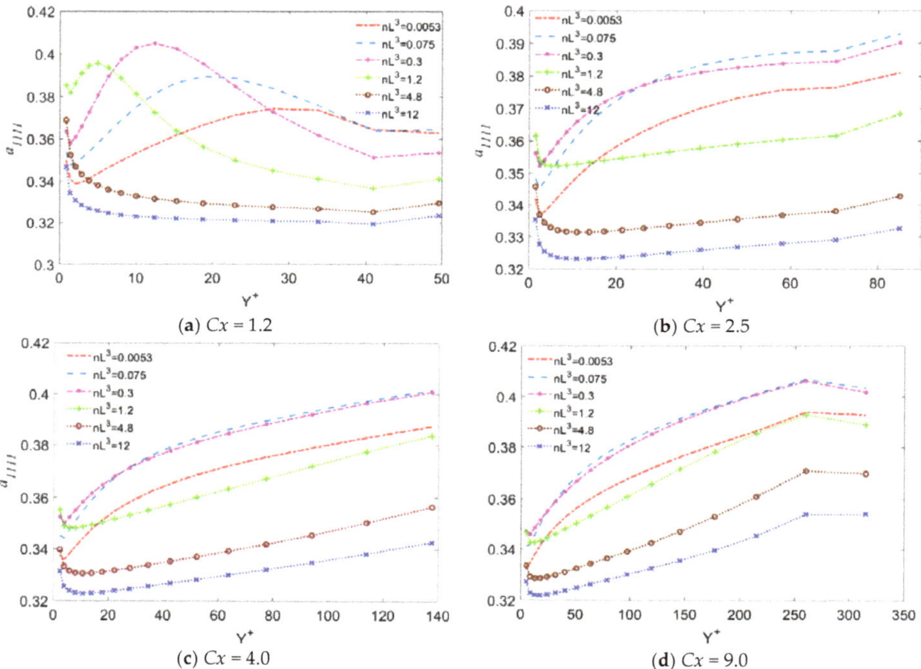

Figure 5. a_{1111} varying with Y$^+$ from the wall to the boundary layer at different nL^3.

It is generally believed that the viscous bottom layer is located at the wall distance $0 < y^+ < 40$; The corresponding region $y^+ < 5$ is the linear bottom layer, where its velocity presents a linear distribution along the normal direction of the wall. It can be seen from the Figure 5 that the semi-dilute phase is the dividing line. When $nL^3 > 1$, it is more difficult for the fibers to align with the increase of phase concentration in $y^+ < 5$. However, when $nL^3 < 1$ fibers will approach the homogeneous orientation of $1/\pi$ more easily with the decrease of phase concentration.

When $40 < y^+ < 300$, the flow is in the logarithmic layer where its velocity presents a logarithmic distribution along the normal direction of the wall. The average viscous shear stress in the layer is very small, so the flow is almost controlled by the turbulent shear stress. When the contraction ratio $C_x < 2$, the turbulent effect is greater than the tensile effect in the boundary layer, and a_{1111} behaves in a trend of increasing at first and then decreasing along the boundary layer thickness. However, when $C_x > 2$, a_{1111} shows a slight upward trend and remains in the range of 0.32~0.40 on the whole, which was close to the uniform orientation.

It can be explained that the viscous damping reduces tangential velocity pulsation and the wall also prevents normal velocity pulsation at the viscous bottom of turbulent boundary so that fibers in this layer are easy to maintain their original orientation. Accordingly, in the influence of the boundary layer the fiber orientation tends to be uniform. Therefore the orientation of fibers near the wall is not easily aligned.

Different from in the turbulent boundary layer, fiber orientation alignment generally increases gradually in the turbulent central region along the direction from the wall to the central streamline, especially when $C_x > 4$, as shown in Figure 6. When $C_x < 4$, the evolution curves of a_{1111} under different phase concentrations is compared. It can be found, obviously, that the higher the phase concentration is, the easier the fibers are to align. The alignment orientation of fiber has the regular characteristics of the fluid viscous interaction and local turbulence structure. At $C_x > 4$, when the tensile effect of the contracting precedes its turbulent effect gradually, a_{1111} increases quantitatively with the increasing of C_x. However, the fibers under the semi-dilute concentration $nL^3 = 0.3$ and $nL^3 = 1.2$ have a lower alignment than those of the dilute phase $nL^3 = 0.0053$ and the semi-dilute phase $nL^3 = 4.8$ and $nL^3 = 12$ when $C_x = 9.0$.

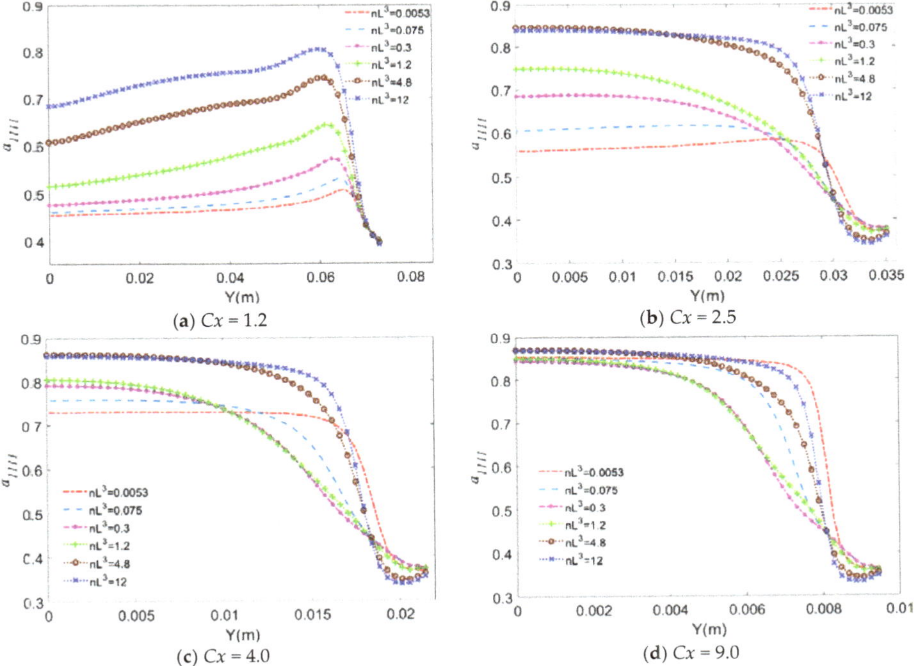

Figure 6. a_{1111} varying with Y from the central streamline to near-wall area at different nL^3.

4.2. Effect of Fibers Concentrations on Suspension Flow

A wall is the main source of vorticity and turbulence in the boundary layer. The flow is basically laminar at the viscous bottom layer near the wall, so the fluid viscosity plays a decisive role in the flow transport. As shown in Figure 7 $nL^3 = 0.0053$, $nL^3 = 0.075$ and $nL^3 = 0.3$ in dilute phase not only have higher wall velocity profile than that in semi-dilute phase $nL^3 = 1.2$, $nL^3 = 4.8$ and $nL^3 = 12$, but also higher than that in Newtonian flow field as C_x increases. But in the complete turbulent layer and blending region, things are not the same. Turbulence is dominant in the complete turbulent layer. In the Blending region, the effects of fluid viscosity and turbulence are equivalent. The phase concentrations $nL^3 = 0.0053$, $nL^3 = 4.8$ and $nL^3 = 12$ have higher wall velocity profiles than the adjacent semi-dilute phases $nL^3 = 0.075$, $nL^3 = 0.3$ and $nL^3 = 1.2$. as C_x increases in the Figure 8. At the same time, the thickness of boundary layer decreases with the increase of wall shear velocity.

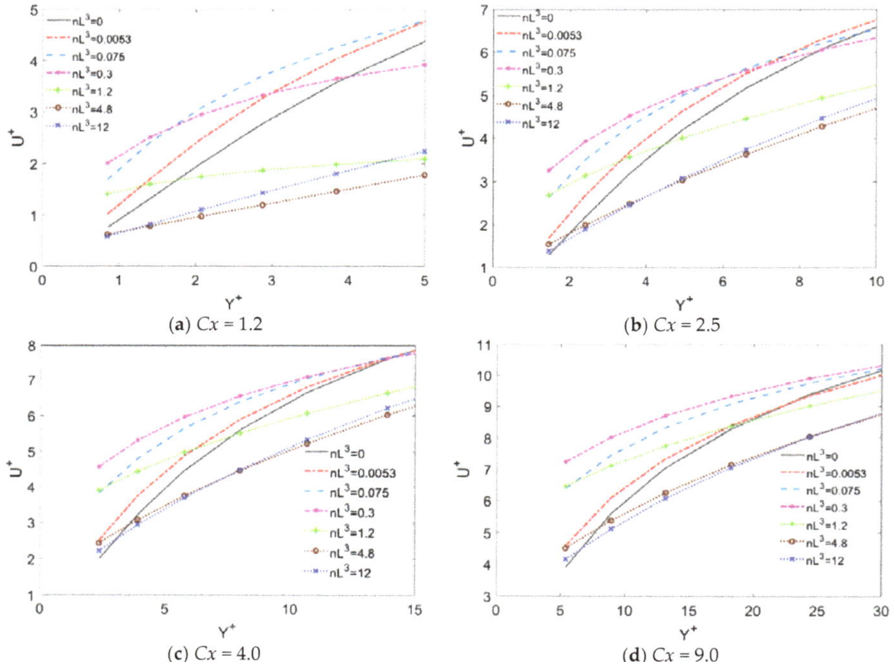

Figure 7. U^+ varying with Y^+ from the wall to the viscous bottom layer at different nL^3.

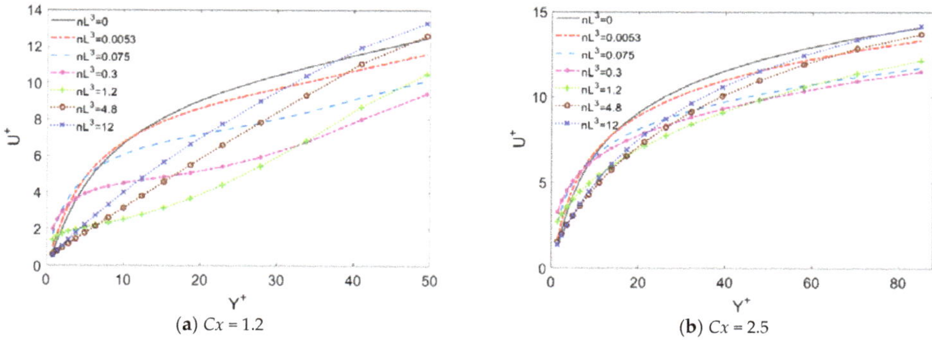

Figure 8. *Cont.*

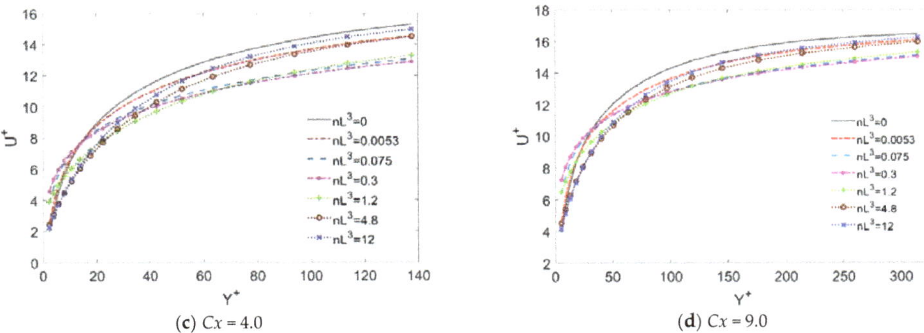

(**c**) $Cx = 4.0$ (**d**) $Cx = 9.0$

Figure 8. U^+ varying with Y^+ from the wall to the boundary layer at different nL^3.

In the central region of turbulence, the velocity profile gradually changes from concave surface to convex surface with the increase of C_x due to the influence of contract wall, shown as Figure 9. Near the center streamline, the velocity profile of $nL^3 = 0.3$, $nL^3 = 0.075$ and $nL^3 = 1.2$ is higher than that of $nL^3 = 0.0053$, $nL^3 = 4.8$ and $nL^3 = 12$, but it is the opposite in the area near the wall. This may be related to the evolution of fiber orientation distribution in the flow field. When $C_x > 2$, fibers in the turbulent central region that are subjected to tensile effect of contract flow strongly behave the obvious alignment while fibers are randomly oriented in the boundary layer. The fibers aligned along the streamlines take advantage of the additional term of Equation (14) to make the calculated average velocity of the flow slightly higher than the original flow field without the additional term. This additional viscous action mechanism changes the velocity profile of the local suspension flow, which behaves with a certain drag reduction trend on the central turbulent region.

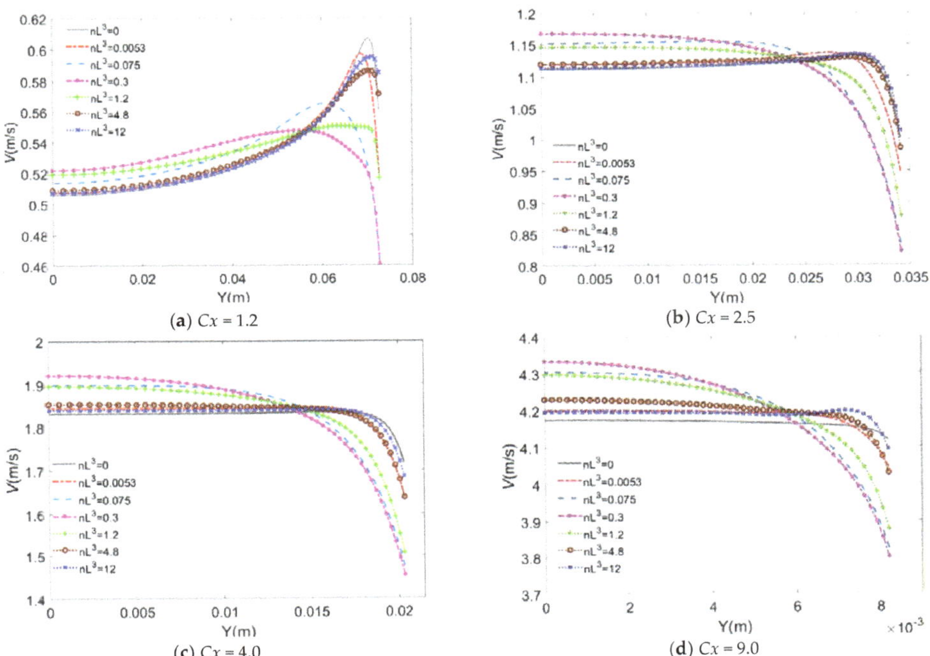

(**a**) $Cx = 1.2$ (**b**) $Cx = 2.5$

(**c**) $Cx = 4.0$ (**d**) $Cx = 9.0$

Figure 9. a_{1111} varying with Y from the central streamline to near-wall area at different nL^3.

5. Conclusions

In order to understand the effect of fiber concentration on the average flow and fiber orientation distribution in the turbulent contraction, a coupling Euler model was used for numerical simulation. In view of the relative independence of displacement and angle space calculation, a semi-discrete approximation form is adopted to simplify the Fokker-Plank type function of fiber orientation angle. At the same time, the explicit fourth-order Runge-Kutta method is introduced to greatly reduce the iterative calculation cost. The velocity profile and fiber orientation distribution of suspension flow can be obtained under different fiber concentrations based on the Reynolds stress model solver of Fluent software.

Due to the local tensile effect in the turbulent contraction whose contract ratio $C_x > 4$, the higher fibers concentration is, the easier it is to move in clusters and earlier align with the flow direction when the fiber concentration exceeds the semi-dilute phase. Fibers in near semi-dilute suspension have more orientations than those in the dilute suspensions because there is hydraulic disturbance and lubrication within the range of fiber length for semi-dilute suspension.

From the mechanism of two-way coupling RSM, the fiber's concentration mainly affects the additional stress of suspension through the additional viscosity term, and then affects the orientation diffusion of the fibers through the flow field, and finally determines the orientation distribution of fibers. Hence the addition of fibers changes the viscosity of the flow field and affects the momentum and mass transport mechanism of the suspension flow. The results of a two-way coupling simulation are basically consistent with the theory and functions of the model here, which can provide a process strategy for fiber orientation optimization and rheological control in the industrial applications of suspension such as paper making and textile.

Author Contributions: Conceptualization, W.Y.; methodology, W.Y.; software, W.Y.; validation, W.Y. and P.H.; resources, W.Y. and P.H.; writing, review and editing, W.Y.; visualization, P.H.; project administration, W.Y. All authors have read and agreed to the published version of the manuscript.

Funding: This research was supported by the National Natural Science Foundation of China (Grant No. 11302110), the Public Project of Science and Technology Department of Zhejiang Province (Grant No. 2015C31152) and Wang Kuancheng Education Foundation Project.

Institutional Review Board Statement: Not applicable.

Informed Consent Statement: Not applicable.

Data Availability Statement: Not applicable.

Conflicts of Interest: The authors declare no conflict of interest.

References

1. Harris, J.B.; Pittman, J.F.T. Alignment of slender rod-like particles in suspension using converging flow. *Trans. Inst. Chem. Eng.* **1976**, *54*, 73.
2. Ullmar, M.; Norman, B. *Observation of Fiber Orientation in a Headbox Nozzle at Low Consistency*; TAPPI Conference Papers; TAPPI: Peachtree Corners, GA, USA, 1997; p. 865.
3. Ullmar, M. On Fiber Orientation Mechanism in a Headbox Nozzle. Licentiate Thesis, Royal Institute of Technology, Stockholm, Sweden, 1998.
4. Zhang, X. Fibre Orientation in a Headbox. Master's Thesis, The University of British Columbia, Vancouver, BC, Canada, 2001.
5. Olson, J.A. The Motion of Fibre in turbulent flow, stochastic simulation of isotropic homogeneous turbulence. *Int. J. Multiph. Flow* **2001**, *27*, 2083–2103. [CrossRef]
6. Olson, J.A.; Frigaard, I.; Chan, C.; Hämäläinen, J.P. Modeling a turbulent fibre suspension flowing in a planar contraction: The one-dimensional headbox. *Int. J. Multiph. Flow* **2004**, *30*, 51–66. [CrossRef]
7. Parsheh, M.; Brown, M.L.; Aidun, C.K. On the orientation of stiff fibres suspended in turbulent flow in a planar contraction. *J. Fluid Mech.* **2005**, *545*, 245–269. [CrossRef]
8. Parsheh, M.; Brown, M.L.; Aidun, C.K. Variation of fiber orientation in turbulent flow inside a planar contraction with different shapes. *Int. J. Multiph. Flow* **2006**, *32*, 1354–1369. [CrossRef]
9. Lin, J.; Liang, X.; Zhang, S. Fibre Orientation Distribution in Turbulent Fibre Suspensions Flowing through an Axisymmetric Contraction. *Can. J. Chem. Eng.* **2011**, *89*, 1416–1425. [CrossRef]

10. Lin, J.; Shen, S.; Ku, X. Characteristics of Fiber Suspension Flow in a Turbulent Boundary Layer. *J. Eng. Fibers Fabr.* **2013**, *8*, 17–29. [CrossRef]
11. Wei, Y. Optimal contract wall for desired orientation of fibers and its effect on flow behavior. *J. Hydrodyn.* **2017**, *29*, 495–503.
12. Olson, J.A.; Kerekes, R.J. The motion of fibres in turbulent flow. *J. Fluid Mech.* **1998**, *377*, 47–64. [CrossRef]
13. Gillissen, J.J.J.; Boersma, B.J.; Mortensen, P.H.; Andersson, H.I. The stress generated by non-Brownian fibers in turbulent channel flow simulation. *Phys. Fluids* **2007**, *19*, 1–8. [CrossRef]
14. Johnson, T.; Röyttä, P.; Mark, A.; Edelvik, F. Simulation of the spherical orientation probability distribution of paper fibers in an entire suspension using immersed boundary methods. *J. Non-Newton. Fluid Mech.* **2016**, *229*, 1–7. [CrossRef]
15. Lin, J.Z.; Zhang, L.X.; Zhang, W.F. Rheological Behavior of Fiber Suspensions in a Turbulent Channel Flow. *J. Colloid Interface Sci.* **2006**, *296*, 721–728. [CrossRef] [PubMed]
16. Lin, J.Z.; Zhang, S.L.; Olson, J.A. Effect of Fibers on the Flow Property of Turbulent Fiber Suspensions in a Contraction. *Fibers Polym.* **2007**, *8*, 60–65. [CrossRef]
17. Lin, W.; Shi, R.; Lin, J. Distribution and Deposition of Cylindrical Nanoparticles in a Turbulent Pipe Flow. *Appl. Sci.* **2021**, *11*, 962. [CrossRef]
18. Yang, W.; Zhou, K.; Zhao, Z.L.; Wan, Z.H. Study on the two-way coupling turbulent model and rheological properties for fiber suspension in the contraction. *J. Non-Newton. Fluid Mech.* **2017**, *246*, 1–9. [CrossRef]
19. Batchelor, G.K. Slender-body theory for particles of arbitrary cross-section in stokes flow. *J. Fluid Mech.* **1970**, *44*, 419–440. [CrossRef]

*applied
sciences*

Review

A Review on the Some Issues of Multiphase Flow with Self-Driven Particles

Chen Liu and Jianzhong Lin *

State Key Laboratory of Fluid Power Transmission and Control, Zhejiang University, Hangzhou 310027, China;
12024039@zju.edu.cn
* Correspondence: mecjzlin@public.zju.edu.cn

Abstract: Multiphase flow with self-driven particles is ubiquitous and complex. Exploring the flow properties has both important academic meaning and engineering value. This review emphasizes some recent studies on multiphase flow with self-driven particles: the hydrodynamic interactions between self-propelled/self-rotary particles and passive particles; the aggregation, phase separation and sedimentation of squirmers; the influence of rheological properties on its motion; and the kinematic characteristics of axisymmetric squirmers. Finally, some open problems, challenges, and future directions are highlighted.

Keywords: multiphase flow with self-driven particles; squirmers; aggregation; phase separation; sedimentation; review

Citation: Liu, C.; Lin, J. A Review on the Some Issues of Multiphase Flow with Self-Driven Particles. *Appl. Sci.* **2021**, *11*, 7361. https://doi.org/10.3390/app11167361

Academic Editors: Miguel R. Oliveira Panão and Maria Grazia De Giorgi

Received: 31 May 2021
Accepted: 9 August 2021
Published: 10 August 2021

1. Introduction

Previous investigations on multiphase flows were mainly focused on the passive particles which are just driven by fluid and external force. However, in the multiphase flow with self-driven particles, the particles are mainly driven by internal force together with some influence of fluid and external force. Meanwhile, self-driven particles inject energy into fluid so as to change the motion of the fluid and then change its own motion in turn.

Multiphase flows with self-driven particles exist in natural and engineering applications. In nature, cells (e.g., Spermatozoa, Leucocyte), bacteria (e.g., Coccus, bacillus, Spirillum, Vibrio), fungus (e.g., Ascomycota), algae (e.g., Diatom, Dinoflagellates), protozoa (e.g., Entamoeba histolytica, Paramecium), movement proteins, etc., are all self-driven particles (as shown in Figure 1). Situations including when spermatozoa pass through the mucus to fuse with an egg [1], when Escherichia coli moves to high nutrient areas inside the human body, etc., all belong to the multiphase flow with self-driven particles [2].

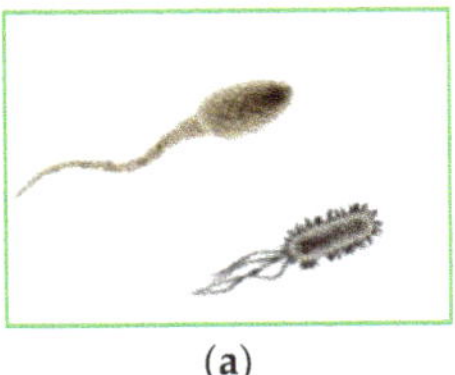 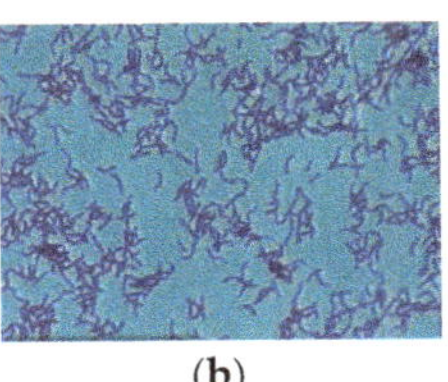 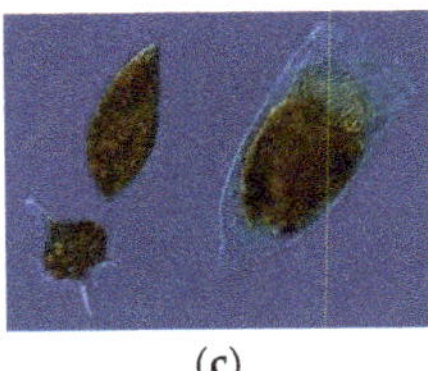

(**a**)　　　　　　　(**b**)　　　　　　　(**c**)

Figure 1. Self-driven particles in nature. (**a**) Spermatozoa and *E. coli*; (**b**) Spirillum; (**c**) Dinoflagellates.

In practice, synthesized self-driven particles contain artificial cell tissues, phosphorus-containing colloidal particles, soft field-responsive gel, catalytic particles for biodegradation, biomarkers and contrast media, miniature swimming devices and robots, etc. (as shown in Figure 2). In the presence of external fields, artificial particles become self-driven and obtain the abilities of targeted drug delivery, precise surgery, self-assembly, environmental modification, and water treatment; such situations also belong to the multiphase flow with self-driven particles.

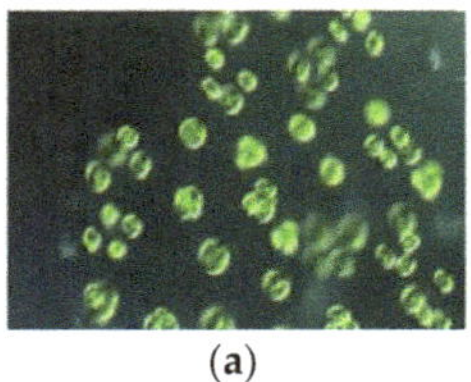
(a)

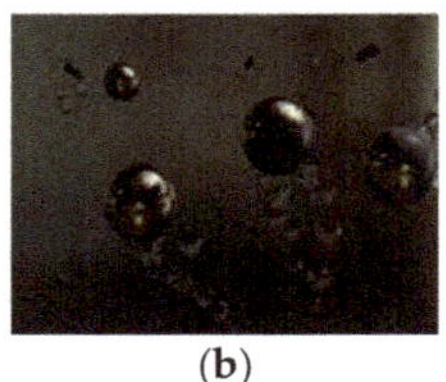
(b)

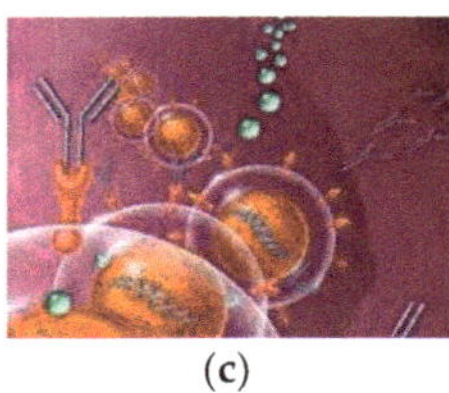
(c)

Figure 2. Synthesized self-driven particles. (**a**) Artificial cell; (**b**) biomarkers; (**c**) miniature swimmer.

When compared with multiphase flow with passive particles, the multiphase flow with self-driven particles involves more complex properties [3]. Firstly, the system is in a non-equilibrium state. Brownian motion of self-driven particles is caused by the interaction between random collision of fluid molecules and particles, which cannot satisfy the fluctuation–dissipation theorem that relies on the assumption that the response of a system in equilibrium to a small applied force is the same as its response to a spontaneous fluctuation, while the system consisting of fluid molecules and particles does not satisfy this assumption because of the interaction between small applied force and self-driving force. Secondly, there is a great diversity of self-driving modes which include gravity, torque, flagella driving, cilia shaking, surface deformation, chemical reaction, bubble release, electromagnetic light energy and actin aggregation and so on. Different driving modes lead to different stresses and patterns of flow, which will affect the particle motion in turn. Thirdly, there exist some abnormal characteristics such as turbulence with small Reynolds number [4], abnormal shear viscosity, weak shear hydrodynamic diffusion, biological convection, cluster structure, non-equilibrium phase transition between disordered and ordered phases, orientational ordering of quasi-liquid crystal and so on [5]. Moreover, the translational and rotational velocities of particles will deviate from the Maxwell distribution [6].

The study of multiphase flow with self-driven particles plays an important role in exploring the laws of nature and practical applications. Firstly, research on the moving mode and efficiency of a natural organism as well as the effect of environment on its kinematic characteristics can deepen the understanding of the tropism and rationality of natural selection in organisms. For example, how does the hydrodynamic interaction between organisms affect swimming efficiency? How do the different characteristics between the flows near the wall and far away from the wall influence the distribution and swimming properties of organisms? Secondly, exploring the energy conversion mechanism of self-driven particles in the flow is beneficial for the development of artificial active materials, such as cell tissue and phosphorus-containing colloid. Moreover, research on the influence of particle shapes on the flow properties contributes to the design of the miniature swimming devices and improvement of self-organization technology of rotating body in a water environment. Understanding the interaction between self-driven particles and passive particles also contributes to the development of catalytic active particles and achieving of the biodegradation of pollutants and environmental remediation in water treatment and water protection. Thirdly, exploring the influence of fluid physical property on particle motion contributes to the realization of the propagation and diffusion mechanism of active organisms in the human system, e.g., manipulating drugs to kill germs and control infections. Finding out the influence of wall surface on the properties of particle motion can ensure that particles give full play to the function of being biomarkers and contrast media, and contribute to particle localization and identification, targeted drug delivery, accuracy improvement of non-invasive surgery, screening of diseased cells and development of detection devices.

The energy injected into the fluid by self-driven particles is dependent on the particle driving modes. The self-driven particles described in this paper are the self-propelled and self-rotary particles and squirmers, which, as the most typical particles in natural and synthetic particles, directly interact with fluid by oscillating the cilia around the body. Based on the different stress applied to the fluid, squirmers can be divided into three kinds of modes, i.e., pushers (e.g., *Escherichia coli*, spermatozoa), pullers (e.g., Chlamydomonas) and neutral squirmers (e.g., paramecium), respectively.

In past research, although the research on the motion of self-propelled/rotary particles and squirmers has made some achievements, there are still some problems that have not been clarified. For example, the effect of number density ratio of self-driven particles to passive particles on the motion of passive particles was not taken into account; the settlement characteristics of squirmers under the combined influence of driving force, gravity, hydrodynamic force, wall effect and Reynolds number are not clear; the combined effect of Reynolds number, power law index, and driving modes on the swimming velocities and hydrodynamic efficiency of squirmers in shear-thickening fluids are still unknown; there is still a lack of studies taking particle volume fraction, shape factor, self-driving mode, and fluid viscosity into account to explore the formation mechanisms of self-organization of squirmers. Therefore, the following part of the paper summarizes the research progress of these related contents.

2. Interactions between Self-Propelled/Rotary Particles and Passive Particles

Self-driven particles frequently collide with passive particles in flow. For example, spermatozoa, algae, bacteria and movement proteins collide with intracellular vesicles or dead bacteria; artificial active particles collide with pollutants. There are some pieces of research on interactions between self-driven particles and passive particles. Ouyang et al. [7] studied the interaction between one self-rotary rotator and two passive particles, and found that when the rotator acted on passive particles, the Saffman force was larger than the Magnus force, which caused the passive particles to simultaneously rotate about rotator and revolve on its axis. In a small Reynolds number range, velocities of passive particles were the superposition of large amplitude and small amplitude pulsations, but the former would disappear if the Reynolds number was large enough. However, studies of interactions between a few self-driven and passive particles are insufficient to understand the properties of particle diffusion and aggregation. In addition, self-driven particles usually translate and rotate simultaneously, rather than only one of them doing so. Based on the experimental results, Kümmel et al. [8] pointed out that increasing the number of self-driven particles would change the structural and dynamic characteristics of passive particles. As the number density of passive particles increased, the particles would aggregate with a self-diffusing function (as shown in Figure 3). In their study, self-driven particles carried out translational self-diffusion under the function of electrophoresis.

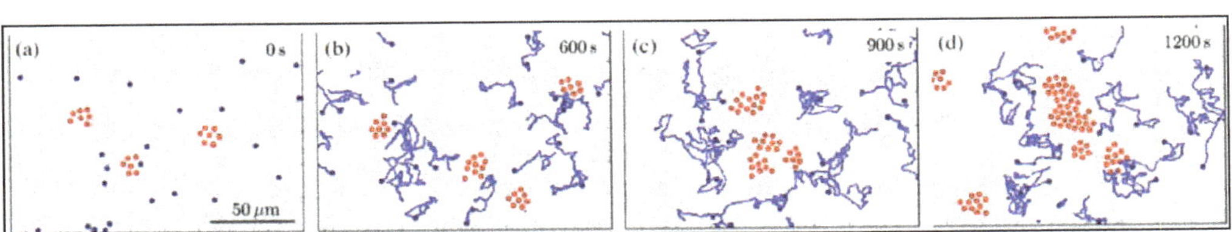

Figure 3. (**a–d**): Passive particles (red) aggregated under the function of self-driven particles (blue) [8]. Adapted with permission from Kümmel et al. (2015).

Natural and synthetic self-driven particles usually move near the wall. Some papers have concluded that cells would move along the circumferential direction, Chlamydomonas cells would disperse or oscillate along the wall [9] (as shown in Figures 4 and 5), tumble of *Escherichia coli* would be restrained, Volvox would become double beat, spermatozoa would change to backward swimming [10], and there existed three kinds of motion states for Chlamydomonas cells after touching the wall surface, i.e., escaping from the wall and swimming parallel with the wall [11].

Figure 4. Chlamydomonas cells disperse near the wall [9]. Adapted with permission from Bechinger et al. (2016).

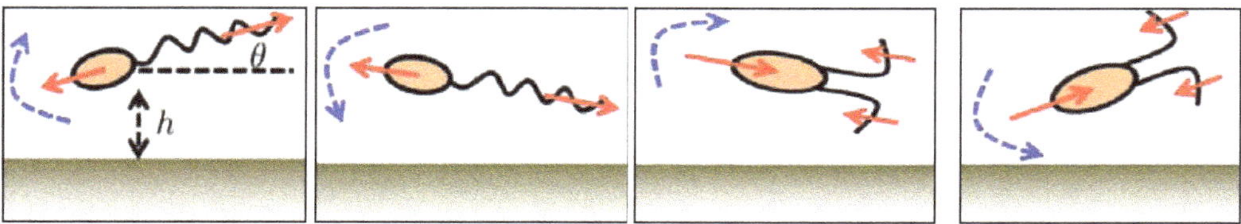

Figure 5. Squirmer oscillating along the wall [9]. Adapted with permission from Bechinger et al. (2016).

Research on the influence of wall surface on the swimming properties of self-driven particles can provide benefits for controlling the natural biological and synthetic particles such as biofilm formation [12], guiding spermatozoa pass through the fallopian tube [13], biochemical sensing [14], targeting drug delivery [15], environmental modification [16], and improving the velocities of self-diffusion electrophoresis particles [17]. Breke et al. [18] discovered that hydrodynamic attraction led to Escherichia coli aggregation near the wall. However, Molaei et al. [9] believed that despite hydrodynamic attraction enhancing particle aggregation, it also appeared without hydrodynamic attraction. Near the wall, particle movements were related to the flow regime caused by the interaction between fluid and the wall, which depended on the wettability of the wall surface [19] and could be described by slip length ls (as shown in Figure 6). In addition, the slip length ls was close to 0 on the hydrophilic surface but a few tens of nanometers away on the smooth hydrophobic surface. Moreover, ls could be increased to the micron scale on a surface coated with hydrophobic molecular film or a surface on which bubble formation took place on the inner concave place. Poddar et al. [4] found that under the condition of $ls \neq 0$, the trajectories of particles would change greatly with the increase in ls, and the results obtained from such cases were totally different from the case of $ls \approx 0$ [20]. The values of ls changed along the wall for the rough surface [21].

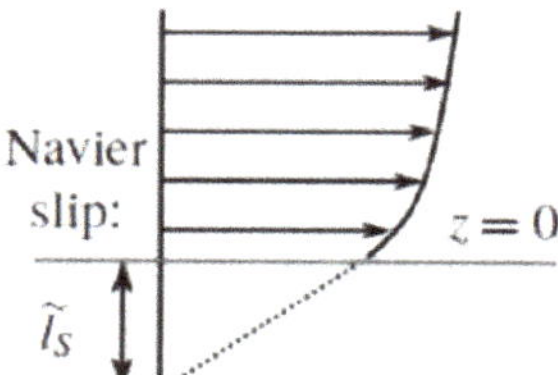

Figure 6. Slip length.

3. Aggregation, Phase Separation and Sedimentation of Squirmers

Natural and synthetic self-driven particles, such as Escherichia coli or Brevibacterium with honeycomb or rafted structure (as shown in Figure 7), artificial Janus granules and synthetic photoactivated colloidal particles, often show the phenomena of aggregation, phase separation and sedimentation [5,22]. Clarifying and controlling such mechanisms can help improve the capability of screening diseased cells, developing detection devices together with particle localization and identification. There are several explanations for the aggregation of squirmers in previous studies. Some researchers believed it was caused by Brownian motion [23,24]; some accepted that high concentration and strong driving properties led to the increase in particle collision rate [25]; some supported that it was caused by the comprehensive influence of geometric dimensions of particles, self-driven properties and collision between particles [26]; and others attributed to the hydrodynamic interactions between particles and fluid [27,28].

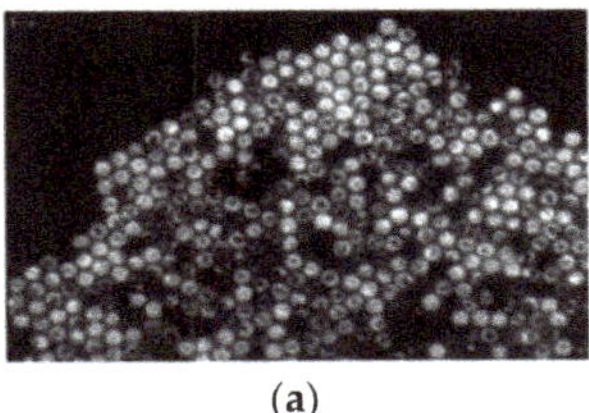

(a)

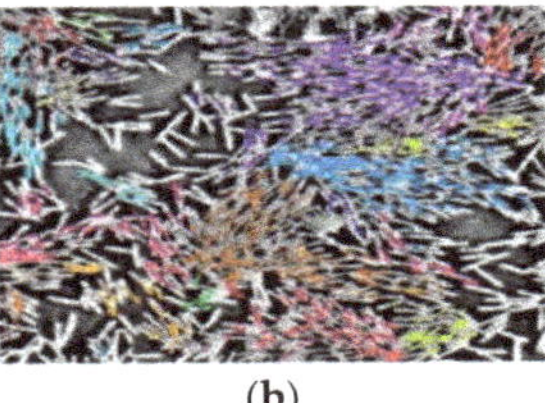

(b)

Figure 7. (**a**) Escherichia coli with honeycomb structure; (**b**) Brevibacterium with rafted structure.

For the particles with different phases, particle aggregation may result in phase separation. Matas-Navarro et al. [29] discovered that phase separation would be enhanced when the hydrodynamic interaction between fluid and particles was weak and would disappear when the interaction was strong. Yoshinaga et al. [30] concluded that hydrodynamic force suppressed phase separation. Phase separation is also related to the driving modes of particles. Theers et al. [31] found that pushers had the largest degree of phase separation, neutral squirmers followed and pullers were the last. However, Zottl et al. [32] and Blaschke et al. [33] discovered that neutral squirmers had the largest degree of phase separation. The reason for the different conclusions could be attributed to the different treatment of change in fluid density. If the compressibility of the flow was not considered, the fluid transport induced by squirmers would lead to the uneven distribution of fluid density. The driving characteristics of squirmers would be weakened in the areas with large fluid density, resulting in squirmers being stable within the group without phase separation. The research of [32,33] belonged to such cases, but the effect of fluid compressibility was taken into account in the research of [31]. The effect of fluid compressibility is related to the number density of particles. The above conclusions were based on the assumption that number density of particles is constant.

Near the wall, particles would present different settlement patterns, such as a stable state together with a fixed position and orientation [34], upright state together with floating above the wall [35], etc. The appearance of such states is correlated with the influence of gravity. The inertia of particles could not be ignored if settling velocities of particles were large enough [36]. Accordingly, it is necessary to explore the settlement characteristics of squirmers under the combined influence of driving force, gravity, hydrodynamic force, wall effect and inertia of particles.

4. Influence of Rheological Properties on the Motion of Squirmers

The fluid in which the microorganism lives frequently has non-Newtonian properties, e.g., Escherichia coli swims in the gastric juice, bacterium passes through the viscous-elastic barriers which are used to protect epithelia. The non-Newtonian properties of fluid contain the dependence of viscosity on shear strain rate, viscoelasticity and yield stress, etc. [37]. These characteristics make the motion of self-driven particles in non-Newtonian fluid different from that in Newtonian fluid. For example, the viscoelasticity will change the swimming stoke of particles, and elastic stress may affect the swimming velocities of particles. The existence of high molecular weight and macromolecules will increase the viscosity and further reduce the velocities of particles [38], while the interaction between driving property of self-driven particles and rheology of fluid may improve the velocities of particles [39–41]. Understanding the influence of rheological properties on the motion of self-driven particles is helpful to manipulate drugs to wipe out germs and control infection.

When squirmers swim in a fluid with viscosity varying with shear rate, the velocity and hydrodynamic efficiency, which is defined as the value of the useful to the total work, are related to the change of viscosity and driving mode caused by fluid shear. In the shear-thinning fluid, the non-local effect caused by the change of flow is more important than that of local viscosity reduction on its swimming [42]. The change of squirmer velocity depends on its starting velocity [43]. Compared with swimming in Newtonian fluid, although squirmers swim slowly, they swim more efficiently [44]. The power consumption of squirmer swimming decreases with the increase in Reynolds number, and the hydrodynamic efficiency is the same at a small Reynolds number for pullers and pushers [45]. The squirmers near the wall collide periodically with the wall with a constant period [46] and will change its trajectory due to rotation in parallel and opposite motion collisions [47].

Another property of non-Newtonian fluid is viscoelasticity. In the viscoelastic fluid, self-driven particles can not only paddle, but also move by the elasticity of fluid [48]. The change of squirmer motion caused by viscoelasticity is related to the driving mode. Whether the pullers and pushers move towards the wall depends on their initial position, while the neutral squirmer does not depend on the initial position [49]. The residence time of a squirmer in the near-wall region depends on the fluid elasticity and the initial position [50]. The elasticity of the fluid makes it easier for a squirmer to move towards the wall [51]. The degree of drift caused by viscoelasticity depends on the Deborah number, and ratio of driving velocity to flow velocity and driving mode [52]. The velocity of a squirmer decreases with the addition of Brinkman medium, but the hydrodynamic efficiency increases [53]. Viscoelasticity of fluid strengthens the rotational diffusion [54]. Squirmers move faster in a third-order viscoelastic fluid than in a Giesekus fluid [55]. Viscoelasticity of fluid slows down and speeds up the pullers and pushers, respectively, but it has no effect on neutral squirmers [56]. Squirmers consume more energy in Newtonian fluid and has higher hydrodynamic efficiency in viscoelastic fluid. For squirmers swimming in upper-convected Maxwell/Oldroyd-B fluids, the elastic stress becomes singular at a critical Weissenberg number [57]. However, the singularity is removed when the exponential Phan–Thien and Tanner model is utilized [58]. The above research was based on the Stokes flow with zero or minimum Reynolds number, i.e., the inertia effect is neglected. In fact, many flows are beyond the range of the Stokes flow [59]. Therefore, the influence of elastic number, which represents the ratio of elasticity to inertia, on squirmer velocity and hydrodynamic efficiency remains to be studied.

5. Characteristics of Suspension Flow of Axisymmetric Squirmers

Natural and synthetic self-driven particles are not limited to spherical shapes. Axisymmetric shape is a typical shape except for sphere, such as protozoa (e.g., Ciliata), biopolymer (e.g., Myoglobin, movement proteins), Bacillus (e.g., Bacillus subtitles, *Escherichia coli*) in nature and some synthetic self-driven particles (as shown in Figure 8).

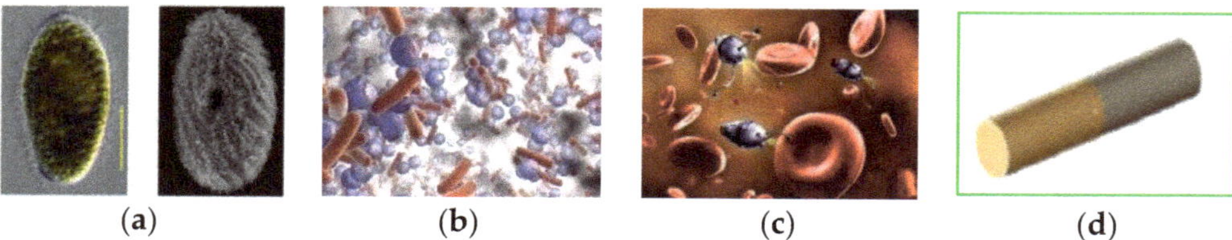

(a)   (b)   (c)   (d)

Figure 8. (**a**) Ciliata; (**b**) Bacillus; (**c**) miniature artificial swimming devices; (**d**) artificial Janus granules.

The study of the shape effect on the flow with self-driven particles is helpful to deepen the understanding of the natural selection tendency of some organisms and the design of micro artificial swimming devices. The non-isotropic shape of axisymmetric particles leads to more complex motion modes and abundant self-organization phenomena, e.g., the swimming and feeding changes were found to be more significant in oblate spheroids than prolate spheroids [60]. For spherical squirmers, the self-organization phenomenon is caused by the interference and blocking between squirmers, but the self-organization of axisymmetric squirmers is caused by its array formed by the interactions. For example, Bacillus subtilis forms polar clusters [61]; Bacteroides dendritic moves along the narrow, long and high-density zone [62]; Tubulin-dynamin forms vortex arrays [63]; and Escherichia coli forms long range array [64].

Axisymmetric particles are more prone to self-organization than spherical particles. Moreover, shape-induced phase separation will occur at low Peclet numbers. However, whether the direct contact between particles or the long-range hydrodynamic effect is the main reason for the self-organization of squirmers has been debated. Based on the Langevin dynamics simulation of columnar [65] and filamentous squirmers [66], it was found that the formation of self-organization is dominated by the interactions between squirmers. Moreover, Brownian dynamics' simulation considering long-range hydrodynamic action [67] also captured the self-organization. However, Pandey et al. [68] believed that particle shape and long-range hydrodynamic force were the factors to form the self-organization.

It has been found that suspension flow of axisymmetric squirmers is more prone to turbulence than that of spherical one [5]. It is generally believed that the turbulence emergence of particle suspension is related to the Peclet number. When the Peclet number is large, i.e., convection is stronger than diffusion, turbulence is more likely to appear. However, it was found that there is no turbulence when the Peclet number in the suspension flow of axisymmetric squirmers is as high as 50 [69]. Therefore, there are other factors at work, e.g., the hydrodynamic interactions, rotating dipoles formed by rotating flagella bundle and a counter-rotating body propulsion of squirmers [70], and induced circular motions [71] on the surface. Reinken et al. [72] pointed out that axisymmetric squirmers had a stronger rotation effect than spherical ones; the coupling of rotation and translation made turbulence appear. If the axisymmetric squirmers are asymmetric along the axis, the order of its orientation would be weakened, which also leads to turbulence [73]. Therefore, the factors leading to turbulence of suspension contain Peclet number, squirmer flexibility, hydrodynamic interactions, effects of strong rotation, anteroposterior asymmetry of squirmers, and self-driving modes. Thus, it is important to explore the correlation between various factors and turbulence.

6. Conclusions and Prospects

In this paper, the interaction between self-propelled/self-rotary particles and passive particles, the aggregation and phase separation of squirmer, the effect of sedimentation and rheological property on the motion of squirmer, and the characteristics of suspension with axisymmetric squirmers are reviewed. The following research can be carried out in the future:

(1) For the interactions between self-propelled/self-rotary particles and passive particles, the following issues should be focused on: the dynamic characteristics and configuration of the passive particles; the critical parameters of configuration transformation under different parameters; and the trajectory and morphology of self-propelled/self- rotary particles near the rough wall with variable roughness element.

(2) For the aggregation, phase separation and sedimentation of squirmers, the following issues should be focused on: the characteristics of aggregation and phase separation of squirmers under different driving modes; the distribution of cluster scale, mean cluster scale for pushers, pullers and neutral squirmers under different parameters; the characteristics of sedimentation under the combined action of different parameters; and the settlement trajectory and morphology under different parameters.

(3) For the influence of rheological property on squirmer movement, the following issues should be focused on: the motion of squirmers in a shear-thickening fluid; the hydrodynamic efficiency under different parameters; the characteristics of squirmer motion

in a viscoelastic fluid by taking inertia into account; and the motion modes and velocity variation near the wall with different Weissenberg numbers and elasticity numbers.

(4) For the suspensions with axisymmetric squirmers, the following issues should be focused on: the characteristics of self-organization of the axisymmetric squirmer group; the turbulent characteristics of suspension with axisymmetric squirmers; and the root mean square of flow and squirmer velocity, Reynolds stress, and probability density distribution function of orientation under different parameters.

(5) Scientists have put effort into computational studies on hydrodynamic interactions of self-driven particles. The immersed boundary–lattice Boltzmann method and the direct-forcing fictitious domain method are the main methods in the studies of multiphase flow with self-driven particles. Both methods have been successfully applied to the study of Newtonian fluid. When the methods are applied to viscoelastic fluid, especially the fluid with a large Weissenberg number, there will be a stress boundary layer. Therefore, how to choose the appropriate discrete scheme is worth studying.

Author Contributions: Conceptualization, J.L.; writing, C.L. and J.L.; review, J.L. Both authors have read and agreed to the published version of the manuscript.

Funding: This work was supported by the National Natural Science Foundation of China (Grant no. 11632016).

Institutional Review Board Statement: Not applicable.

Informed Consent Statement: Not applicable.

Data Availability Statement: Not applicable.

Conflicts of Interest: There are no conflict of interest regarding the publication of this paper.

References

1. Taketoshi, N.; Omori, T.; Ishikawa, T. Elasto-hydrodynamic interaction of two swimming spermatozoa. *Phys. Fluids* **2020**, *32*, 101901. [CrossRef]
2. Japaridze, A.; Gogou, C.; Kerssemakers, J.W.J.; Nguyen, H.M. Direct observation of independently moving replisomes in Escherichia coli. *Nat. Commun.* **2021**, *11*, 3109. [CrossRef]
3. Pedley, T.J. Spherical squirmers: Models for swimming micro-organisms. *IMA J. Appl. Math.* **2016**, *81*, 488–521. [CrossRef]
4. Poddar, A.; Bandopadhyay, A.; Chakraborty, S. Near-wall hydrodynamic slip triggers swimming state transition of micro-organisms. *J. Fluid Mech.* **2020**, *894*, A11-1-34. [CrossRef]
5. Wensink, H.H.; Dunkel, J.; Heidenreich, S.; Drescher, K.; Goldstein, R.E.; Lowen, H.; Yeomans, J.M. Meso-scale turbulence in living fluids. *Proc. Natl. Acad. Sci. USA* **2012**, *109*, 14308. [CrossRef] [PubMed]
6. Ouyang, Z.Y.; Lin, J.Z.; Ku, X.K. Dynamics of a self-propulsion particle under different driving modes in a channel flow. *Chin. Phys. B* **2017**, *26*, 014701. [CrossRef]
7. Ouyang, Z.Y.; Lin, J.Z.; Ku, X.K. Hydrodynamic interactions between a self-rotation rotator and passive particles. *Phys. Fluids* **2017**, *29*, 103301. [CrossRef]
8. Kümmel, F.; Shabestari, P.; Lozano, C.; Volpe, G.; Bechinger, C. Formation, compression and surface melting of colloidal clusters by active particles. *Soft Matter* **2015**, *11*, 6187–6191. [CrossRef]
9. Bechinger, C.; Di Leonardo, R.; Löwen, H.; Reichhardt, C.; Volpe, G.; Volpe, G. Active Particles in Complex and Crowded Environments. *Rev. Mod. Phys.* **2016**, *88*, 045006. [CrossRef]
10. Miki, K.; Clapham, D.E. Rheotaxis Guides Mammalian Sperm. *Curr. Biol.* **2013**, *23*, 443–452. [CrossRef] [PubMed]
11. Li, G.; Ardekani, A.M. Hydrodynamic interaction of microswimmers near a wall. *Phys. Rev. E* **2014**, *90*, 013010. [CrossRef]
12. Li, Y.; Zhai, H.; Sanchez, S.; Kearns, D.B.; Wu, Y. Noncontact Cohesive Swimming of Bacteria in Two-Dimensional Liquid Films. *Phys. Rev. Lett.* **2017**, *119*, 018101. [CrossRef]
13. Guidobaldi, H.A.; Jeyaram, Y.; Condat, C.; Oviedo, M.; Berdakin, I.; Moshchalkov, V.; Giojalas, I.; Silhanek, A.; Marconi, V. Disrupting the wall accumulation of human sperm cells by artificial corrugation. *Biomico Fluidics* **2015**, *9*, 024122. [CrossRef] [PubMed]
14. Duan, W.; Wang, W.; Das, S.; Yadav, V.; Mallouk, T.E.; Sen, A. Synthetic nano- and micro-machines in analytical chemistry: Sensing, migration, capture, delivery, and separation. *Annu. Rev. Analyt. Chem.* **2015**, *8*, 311–333. [CrossRef]
15. Campuzano, S.; De Ávila, B.E.F.; Yáñez-sedeño, P.; Pingarrón, J.M.; Wang, J. Nano/microvehicles for efficient delivery and (bio) sensing at the cellular level. *Chem. Sci.* **2017**, *8*, 6750–6763. [CrossRef]
16. Richard, C.; Simmchen, J.; Eychmüller, A. Photocatalytic Iron Oxide Micro-Swimmers for Environmental Remediation. *Z. Phys. Chem.* **2018**, *232*, 747–757. [CrossRef]

17. Ketzetzi, S.; De Graaf, J.; Doherty, R.P.; Kraft, D.J. Slip Length Dependent Propulsion Speed of Catalytic Colloidal Swimmers near Walls. *Phys. Rev. Lett.* **2020**, *124*, 048002. [CrossRef] [PubMed]

18. Berke, A.P.; Turner, L.; Berg, H.C.; Lauga, E. Hydrodynamic Attraction of Swimming Microorganisms by Surfaces. *Phys. Rev. Lett.* **2008**, *101*, 038102. [CrossRef] [PubMed]

19. Dey, P.; Saha, S.K.; Chakraborty, S. Confluence of channel dimensions and groove width dictates slippery hydrodynamics in grooved hydrophobic confinements. *Microfluid. Nanofluidics* **2020**, *24*, 1–15. [CrossRef]

20. Ishimoto, K. Guidance of microswimmers by wall and flow: Thigmotaxis and rheotaxis of unsteady squirmers in two and three dimensions. *Phys. Rev. E* **2017**, *96*, 043103. [CrossRef]

21. Nizkaya, T.V.; Asmolov, E.S.; Harting, J.; Vinogradova, O.I. Inertial migration of neutrally buoyant particles in superhydrophobic channels. *Phys. Rev. Fluids* **2020**, *5*, 014201. [CrossRef]

22. Marchetti, M.C.; Fily, Y.; Henkes, S.; Patch, A.; Yllanes, D. Minimal model of active colloids highlights the role of mechanical interactions in controlling the emergent behavior of active matter. *Curr. Opin. Colloid Interface Sci.* **2016**, *21*, 34–43. [CrossRef]

23. Wysocki, A.; Winkler, R.G.; Gompper, G. Propagating interfaces in mixtures of active and passive Brownian particles. *New J. Phys.* **2016**, *18*, 123030. [CrossRef]

24. Stenhammar, J.; Marenduzzo, D.; Allen, R.J.; Cates, M.E. Phase behaviour of active Brownian particles: The role of dimensionality. *Soft Matter* **2014**, *10*, 1489–1499. [CrossRef]

25. Cates, M.E.; Tailleur, J. Motility-Induced Phase Separation. *Annu. Rev. Condens. Matter Phys.* **2015**, *6*, 219–244. [CrossRef]

26. Abkenar, M.; Marx, K.; Auth, T.; Gompper, G. Collective behavior of penetrable self-propelled rods in two dimensions. *Phys. Rev. E* **2013**, *88*, 062314. [CrossRef] [PubMed]

27. Alarcón, F.; Valeriani, C.; Pagonabarraga, I. Morphology of clusters of attractive dry and wet self-propelled spherical particle suspensions. *Soft Matter* **2017**, *13*, 814–826. [CrossRef] [PubMed]

28. Delmotte, B.; Keaveny, E.E.; Plouraboué, F.; Climent, E. Large-scale simulation of steady and time-dependent active suspensions with the force-coupling method. *J. Comput. Phys.* **2015**, *302*, 524–547. [CrossRef]

29. Matas-Navarro, R.; Golestanian, R.; Liverpool, T.B.; Fielding, S.M. Hydrodynamic suppression of phase separation in active suspensions. *Phys. Rev. E* **2014**, *90*, 032304. [CrossRef] [PubMed]

30. Yoshinaga, N.; Liverpool, T.B. Hydrodynamic interactions in dense active suspensions: From polar order to dynamical clusters. *Phys. Rev. E* **2017**, *96*, 020603. [CrossRef]

31. Theers, M.; Westphal, E.; Qi, K.; Winkler, R.G.; Gompper, G. Clustering of microswimmers: Interplay of shape and hydrodynamics. *Soft Matter* **2018**, *14*, 8590–8603. [CrossRef] [PubMed]

32. Zöttl, A.; Stark, H. Hydrodynamics Determines Collective Motion and Phase Behavior of Active Colloids in Quasi-Two-Dimensional Confinement. *Phys. Rev. Lett.* **2014**, *112*, 118101. [CrossRef]

33. Blaschke, J.; Maurer, M.; Menon, K.; Zöttl, A.; Stark, H. Phase separation and coexistence of hydrodynamically interacting microswimmers. *Soft Matter* **2016**, *12*, 9821–9831. [CrossRef]

34. Rühle, F.; Blaschke, J.; Kuhr, J.; Stark, H. Gravity-induced dynamics of a squirmer microswimmer in wall proximity. *New J. Phys.* **2018**, *20*, 025003. [CrossRef]

35. Fadda, F.; Molina, J.J.; Yamamoto, R. Dynamics of a chiral swimmer sedimenting on a flat plate. *Phys. Rev. E* **2020**, *101*, 052608. [CrossRef]

36. Ishikawa, T.; Hota, M. Interaction of two swimming Paramecia. *J. Exp. Biol.* **2006**, *209*, 4452–4463. [CrossRef]

37. Yu, Z.S.; Lin, J.Z. Numerical research on the coherent structure in the viscoelastic second-order mixing layers. *Appl. Math. Mech.* **1998**, *19*, 717–723.

38. Datt, C.; Natale, G.; Hatzikiriakos, S.G.; Elfring, G.J. An active particle in a complex fluid. *J. Fluid Mech.* **2017**, *823*, 675–688. [CrossRef]

39. Yu, Z.; Wang, P.; Lin, J.Z.; Hu, H. Equilibrium positions of the elasto-inertial particle migration in rectangular channel flow of Oldroyd-B viscoelastic fluids. *J. Fluid Mech.* **2019**, *868*, 316–340. [CrossRef]

40. D'Avino, G.; Maffettone, P.L. Particle dynamics in viscoelastic liquids. *J. Non-Newton. Fluid Mech.* **2015**, *215*, 80–104. [CrossRef]

41. Zöttl, A.; Yeomans, J.M. Enhanced bacterial swimming speeds in macromolecular polymer solutions. *Nat. Phys.* **2019**, *15*, 554–563. [CrossRef]

42. Pietrzyk, K.; Nganguia, H.; Datt, C.; Zhu, L.L.; Elfring, G.J.; Pak, O.S. Flow around a squirmer in a shear-thinning fluid. *J. Non-Newton Fluid Mech.* **2019**, *268*, 101–110. [CrossRef]

43. Datt, C.; Zhu, L.; Elfring, G.J.; Pak, O.S. Squirming through shear-thinning fluids. *J. Fluid Mech.* **2015**, *784*, R1. [CrossRef]

44. Nganguia, H.; Pietrzyk, K.; Pak, O.S. Swimming efficiency in a shear-thinning fluid. *Phys. Rev. E* **2017**, *96*, 062606. [CrossRef]

45. Ouyang, Z.Y.; Lin, J.Z.; Ku, X.K. The hydrodynamic behavior of a squirmer swimming in power-law fluid. *Phys. Fluids* **2018**, *30*, 083301 [CrossRef]

46. Ouyang, Z.Y.; Lin, J.Z.; Ku, X.K. Hydrodynamic properties of squirmer swimming in power-law fluids near a wall. *Rheol. Acta* **2018**, *57*, 655–671. [CrossRef]

47. Ouyang, Z.Y.; Lin, J.Y.; Ku, X.K. Hydrodynamic interaction between a pair of swimmers in the power-law fluid. *Int. J. Non-linear Mech.* **2019**, *108*, 72–80. [CrossRef]

48. Keim, N.C.; Garcia, M.; Arratia, P.E. Fluid elasticity can enable propulsion at low Reynolds number. *Phys. Fluids* **2012**, *24*, 081703. [CrossRef]

49. Yazdi, S.; Ardekani, A.M.; Borhan, A. Locomotion of microorganisms near a no-slip boundary in a viscoelastic fluid. *Phys. Rev. E* **2014**, *90*, 043002. [CrossRef]
50. Yazdi, S.; Ardekani, A.M.; Borhan, A. Swimming Dynamics near a Wall in a Weakly Elastic Fluid. *J. Nonlinear Sci.* **2015**, *25*, 1153–1167. [CrossRef]
51. Li, G.; Ardekani, A.M. Near wall motion of undulatory swimmers in non-Newtonian fluids. *Eur. J. Comput. Mech.* **2017**, *26*, 44–60. [CrossRef]
52. Corato, M.D.; D'Avino, G. Dynamics of a microorganism in a sheared viscoelastic liquid. *Soft Matter* **2017**, *131*, 96–211. [CrossRef]
53. Nganguia, H.; Pak, O.S. Squirming motion in a Brinkman medium. *J. Fluid Mech.* **2018**, *855*, 554–573. [CrossRef]
54. Qi, K.; Westphal, E.; Gompper, G.; Winkler, R.G. Enhanced Rotational Motion of Spherical Squirmer in Polymer Solutions. *Phys. Rev. Lett.* **2020**, *124*, 068001. [CrossRef]
55. Datt, C.; Elfring, G.J. A note on higher-order perturbative corrections to squirming speed in weakly viscoelastic fluids. *J. Non-Newton. Fluid Mech.* **2019**, *270*, 51–55. [CrossRef]
56. De Corato, M.; Greco, F.; Maffettone, P.L. Locomotion of a microorganism in weakly viscoelastic liquids. *Phys. Rev. E* **2015**, *92*. [CrossRef]
57. Housiadas, K.D.; Binagia, J.P.; Shaqfeh, E.S.G. Squirmers with swirl at low Weissenberg number. *J. Fluid Mech.* **2021**, *911*, A16. [CrossRef]
58. Housiadas, K.D. An active body in a Phan-Thien and Tanner fluid: The effect of the third polar squirming mode. *Phys. Fluids* **2021**, *33*, 043110. [CrossRef]
59. Gagnon, D.A.; Keim, N.C.; Arratia, P.E. Undulatory swimming in shear-thinning fluids: Experiments with Caenorhabditis elegans. *J. Fluid Mech.* **2014**, *758*, R3. [CrossRef]
60. Eastham, P.S.; Shoele, K. Axisymmetric squirmers in Stokes fluid with nonuniform viscosity. *Phys. Rev. Fluids* **2020**, *5*, 063102. [CrossRef]
61. Zhang, Z.; Igoshin, O.A.; Cotter, C.R.; Shimkets, L.J. Agent-Based Modeling Reveals Possible Mechanisms for Observed Aggregation Cell Behaviors. *Biophys. J.* **2018**, *1152*, 499–511. [CrossRef]
62. Be'Er, A.; Strain, S.K.; Hernández, R.A.; Ben-Jacob, E.; Florin, E.L. Periodic Reversals in Paenibacillus dendritiformis Swarming. *J. Bacteriol.* **2013**, *195*, 2709–2717. [CrossRef]
63. Sumino, Y.; Nagai, K.H.; Shitaka, Y.; Tanaka, D.; Yoshikawa, K.; Chaté, H.; Oiwa, K. Large-scale vortex lattice emerging from collectively moving microtubules. *Nature* **2012**, *483*, 448–452. [CrossRef]
64. Nishiguchi, D.; Nagai, K.H.; Chaté, H.; Sano, M. Long-range nematic order and anomalous fluctuations in suspensions of swimming filamentous bacteria. *Phys. Rev. E* **2017**, 95020601. [CrossRef]
65. Bott, M.C.; Brader, J.M.; Wittmann, R.; Winterhalter, F.; Marechal, M.; Sharma, A. Isotropic-nematic transition of self-propelled rods in three dimensions. *Phys. Rev. E* **2018**, *98*, 012601. [CrossRef]
66. Prathyusha, K.; Henkes, S.; Sknepnek, R. Dynamically generated patterns in dense suspensions of active filaments. *Phys. Rev. E* **2018**, *97*, 022606. [CrossRef]
67. Hennes, M.; Wolff, K.; Stark, H. Self-Induced Polar Order of Active Brownian Particles in a Harmonic Trap. *Phys. Rev. Lett.* **2014**, *112*, 238104. [CrossRef]
68. Pandey, A.; Kumar, P.B.S.; Adhikari, R. Flow-induced nonequilibrium self-assembly in suspensions of stiff, apolar, active filaments. *Soft Matter* **2016**, *12*, 9068–9076. [CrossRef]
69. Drescher, K.; Dunkel, J.; Cisneros, L.H.; Ganguly, S.; Goldstein, R.E. Fluid dynamics and noise in bacterial cell-cell and cell-surface scattering. *Proc. Natl. Acad. Sci. USA* **2011**, *108*, 10940–10945. [CrossRef]
70. Hu, J.; Wysocki, A.; Winkler, R.G.; Gompper, G. Physical Sensing of Surface Properties by Microswimmers—Directing Bacterial Motion via Wall Slip. *Sci. Rep.* **2015**, *5*, 9586. [CrossRef] [PubMed]
71. Lemelle, L.; Palierne, J.F.; Chatre, E.; Vaillant, C.; Place, C. Curvature reversal of the circular motion of swimming bacteria probes for slip at solid/liquid interfaces. *Soft Matter* **2013**, *9*, 9759–9762. [CrossRef]
72. Reinken, H.; Klapp, S.H.L.; Bär, M.; Heidenreich, S. Derivation of a hydrodynamic theory for mesoscale dynamics in microswimmer suspensions. *Phys. Rev. E* **2018**, *97*, 022613. [CrossRef] [PubMed]
73. Chen, Q.S.; Patelli, A.; Chaté, H.; Ma, Y.Q.; Shi, X.Q. Fore-aft asymmetric flocking. *Phys. Rev. E* **2017**, *96*, 020601. [CrossRef] [PubMed]

Article

Research on the Inertial Migration Characteristics of Bi-Disperse Particles in Channel Flow

Dongmei Chen, Jianzhong Lin * and Xiao Hu

State Key Laboratory of Fluid Power Transmission and Control, Zhejiang University, Hangzhou 310027, China; chendm@zju.edu.cn (D.C.); 11824035@zju.edu.cn (X.H.)
* Correspondence: mecjzlin@public.zju.edu.cn

Abstract: The inertial focusing effect of particles in microchannels shows application potential in engineering practice. In order to study the mechanism of inertial migration of particles with different scales, the motion and distribution of two particles in Poiseuille flow are studied by the lattice Boltzmann method. The effects of particle size ratio, Reynolds number, and blocking rate on particle inertial migration are analyzed. The results show that, at a high blocking rate, after the same scale particles are released at the same height of the channel, the spacing between the two particles increases monotonically, and the change in the initial spacing has little effect on the final spacing of inertial migration. For two different size particles, when the smaller particle is downstream, the particle spacing will always increase and cannot remain stable. When the larger particle is downstream, the particle spacing increases firstly and then decreases, and finally tends to be stable.

Keywords: microfluidics; inertial focusing; two scale particles; lattice Boltzmann method

Citation: Chen, D.; Lin, J.; Hu, X. Research on the Inertial Migration Characteristics of Bi-Disperse Particles in Channel Flow. *Appl. Sci.* **2021**, *11*, 8800. https://doi.org/10.3390/app11198800

Academic Editor: Richard Yongqing Fu

Received: 23 August 2021
Accepted: 18 September 2021
Published: 22 September 2021

Publisher's Note: MDPI stays neutral with regard to jurisdictional claims in published maps and institutional affiliations.

1. Introduction

The precise focusing process of particles is a critical step of separation and screening techniques [1–3] and is widely used in the fields of biochemical engineering and medical areas. In recent decades, microfluidic technology has been widely used, owing to its unique advantages in many fields and rapid development, among which inertial microfluidic technology is one of the typical representatives [4]. Inertial microfluidic, as a passive method, has attracted wide attention for its advantages of simple operation, simple structure, being harmless to cell viability, and high-throughput.

The suspended particles naturally gathered together and migrated to the equilibrium position, under specific flow fields and geometric conditions, confirming, by Segré and Siberberg [5] with extensive experiments, that the particles gathered into a concentric ring on the cross section of the channel and continued to move in the flow direction. This focusing was thought to be a balance of shear-induced, wall-induced, and rotation-induced lift forces, and the underlying mechanisms have been extensively investigated [6]. Remarkably, Segré and Siberberg [5] proposed that the particles not only migrated by inertia to the equilibrium position of the cross section, but also ordered longitudinally along the main flow direction to form particle trains that may result from particle–particle interactions.

Matas et al. [7] observed that, after particles randomly enter the pipe, the particles would be arranged along the flow direction to form a multi-particle train structure, defined as the particle train [7,8] when three or more particles are aligned with a regular inter-particle spacing. Gao et al. [8] found that increasing the Reynolds number was beneficial to the formation of particle trains, but it reduced the number of particles in the particle trains. The distance between adjacent particles decreases with the increase in Reynolds number. Hu et al. [9] found in numerical simulations that, during inertial migration, owing to the force between particles and the fluid, with the effect of inertia, the particles moved to the equilibrium position one by one, forming a line of evenly spaced particle structures. However, the particle spacing increases slowly with the increase in the inertial migration length; the particle inertial migration length decreases with the decrease in the power-law exponent, and the shear thinning effect will increase the formation of ordered particle trains; the particle spacing decreases with the increase in Reynolds number and blocking ratio. Hu et al. [10] showed that, for single-line particle pairs, the inter-particle spacing increased to a larger value for further downstream, while two lines of 12 particles would self-organize the staggered particle trains, which were dependent on the Reynolds number and blockage ratio.

However, the orderly arrangement technology of particle trains is difficult to apply to cell populations because of size dispersion and deformability of cells [11]. The particle size not only affects the equilibrium position of the particles [12], but also affects the migration speed of the particles [13] and the arrangement of the flow direction [14]; therefore, label-free enrichment or separation of particles in polydisperse suspensions can be achieved. However, most of these works only focus on the separation efficiency, and there is little research on the physical mechanism of particle inertial migration by the size dispersion of particles. Up to now, a large number of theoretical, numerical, and experimental studies have focused on exploring the physical mechanism of particle migration in a closed environment. Only a few works have studied the effect of the interaction between particles of different sizes in multi-scale situations. The effect of particle multiscale on inertial behavior is still unclear and needs further study. In order to explore the effect of particle multiscale on inertial migration, in this paper, the lattice Boltzmann method is used to study the characteristics of inertial migration of two scale particles in channel flow, and the influence of important parameters such as particle size ratio and Reynolds number on the equilibrium position of the particles and the inter-particle spacing is discussed.

2. Materials and Methods

2.1. Lattice Boltzmann Method

The lattice Boltzmann method (LBM) comes from lattice gas automata, which is a numerical simulation method based on the discrete Boltzmann equation. LBM is considered to be an effective numerical simulation method for studying multiphase flow. It is a kind of mesoscopic model that has the advantages of both macroscopic and microscopic models.

The main idea of LBM is to numerically solve the discrete Boltzmann equation to simulate the macroscopic motion of fluids. LBM models usually include discrete velocity models, equilibrium distribution function, and evolution equation for the distribution function. The discrete velocity model adopted in this paper is the D2Q9 model [15], which applies to two-dimensional space and contains nine discrete velocity directions [16]:

$$e_i = \begin{cases} (0,0) & i = 0 \\ c\left(\cos\left[(i-1)\frac{\pi}{2}\right], \sin\left[(i-1)\frac{\pi}{2}\right]\right) & i = 1,2,3,4 \\ \sqrt{2}c\left(\cos\left[(2i-1)\frac{\pi}{4}\right], \sin\left[(2i-1)\frac{\pi}{4}\right]\right) & i = 5,6,7,8 \end{cases}, \tag{1}$$

where i represents the component of the function in the i direction; e_i represents the direction vector of the discrete velocity in the i direction; and $c = \Delta x / \Delta t$, where Δx, and Δt are the grid step size and the unit lattice time, respectively, in the standard LBM $\Delta x = 1$, $\Delta t = 1$.

The equilibrium distribution function is as follows:

$$f_i^{eq} = \rho w_i \left[1 + \frac{e_i \cdot u}{c_s^2} + \frac{(e_i \cdot u)^2}{2c_s^4} - \frac{u^2}{2c_s^2}\right]$$

$$c_s = \frac{1}{\sqrt{3}}, \; w_i = \begin{cases} 4/9 & i = 0 \\ 1/9 & i = 1,2,3,4 \\ 1/36 & i = 5,6,7,8 \end{cases}, \tag{2}$$

where c_s is the speed of sound; w_i is the weight factor; and ρ and u represent the fluid density and velocity, respectively. The evolution equation of the distribution function with the external force term is as follows:

$$f_i(x + \Delta t e_i, t + \Delta t) = f_i(x, t) + \frac{1}{\tau}\left[f_i^{eq}(x, t) - f_i(x, t)\right] + \Delta t \cdot F_p, \tag{3}$$

where τ is the relaxation time, $f_i(x,t)$ is the distribution function at the position x and time t, and F_p is the external force term that drives the Poiseuille flow. Using the external force model with good stability proposed by He et al. [17],

$$F_p = \left(1 - \frac{1}{2\tau}\right)\frac{(e_i - u) \cdot F_b}{c_s^2} f_i^{eq}(r, t), \tag{4}$$

where F_b is the body force. The fluid density and velocity are calculated as follows:

$$\rho = \sum f_i, u = \frac{1}{\rho}\sum f_i e_i + \frac{\Delta t}{2\rho}F_b. \tag{5}$$

Navier–Stokes equations can be derived through the Chapman–Enskog expansion and have second-order accuracy in both time and space [18].

The hydrodynamic force experienced by the particles is calculated by means of momentum exchange, and the specific process is as described in [10].

2.2. Repulsive Force Model

When the distance between particles or between the particles and the wall is less than a lattice length, the hydrodynamic force on the particles cannot be calculated. Therefore, the following repulsive force model is introduced to analyze the repulsive force between the two particles or walls that will collide.

When the distance between the centre of the particle and the wall is less than $2\Delta x$ [19], the repulsive force is introduced:

$$f_r = \begin{cases} \frac{C_m}{\varepsilon}\left(\frac{d - d_{\min} - \Delta r}{\Delta r}\right)^2 e_r, & d \leq d_{\min} + \Delta r \\ (0,\ 0), & d > d_{\min} + \Delta r \end{cases}, \tag{6}$$

where $C_m = MU^2/a$, M is the particle mass, U is the velocity, and a is the particle radius. $E = 10^{-4}$ is a positive coefficient, d is the distance between the center of the particles or the direction from the center of the particle to the wall, and e_r is the direction vector; $d_{min} = 2a$, $\Delta r = 2\Delta x$ represents two lattices when repulsive force exists in the simulation.

2.3. Problem Definition

The migration of particles in the Poiseuille flow is shown in Figure 1. Periodic boundary conditions are selected in the x direction, the upper and lower walls adopt the standard rebound boundary, and the boundary conditions of the particle surface adopt the moving wall rebound format.

During the simulation, when the calculation domain length changes from $1500\Delta x$ to $3500\Delta x$, the result obtained does not change much, so the length of $1500\Delta x$ and $2000\Delta x$ is adopted, and the channel height $H = 150\Delta x$. The particle density is equal to the fluid density, the diameter $D = 18{\sim}45\Delta x$, and the blocking ratio $k = D/H$. $\text{Re} = \rho U_{max}H/m$, ρ and U_{max} are fluid density and maximum velocity, respectively.

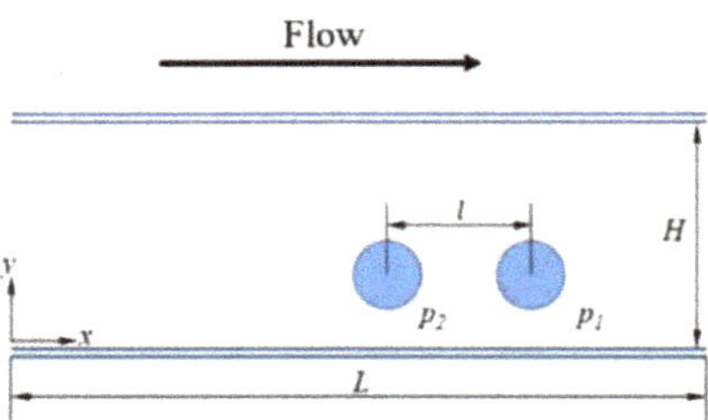

Figure 1. Schematic diagram of particle migration.

3. Validation

3.1. Velocity Profile in a Poiseuille Flow

Figure 2 shows the comparison between the velocity profile of the Poiseuille flow simulated by the numerical simulation and the analytical solution (7), which shows that the method is reliable.

$$u_y = 0$$
$$u_x = U_{\max}\left[1 - \left(\left|1 - \tfrac{2y}{H}\right|\right)^2\right] \text{ for } 0 \leq y \leq H \tag{7}$$

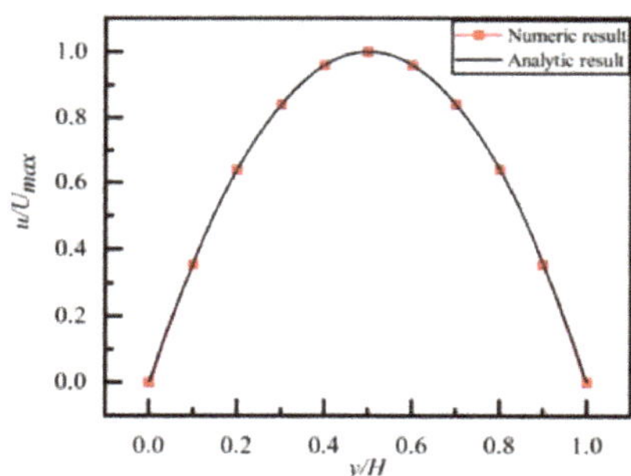

Figure 2. Comparison of velocity profiles.

3.2. Trajectory of a Particle in Shear Flow

Figure 3 shows the trajectory of a particle in the shear flow of Newtonian fluid. The flow domain is $2000 \times 80\Delta x$, the particle diameter is $20\Delta x$, Re = 40, and the upper and lower walls move in opposite directions at a speed of $U_W = 1/120$. Under the same simulated conditions, it can be seen that the numerical simulation results are very consistent with the results given by Feng and Michaelides [20]. Hu et al. [9] also verified this result with the IB-LBM under the same experimental conditions.

3.3. Trajectory of a Particle in Poiseuille Flow

Figure 4 shows the trajectory of particles after they are released at different initial vertical heights. The flow domain is set to $1000 \times 120\Delta x$ and the particle diameter is $36\Delta x$. It can be seen that, after the particles are released at y_0 below the channel centerline, they always migrate to the same equilibrium position y^{eq}, which is consistent with the Segré and Silberberg effects.

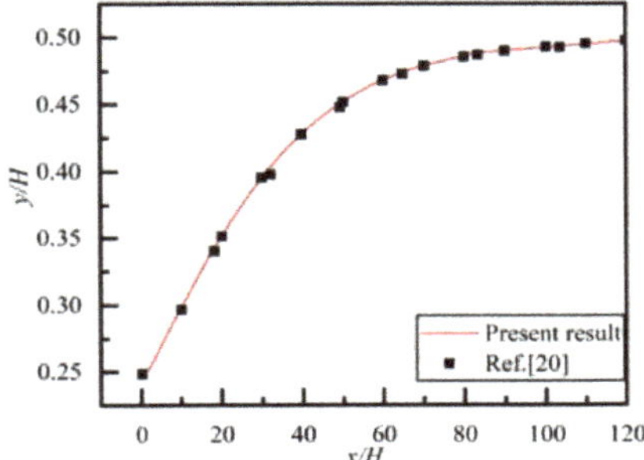

Figure 3. Particle trajectory in shear flow.

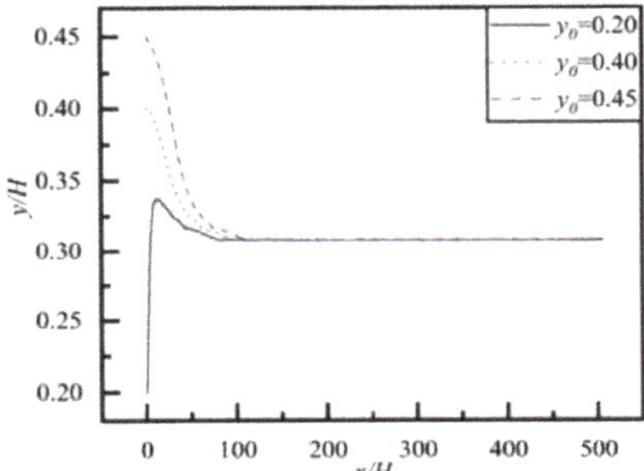

Figure 4. Particle trajectories in Poiseuille flow.

4. Results and Discussion

4.1. A Pair of Single-Scale Particles

4.1.1. The Effect of Initial Spacing

Figure 5 shows the variation of the spacing l with the migration distance of a pair of single-scale particles in the migration process under different grid resolutions. The figure shows the preliminary process of the migration. It can be seen that the evolution of inter-particle spacing under different initial spacing is relatively similar. Comparing (a) and (b), it can be seen that the results are almost the same in different flow domains and different particle diameters.

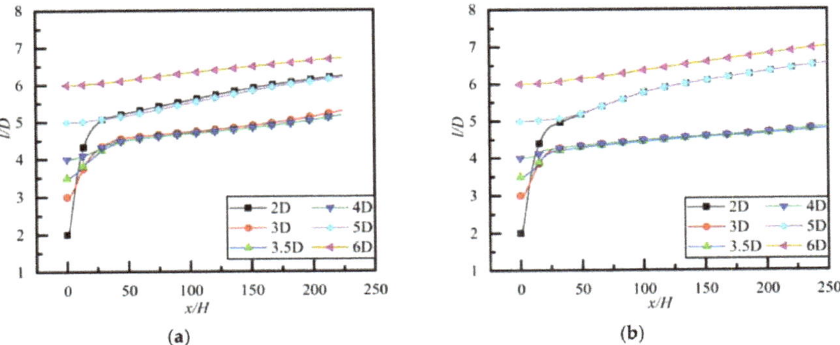

Figure 5. Inter-particle spacing at the initial stage for a single-scale particle pair ($k = 0.4$, Re = 20); (**a**) flow domain $2000 \times 150\Delta x$ (D = $60\Delta x$); (**b**) flow domain $2000 \times 80\Delta x$ (D = $32\Delta x$).

Figure 6 shows the change in the distance *l* with the migration distance after the particles have migrated for a long distance. It can be seen that the spacing of the particle pair increases rapidly at first, and then keeps increasing slowly, especially for the particle pair with a small initial spacing, which is consistent with Hu et al. [10] and Lee et al. [6]; the final spacing of the particle pair under different initial spacing reached the same value. It shows that, at a high blocking ratio, the initial particle spacing has little effect on the final particle spacing.

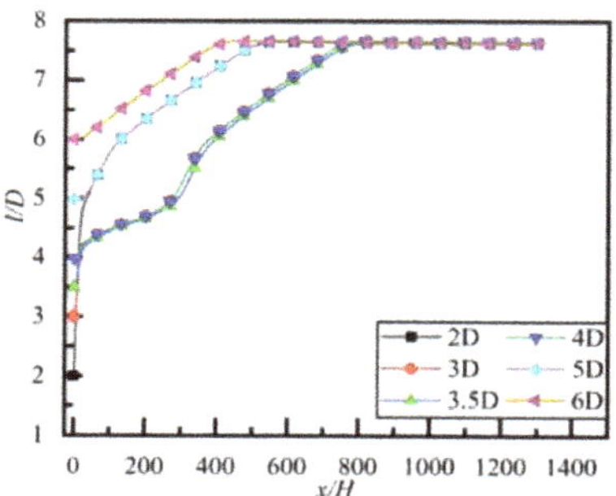

Figure 6. Changes of inter-particle spacing along the flow direction for a single-scale particle pair (*k* = 0.4, Re = 20).

4.1.2. Effect of Blocking Ratio

Figure 7 shows the change in the distance between a pair of single-scale particles with different blocking ratios calculated by the $2000 \times 150\Delta x$ flow domain during the migration process. The initial distance is *l* = 2D and Re = 20. It can be seen that, the smaller the blocking rate, the larger the horizontal spacing between particles, which is consistent with the numerical results of Hu et al. [10]; when the blockage ratio is small, the restriction of the pipeline to the particles is weaker, and the spacing of the particles cannot be kept stable.

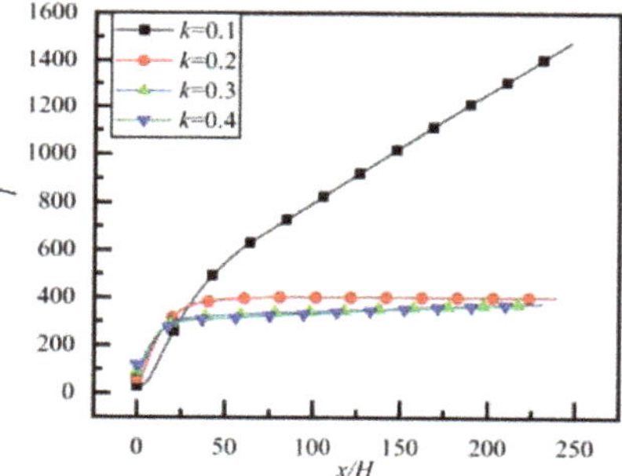

Figure 7. Changes in the spacing of a pair of single-scale particles at different blocking ratios (Re = 20).

4.2. A Pair of Dual-Scale Particles

In order to study the effect of the interaction between particles of different sizes, the following provides the results of the influence of size ratios of particles, Reynolds number, and blocking ratio on particle inertial migration. The flow field and the position of the particles are shown in Figure 8. The particles migrate from left to right.

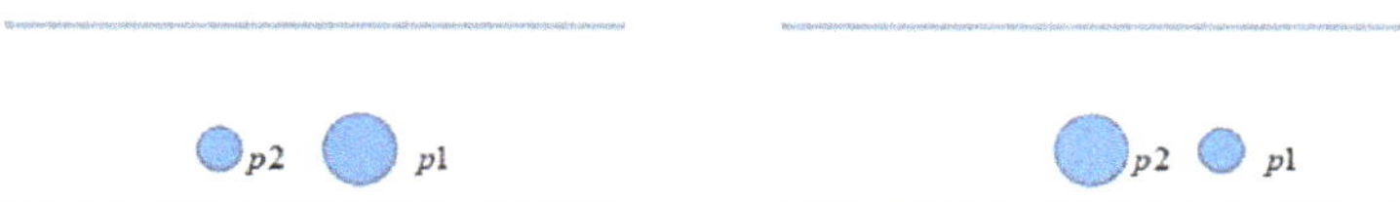

Figure 8. A schematic diagram of the migration of a pair of particles of different sizes.

4.2.1. Effect of Size Ratio of Particles

Figure 9 shows the effect of the size ratio of two particles on the distance between the two particles. The particle size ratio is defined $\beta = D_{p1}/D_{p2}$, which represents the ratio of the downstream particle diameter to the upstream particle diameter, blocking ratio $k = 0.125{\sim}0.3$ ($k = D/H$), particle diameter $D_p = 18.75\Delta x, 22.5\Delta x, 30\Delta x, 37.5\Delta x, 45\Delta x$. As shown in Figure 9a, when the small particle is downstream, the inter-particle spacing will continue to increase and cannot remain stable; when the large particle is downstream, the inter-particle spacing increases at the beginning and then decreases, and finally stabilizes, Gao et al. [14] found that mixed particle trains often begin with a large particle and end with a small one; two particles of the same size and the spacing increases monotonously, which is consistent with the numerical results of Hu et al. [10] and Lee et al. [6]. The reason is that, when the large particle is downstream, the weak production by the large particle forms a large reversing streamline zone, which has a very large impact on the small particle downstream. The small particle and the large particle form a stable structure; the difference between the velocity of the particles is small, so the spacing between particles can eventually remain stable. In this case, when the small particle is downstream, the reverse streamline area formed by the wake of the small particle has little effect on the large particle. The velocity of the small particle is relatively higher, and the distance between the particles cannot be kept stable.

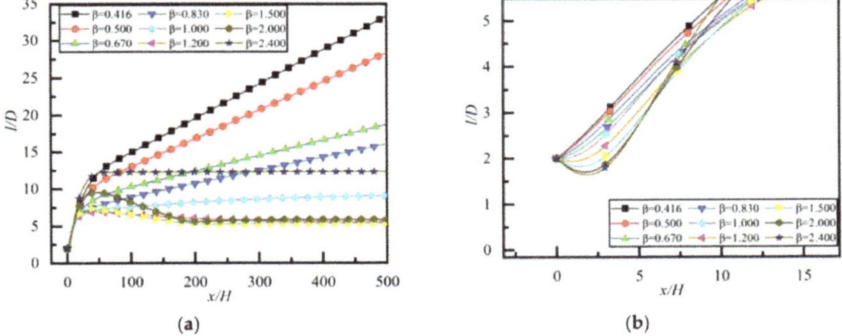

Figure 9. Effect of size ratio of particles on the distance between two particles ($2000 \times 150\Delta x$, Re = 20); (**a**) for a long distance along the flow direction; (**b**) at the initial stage.

As shown in Figure 9b, at the initial stage of particle movement, if the large particle is downstream and the small particle is upstream, the inter-particle spacing will first decrease and then increase; if the small particle is downstream and large particle is upstream, the distance between particles will increase monotonously, and there will be no collisions between particles. This is because of the small inertia of the small particle, which shows that the small particle follows well and, at the initial stage, it accelerates faster.

Figure 10 is a schematic diagram of particle movement from t0 to t6, and the time interval is equal. (a) shows the situation of small particle downstream; the spacing between particles keeps increasing and the relative velocity between particles increases first and then tends to level off. (b) shows the situation of large particle downstream; it can be seen that the spacing between particles first increases and then decreases.

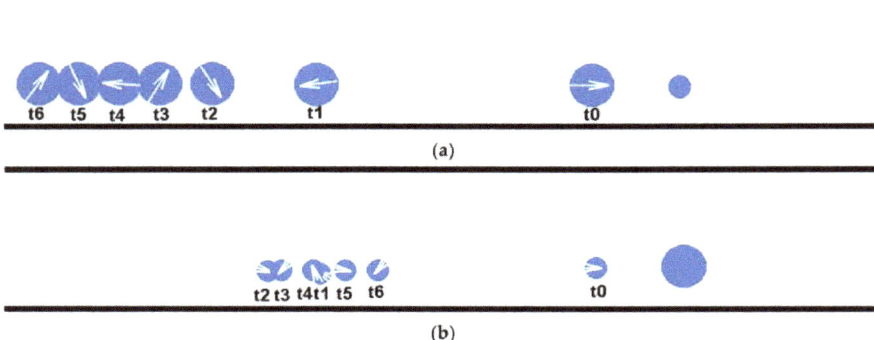

Figure 10. Schematic diagram of particle movement (the downstream particle is relatively immobile); (**a**) Small particle is downstream; (**b**) Big particle is downstream.

4.2.2. Effect of Reynolds Number

Figure 11 shows the effect of Reynolds number on the distance between two particles. It can be seen that, when β = 0.5, that is, when the small particle are downstream, the larger the Reynolds number, the larger the inter-particle spacing, and the particle spacing cannot be kept stable. The larger the Reynolds number, the greater the resistance to the large particle, so the spacing becomes wider and wider. When β = 2.0, that is, when the large particle is downstream, the larger the Reynolds number, the smaller the inter-particle spacing, and the inter-particle spacing can remain stable within the studied Reynolds number range. Gao et al. [14] and Hu et al. [10] used experimental and numerical simulation methods, respectively, to find that the average distance between particles in a single-line particle trains decreased with the increase in Re. The larger the Reynolds number, the greater the resistance to the large particle, and the greater the effect of wake on the small particle downstream, so the spacing remains stable.

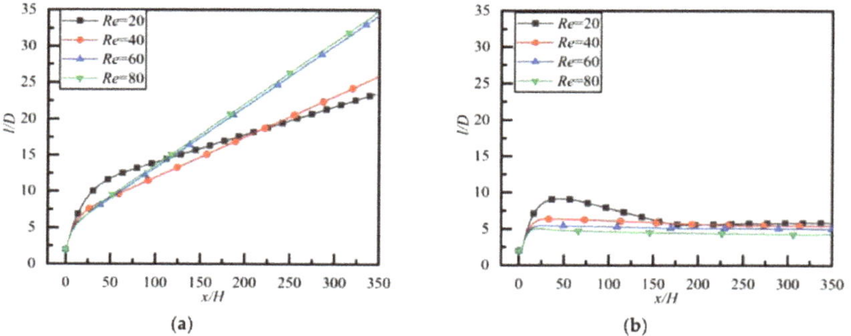

Figure 11. Effect of Reynolds number on the distance between two particles; (**a**) β = 0.5; (**b**) β = 2.0.

4.3. The Equilibrium Position of the Particles

The equilibrium position of a single particle is shown in Figure 12. It can be seen that the particles tend to the equilibrium position quickly. For particles with a low blocking rate, the equilibrium position of the particles is closer to the wall, which is consistent with the numerical results of Hu et al. [10]. The equilibrium positions of two particles of different scales are shown in Figure 13. When small particles are downstream, their equilibrium positions are closer to the center-line of the pipeline, while the equilibrium positions of large particles remain unchanged. The speed of small particles is greater than that of large particles, resulting in a continuous increase in the spacing of particles. When large particles are downstream, their equilibrium position is basically unaffected, while the equilibrium position of downstream small particles is closer to the wall. The speed of small particles is lower than that of large particles, and the distance between the particles remains unchanged after a series of oscillating migration. Figure 14 shows the change in the equilibrium position of the smaller particle when compared with a single particle.

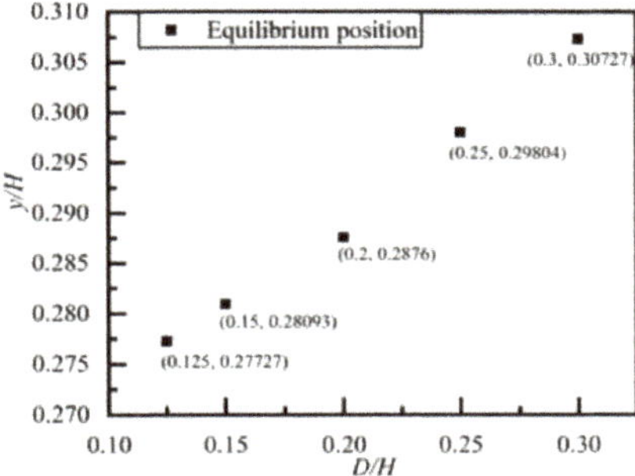

Figure 12. The equilibrium position of a single particle at different blocking ratios.

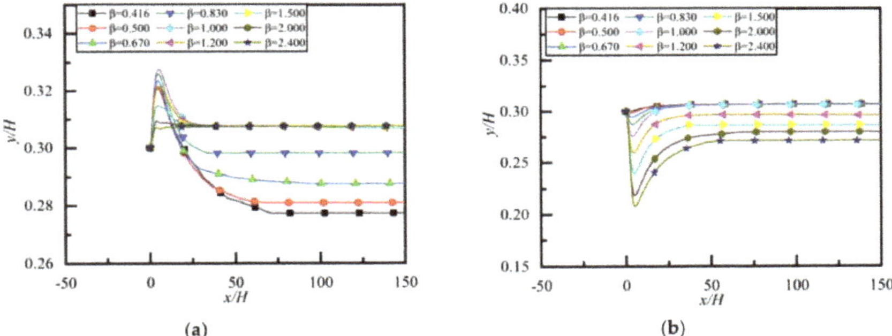

(a)

(b)

Figure 13. Changes in the equilibrium position of upstream and downstream particles; (**a**) equilibrium position of p1 particles; (**b**) equilibrium position of p2 particles.

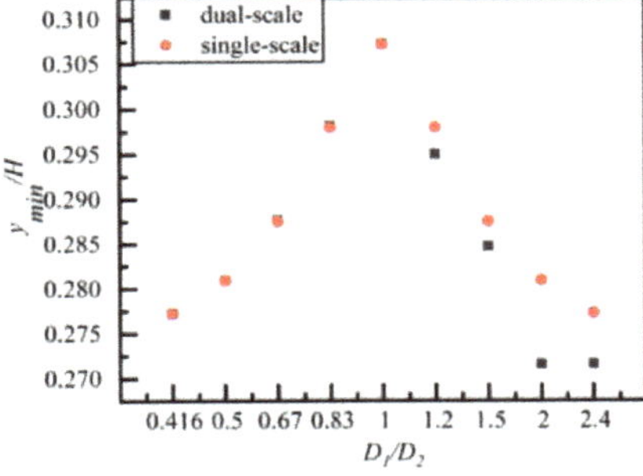

Figure 14. Changes in the equilibrium position of the smaller particle.

5. Conclusions

In this paper, the LBM method is used to study the inertial migration characteristics of single-scale and dual-scale particles in channel flow. The results show that, in the case of a high blocking ratio, the final particle spacing of two particles of equal diameter released at the same height does not change with the change in the initial spacing of the particles. For two particles of different sizes, the equilibrium position of the large particle is almost the same as that of a single particle, while the equilibrium position of the small particle has changed. When the large particle is upstream, the equilibrium position of the small particles is closer to the wall; when the small particle is upstream, the equilibrium position of the small particle is closer to the center line. When the large particle is downstream, the inter-particle spacing can eventually remain stable, while, when the small particle is downstream, the spacing between the two particles will continue to increase and cannot be stabilized. When the small particle is downstream, the larger the Reynolds number, the larger the inter-particle spacing, and the particle spacing cannot be balanced. When the large particle is downstream, the larger the Reynolds number, the smaller the inter-particle spacing, and the spacing remains stable within the studied Reynolds number range.

Author Contributions: Conceptualization, J.L. and D.C.; Methodology, D.C. and X.H.; Mathematical modeling and solution, D.C. and X.H.; Writing—original draft preparation, D.C.; Writing—review and editing, J.L. All authors have read and agreed to the published version of the manuscript.

Funding: This work was supported by the National Natural Science Foundation of China (Grant no. 11632016).

Institutional Review Board Statement: Not applicable.

Informed Consent Statement: Not applicable.

Data Availability Statement: Not applicable.

Conflicts of Interest: There are no conflict of interest regarding the publication of this paper.

References

1. Zhang, Y.; Zhang, J.; Tang, F.; Li, W.; Wang, X. Design of a Single-Layer Microchannel for Continuous Sheathless Single-Stream Particle Inertial Focusing. *Anal. Chem.* **2018**, *90*, 1786–1794. [CrossRef] [PubMed]
2. Yan, S.; Zhang, J.; Yuan, D.; Li, W. Hybrid microfluidics combined with active and passive approaches for continuous cell separation. *Electrophoresis* **2017**, *38*, 238–249. [CrossRef] [PubMed]
3. Godino, N.; Jorde, F.; Lawlor, D.; Jaeger, M.; Duschl, C. Purification of microalgae from bacterial contamination using a disposable inertia-based microfluidic device. *J. Micromech. Microeng.* **2015**, *25*, 84002. [CrossRef]
4. Xuan, X.; Zhu, J.; Church, C. Particle focusing in microfluidic devices. *Microfluid. Nanofluid.* **2010**, *9*, 1–16. [CrossRef]
5. Segré, G.; Silberberg, A. Radial particle displacements in poiseuille flow of suspensions. *Nature* **1961**, *189*, 209. [CrossRef]
6. Lee, W.; Amini, H.; Stone, H.A.; Di Carlo, D. Dynamic self-assembly and control of microfluidic particle crystals. *Proc. Natl. Acad. Sci. USA* **2010**, *107*, 22413–22418. [CrossRef] [PubMed]
7. Matas, J.; Glezer, V.; Guazzelli, É.; Morris, J.F. Trains of particles in finite-Reynolds-number pipe flow. *Phys. Fluids* **2004**, *16*, 4192–4195. [CrossRef]
8. Gao, Y.; Magaud, P.; Baldas, L.; Lafforgue, C.; Abbas, M.; Colin, S. Self-ordered particle trains in inertial microchannel flows. *Microfluid. Nanofluid.* **2017**, *21*, 154. [CrossRef]
9. Hu, X.; Lin, J.; Ku, X. Inertial migration of circular particles in Poiseuille flow of a power-law fluid. *Phys. Fluids* **2019**, *31*, 72206.
10. Hu, X.; Lin, J.; Chen, D.; Ku, X. Stability condition of self-organizing staggered particle trains in channel flow. *Microfluid. Nanofluidics* **2020**, *24*, 1–12. [CrossRef]
11. Morris, J.F. High-speed trains: In microchannels? *J. Fluid Mech.* **2016**, *792*, 1–4. [CrossRef]
12. Mach, A.J.; Di Carlo, D. Continuous scalable blood filtration device using inertial microfluidics. *Biotechnol. Bioeng.* **2010**, *107*, 302–311. [CrossRef] [PubMed]
13. Zhou, J.; Papautsky, I. Fundamentals of inertial focusing in microchannels. *Lab Chip* **2013**, *13*, 1121–1132. [CrossRef] [PubMed]
14. Gao, Y.; Magaud, P.; Lafforgue, C.; Colin, S.; Baldas, L. Inertial lateral migration and self-assembly of particles in bidisperse suspensions in microchannel flows. *Microfluid. Nanofluid.* **2019**, *23*, 93. [CrossRef]
15. Qian, Y.H.; Dhumieres, D.; Lallemand, P. Lattice Bgk Models for Navier-Stokes Equation. *Europhys. Lett.* **1992**, *17*, 479–484. [CrossRef]
16. He, Y.L.; Wang, Y.; Li, Q. *Theory and Application of Lattice Boltzmann Method*; Science Press: Beijing, China, 2009.
17. He, X.Y.; Shan, X.W.; Doolen, G.D. Discrete Boltzmann equation model for nonideal gases. *Phys. Rev. E* **1998**, *57*, R13–R16. [CrossRef]
18. Chen, S.; Doolen, G.D. Lattice Boltzmann method for fluid flows. *Annu. Rev. Fluid Mech.* **1998**, *30*, 329–364. [CrossRef]
19. Glowinski, R.; Pan, T.W.; Hesla, T.I.; Joseph, D.D.; Périaux, J. A Fictitious Domain Approach to the Direct Numerical Simulation of Incompressible Viscous Flow past Moving Rigid Bodies: Application to Particulate Flow. *J. Comput. Phys.* **2001**, *169*, 363–426. [CrossRef]
20. Feng, Z.; Michaelides, E.E. The immersed boundary-lattice Boltzmann method for solving fluid–particles interaction problems. *J. Comput. Phys.* **2004**, *195*, 602–628. [CrossRef]

Article

Numerical Study on the Rising Motion of Bubbles near the Wall

Kaixin Zhang, Yongzheng Li, Qi Chen and Peifeng Lin *

Key Laboratory of Fluid Transmission Technology of Zhejiang Province, Zhejiang Sci-Tech University, Hangzhou 310018, China; 202030606392@mails.zstu.edu.cn (K.Z.); 201920501055@mails.zstu.edu.cn (Y.L.); 202130606395@mails.zstu.edu.cn (Q.C.)
* Correspondence: linpf@zstu.edu.cn

Abstract: Based on the volume of fluid method (VOF), the rising characteristics of bubbles in near-wall static water are studied. In this study, the influence of the wall on the rising motion of the bubble was studied by changing the distance of the bubble wall, the diameter of the bubble, the arrangement of the bubble and the size ratio, etc. The influence is expressed as the average swing amplitude of the "Z"-shaped motion when the bubble rises. The study found that in the case of a single bubble, the wall surface has a certain influence on the rise of the bubble, and its degree is affected by the bubble wall distance and the bubble diameter. The influence of bubble wall distance is more obvious. The greater the bubble wall distance, the less the bubble is affected by the wall; in the case of double bubbles, the influence of the interaction force between the bubbles is significantly greater than the wall surface.

Keywords: gas-liquid two-phase flow; bubbles near the wall; numerical simulation; volume of fluid method

Citation: Zhang, K.; Li, Y.; Chen, Q.; Lin, P. Numerical Study on the Rising Motion of Bubbles near the Wall. *Appl. Sci.* **2021**, *11*, 10918. https://doi.org/10.3390/app112210918

Academic Editor: Artur Tyliszczak

Received: 20 October 2021
Accepted: 15 November 2021
Published: 18 November 2021

Publisher's Note: MDPI stays neutral with regard to jurisdictional claims in published maps and institutional affiliations.

1. Introduction

Two-phase flow is a very common phenomenon. As an important branch of fluid mechanics, it began to develop rapidly in the 1960s. It is mainly used to study the interaction between two phases and the changes in flow patterns and motion disciplines. Generally, it is divided into gas-liquid two-phase flow, solid-liquid two-phase flow and liquid-liquid two-phase flow according to the phase state of the substances constituting the flow system [1]. Gas-liquid two-phase flow is one of the most common types of multi-phase flow. It refers to the flow phenomenon of gas-phase fluid and liquid-phase fluid in the same flow system [2,3]. The motion and change of the gas phase in the flow will affect the characteristics of the two-phase flow. Therefore, studying the motion discipline of the gas phase is the key to studying the characteristics of the two-phase flow.

The rise of bubbles in water is a very complicated and unstable process. The bubbles continue to rise in the water. Due to the combined action of gravity, buoyancy and surface tension, bubbles will deform, burst and coalesce. Eventually, the rising path of the bubble will be unstable, usually spiral, "Z"-shaped motion, etc. [4,5]. Bubbles deform and break into many μm-level micro-bubbles during their rising motion. The bubbles usually appear in the form of micro-bubble groups, so it is also very important to study the interaction between bubbles. In this article, the influence of the wall surface on the motion characteristics of single and double bubbles will be explored, and the discipline of motion of bubbles near the wall will be studied.

Since the discipline of bubble motion in liquid is widely used in the chemical industry, bubble dynamics theory was established to study the bubble motion and the interaction between bubbles [6]. At present, many scholars have conducted researches on the motion discipline of a single bubble and the motion discipline of bubble groups. The American scientist Clift et al. [7,8] studied the shape change of bubbles in the liquid after consulting a large number of data in the literature. According to the dimensionless criterion, they drew the bubble shape phase diagram, which is called the Grace diagram. Some scholars [9–11] also verified the bubble shape phase diagram obtained by Clift, and found that the result is consistent with the bubble phase diagram. Duineveld [12] found that when the equivalent diameter of the bubble is less than 1.8 mm, because the bubble shape tends to be spherical, the rising path presents a straight line; when the equivalent diameter of the bubble exceeds 1.8 mm, the path of bubble will change from a straight line to a "Z" shape. The bubble-free surface interaction has been experimentally investigated by Robinson et al. [13], when bubbles are close together, their mutual interactions can influence the existence of free surfaces. These factors can influence the migratory behavior and lifetime of the bubbles. Sugiyam et al. [14] studied the near-wall motion of deformable bubbles in viscous fluids, and found that the bubbles have a significant lateral deviation in the wall domain. When the distance between the bubble and the wall changes, the bubble will bounce due to the pressure difference between the two sides and the lift between the wall, which is the "Z"-shaped motion path mentioned above. Chen et al. [15] tracked the three-dimensional deformation of the two-phase interface based on the numerical simulation method of Front Tracking and compared the data with unbounded still water. They found that the bubbles around the wall would be suppressed by the wall, causing the bubbles to gradually deviate from the wall. Tatineni et al. [16]further proposed a high-resolution numerical method based on the level set method to solve the motion and deformation of the gas-liquid interface. It is found that the rising bubbles will be affected by the wall surface and migrate laterally to the central domain when they are close to the wall surface. And the closer the bubble wall is, the greater the influence of the wall on the bubble. Many scholars have also conducted research on the rise of multiple bubbles. Komasawa et al. [17] studied the motion characteristics of stationary bubbles in downward flowing water, and found that the experimental results are consistent with the motion characteristics of bubbles rising freely. At the same time, they also studied the effect of bubble wake on bubbles. Ohta et al. [18] examined the influence of initial bubble conditions on bubble rise motion, two-dimensional direct numerical simulations of the motion of a gas bubble rising in viscous liquids were carried out by a coupled level set/volume-of-fluid method. The results show that the smaller the distance between two bubbles, the greater the influence on their respective velocity fields, and the easier it is for the bubbles to attract and fuse with each other.

In this article, the motion characteristics of bubbles in water are studied by using the VOF method in Fluent. By changing the bubble diameter, bubble wall distance, etc., the motion path, rising speed, and surrounding flow field changes of the bubbles in the near-wall domain are studied to analyze the changes in the bubble motion characteristics. On the basis of the single-bubble research, the double-bubble research is carried out. The double-bubble is used to analyze the interaction between the bubbles, and the bubble interaction and wall influence are analyzed and studied by changing the arrangement of the bubbles.

2. Numerical Simulation Method

2.1. Governing Equation

The problem of two-phase interface is usually calculated by capturing the phase interface and performing numerical simulation. The more commonly used methods are the Volume of Fluid (VOF) method [19–21] and the Level Set (LS) method [22,23]. In this article, the VOF method is used to track the gas-liquid interface to study the motion of bubbles. The VOF method establishes the two-phase intersection interface based on the volume ratio function. The sum of the volume fraction of each phase is 1, so the maximum value is 1 [24]. Since the phases are not interspersed with each other, each additional phase only needs to increase the volume fraction function of the corresponding phase. In the VOF model, suppose there is a two-phase fluid, and mark the calculation domain as S, then the domain where fluid A and fluid B are located can be represented by S^A and S^B.

For the continuity equation of incompressible fluid, the governing equation of bubble motion is:

$$\nabla \cdot u = 0 \tag{1}$$

$$\frac{\partial \alpha_A}{\partial t} + u_A \nabla \alpha_A = \frac{S^A}{\rho_A} + \frac{1}{\rho_A}\sum_{B=1}^{n} = 1(\dot{m}_{BA} - \dot{m}_{AB}) \tag{2}$$

where α_A is the volume fraction of the fluid A; u_A is the velocity vector of the fluid A, $m \cdot s^{-1}$; ρ is the density, $kg \cdot m^{-3}$; m_{BA} is the mass transport from the B (A) phase to the A(B) phase, kg.

Where $\overline{V}(u,v)$ is the velocity field of the fluid, ΔV_{ij} is the volume of a single grid, and Q_{ij} is defined on each grid I_{ij} as the integral of $\alpha(\overline{x}, t)$ on the grid:

$$Q_{ij} = \frac{1}{\Delta V_{ij}} \int_{I_{ij}} \alpha(\overline{x}, t)dV \tag{3}$$

Equation (3) is the VOF function, and it also satisfies:

$$\frac{\partial Q}{\partial t} + u\frac{\partial Q}{\partial x} + v\frac{\partial Q}{\partial y} = 0 \tag{4}$$

Equation (4) is the VOF equation. From the above, it can be seen that the volume function of each phase is essentially the ratio of the phase volume to the grid volume in the grid.

The momentum conservation equation considering surface tension is as follow:

$$\rho\left[\frac{\partial u}{\partial t} + (u \cdot \nabla)u\right] = -\nabla p + \nabla \cdot (2\mu D) + \rho g + \varphi \tag{5}$$

where φ is surface tension, p is pressure, μ is dynamic viscosity coefficient.

2.2. Geometric Model

In the calculation of the two-dimensional plane domain, in order to ensure that the bubble has obvious deformation, and will not cause the bubble rising instability due to excessive deformation, the initial bubble with a diameter of $d = 4$ mm is selected and simulated. The entire domain is 80 mm long and 160 mm high. The height of the liquid level is 140 mm and the initial height of the bubble is 20 mm. The distance from the bubble to the bottom surface is 5 times its diameter, and the distance from the non-researched side wall is greater than 10 times the diameter, which can eliminate the influence of the non-researched side wall and the bottom surface of the bubble motion as much as possible. Taking a bubble with an initial diameter of 4 mm and a bubble wall distance of 4 mm as an example, the calculation domain is shown in Figure 1. Other bubbles with different diameters are the same as in this case.

The mesh of the model is drawn by ICEM software. The two groups of models in this article have regular structures and simple shapes, and the mesh is divided into structured grids.

Figure 2 is the grid division of the two-dimensional calculation model. The quadrilateral structure grid is used. The minimum size of the grid is 0.2 mm. Due to the need to study the motion of the wall bubbles, boundary refinement is used, and the overall grid number is 150,000. The gas used in the simulation is air, and the liquid is liquid water. Both physical properties and parameters under normal temperature and pressure are used. Except for the verification of the VOF method, the same gravity and surface tension are used. The surface tension of liquid is 0.0728 N/m.

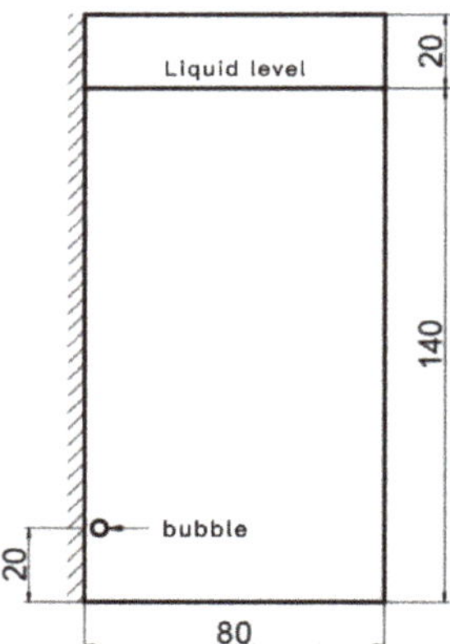

Figure 1. Two-dimensional calculation domain of the near-wall bubble with an initial diameter of 4 mm.

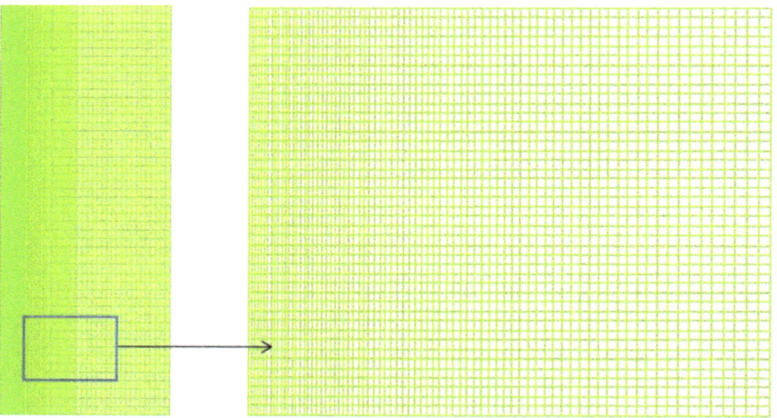

Figure 2. Global grid and local grid of 2D model.

In the two-dimensional model, the top is set to PRESSURE-OUTLET, and the gauge pressure is 0 Pa; the rest of the walls are set to WALL, and the wall uses no-slip boundary conditions.

2.3. Grid Independence and Algorithm Verification

For the research on the rise of bubbles with a diameter of 4 mm in the two-dimensional calculation domain, this article divides into four kinds of grids of 80,000, 100,000, 150,000 and 200,000 to verify the independence of the grid. This research refers to the verification method for grid independence in the article by Wang [25]. The position change of the top and bottom of the bubble over time was used to verify grid independence. The top and bottom positions of the bubble are shown in Figure 3.

Figure 4a,b are the curves of the height of the top and bottom of the bubble rising with time. It can be seen from the curve that the number of grids in the four cases basically coincides with the curve, and there is no big difference. Therefore, the grid independence is verified. In this study, 150,000 grids are used for numerical simulation.

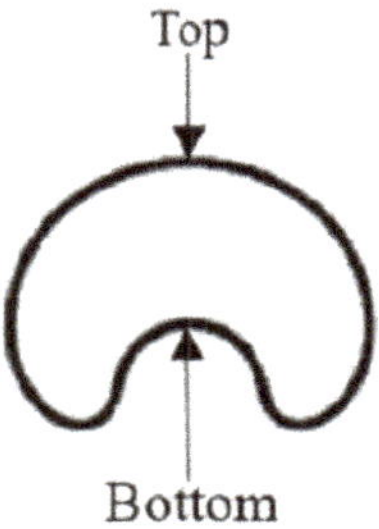

Figure 3. Schematic diagram of the top and bottom of the bubble in the literature.

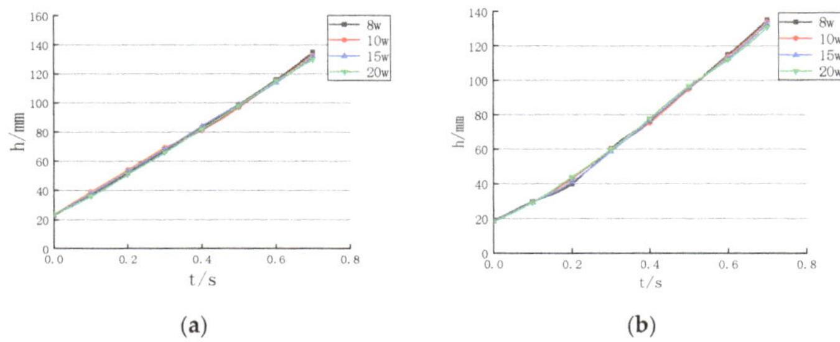

(a)   (b)

Figure 4. The change curve of bubble position with time under different grid numbers: (**a**) Top (**b**) Bottom.

Before the numerical simulation, the correctness of choosing the VOF model for calculation is first verified in this article. In Figure 5, Wang et al. [25] studied the rising deformation of bubbles with different diameters. In our current project, the bubble diameters are all below 10 mm, the rising deformation of 7.5 mm bubbles is verified in Figure 6, so it is proved that this article chooses to use VOF for calculation.

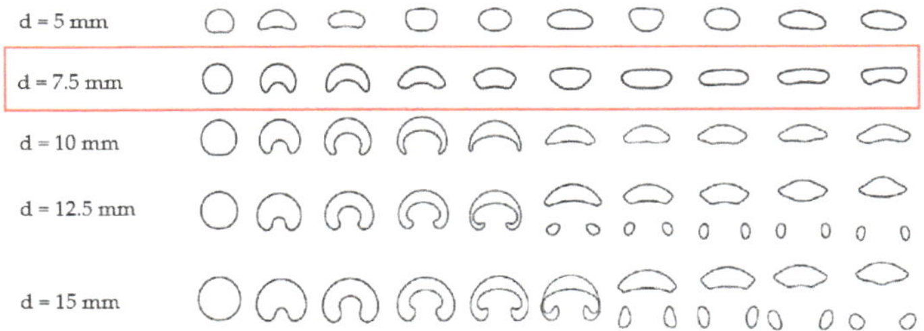

Figure 5. Deformation during rising of bubbles of different diameters.

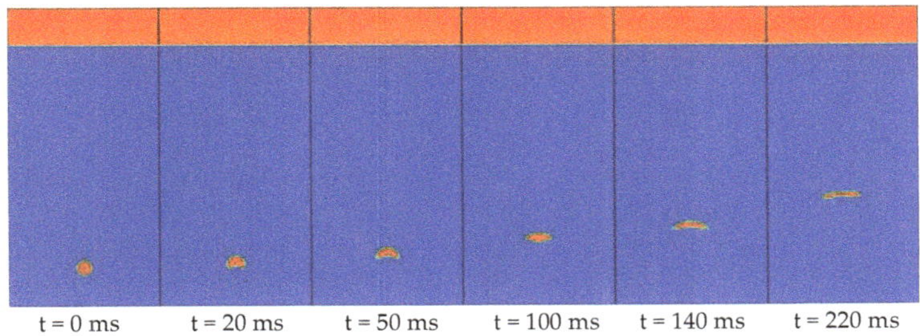

Figure 6. The rising and deformation process of a single central circular bubble without boundary.

3. Numerical Simulation Results

3.1. Analysis of Single Bubble Motion near the Wall

When the bubble rises freely, the bubble will rise in a straight line; when the bubble is located near the wall, the bubble will swing and rise in a "Z" shape. In this section, when the bubble diameter is fixed at 4 mm, the bubble wall distance and bubble diameter are changed, and the influence of the wall surface on the rise of the bubble is analyzed. In this article, the distance is defined as the dimensionless quantity S^*.

$$S^* = \frac{D_e}{D_0} \tag{6}$$

where D_e is the distance between the wall and the center of the bubble, that is, the distance from the bubble wall, D_0 is bubble diameter, L_n is the last observable swing amplitude of the bubble, T_n is the last observable full cycle of the bubble swing.

3.1.1. The Influence of Bubble Wall Distance

Figure 7a is the ascending path of the 4 mm bubble at $S^* = 0.75, 1.0, 1.25, 1.5$. The bubble rises linearly in a certain path, and then begins to deviate to the side away from the wall to swing up in a "Z" shape. Figure 7b adjusts the origin of the X axis of the four types of bubbles. The origin of the X axis is set to the X coordinate corresponding to the center of the bubble, so that the starting points of the bubble path are all fitted together. The path difference between the bubbles can be seen more intuitively.

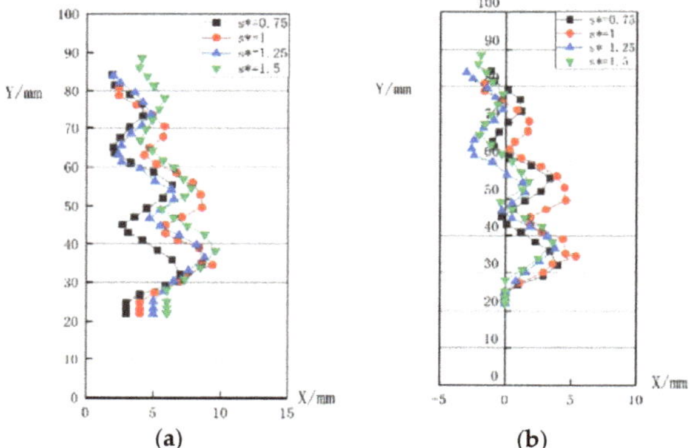

Figure 7. Bubble motion path diagram under different S*: (**a**) Different initial position, (**b**) Same initial position.

In the Table 1, L is the average swing amplitude of the bubble, and F is the average swing frequency of the bubble. When S^* becomes larger, the bubble gradually moves away from the wall, and the swing amplitude of the bubble gradually decreases, while the swing frequency of the bubble increases. The influence of the wall on the bubble gradually weakens as the bubble moves away. In the table, H_{max} represents the maximum rise height of the bubble during the 500 ms monitoring time. In H_{max}, the rise height is the lowest when $S^* = 1$, and when S^* becomes larger, the bubble height also becomes higher.

Table 1. Numerical table of bubble rise swing under different S*.

S*	L_1/mm	L_2/mm	L_3/mm	L_4/mm	L_5/mm	L/mm	H_{max}/mm	F/s^{-1}
0.75	4.0	4.3	3.4	4.4	2.2	3.66	84.4	4.16
1	5.4	3.5	2.7	4.3	1.5	3.48	80.8	4.42
1.25	3.8	4.1	1.8	4.1	2.4	3.22	84	4.69
1.5	3.6	4.0	2.2	3.8	1.8	3.08	88.6	4.85

Figure 8 shows the average rising speed of the bubble every 20 ms in 500 ms. From Table 2, it can be seen that when the bubble rises, the speed will gradually increase, and when it reaches a certain value, it will gradually stabilize and fluctuate up and down within a certain range. The farther the bubble is from the wall, the faster the initial rising speed increases. From the two curves of $S^* = 1$ and $S^* = 0.75$, it can be found that when the bubble rises in contact with the wall, the speed will be faster than the free rise of the bubble. It can be seen from Table 2 that the overall rising speed of the bubble within 500 ms can also prove that the bubble bounce motion will rise faster than the free motion.

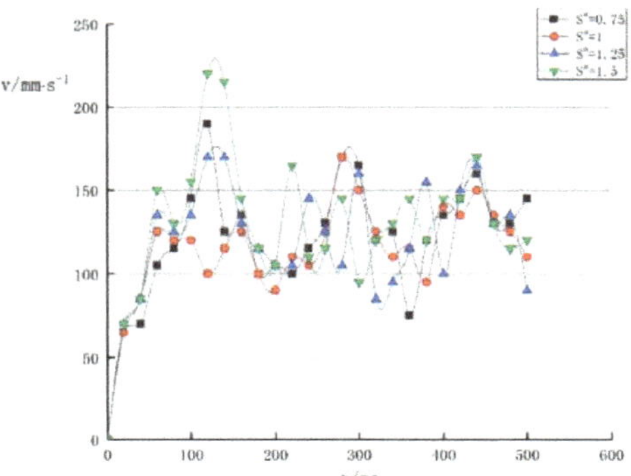

Figure 8. Graphs of the average rising velocity of bubbles under different S*.

Table 2. Numerical table of rising swing amplitude of bubbles with different diameters.

Bubble Diameter /mm	L_1/mm	L_2/mm	L_3/mm	L_4/mm	L_5/mm	L/mm	H_{max}/mm	F/s^{-1}
4	3.6	4.0	2.2	3.8	1.8	3.08	88.6	4.85
5	3.7	5	4.2	3.1	–	4.0	94.4	4.24
6	3.4	3.7	7.3	4.6	–	4.75	99	3.57

It can be seen from Figure 9a,b that the flow field of bubbles rising near the wall is different from the flow field of bubbles rising in unbounded still water. Due to the influence of the left wall, the flow field on the left side of the fluid flows closer to the left side of the bubble, and the flow velocity direction is more. It is the tangent direction of the left side of the bubble. The flow velocity on the left side will be faster than that of unbounded static water, resulting in the formation of the flow field at the bottom of the bubble forming a situation where the left side is less and the right side is more, which further causes the clockwise deflection of the bubble.

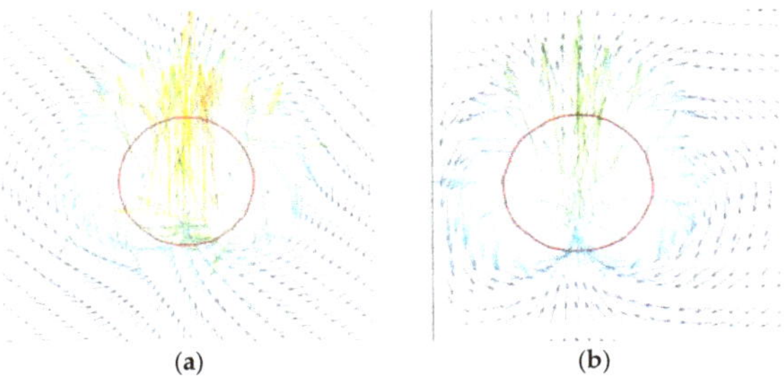

(a)   (b)

Figure 9. The velocity vector generated by the near-wall bubble and the central bubble rising 10 ms: (**a**) The central bubble, (**b**) The near-wall bubble.

3.1.2. Influence of Bubble Diameter

Table 2 shows the swing amplitude when the bubble rises with diameters of 4, 5, and 6 mm and the rise height within 500 ms when $S^* = 1.5$. It can be seen from the table that when the bubble diameter becomes larger, the average swing amplitude of the bubble increases.

Figure 10 during the rising process of the bubble, the overall upward path is still a straight upward first, and then a "Z"-shaped swing upward. However, it can be found that as the diameter increases, each deflection point of the bubble is rising, which means that the bubble swing frequency is decreasing, the bubble swing amplitude is increasing, and the average rising speed within 500 ms is also increasing. But the difference from the previous section is that the initial bubble rise speed decreases as the bubble diameter increases. It can also be seen in the figure that as the diameter of the bubble increases, the overall upward path of the bubble gradually deviates from the wall surface.

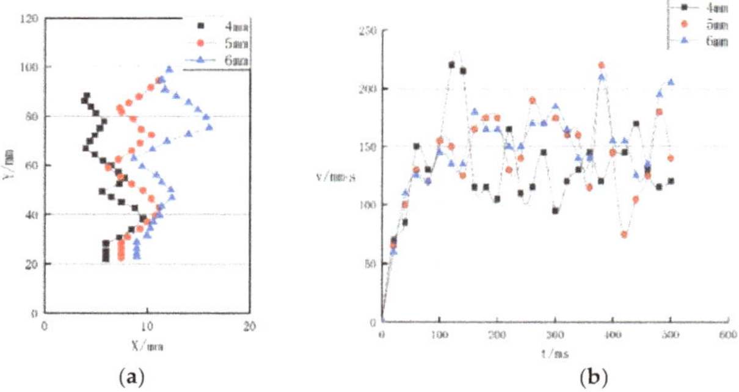

Figure 10. Bubble motion path and rising speed diagram under different diameters: (**a**) Motion path, (**b**) Ascent speed.

3.2. Analysis of the Motion of Double Bubbles near the Wall

3.2.1. Vertically Rising Bubbles

(1)　Double bubbles of equal diameter

Figure 11 shows the upward motion of two vertically arranged bubbles in the near-wall domain. The diameter of the bubbles is 4 mm, and the two bubbles are arranged vertically with a distance of 8 mm. At 100 ms, it can be found that the two bubbles are deflected away from the wall under the influence of the wall; At 115 ms, the deflection of the tail bubble recovers and it approaches the wall again, while the head bubble continues to move away from the wall; A large bubble is formed after two bubbles come into contact at 140 ms. From the bubble motion in the figure and the previous research, we can find that two bubbles with the same diameter and the same distance from the bubble wall produce different swing amplitudes in the near-wall domain. This shows that the effect of the near wall on the double bubble is different from that of the single bubble.

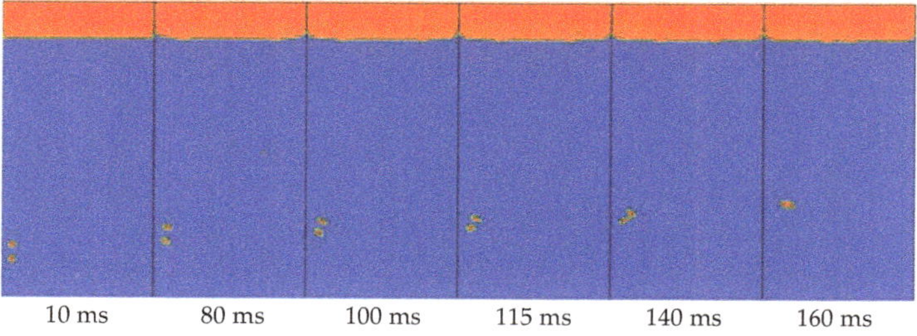

Figure 11. The shape change diagram of the rising double bubbles vertically arranged near the wall.

Figure 12 is the flow field diagram of the bubble at different moments. At 80 ms, the bubble moves away from the wall due to the influence of the wall at this time. At 110 ms, the bubble forms a wake vortex due to the deflection, and the right wake vortex of the head bubble has an impact on the tail bubble, causing the bubble to rotate counterclockwise to restore the deflection, resulting in a difference in the swing amplitude of the two bubbles.

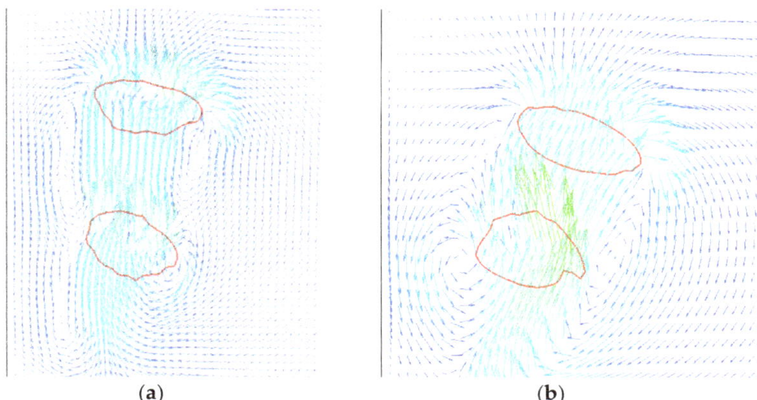

(**a**)　　　　(**b**)

Figure 12. Upward flow field diagrams of vertically arranged double bubbles at different moments: (**a**) 80 ms, (**b**) 110 ms.

(2)　The upper small and the lower large double bubbles

Figure 13 is a simulation of the rising motion of double bubbles of different sizes arranged vertically, with small head bubbles and large tail bubbles. From the figure, it can be found that the double bubbles of the same size are similar to those in the previous article. Both bubbles deflected away from the wall, and then merged.

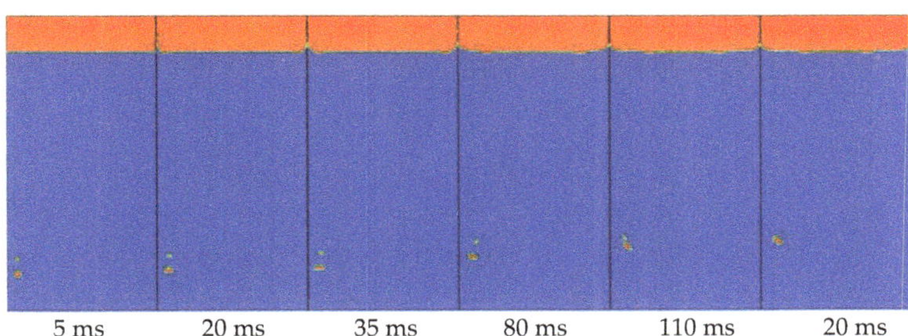

Figure 13. The rising shape of double bubbles of different sizes near the wall (upper small and lower large).

In Figure 14a, it can be found that the flow field of large bubbles is denser than that of small bubbles. This is the reason why the rising speed of large bubbles is faster than that of small bubbles; the big bubble is moving away from the wall, while the small bubble has recovered its deflection and is moving close to the wall. This result can be mutually confirmed with the near-wall motion of single bubbles with different diameters. Large bubbles are affected by the wall surface more obviously, with larger average swing amplitude and lower frequency.

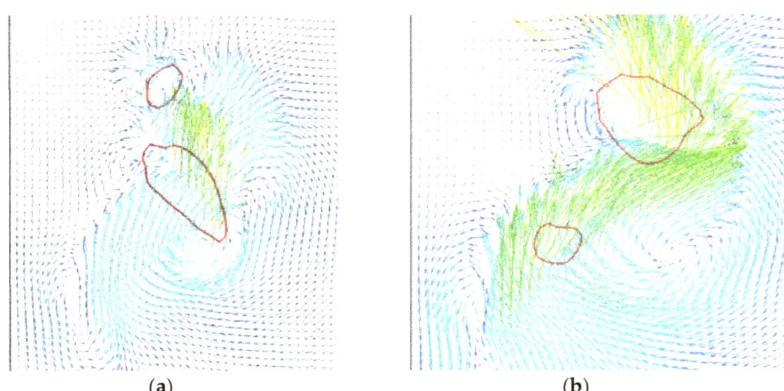

(a)   (b)

Figure 14. Upward flow field diagram of double bubbles of different sizes near the wall at 110 ms: (**a**) Upper small and lower large, (**b**) Upper big and lower small.

(3) The upper large and the lower small double bubbles

Figure 15 is a simulation of the rising motion of double bubbles of different sizes arranged vertically. The head bubble is large and the tail bubble is small. Contrary to the previous section, the bubbles still coalesce. It can be seen from the figure that it is different from the previous section. The big bubble first deflects at 70 ms, while the small bubble starts to deflect for the first time at 135 ms. The speed of the small bubble is faster than that of the big bubble. The two bubbles come into contact at 160 ms and then merge into one large bubble.

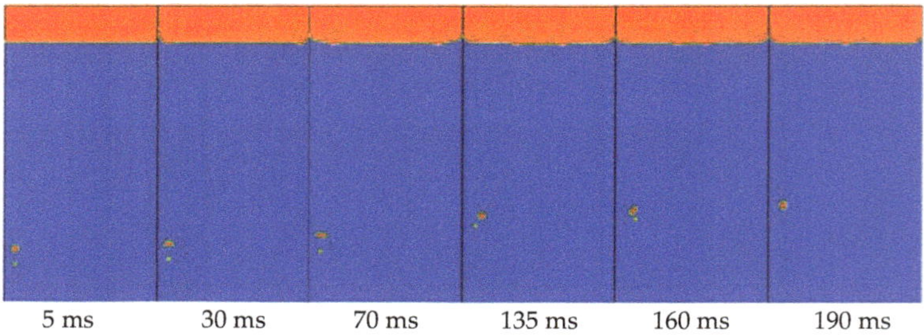

Figure 15. The rising shape of double bubbles of different sizes near the wall (upper large and lower small).

From Figure 14b, it can be seen that when the big bubble rises, a wake vortex is left at the tail. The small bubbles rise rapidly along the jet formed by the rising of the large bubbles, thus coming into contact with the large bubbles.

3.2.2. Horizontally Arranged Rising Bubbles

(1) Horizontal arrangement with 2 times diameter spacing

Figure 16 is a simulation of the upward motion of double bubbles arranged horizontally. The motion of the double bubble near the wall is similar to the motion of the free double bubble. The two bubbles separated first, then approached, and finally merged together. Compared with a single bubble, it can be found that the left bubble is not affected by the wall surface, and first deviates from the wall surface.

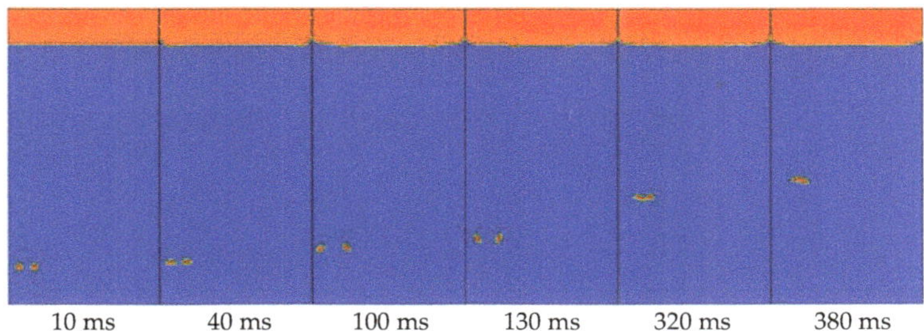

Figure 16. The shape change of the rising double bubbles arranged vertically near the wall.

Figure 17 shows the surrounding flow field distribution of two bubbles at 50 ms. At this time, the bubbles are beginning to move away from each other. When there is a single bubble near the wall, due to the influence of the left wall, the flow field on the left side of the fluid will flow closer to the left side of the bubble. The direction of the flow velocity is more the tangent direction of the left side of the bubble, and the flow velocity on the left will be faster than that of unbounded still water. As a result, the flow field at the bottom of the bubble forms a situation where the left side is less and the right side is more. In the case of double bubbles, it can be seen from the figure that two jets merge between the two bubbles, causing the two bubbles to have a fast flow velocity in the middle of the bubble and a slow flow velocity on both sides, thus forming a deflection of the two bubbles away from each other. The flow field on the left side of the left bubble is affected by the wall, and the flow field on the right side of the right bubble has no boundary. The bubble on the left will swing wider than the bubble on the right, and the overall path of the two bubbles will gradually deviate from the wall.

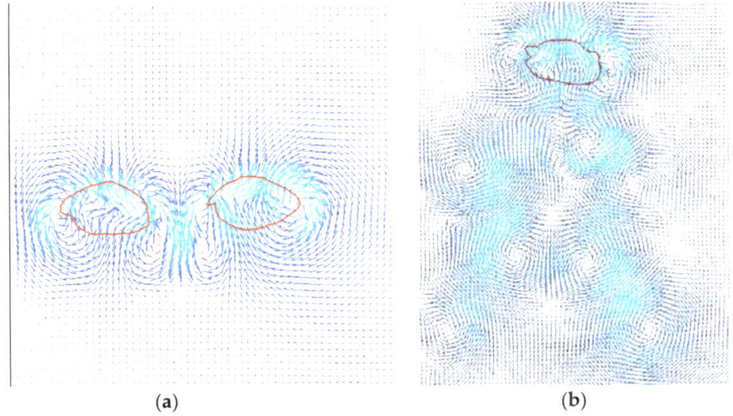

Figure 17. The flow field distribution diagram of the horizontally arranged near-wall double bubbles at the initial stage of rise and after the coalescence: (**a**) Bubbles before merging, (**b**) The merged bubbles.

(2)   Double bubbles arranged horizontally at 3 times diameter spacing

Figure 18 is the rising deformation diagram of the horizontally arranged double bubbles with the bubble spacing of 3 times the bubble diameter. It can be seen from the figure that the two bubbles did not coalesce, and the interaction between the bubbles became smaller due to the increase in the distance between the bubbles. So unlike the previous article, the bubbles are far away from each other, The left bubble also appeared to move away from the wall at 90 ms, and the left bubble came into contact with the wall at 500 ms. The rising form changes to bounce rising, and it is obvious that the left bubble rises faster at 850 ms. It is mutually corroborated with the conclusion of the bubble rising speed in the previous article.

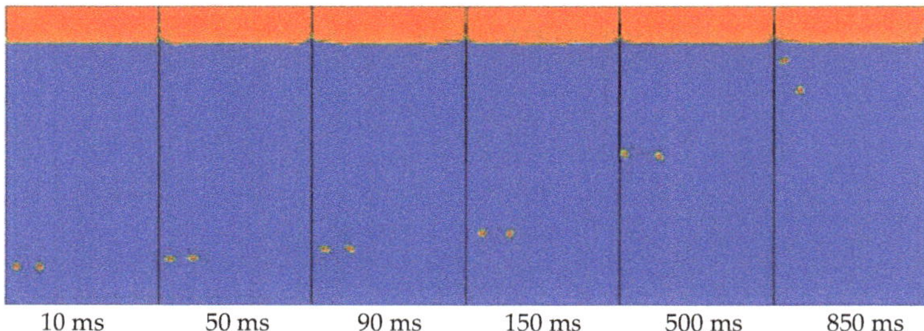

Figure 18. The shape change of the rising double bubbles arranged horizontally near the wall.

Figure 19 shows the flow field distribution of the bubble at 90 ms. It can be found that the deflection of the left bubble is slightly smaller than that of the right bubble. This is because the inducement of the deflection of the left bubble is that the influence of the wall surface is more obvious than the influence between the bubbles, and the jet formed on the wall promotes the deflection of the left bubble; The right bubble is the bubble deflection caused by the interaction between the bubbles, so compared with the two, the right bubble deflection is greater.

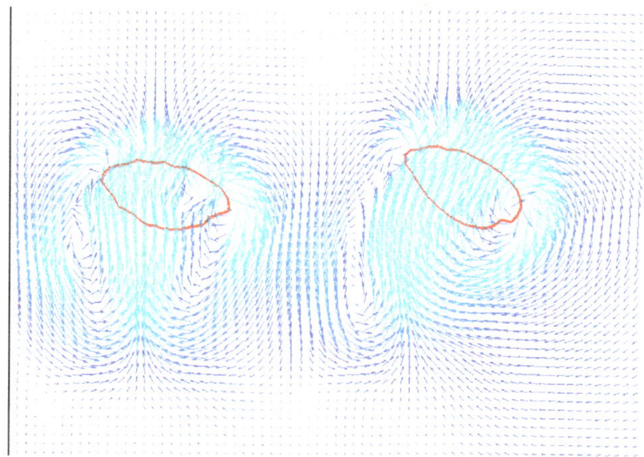

Figure 19. The upward flow field of double bubbles arranged horizontally near the wall at 90 ms.

(3)   Double bubbles arranged horizontally at 4 times diameter spacing

Figure 20 shows the rising deformation of horizontally arranged double bubbles with a bubble spacing of four times the diameter. It can be seen from the figure that at four times the diameter, the interaction between the bubbles becomes very insignificant, the right bubble basically rises in a straight line, and the rising speed of the right bubble is significantly faster than the left bubble at 850 ms. It can be confirmed that when the distance between the bubble wall and the bubble wall gradually increases, the influence of the wall surface on the bubble will gradually weaken, and the rising speed of the bubble will gradually increase.

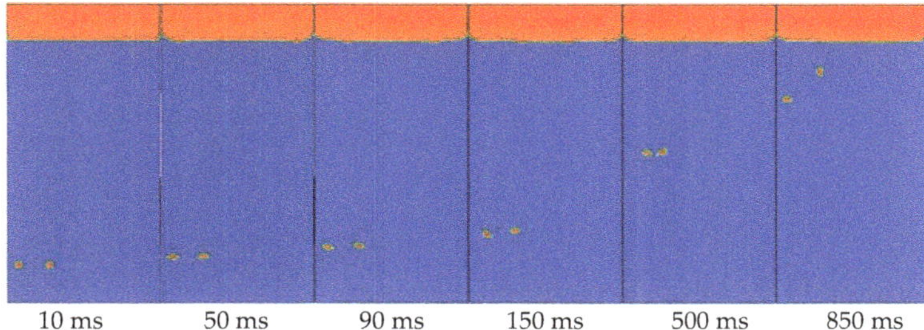

Figure 20. The shape change of the rising double bubbles arranged horizontally near the wall.

In summary, when the vertically arranged double bubbles of different sizes rise, with proper bubble spacing, coalescence can occur regardless of whether it is an arrangement of large top and small bottom or large top and small bottom. When the head bubbles are small, the reason for coalescence is that the big bubbles rise faster than the small bubbles; when the head bubbles are large, the coalescence is due to the jet flow generated when the large bubbles rise to accelerate the rising speed of the small bubbles.

4. Conclusions

This article takes the rising motion of bubbles in the near-wall domain as the research topic. Numerical simulations are used to analyze the rising motion characteristics of a single circular bubble and double circular bubbles in the domain near the wall, and explore the influence of the wall on the bubble rising, and the following conclusions are obtained:

(1)　When a single bubble rises near the wall, the bubble will be affected by the wall and change its original state of motion. The bubble first rises in a straight line, and then begins to swing upward. When S^* becomes larger, the height of bubble rising also becomes higher.

(2)　Under the condition that the diameter of the bubble is fixed, when $S^* < 1$, the bubble will touch the wall when it rises, and then form a bouncing upward motion; and when $S^* \geq 1$, the bubble will not touch the wall, and the bubble will rise straight up for a certain distance and then rise in a "Z" shape.

(3)　Numerical simulation results of the rising motion of a single bubble with a fixed diameter show that when S^* increases from 0.75 to 1.5, the bubble's average swing amplitude decreases from 3.66 mm to 3.08 mm, while the bubble's swing frequency decreases from 4.16 s^{-1} increases to 4.85 s^{-1}. The results of this study show that the distance of the bubble wall has an effect on the rising movement of the bubble. It is concluded that when the diameter is fixed, when S^* gradually becomes larger, that is, when the bubble gradually moves away from the wall, the swing amplitude of the bubble gradually decreases, and the swing frequency of the bubble follows. As the bubble increases, the influence of the wall on the bubble gradually weakens as the bubble moves away.

(4)　The result of numerical simulation of the rising motion of a single bubble with $S^* < 1$ shows that when the diameters are 4, 5, and 6 mm, the average swing amplitude of the bubble increases from 3.08 mm to 4.75 mm, and the swing frequency of the bubble increases from 4.85 s^{-1}. The law of change reduced to 3.57 s^{-1}. The results of this study indicate that the bubble diameter has an effect on the bubble's rising motion. It is concluded that when the bubble diameter gradually increases in the area near the wall, the swing amplitude of the bubble gradually increases, while the swing frequency of the bubble decreases accordingly. It is concluded that the influence of the size of the bubble on the rising movement of the bubble gradually increases with the larger the bubble diameter.

(5) The double bubbles in the near-wall domain will be affected by the wall and move away from the wall. The swing amplitude of the head bubble is greater than that of the tail bubble.

(6) When the double bubbles are arranged horizontally, the influence of the wall surface on the bubbles is not obvious. The bubbles first move away from each other and then approach, and the flow field after the bubbles merge is symmetrically distributed. When the distance between the horizontally arranged double bubbles gradually increases, the influence of the wall surface on the left bubble will gradually become obvious. When the vertically arranged double bubbles of different sizes rise, with proper bubble spacing, coalescence can occur regardless of whether it is an arrangement of large top and small bottom or large top and small bottom.

Author Contributions: Conceptualization, P.L.; Formal analysis, Y.L. and K.Z.; Investigation, Q.C. and P.L.; writing-original draft preparation, K.Z.; writing-review and editing, Y.L. All authors have read and agreed to the published version of the manuscript.

Funding: The present work is financially supported by the Key R&D Program of Zhejiang Province (Grant No. 2020C03081), the Joint Funds of the National Natural Science Foundation of China (Grant No. U2006221), the National Natural Science Foundation of China (Grant No. 51676173).

Conflicts of Interest: The authors declare no conflict of interest.

References

1. Yonemoto, Y.; Kunugi, T. Development of multi-scale multiphase flow equation and thermodynamic modeling of gas-liquid interface. *Therm. Sci. Eng.* **2008**, *16*, 11–29.
2. Mansour, M.; Landage, A.; Khot, P.; Nigam, K.; Zhringer, K. Numerical study of gas–liquid two-phase flow regimes for upward flow in a helical pipe. *Ind. Eng. Chem. Res.* **2019**, *59*, 3873–3886. [CrossRef]
3. Wang, H.; Long, B.; Wang, C.; Han, C.; Li, L. Effects of the Impeller Blade with a Slot Structure on the Centrifugal Pump Performance. *Energies* **2020**, *13*, 1628–1644. [CrossRef]
4. Wang, B.; Socolofsky, S.A. On the bubble rise velocity of a continually released bubble chain in still water and with crossflow. *Phys. Fluids* **2015**, *27*, 3537–3757. [CrossRef]
5. Wang, H.; Qian, Z.; Zhang, D.; Wang, T.; Wang, C. Numerical Study of the Normal Impinging Water Jet at Different Impinging Height, Based on Wray–Agarwal Turbulence Model. *Energies* **2020**, *13*, 1744–1758. [CrossRef]
6. Mirsandi, H.; Kong, G.; Buist, K.A.; Baltussen, M.W.; Kuipers, J. Numerical study on the interaction of two bubbles rising side-by-side in viscous liquids. *Chem. Eng. J.* **2020**, *410*, 128257. [CrossRef]
7. Clift, R.; Grace, J.R.; Weber, M.E. *Bubbles, Drops, and Particles*; Academic Press: Mineola, NY, USA, 1978.
8. Grace, J.R. Shapes and velocities of bubbles rising in infinite liquids. *Trans. Inst. Chem. Eng.* **1973**, *51*, 116–120.
9. Wu, M.; Gharib, M. Experimental studies on the shape and path of small air bubbles rising in clean water. *Phys. Fluids* **2002**, *14*, L49–L52. [CrossRef]
10. Wang, E.N.; Devasenathipathy, S.; Hao, L.; Hidrovo, C.H.; Santiago, J.G.; Goodson, K.E.; Kenny, T.W. A hybrid method for bubble geometry reconstruction in two-phase microchannels. *Exp. Fluids* **2006**, *40*, 847–858. [CrossRef]
11. Hua, J.; Jing, L. Numerical simulation of bubble rising in viscous liquid. *J. Comput. Phys.* **2007**, *222*, 769–795. [CrossRef]
12. Duineveld, P.C. The rise velocity and shape of bubbles in pure water at high Reynolds number. *J. Fluid Mech.* **1995**, *292*, 325–332. [CrossRef]
13. Robinson, P.B.; Blake, J.R.; Kodama, T.; Shima, A.; Tomita, Y. Interaction of cavitation bubbles with a free surface. *J. Appl. Phys.* **2001**, *89*, 8225. [CrossRef]
14. Sugiyama, K.; Takemura, F. On the lateral migration of a slightly deformed bubble rising near a vertical plane wall. *J. Fluid Mech.* **2010**, *662*, 209–231. [CrossRef]
15. Chen, B.; Kawamura, T.; Kodama, Y. Direct numerical simulation of a single rising bubble in still water. *J. Eng. Thermophys.* **2005**, *26*, 980–982.
16. Tatineni, M.; Zhong, X. Numerical study of two-phase flows in microchannels using the level set method. In Proceedings of the 42nd AIAA Aerospace Sciences Meeting and Exhibit, Reno, NE, USA, 5–8 January 2004.
17. Komasawa, I.; Otake, T.; Kamojima, M. Wake behavior and its effect on interaction between spherical-cap bubbles. *J. Chem. Eng. Jpn.* **2006**, *13*, 103–109. [CrossRef]
18. Ohta, M.; Imura, T.; Yoshida, Y.; Sussman, M. A computational study of the effect of initial bubble conditions on the motion of a gas bubble rising in viscous liquids. *Int. J. Multiph. Flow* **2005**, *31*, 223–237. [CrossRef]
19. Wright, M.D.; Gambioli, F.; Malan, A.G. CFD based non-dimensional characterization of energy dissipation due to verticle slosh. *Appl. Sci.* **2021**, *11*, 10401. [CrossRef]

20. Wan, Z.; Li, Y.; Wang, S. A comprehensive simulation and optimization on heat transfer characteristics of subcooled seawater falling film around elliptical tubes. *Appl. Therm. Eng.* **2021**, *189*, 116675. [CrossRef]

21. Scapin, N.; Costa, P.; Brandt, L. A volume-of-fluid method for interface-resolved simulations of phase-changing two-fluid flows. *J. Comput. Phys.* **2020**, *407*, 109251. [CrossRef]

22. Tsui, Y.Y.; Liu, C.Y.; Lin, S.W. Coupled level-set and volume-of-fluid method for two-phase flow calculations. *Numer. Heat Transf. Part. B Fundam.* **2017**, *71*, 173–185. [CrossRef]

23. Zhang, X.; Wang, J.; Wan, D. An improved multi-scale two phase method for bubbly flows. *Int. J. Multiphas. Flow* **2020**, *133*, 103460. [CrossRef]

24. Nguyen, V.T.; Park, W.G. A Volume-of-Fluid (VOF) interface-sharpening method for two-phase incompressible flows. *Comput. Fluids* **2017**, *152*, 104–119. [CrossRef]

25. Wang, C.; Gai, J. Numerical simulation of bubble rising behavior in liquid LBE using diffuse interface method. *Nucl. Eng. Des.* **2018**, *340*, 219–228. [CrossRef]

Article

Numerical Simulation of Non-Spherical Submicron Particle Acceleration and Focusing in a Converging–Diverging Micronozzle

Yanru Wang, Jiaxin Shen, Zhaoqin Yin * and Fubing Bao

Zhejiang Provincial Key Laboratory of Flow Measurement Technology, China Jiliang University, Hangzhou 310018, China; s20020804055@cjlu.edu.cn (Y.W.); P20020854067@cjlu.edu.cn (J.S.); dingobao@cjlu.edu.cn (F.B.)
* Correspondence: yinzq@cjlu.edu.cn

Abstract: Submicron particles transported by a Laval-type micronozzle are widely used in micro- and nano-electromechanical systems for the aerodynamic scheme of particle acceleration and focusing. In this paper, the Euler–Lagrangian method is utilized to numerically study non-spherical submicron particle diffusion in a converging–diverging micronozzle flow field. The influence of particle density and shape factor on the focusing process is discussed. The numerical simulation shows how submicron particle transporting with varying shape factors and particle density results in different particle velocities, trajectories and focusing in a micronozzle flow field. The particle with a larger shape factor or larger density exhibits a stronger aerodynamic focusing effect in a supersonic flow field through the nozzle. In the intersection process, as the particle size increases, the position of the particle trajectory intersection moves towards the throat at first and then it moves towards the nozzle outlet. Moreover, the influence of the thermophoretic force of the submicron particle on the aerodynamic focusing can be ignored. The results will be beneficial in technological applications, such as micro-thrusters, microfabrication and micro cold spray.

Keywords: micronozzle; particle acceleration; non-spherical submicron particles; aerodynamic focusing

Citation: Wang, Y.; Shen, J.; Yin, Z.; Bao, F. Numerical Simulation of Non-Spherical Submicron Particle Acceleration and Focusing in a Converging–Diverging Micronozzle. *Appl. Sci.* **2022**, *12*, 343. https://doi.org/10.3390/app12010343

Academic Editor: Johann Michael Köhler

Received: 22 October 2021
Accepted: 27 December 2021
Published: 30 December 2021

Publisher's Note: MDPI stays neutral with regard to jurisdictional claims in published maps and institutional affiliations.

1. Introduction

In recent years, there has been a considerable increase in the attention of many researchers in the field on MEMS techniques, such as micro-thrusters, microfabrication and micro cold spray [1]. In these studies, the most important micro-device is a Laval-type micronozzle, which has an appropriate geometry, including a convergent section, a throat and a divergent section to induce particle acceleration via a supersonic propulsive gas. Two advantages of the fluid field in a nozzle are the supersonic flow velocity and particle focusing. A supersonic gas in combination with micro particles or liquid droplets in a two-phase flow could be used for cooling microchips, cold spray technology or a new collimated aerosol beam-direct write technology (CAB-DW), etc. [2]. Both in experimental and numerical simulation studies, the main purpose is to create a narrow and collimated beam with high-speed particles in a supersonic nozzle.

Much of the past computational work has focused on comparing the results of simulations and experiments to investigate particle velocity in a micronozzle with a wedge or conical shape for different manufacturing processes [3]. Because of the very small size of a micronozzle, the influence of viscosity and the characteristics of rarefied gas aerodynamics are significant, while the fluid dynamics of the micronozzle are substantially different from that of the macroscopic nozzle. Many numerical simulations based on the direct simulation Monte Carlo (DSMC) method in micronozzles have been performed recently [4–6]. When the Knudsen number (Kn) is smaller than approximately 0.1, the continuum approach based on the Navier–Stokes (N-S) equations with velocity slip and temperature jump boundary conditions is employed. The effect of nozzle geometries, such as the ratio of throat width to divergent length, the spay angle and the standoff distance, has been studied to successfully induce higher acceleration [7]. Particles need to be accelerated faster during the cold spraying process to ensure that the impact between particles and the substrate is sufficient to form a dense coating.

For the dispersed phase, either solid particles or liquid droplets with a carrier gas transported in a micronozzle are sharply accelerated and focused into a narrow particle beam via aerodynamic focusing. This has attracted widespread interest in the problem of forming a collimated particle beam and controlling the speed of a particle beam in a micronozzle. Israel et al. [5] first indicated that aerosol focusing is the result of the inertial effect, where particles accelerate through the convergent part of the micronozzle and gather downstream. Akhatov et al. [8] studied the flow focusing of particles and verified that the velocity of the particle beam can be accelerated to 100 m/s in a contracting subsonic nozzle through experimental and numerical simulation methods. Bhattacharya et al. [9] applied the Lagrangian particle tracking algorithm combined with the N-S equation to simulate the motion of aerosol particles whose diameters varied from 2 μm to 6 μm through a converging–diverging nozzle. They compared the Magnus force with the Saffman lift force and observed that the influence of the Magnus force on 2 μm diameter particles can be ignored. Kudryavtsev et al. [3] mentioned aerodynamic focusing and conducted a numerical study on the micro particle flow in plane-shaped, axisymmetric and three-dimensional supersonic micronozzles with the Euler–Lagrangian method. Particle beam collimation occurred in two different ranges of particle sizes. Shershnev and Kudryavtsev [10] also noted this phenomenon and continued their previous research, studying particle-laden flows in a micronozzle with rectangular cross-sections and a convergent/divergent sidewall. The obtained results agreed well with previous data for axisymmetrical and plane-shaped micronozzles. Kudryavtsev et al. [3] also considered the fact that the aerodynamic focusing of particles in the supersonic convergence–divergence nozzle significantly increased the speed of the collimated beam. Table 1 is the summary of the previous studies on aerosol focusing.

Table 1. The previous studies on aerosol focusing in nozzles.

Authors	Particle Size	Method	Findings
Israel et al. [5]	0.12–1.3 μm	Experiment	1. Aerosol focusing is the result of the inertial effect. 2. Particle velocity is up to 190 m/s.
Akhatov et al. [8]	100 μm	Experiment and a mathematical model	The Saffman force acting on aerosol particles becomes significant, causing a noticeable migration of particles toward the center line of the capillary.
Bhattacharya et al. [9]	2–6 μm	CFD numerical simulation	1. The influence of the Magnus force on 2 μm diameter particles can be ignored compared with the Saffman lift force. 2. A silver particle velocity of 600 m/s can be reached and the aerosol beam width is as thin as 50 μm.
Kudryavtsev et al. [3]	0.05–5.0 μm	CFD numerical simulation	Particle beam collimation occurred in two different ranges of particle sizes for the plane-shaped and axisymmetrical nozzle.
Shershnev and Kudryavtsev [10]	0.05–5.0 μm	CFD numerical simulation	Particle beam collimation occurred in two different ranges of particle sizes in the nozzle with a rectangular cross-section.

Although many studies have been carried out on particle dynamics in micronozzles, far too little attention has been paid to the impact of non-spherical shape characteristics and rarefied gas on particle motion to date. Based on the microscopic observation of the morphology of particles, most of the micro particles are irregular and non-spherical [11,12].

Only Song et al. [13] numerically studied the non-spherical silicon particles in different gas streams, and the results showed that the particle impact velocity and temperature can be altered by the change of the sizes and shapes of sprayed particles. Therefore, based on the N-S equation with the first-order slip boundary conditions and drag force equation for non-spherical particles, we combine the Euler–Lagrangian method to discuss the particle trajectory and diffusion range in a pressure-driven micronozzle in this paper. The obtained results are important for optimizing the performance of micronozzles, such as controlling the speed of the submicron particle beam in a micronozzle and forming a collimated submicron particle beam.

2. Model Formulation

The gas in the micronozzle follows the conservation laws of mass, momentum and energy. The corresponding governing equations are N-S equations, written as [14,15]:

$$\frac{\partial \rho}{\partial t} + \frac{\partial (\rho u_i)}{\partial x_i} = 0, \tag{1}$$

$$\frac{\partial (\rho u_j u_i)}{\partial x_i} = -\frac{\partial p}{\partial x_i} + \mu \frac{\partial^2 u_i}{\partial x_j^2}, \tag{2}$$

$$\frac{\partial (\rho c T)}{\partial t} + \frac{\partial (\rho u_j c T)}{\partial x_j} = u_j \frac{\partial p}{\partial x_j} + \sigma_{ij} \frac{\partial u_i}{\partial u_j} - \frac{\partial q_j}{\partial x_j}, \tag{3}$$

where i and j represent Cartesian coordinates, ρ is the gas density, u is the gas velocity, p is the gas pressure, μ is the gas dynamic viscosity, σ is the viscosity tensor, c is the specific heat capacity, T is the temperature and q is the heat flow, referring to the heat transfer between the fluid and the wall and the inner fluid in the adjacent grids. Sutherland's law, using the three coefficients of gas dynamic viscosity method depending on the gas temperature, is expressed as [16]:

$$\mu = T^{3/2} \left(\frac{T_0 + S}{T + S} \right) \tag{4}$$

where $T_0 = 273$ K is the reference temperature and $S = 144.4$ K is Sutherland's constant. It is necessary to consider the impact of gas compressibility because of the significant change to the gas density in the flow field of a micronozzle, and the equation of compressible ideal gas is:

$$pV = mR_g T \tag{5}$$

where V represents the gas volume, m represents the mass of substance for gas and R_g represents the gas constant. Considering the rarefaction effects on the wall, the first-order slip boundary conditions have been proposed [17], which can be written as follows:

$$(u_\tau)|_s = \alpha_u \lambda_s \left(\frac{\partial u_\tau}{\partial n} \right)|_s \tag{6}$$

$$T_s - T_w = \alpha_T \frac{k}{k-1} \frac{\lambda_s}{Pr} \left(\frac{\partial T}{\partial n} \right)\bigg|_s \tag{7}$$

where u_τ denotes the tangential component of velocity, and T_w and T_s stand for wall temperature and gas temperature near the wall, respectively. λ_s is the mean free path near the wall, $Pr = 2/3$ is the Prandtl number and $k = 5/3$ is the specific heat ratio of argon, while n represents the coordinate normal to the wall. For the values of the coefficients, $\alpha_u = 1.142$ and $\alpha_T = 0.5865$.

The dispersed phase simulation is conducted using the motion equation for each submicron particle, which is:

$$m_p \frac{du_p}{dt} = F_D + m_p \frac{g(\rho_p - \rho)}{\rho_p} + F \tag{8}$$

where F_D is the drag force, F is the external force, m_p is the particle mass, u_p is the particle velocity, g is the gravitational acceleration and ρ_p is the particle density. Among the factors which affect particle movement, the drag force plays a significant role, and other factors can be ignored in this paper.

F_D is defined as:

$$F_D = \frac{18\mu C_D Re}{24 d_p^2 \rho_p}(u - u_p) \tag{9}$$

where d_p is the particle diameter, C_D is the drag coefficient, and Re is the relative Reynolds, which is expressed as:

$$Re = \frac{\rho d_p |u - u_p|}{\mu} \tag{10}$$

Note that C_D can be calculated as [18]:

$$C_D = \frac{24}{Re_{sph}}\left(1 + b_1 Re_{sph}{}^{b_2}\right) + \frac{b_3 Re_{sph}}{b_4 + Re_{sph}} \tag{11}$$

where:

$$\begin{aligned}
b_1 &= \exp\left(2.3288 - 6.4581 S_f + 2.4486 S_f{}^2\right) \\
b_2 &= 0.0964 + 0.5565 S_f \\
b_3 &= \exp\left(4.905 - 13.8944 S_f + 18.4222 S_f{}^2 - 10.2599 S_f{}^3\right) \\
b_4 &= \exp\left(1.4681 + 12.2584 S_f - 20.7322 S_f{}^2 + 15.8855 S_f{}^3\right)
\end{aligned} \tag{12}$$

The shape factor S_f is defined as:

$$S_f = \frac{s}{S} \tag{13}$$

where s is the surface area of a sphere with the same volume as the particle, and S is the actual surface area of the particle. Particles with high sphericity are almost spherical ($S_f \approx 1$). To calculate the particle mass, drag force and Re_{sph}, particle size d_p is the diameter of a sphere with the same volume.

3. Numerical Procedure

The micronozzle operating regime depends on the ratio of the outlet pressure p_2 to the inlet pressure p_1. When p_2 is equal to the ambient pressure and p_2/p_1 is equal to or less than a critical pressure ratio η_{cr}, the flow becomes sonic at the nozzle throat and it continues accelerate in the diverging section. The flow is fully expanded and a supersonic flow velocity forms at the nozzle exit. This is the normal operating regime of a supersonic nozzle and is desirable in many applications. Moreover, η_{cr} is a significant value for analyzing the flow in the nozzle as it changes from a subsonic to a supersonic velocity. η_{cr} can be calculated using the following expression from a one-dimensional isentropic relation:

$$\eta_{cr} = \frac{p_2}{p_1} = \left(\frac{2}{k+1}\right)^{\frac{k}{k-1}} = 0.487 \tag{14}$$

The physical model and grid model in this paper are shown in Figure 1. It is a typical convergent–divergent nozzle and is based on the shape parameters of the nozzle used in the experimental study of Rothe [19] and the numerical study of Kudryavtsev et al. [3]. The angles of the converging and diverging parts are $\alpha = 45°$ and $\beta = 20°$, respectively. The nozzle throat half-width h is 100 µm. Local grid refinement was carried out in the convergent part, divergent part and the nozzle throat. The simulation was carried out in the fully expanded condition and the flow was assumed to be steady and two-dimensional. The flow field of argon was driven by the pressure ratio of the outlet and inlet, and the inlet pressure was 101,325 Pa, with the initial outlet and ambient pressure of 3739 Pa. The wall temperature was set to 300 K. The average velocity at the throat was near the local speed of sound $c^* = \sqrt{kR_gT}$ = 337 m/s, with the Reynolds number $Re = \rho uh/\mu$ equaling 178. It was regarded as a laminar flow when the Reynolds number in the nozzle throat was less than 1000 [20]. The flow was assumed to be compressible and the density-based solver was employed. The convective terms were calculated based on a MUSCL (monotonic upstream-centered scheme for conservation laws) reconstruction, and the flow variable unit centered on the boundary of the grid was reconstructed with third-order accuracy [21]. The Roe-FDS was selected as the flux type. The double-precision floating point operation was chosen. Moreover, the convergence criterion for iteratively solving continuity, momentum and energy equations was set at 10^{-8}.

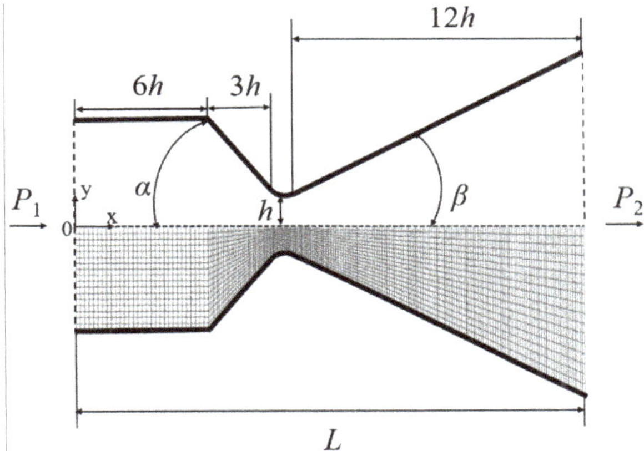

Figure 1. Micronozzle model and grid model.

The following assumptions were used for the discrete phase. On the one hand, it was assumed that the particles at the entrance were evenly distributed, and the type of nozzle wall was set to trap. This means that particles would be removed from the simulation if they hit the wall. On the other hand, one-way coupling was adopted owing to the volume fraction of particles being less than 10%; thus, the interaction between particles was ignored as well as the reverse influence of the particles on the fluid. The combined approach of computational fluid dynamics and the discrete particle method (CFD-DPM) was employed to investigate the motion characteristics of micro-/nano-particles in this study [22,23]. When submicron particles collided with the nozzle wall, they were considered to stick to the surface. Particles are seeded with the gas velocity at the left boundary of the simulation domain. All numerical simulations were carried out with the commercial software package ANSYS FLUENT15.0.

4. Validation of Solvers

Figure 2 shows the distribution of the dimensionless gas temperature along the micronozzle centerline. From the inlet to the convergent section, there was a slight decrease in T/T_t. When the gas moved to the nozzle throat, there was a sharp drop in T/T_t from 1.1 to 0.4, approximately. Thus, it can be suggested that there was a slight dependency on temperature distribution in x/L = 0.3–0.6. As can be seen, the predicted dimensionless gas temperature along the micronozzle centerline agrees favorably with the result of Kudryavtsev et al. [3] and the experimental results obtained by Rothe [19] using nitrogen. Kudryavtsev et al. [3], using N-S equations for a numerical simulation, found the same flow condition as our present work, while the region of their model is larger than that of our model due to their adding a small part of ambient space near the nozzle outlet in their work. Therefore, we can conclude that the numerical simulation of gas with rarefaction effects in a micronozzle can be acquired using compressible N-S equations in addition to the velocity slip and temperature boundary conditions.

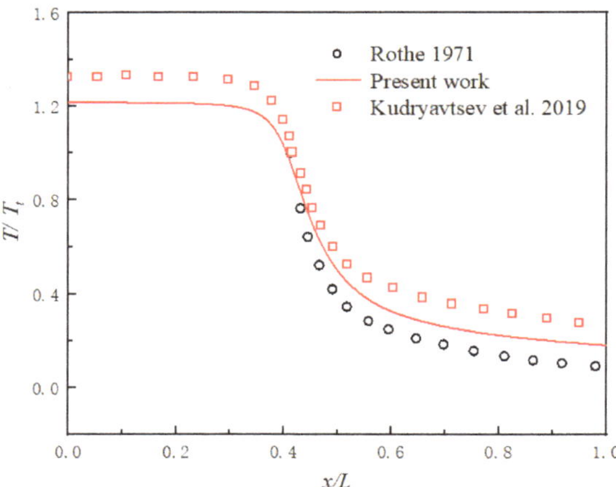

Figure 2. Distribution of the dimensionless temperature of gas along micronozzle centerline.

A series of computations for five different grid sizes of 180,000, 240,000, 320,000, 400,000 and 480,000 were performed to ensure the production of the grid-independent solution in Figure 3. Comparing the gas velocity at the throat under these numbers of grids with the calculated local speed of sound c^*, it was found that when the number of grids is more than 400,000, the deviation is less than 1.3%. However, when the number of grids contains less than 400,000, the deviation is greater than approximately 2%. Comprehensively considering the computational efficiency and precision, we deemed 400,000 grids to be sufficient for the present numerical simulation.

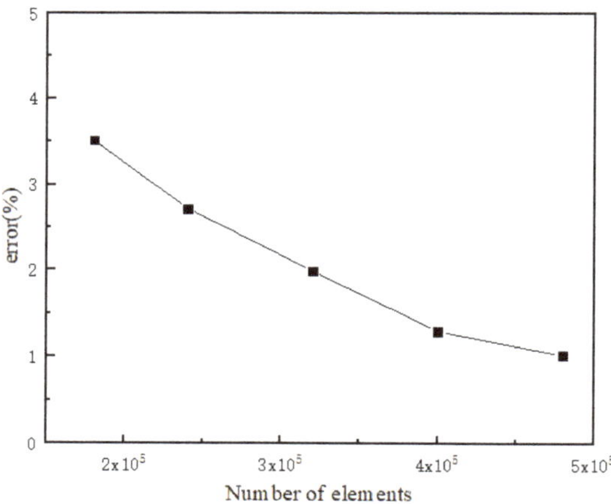

Figure 3. The test of grid independence in the flow field of the micronozzle.

5. Results and Discussion

5.1. Flow Field Characteristics in the Micronozzle

Figure 4 show the isolines of the Mach number (*Ma*) and temperature (*T*) in the fully expanded flow fields of the micronozzle. As can be observed in Figure 4a, *Ma* keeps growing. In the convergent section, *Ma* is less than 1 (*Ma* ≈ 0.4), and it is a subsonic flow.

As the cross-section of the nozzle decreases gradually, the gas velocity increases, and *Ma* is about 1 at the nozzle throat. After the gas flow expands along the micronozzle in the divergent section, the gas velocity continues to increase with *Ma* > 1. The results suggest that *Ma*, as well as *T*, has the opposite changes (Figures 4 and 5). *Ma* is at the highest value around the nozzle outlet, where *T* is the lowest due to the thermodynamic energy being converted into kinetic energy in the flow fields. In accordance with the gas equation of state and the energy equation, the ideal gas flow velocity is restricted to $U_{max} = c_0 \sqrt{2/(\gamma - 1)}$, where c_0 is the speed of sound under stagnation conditions, as mentioned by Shershnev and Kudryavtsev [24]. Figure 4a also shows a thick boundary layer in the diverging part of the nozzle, which is a typical feature of the small Reynolds number nozzle.

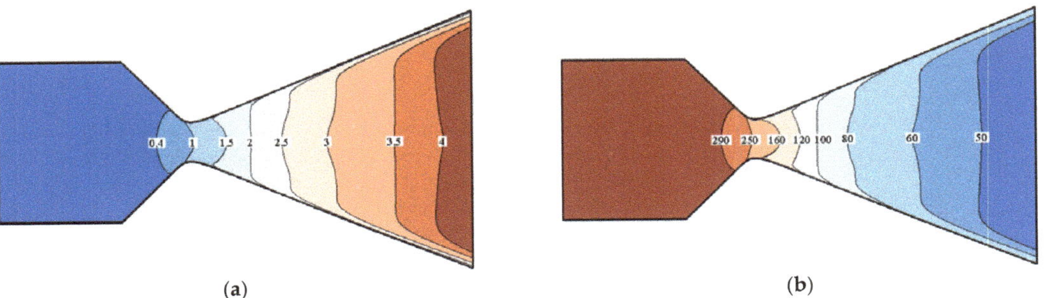

Figure 4. Isolines of Mach number and gas temperature in a fully expanded micronozzle: (**a**) Mach number; (**b**) gas temperature (K).

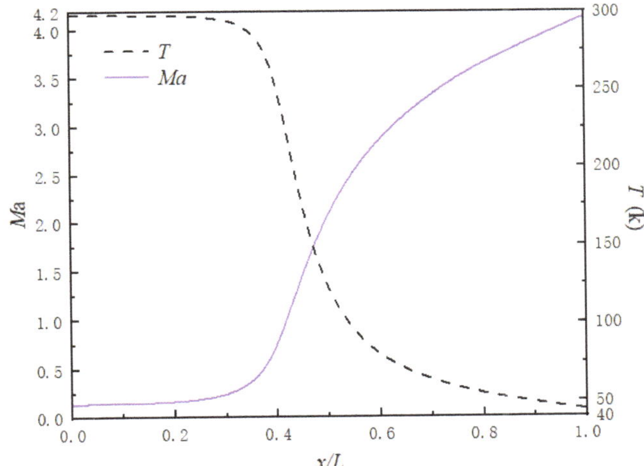

Figure 5. Centerline Mach number and temperature distribution in a micronozzle.

The centerline Mach number and gas temperature distributions are illustrated in Figure 5. As *T* decreases, the viscosity coefficient of gas decreases, which hinders the development of a boundary layer and promotes gas expansion. Furthermore, the effect of rarefied gas increases owing to the decrease in the gas density. Therefore, the wall viscous effects on the nozzle flow increase and the boundary layer gradually becomes thicker, decreasing the velocity gradient near the outlet. *Ma* is approximately 4.2 in the nozzle outlet in Figure 5, which is near the theoretical value of the isentropic condition. It can be concluded that the boundary layer affects the Mach number distribution along with the change in temperature and gas density.

The characteristics of the flow fields in the micronozzle are discussed above. There are considerable changes in the parameters, such as gas velocity and temperature, thus affecting the velocity and trajectory of submicron particles.

5.2. Distributions of Non-Spherical Submicron Particle Velocity

Figure 4b shows the large temperature difference in the micronozzle. Particles tend to move from the higher-temperature area to the lower-temperature area through thermophoresis when there is a relatively large gradient in the fluid temperature. The thermophoretic force is formulated as [25]:

$$F_T = 4.5\pi\frac{\mu^2}{\rho}d_p\frac{1}{1+3\frac{2\lambda}{d_p}}\frac{\frac{C_s}{C_p}+2.48\frac{2\lambda}{d_p}}{1+2\frac{C_s}{C_p}+4.48\frac{C_s}{C_p}}\frac{\nabla T}{T} \tag{15}$$

where C_s represents the thermal conductivity of air, C_p represents the thermal conductivity of the particle and λ represents the mean free path. According to the temperature distribution in Figure 4b, there is a more than 200 K temperature difference in the nozzle which induces the thermophoretic force to affect the particles. At present, the influence of the thermophoretic force on submicron particle focusing in a micronozzle is vague. Therefore, we compared the velocity in the y-direction (u_{p_y}) of the particle ($d_p = 0.6$ μm) released from the same initial position under two working conditions in Figure 6. One condition is that the thermophoretic force acting on the particles is considered, where $F = F_T$ in Equation (8), and another condition is that the thermophoretic force is ignored, where $F = 0$.

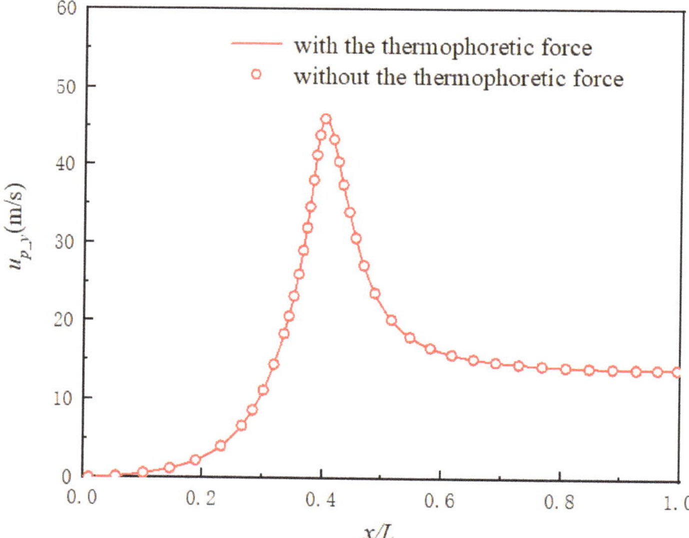

Figure 6. The change in the particle velocity in the nozzle considering the effect of the thermophoretic force.

The result shows that there is almost no effect of thermophoretic force on aerodynamic focusing, so the thermophoretic force can be ignored in this paper. The factor that determines particle focusing is inertial force, which will be discussed later.

Most particles are non-spherical, which leads to different aerodynamic properties [26,27]. According to the definition of the shape factor (Equation (13)), particles with smaller shape factors have lower sphericity. It is expected that those particles are more rod-like or disk-like in shape. Table 2 shows the sphericity of the regular-shaped particles.

Table 2. The sphericity of several regular-shaped particles.

Particle Shape		Model	Shape Factor (S_f)
Sphere			1
Cube			0.806
Disk-like	$(h = r)$		0.827
	$(h = r/3)$		0.594
	$(h = r/10)$		0.323
Rod-like	$(h = 3r)$		0.86
	$(h = 10r)$		0.691
	$(h = 20r)$		0.580

The submicron particle velocity is obtained by injecting Al particles ($\rho_{Al} = 2688 \text{ kg/m}^3$) with different shape factors and sizes into the nozzle inlet, as shown in Figure 7. The gas velocity in the flow field centerline and the particle velocity are defined as u_c and u_p, respectively. With the rapid growth in the gas velocity, particle velocities have different degrees of increase with different shape factors. u_p with $S_f = 0.4$ coincides relatively well with u_c for $d_p = 0.3$ μm, while this coincidence degree becomes lower as S_f increases. This implies that particles with small shape factors show a stronger momentum exchange between the gas and particles, which makes it easier for particles to be accelerated. As a result, the outlet velocity of particles with small shape factors is relatively greater. In addition, the difference between u_p and u_c with a different S_f becomes more obvious with the increase in d_p, because the shape factor has little effect on the particle velocity of small particles (Figure 7a,d). We can also observe that as the particle size increases, the coincidence degree becomes lower between u_p and u_c, which means that large particles show poor airflow followability due to their large inertia.

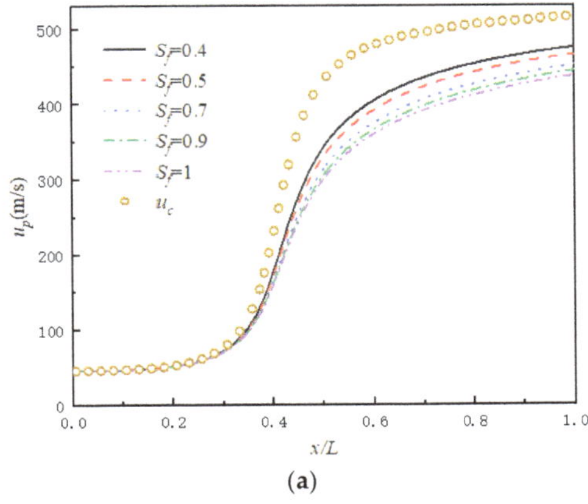

(a)

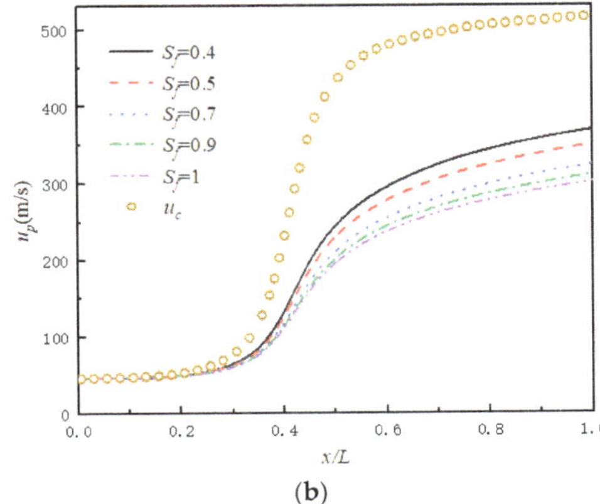

(b)

Figure 7. *Cont.*

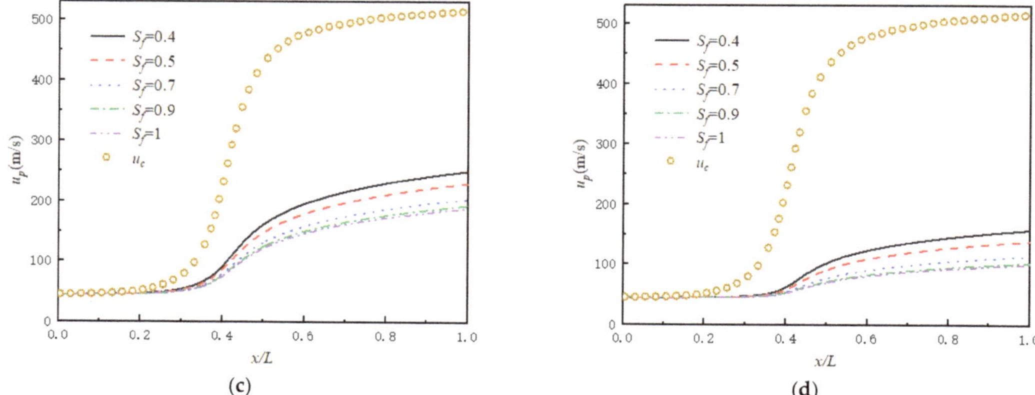

(c)   **(d)**

Figure 7. Velocity of particles along the micronozzle axis with different shape factors for: (**a**) $d_p = 0.3$ μm; (**b**) $d_p = 0.7$ μm; (**c**) $d_p = 1.6$ μm; (**d**) $d_p = 4.5$ μm.

In order to better understand the mechanism of aerodynamic focusing, we compared the velocity in the y-direction of the Al particle released from the same initial position with variable shape factors for $d_p = 0.7$ μm in Figure 8. Here, u_{c_y} is defined as the flow field velocity in the y-direction. With the increase in S_f, the gradient of u_{p_y} decreases in the diverging section of the micronozzle; in other words, u_{p_y} at the outlet increases, making the aerodynamic focusing more obvious. It can be concluded that by reducing the shape factors, the particle focusing is weaker, but the particle velocity can be higher. Figure 9 shows the particle velocity in the y-direction with $S_f = 0.5$ for $d_p = 0.7$ μm using three kinds of material particles, Al, Ti and Cu. The densities are $\rho_{Al} = 2688 \text{kg/m}^3$, $\rho_{Ti} = 4506 \text{ kg/m}^3$ and $\rho_{Cu} = 8880 \text{ kg/m}^3$, respectively. It is observed that the heavier Cu particle is easier to focus. Therefore, by increasing particle sizes and particle densities, the particle focusing is stronger due to their gained inertia. Therefore, the decisive influence of the aerodynamic focusing of submicron particles is inertial force.

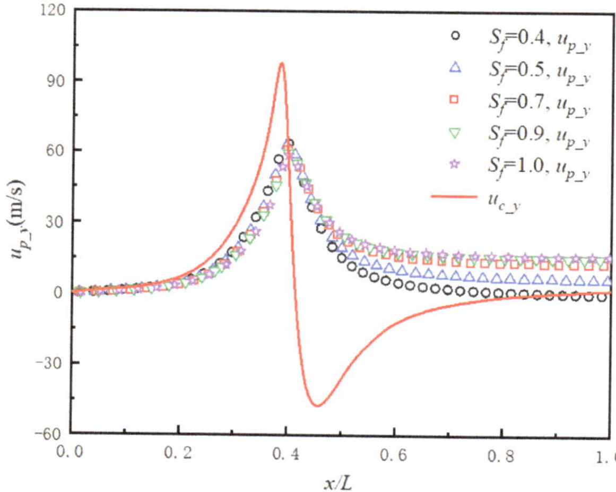

Figure 8. Velocity in the y-direction of the particle released from the same initial position with variable shape factors.

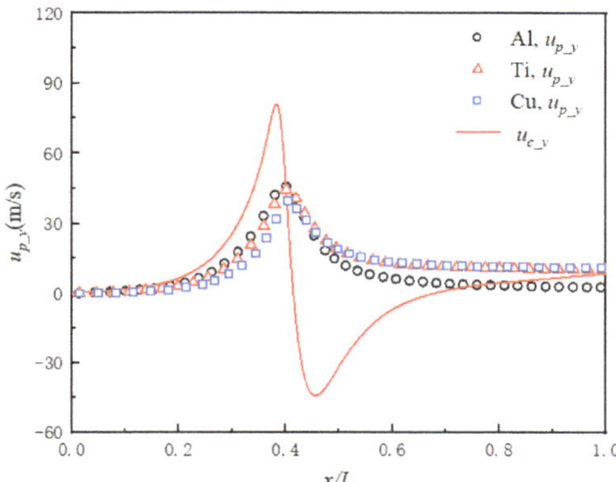

Figure 9. Velocity in the *y*-direction of the particle released from the same initial position with variable densities.

5.3. Effect of the Diffusion of Submicron Particles

To explore the changes in particle trajectories and the gathering effect in the fully expanded flow field, submicron particles evenly released at the inlet were tracked. Figure 10 shows the particle trajectory of Al with different submicron particle sizes and with $S_f = 0.5$. The streamline of the flow field is illustrated in Figure 11. The gas continues to expand and accelerate between the divergent section and outlet of the micronozzle, promoting submicron particle focusing. This implies that the drag force further increases with the gas flow as a result of the increasing particle velocity, weakening particle diffusion and enhancing the dynamic focusing of particles. As mentioned in the reference paper by Kudryavtsev et al. [3], when particle diameters increase, the particle trajectory undergoes the processes of repeated changes: the divergence process(I-a), the collimation process(I-b), a focused beam(I-c), the intersection process(II), a focused beam(III-c), the collimation process(III-b) and the divergence process (III-a). These processes can be divided into three stages. The divergence process(I-a), collimation process(I-b) and a focused beam(I-c) are included in the first stage; the intersection process(II) is included in the second stage; the divergence process(III-a), collimation process(III-b) and a focused beam(III-c) are included in the third stage.

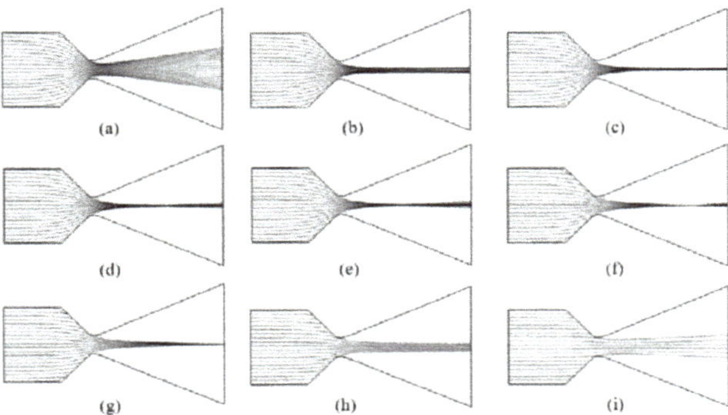

Figure 10. Al particle trajectory in the micronozzle with $S_f = 0.5$ for: (**a**) $d_p = 0.3$ μm (divergence process(I-a)); (**b**) $d_p = 0.6$ μm (collimation process(I-b)); (**c**) $d_p = 0.7$ μm (a focused beam(I-c)); (**d**) $d_p = 0.8$ μm (intersection process(II)); (**e**) $d_p = 1.0$ μm (intersection process(II)); (**f**) $d_p = 1.4$ μm (intersection process(II)); (**g**) $d_p = 1.6$ μm (a focused beam(III-c)); (**h**) $d_p = 2.2$ μm (collimation process(III-b)); (**i**) $d_p = 4.5$ μm (divergence process(III-a)).

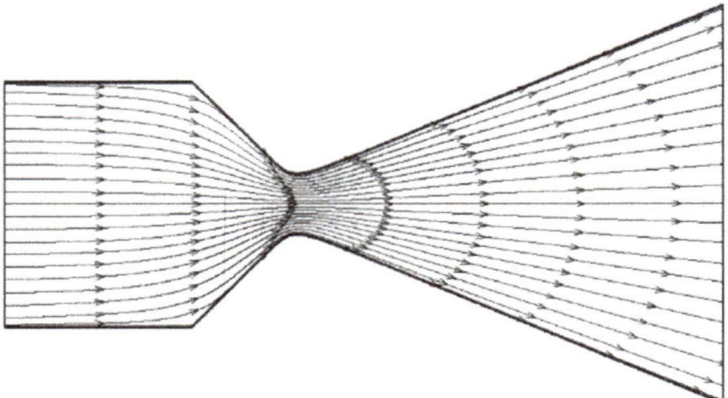

Figure 11. The streamline in a fully expanded micronozzle.

In Figure 10, the particles diffuse slightly for d_p = 4.5 µm owing to their large inertia. When d_p is about 0.6–0.7 µm or 2.2–4.5 µm, a collimated or focused particle beam forms, both of which are desirable in the field of cold spraying. When d_p = 0.7 µm and d_p = 1.6 µm, aerodynamic focusing is observed, which is the best working state. Some relatively large particles converge so fast that their trajectories cross inside the nozzle, as shown in Figure 10d–f. If the particle trajectories cross, the nozzle exit is not in the best focus position.

Moreover, the critical diameter of Al particles for the occurrence of these processes is also different under various shape factors, as indicated in Figure 12. As S_f increases, the critical diameter becomes smaller. When S_f = 0.7, 0.9 and 1.0, a collimation process(I-b) occurs when d_p is about 0.5–0.6 µm and an intersection process(II) occurs for d_p = 0.7 µm. This explains why u_{p_y} is a relatively larger positive value at the nozzle exit for d_p = 0.7 µm in Figure 8, indicating that the beam is defocusing. When S_f = 0.4 and 0.5, the collimation process(I-b) occurs when d_p is approximately 0.6–0.8µm, which corresponds to the value of u_{p_y}, which is near zero in Figure 8, forming a focused particle beam.

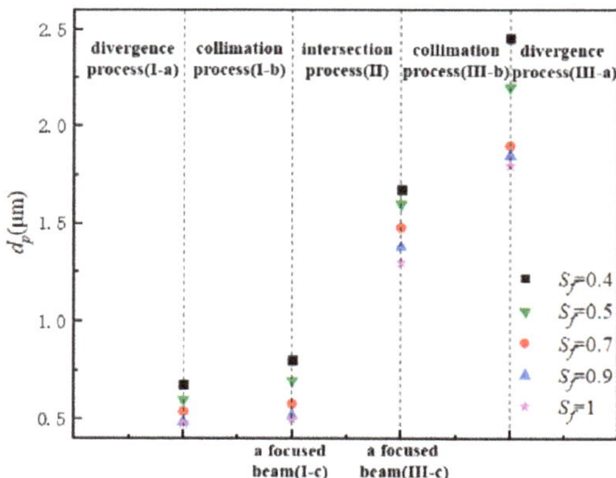

Figure 12. Al particle with variable shape factors in different processes.

Figure 13 demonstrates the diffusion range of the submicron particles of the nozzle outlet with S_f = 0.5 of particles when d_p = 0.2 µm to 2.4 µm under three different densities. The exit radius of particle diffusion is represented as R. All three materials have two minimum particle diffusion radii which were marked with triangles, and at this moment particles are focused. In the first stage, when small particle trajectories change from diffusion to focus, R decreases rapidly as d_p increases. The reason for this is that the increase in particle inertia and the flow drag force weakens the particles escaping from the axial direction, promoting the aerodynamic focusing of the particles. As d_p continues to increase, the intersection process(II) for the particles appears, which is the second stage. R gradually increases at first and then decreases. This is because the position of the particle trajectory intersection moves towards the throat at first. After a particle size increases beyond a special particle size, the intersection moves to the nozzle outlet. This can be also observed in Figure 10d–f. At the third stage, the particle inertial force dominates the behavior of the submicron particles. The fluid drag force seems less obvious, so the diffusion radius of the particles increases slightly when d_p increases. As the particle density increases, the critical diameter of the particle diffusion radius decreases in these three stages; that is, the diffusion radius of the particles changes at a smaller size. The change in R of the Al particles in the first stage is particularly more obvious than that of the Cu particles. On the contrary, the change in R of the Al particles is smaller in the third stage. Figures 12 and 13 suggest that the different properties of particle trajectories with the same shape factor are determined by the particle size and particle density.

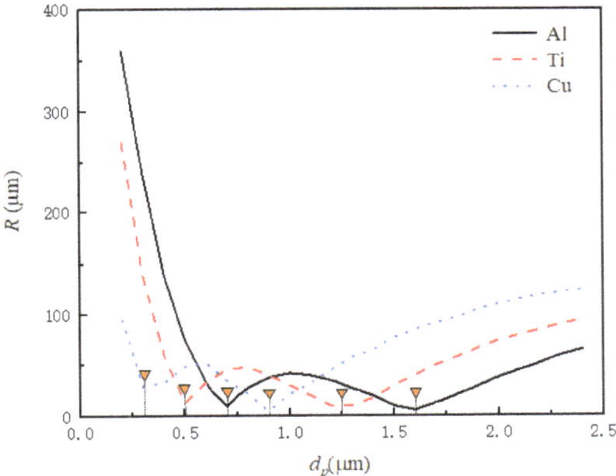

Figure 13. Diffusion radius of particles at the nozzle outlet.

In conclusion, a converging–diverging micronozzle with a fully expanded supersonic flow is significant for the aerodynamic scheme of particle focusing in micro cold spay. The dynamic focusing of particles is the result of the competition between inertial force and drag force. Submicron particles with larger inertias will be useful in aerodynamic focusing in a higher drag force flow field.

6. Conclusions

This paper numerically demonstrates the flow characteristic and motion trajectory of submicron particles in a converging–diverging micronozzle using the Euler–Lagrangian method. The results show that a particle beam can be produced through the effect of aerodynamic focusing in the supersonic part of a fully expanded micronozzle flow field. The performance of the shape factor and particle density with various levels of inertia can be determined, allowing us to observe the resulting different particle velocities and trajectories. By increasing the particle densities and shape factors, the particle focusing is stronger due to their high inertia, while the particle velocity is smaller with a larger shape factor. The velocity of the particles with small inertia better coincides with their gas velocity compared with that of larger ones. The dynamic focusing of particles is the result of the competition between inertia force and drag force. Both of the two forces are beneficial for the aerodynamic focusing of particles. Furthermore, the position of submicron particle focusing changes with particle inertia. As the particle size increases, the position of the particle trajectory intersection moves towards the nozzle throat at first and then it moves inversely. Moreover, the thermophoretic force of the submicron particles has almost no effect on aerodynamic focusing in a micronozzle. The result of this study is important in technological applications, such as controlling the speed of the submicron particle beam in a micronozzle or forming a collimated submicron particle beam, etc. The diffusion and focusing process of particles can be affected by the particle shape. These results can be obtained by other simulation algorithms, such as discrete element methods (DEM), which can calculate the characteristics of the movement and rotation of particles with different particle shapes in the flow field. Further research on the effect of particles on the flow field and the interaction between particles will be considered.

Author Contributions: Conceptualization, Z.Y. and Y.W.; methodology, F.B. and Z.Y.; software, J.S. and Y.W.; validation, Y.W. and J.S.; resources, J.S. and Y.W.; writing, Y.W.; review, Z.Y. All authors have read and agreed to the published version of the manuscript.

Funding: This work was supported by the National Natural Science Foundation of China (No. 11972335, No. 11972334)

Conflicts of Interest: The authors declare no conflict of interest.

References

1. Pourfattah, F.; Sabzpooshani, M. Thermal management of a power electronic module employing a novel multi-micro nozzle liquid-based cooling system: A numerical study. *Int. J. Heat Mass Transf.* **2020**, *147*, 118928. [CrossRef]
2. He, L.; Hassani, M. A review of the mechanical and tribological behavior of cold spray metal matrix composites. *J. Therm. Spray Technol.* **2020**, *29*, 1565–1608. [CrossRef]
3. Kudryavtsev, A.; Shershnev, A.; Rybdylova, O. Numerical simulation of aerodynamic focusing of particles in supersonic micronozzles. *Int. J. Multiph. Flow* **2019**, *114*, 207–218. [CrossRef]
4. Darbandi, M.; Roohi, E. Study of subsonic–supersonic gas flow through micro/nanoscale nozzles using unstructured DSMC solver. *Microfluid. Nanofluidics* **2011**, *10*, 321–335. [CrossRef]
5. Israel, G.W.; Gerhard, W.; Friedlander, S.K. High-speed beams of small particles. *J. Colloid Interface Sci.* **1967**, *24*, 330–337. [CrossRef]
6. Liu, M.; Zhang, X.; Zhang, G.; Chen, Y. Study on micronozzle flow and propulsion performance using DSMC and continuum methods. *Acta Mech. Sin.* **2006**, *22*, 409–416. [CrossRef]
7. Cao, C.; Han, T.; Xu, Y.; Li, W.; Yang, X.; Hu, K. The associated effect of powder carrier gas and powder characteristics on the optimal design of the cold spray nozzle. *Surf. Eng.* **2020**, *36*, 1081–1089. [CrossRef]
8. Akhatov, I.S.; Hoey, J.M.; Thompson, D.; Lutfurakhmanov, A.; Mahmud, Z.; Swenson, O.F.; Schulz, D.L.; Osiptsov, A.N. Aerosol flow through a micro-capillary. *Int. Conf. Micro/Nanoscale Heat Transf.* **2009**, *43895*, 223–232.
9. Bhattacharya, S.; Lutfurakhmanov, A.; Hoey, J.M.; Swenson, O.F.; Mahmud, Z.; Akhatov, I.S. Aerosol flow through a converging-diverging micro-nozzle. *Nonlinear Eng.* **2013**, *2*, 103–112. [CrossRef]
10. Shershnev, A.; Kudryavtsev, A. Numerical simulation of particle beam focusing in a supersonic nozzle with rectangular cross-section. *J. Phys. Conf. Ser.* **2019**, *1404*, 012042. [CrossRef]
11. Lin, W.; Zhang, P.; Lin, J. Flow and heat transfer property of Oldroyd-B-fluid-based nanofluids containing cylindrical particles in a pipe. *Processes* **2021**, *9*, 647. [CrossRef]
12. Shi, R.; Lin, J.; Yang, H.; Yu, M. Distribution of non-spherical nanoparticles in turbulent flow of ventilation chamber considering fluctuating particle number density. *Appl. Math. Mech.* **2021**, *42*, 317–330. [CrossRef]
13. Song, J.; Liu, J.; Chen, Q.; Li, K. Effect of the shape factor on the cold-spraying dynamic characteristics of sprayed particles. *J. Therm. Spray Technol.* **2017**, *26*, 1851–1858. [CrossRef]
14. Ye, Y.; Tu, C.; Zhang, Z.; Xu, R.; Bao, F.; Lin, J. Deagglomeration of airborne nanoparticles in a decelerating supersonic round jet. *Adv. Powder Technol.* **2021**, *32*, 1488–1501. [CrossRef]
15. Liu, M.; Peskin, R.L.; Muzzio, F.J.; Leong, C.W. Structure of the stretching field in chaotic cavity flows. *AIChE J.* **1994**, *40*, 1273–1286. [CrossRef]
16. De Vanna, F.; Picano, F.; Benini, E. A sharp-interface immersed boundary method for moving objects in compressible viscous flows. *Comput. Fluids* **2020**, *201*, 104415. [CrossRef]
17. Ambruş, V.E.; Sofonea, V. Half-range lattice Boltzmann models for the simulation of Couette flow using the Shakhov collision term. *Phys. Rev. E* **2018**, *98*, 063311. [CrossRef]
18. Haider, A.; Levenspiel, O. Drag coefficient and terminal velocity of spherical and nonspherical particles. *Powder Technol.* **1989**, *58*, 63–70. [CrossRef]
19. Rothe, D.E. Electron-beam studies of viscous flow in supersonic nozzles. *AIAA J.* **1971**, *9*, 804–811. [CrossRef]
20. Liu, Z.M.; Zhang, T. Numerical investigation on gas flow in Laval micronozzle. *J. Aerosp. Power* **2009**, *24*, 1556–1563.
21. Celik, I.B.; Ghia, U.; Roache, P.J.; Freitas, C.J. Procedure for estimation and reporting of uncertainty due to discretization in CFD applications. *J. Fluids Eng.* **2008**, *130*, 078001.

22. Bao, F.; Hao, H.; Yin, Z.; Tu, C. Numerical study of nanoparticle deposition in a gaseous microchannel under the influence of various forces. *Micromachines* **2021**, *12*, 47. [CrossRef]
23. Zhang, H.; Li, G.; An, X.; Ye, X.; Wei, G.; Yu, A. Numerical study on the erosion process of the low temperature economizer using computational fluid dynamics-discrete particle method. *Wear* **2020**, *450*, 203269. [CrossRef]
24. Shershnev, A.; Kudryavtsev, A. Kinetic simulation of near field of plume exhausting from a plane micronozzle. *Microfluid. Nanofluid.* **2015**, *19*, 105–115. [CrossRef]
25. Talbot, L.; Cheng, R.K.; Schefer, R.W.; Willis, D.R. Thermophoresis of particles in a heated boundary layer. *J. Fluid Mech.* **1980**, *101*, 737–758. [CrossRef]
26. Lin, W.; Shi, R.; Lin, J. Distribution and deposition of cylindrical nanoparticles in a turbulent pipe flow. *Appl. Sci.* **2021**, *11*, 962. [CrossRef]
27. Hu, X.; Lin, J.; Guo, Y.; Ku, X. Motion and equilibrium position of elliptical and rectangular particles in a channel flow of a power-law fluid. *Powder Technol.* **2021**, *377*, 585–596. [CrossRef]

Article

Pressure Drop and Particle Settlement of Gas–Solid Two-Phase Flow in a Pipe

Wenqian Lin [1], Liang Li [2,3] and Yelong Wang [2,*]

[1] School of Media and Design, Hangzhou Dianzi University, Hangzhou 310018, China; lwq@hdu.edu.cn
[2] State Key Laboratory of Fluid Power Transmission and Control, Zhejiang University, Hangzhou 310027, China; liliang@zju.edu.cn
[3] Guangdong Infore Intelligent Sanitation Technology Co., Ltd., Foshan 528322, China
* Correspondence: wyl@zju.edu.cn

Abstract: Particle settlement and pressure drop in a gas–solid two-phase flow in a pipe with a circular cross-section are studied at mixture inlet velocities (V) ranging from 1 m/s to 30 m/s, particle volume concentrations (α_s) ranging from 1% to 20%, particle mass flows (m_s) ranging from 5 t/h to 25 t/h, and particle diameters (d_p) ranging from 50 μm to 1000 μm. The momentum equations are based on a two-fluid model and are solved numerically. Some results are validated through comparison with the experimental results. The results showed that the gas and particle velocity distributions are asymmetrical around the center of the pipe and that the maximum velocity point moves up. The distance between the radial position of the maximum velocity and the center line for the gas is larger than that for the particles. The particle motion lags behind that of the gas flow. The particle settlement phenomenon is more serious, and the particle distribution on the cross-section is more inhomogeneous as the V, α_s, and m_s decrease and as d_p increases. It can be divided into three areas according to the pressure changes along the flow direction, and the distinction between the three areas is more obvious as the α_s increases. The pressure drop per unit length increases as the V, α_s and m_s increases and as d_p decreases, Finally, the expressions of the settlement index and pressure drop per unit length as functions of V, α_s, m_s, and d_p are derived based on the numerical data.

Keywords: gas–solid two-phase flow; pipe with circular cross-section; settlement; pressure drop; numerical simulation

Citation: Lin, W.; Li, L.; Wang, Y. Pressure Drop and Particle Settlement of Gas–Solid Two-Phase Flow in a Pipe. *Appl. Sci* **2022**, *12*, 1623. https://doi.org/10.3390/app12031623

Academic Editor: Kambiz Vafai

Received: 29 December 2021
Accepted: 28 January 2022
Published: 3 February 2022

Publisher's Note: MDPI stays neutral with regard to jurisdictional claims in published maps and institutional affiliations.

1. Introduction

Particle transport through a pipe is quite common in the power generation, metallurgy, machinery manufacturing, pharmaceutical and food production, and material engineering industries, among others. In transport processes, it is important to characterize the pressure drops and particle settlement [1–4], which are directly related to the transport efficiency and particle deposition to the wall-even blockage, well.

Some research has already been published on particle settlement and pressure drops in gas–solid two-phase flow in a pipe. Tong et al. [5] showed that vortex shedding resulting from natural convection changed the sedimentation velocity and induced horizontal oscillation. Balakin et al. [6] performed a study on particle sedimentation in suspensions with high particle concentrations and pointed out that Eulerian–Eulerian simulations could account for some of the detailed particle-settling processes. Tao et al. [7] found that the initial geometric arrangement of multiple particles had a great effect on sedimentation behavior. Chiodi [8] indicated that the transport of dense particles depended on the ratio of the shear velocity of the flow to the settling velocity of the particles and the Reynold's number of the sedimentation. Senapati and Dash [9] reported that the pressure drops showed completely opposite trends in two situations with different particle concentrations were used. The pressure drops increased as the particle volume concentration increased. Naveh et al. [10] found that the pressure-drop increase rate depended strongly on the Archimedes number.

Ariyaratne et al. [11] indicated that at higher gas velocities, the pressure drops predicted using the standard k-ω turbulence model are higher than those obtained when using the standard k-ε model. Narimatsu and Ferreira [12] presented the minimum pressure gradient point experimentally through pressure gradient versus gas velocity curves and indicated that the transition velocity between dense and diluted flows enhanced as the particle density and diameter increased. Herbreteau and Bouard [13] presented a pressure drop- and Froude number-dependence on the particle size and density.

As shown above, although there have been some studies on particle settlement and pressure drop in gas–solid two-phase flow, few studied both at the same time. In addition, the factors affecting particle settlement and pressure drop include inlet velocity, particle volume concentration, particle mass flow, particle diameter, and so on, but there is no correlation expression between particle settlement, pressure drop, and these factors. Therefore, in the present study, the momentum equations based on a two-fluid model are solved numerically, and the distributions of velocity and particle concentration as well as pressure drop are analyzed. The effects of inlet velocity, particle volume concentration, particle mass flow, and particle diameter on particle settlement and pressure drop are discussed. Finally, the relationship between the settlement index, pressure drop, and related synthetic parameters is determined based on the numerical data.

2. Basic Equations

Figure 1 shows gas–solid two-phase flow in a pipe with diameter D and length L. A two-fluid model is used to simulate three-dimensional gas–solid two-phase flow [14]. The particle phase is also considered to be a continuous medium in the two-fluid model, so particle-to-particle interaction has been reflected by the relationship between the stress and strain rates in the second term on the left-hand side of Equation (2). The two phases are regarded as two interacting continuous phases for the model, so the two phases have the same structure of the governing equations. Assuming that the flow field is steady and isothermal, there is no mass exchange between phases, and the particle stress tensor is ignored. Then, the continuity equation, momentum equation, and state equation are:

$$\nabla \cdot \left(\alpha_{g,s} \rho_{g,s} v_{g,s} \right) = 0, \tag{1}$$

$$\nabla \left[\alpha_{g,s} \rho_{g,s} v_{g,s} v_{g,s} + \alpha_{g,s} \Gamma_{g,s} \left(\nabla v_{g,s} + \nabla v_{g,s}^T \right) \right] = -\nabla \left(\alpha_{g,s} p \right) + \alpha_{g,s} \rho_{g,s} g + M_{g,s}, \tag{2}$$

$$p = \rho_g R T_g, \tag{3}$$

where subscript "g, s" indicates the gas or solid phase; α is the phase composition; ρ is the density; v is the velocity; $\Gamma = \rho(v_l + v_t)$ is the diffusion coefficient; v_l and v_t are the molecular and turbulent viscosity coefficients, respectively; p is the pressure; g is the gravitational acceleration; R is the gas constant; T is the temperature; and M is the interphase momentum exchange term:

$$M_{g,s} = K \left(v_{g,si} - v_{g,s} \right) + p_{g,s} \nabla \alpha_{g,s}, \tag{4}$$

where subscript "i" indicates the different phases, and K is the interphase friction coefficient and can be expressed as follows when the particle volume concentration is larger than 0.2:

$$K = 150 \frac{\alpha_s^2}{\alpha_g} \frac{\mu}{d_s^2} + 1.75 \alpha_g \frac{1}{d_s} \rho_g \left| v_g - v_s \right|, \tag{5}$$

where d is the particle diameter, and μ is the gas viscosity coefficient. When the particle volume concentration is less than 0.2, K can be expressed based on the aerodynamic force acting on solid particles as follows:

$$K = \left(C_D \alpha_g^{-2.65} \right) \left(\frac{3 \alpha_s}{2 d_s} \right) \frac{1}{2} \alpha_g \rho_g \left| v_g - v_s \right|, \tag{6}$$

where the drag coefficient of a single particle C_D and particle's Reynolds number Re are:

$$C_D = Max\left\{\frac{24}{Re}\left(1 + 0.15Re^{0.687}\right), \, 0.44\right\}, \; Re = \frac{\rho_g d_s \left(\alpha_g |v_g - v_s|\right)}{\mu} \tag{7}$$

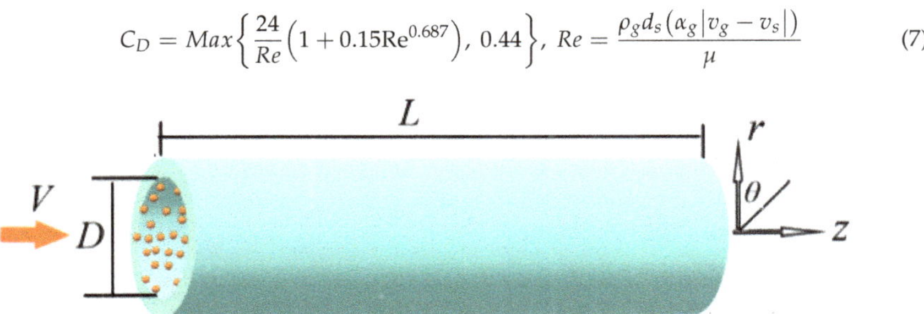

Figure 1. Schematic diagram of gas–solid two-phase flow in a pipe.

In the computation, the turbulent stress in the momentum equation adopts the Buossinesq eddy viscosity model, and the value of the eddy viscosity is determined with the corrected k-ε turbulence model.

The friction between the gas and the pipe wall can be represented by adding a source phase to the gas phase momentum equation of the control body near the pipe wall. Assuming that there is no slip between the flow and the wall, the velocity near the wall is distributed logarithmically, and the wall friction is calculated according to the smooth pipe. The friction between the solid phase and the pipe wall can be calculated by the method in reference [15], i.e., a source phase is added to the momentum equation of the solid phase of the control body near the tube wall.

3. Numerical Simulation

3.1. Parameters

The IPSA_FULL method was used to numerically simulate Equations (1)–(7). IPSA refers to the Inter-phase Slip Algorithm, and FULL refers to the full elimination algorithm, which is full coupled with the implicit approach used in Flent-4.5. This method has been proven to significantly enhance the convergence of the numerical scheme [16].

On the wall, the velocity of the gas and particles satisfies the no-slip condition. The related parameters in the simulation are particle diameter $d_p = 50$ μm, 100 μm, 500 μm, 750 μm, 1000 μm; mixture inlet velocity $V = 1$ m/s, 7 m/s, 15 m/s, 23 m/s, 30 m/s; particle volume concentration $\alpha_s = 1\%$, 5%, 10%, 15%, 20%; particle mass flow $m_s = 5$ t/h, 10 t/h, 15 t/h, 20 t/h, 25 t/h; gas density $\rho_g = 1.189$ kg/m^3; gas viscosity $v = 1.5440 \times 10^{-5}$ m^2/s; the pipe outlet is 1 atmospheric pressure.

3.2. Validation

The grid system was composed of $32(r) \times 32(\theta) \times 208(z) = 212992$ grid points. Grid independence was tested by changing the values of the grid points from 24 to 40, 24 to 40, and 192 to 224 in the r, θ, and z directions, respectively. Table 1 shows the tested results, where a convergence criterion is specified with all of the residual errors being less than 10^{-4}.

Table 1. Values of $\Delta p/L$ when changing grid points.

$r \times \theta \times S$	$\Delta p/L$	$r \times \theta \times S$	$\Delta p/L$	$r \times \theta \times S$	$\Delta p/L$
24 × 32 × 208	50,891	32 × 24 × 208	50,889	32 × 32 × 192	50,893
28 × 32 × 208	50,880	32 × 28 × 208	50,879	32 × 32 × 200	50,881
32 × 32 × 208	50,872	32 × 32 × 208	50,872	32 × 32 × 208	50,872
36 × 32 × 208	50,868	32 × 36 × 208	50,869	32 × 32 × 216	50,867
40 × 32 × 208	50,865	32 × 40 × 208	50,867	32 × 32 × 224	50,864

In order to verify the numerical method and program used in the gas–solid two-phase flow simulation, we compared the present numerical results with the previous results [17], as shown in Figures 2 and 3, where α_{sa} and v_{gza} are the average particle volume concentration and average gas velocity on the cross-section, respectively. We can see that the present numerical results and experimental results are qualitatively consistent.

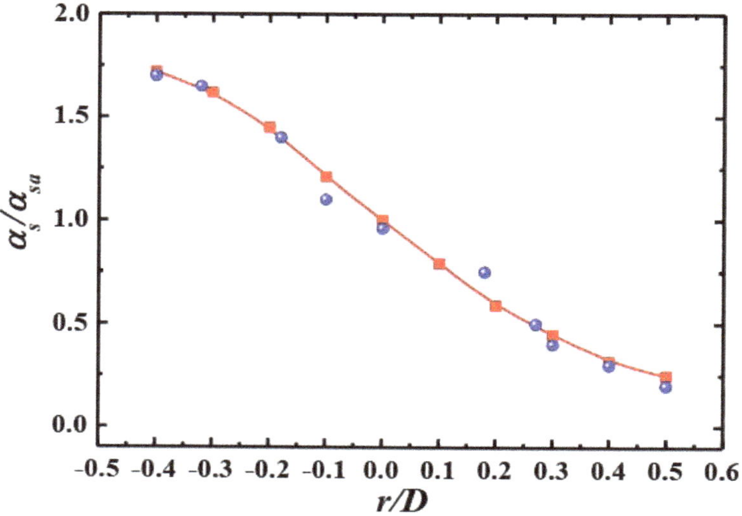

Figure 2. Distribution of particle concentration along the radial direction (α_s = 5%, V = 7 m/s). ■: present results; ●: experimental results [17].

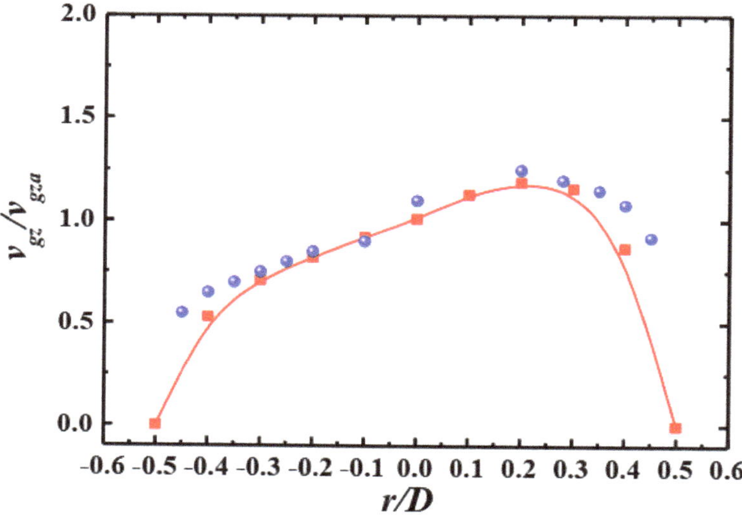

Figure 3. Distribution of gas velocity along the radial direction (α_s = 5%, V = 7 m/s). ■: present results ●: experimental results [17].

4. Results and Discussion

4.1. Distribution of Pressure along the Flow Direction

The pressure distributions along the flow direction for different particle volume concentrations are shown in Figure 4, where the pressure values are relative to the atmospheric pressure at the pipe outlet. It can be seen that four curves have the same change trend. The pressure at the inlet is the maximum, and it then decreases gradually to atmospheric pressure at the outlet because it is the flow caused by the pressure difference between the inlet and outlet. It can be divided into three areas according to the changes in the pressure. The pressure is high and changes slowly in the inlet area ($0 \leq z/L \leq 0.2$). The pressure change begins to increase in the transition area ($0.2 \leq z/L \leq 0.8$). The pressure decreases approximately linearly as the pipe length increases in the fully developed area ($0.8 \leq z/L \leq 1$) where the pressure drop per unit length is a constant that increases as the particle volume concentration increases. The distinction between the three areas is more obvious as the particle volume concentration increases.

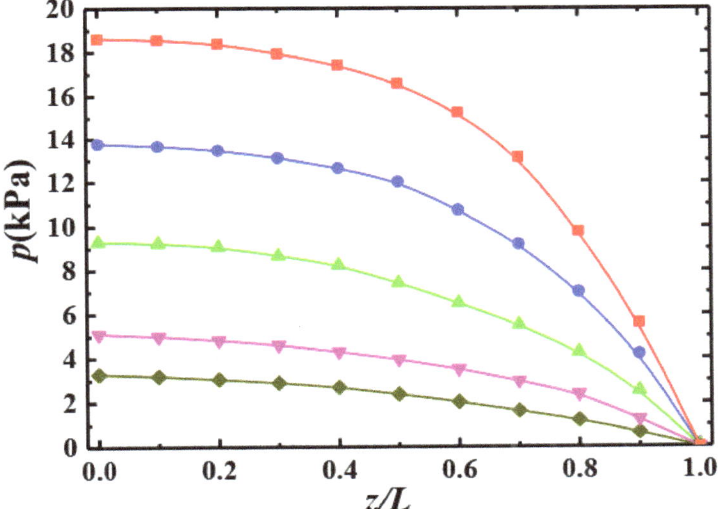

Figure 4. Pressure distributions along the flow direction (d_p = 100 μm, V = 7 m/s, m_s = 15 t/h). ■: α_s = 20%; ●: α_s = 15%; ▲: α_s = 10%; ▼: α_s = 5%; ◆: α_s = 1%.

4.2. Distribution of Velocity along the Flow Direction

Figure 5 shows the velocity distribution of the gas and solid phases along the flow direction of the pipe. We can see that unlike single-phase flow, the gas velocity distribution is asymmetrical around the center of the pipe and that the maximum velocity point moves up because the particles are gradually moved to the lower part of the pipe by gravity, obstructing the motion of the lower gas flow, thus decreasing the lower gas velocity and increasing the upper gas velocity. The particle velocity distribution is similar to that of gas flow, and the difference is that the velocity is smaller. The gas and particle velocities are distributed uniformly at the inlet and show a parabolic velocity profile at z/L = 0.2. Then, the velocity profile changes continuously along the flow direction until z/L = 0.8, where the flow reaches a fully developed stable state. From the inlet area to the fully developed area, the gas velocity increases slightly, and the velocity profile becomes asymmetric around the center, and the overall gas velocity is higher than that of the particles. The maximum gas velocity occurs at r/D = 0.35, while the maximum particle velocity appears near r/D = 0.22. The distance between the radial position of the maximum velocity and the center line for the gas is larger than that for the particles. The particle motion lags behind that of the gas flow.

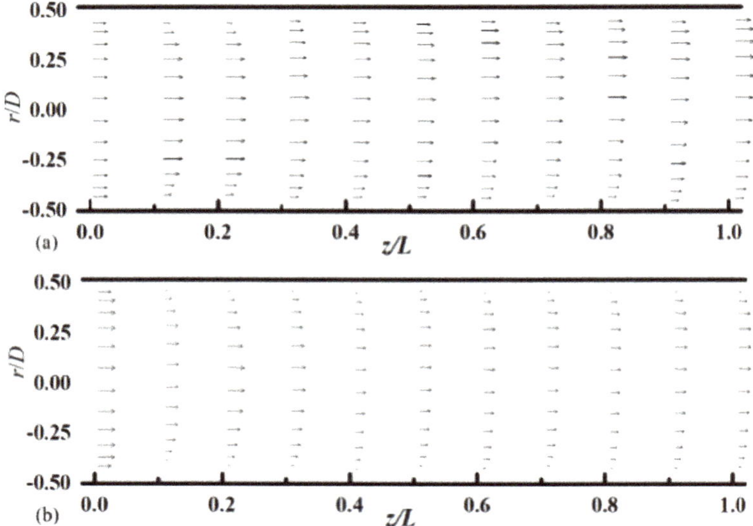

Figure 5. Velocity vector distribution at different sections (d_p = 100 μm, V = 7 m/s, α_s = 5%, m_s = 15 t/h). (**a**) gas phase; (**b**) solid phase.

4.3. Distribution of Particle Volume Concentration

Particle volume concentration distributions on different cross-sections along the flow direction are shown in Figure 6, where the darker the color, the higher the concentration. The particle volume concentration is distributed uniformly at the inlet. As the flow develops downstream, the particle volume concentration increases and decreases gradually at the bottom and the upper part of the pipe, respectively, showing obvious particle sedimentation.

4.4. Relationship between the Settlement Index and Mixture Inlet Velocity

On the cross-section at the outlet, we can define a dimensionless settlement index:

$$Se = \frac{\alpha_{sb} - \alpha_{su}}{\alpha_{si}}, \tag{8}$$

where α_{sb}, α_{su}, and α_{si} are the particle volume concentration near the lower wall (l/D = 0.125 as shown in Figure 6), near the upper wall (l/D = 0.125), and at the inlet, respectively. Se indicates the sedimentation degree of the particles. The larger the value of Se, the larger the particle volume concentration difference near the upper and lower walls, i.e., the more obvious the particle settlement.

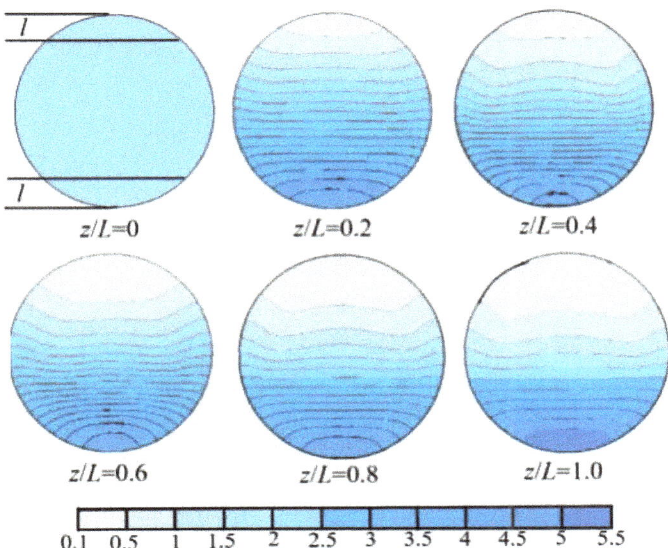

Figure 6. Particle volume distributions on different cross-sections along the flow direction ($d_p = 100$ µm, $V = 7$ m/s, $\alpha_s = 5\%$, $m_s = 15$ t/h).

4.4.1. Effect of Particle Volume Concentration

Figure 7 shows the relationship between the settlement index Se and mixture inlet velocity V for different particle volume concentrations. It can be seen that Se increases as V decreases, i.e., the particle settlement phenomenon is more serious and the particle distribution on the cross-section is more inhomogeneous with the decrease in the mixture inlet velocity. The reason for this is that the conveying time that the particles spend in the pipe is longer at a small inlet velocity, so the settling time due to gravity is longer. Se decreases as the α_s increases, which can be seen in the figure. This is partly due to the fact that the value of Se is inversely proportional to α_s, as shown in expression (8); on the other hand, a high particle volume concentration will hinder particle settlement.

4.4.2. Effect of Particle Mass Flow

The relationship between the settlement index Se and mixture inlet velocity V for different particle mass flow rates is shown in Figure 8, where it can be seen that the value of Se decreases as the V and particle mass flow m_s increase. Actually, the particle mass flow is proportional to the particle volume flow when the particle density remains unchanged, while the particle volume flow is proportional to the volume concentration within a fixed time. Therefore, the principle of Se increasing with m_s is the same as that in Figure 7.

4.4.3. Effect of Particle Diameter

Figure 9 shows the relationship between the settlement index Se and mixture inlet velocity V for different particle diameters. It can be seen that Se increases as the particle diameter d_p increases. It is obvious that the larger the particle diameter, the more significant the particle settlement is, resulting in the particles having a more inhomogeneous distribution on the cross-section at the outlet. In addition, under the parameters considered in the present study, the values of Se are larger in the case of different particle diameters than they are that in other cases, which shows that the particle diameter has a more significant effect on the uniformity of the particle distribution on the cross-section at the outlet.

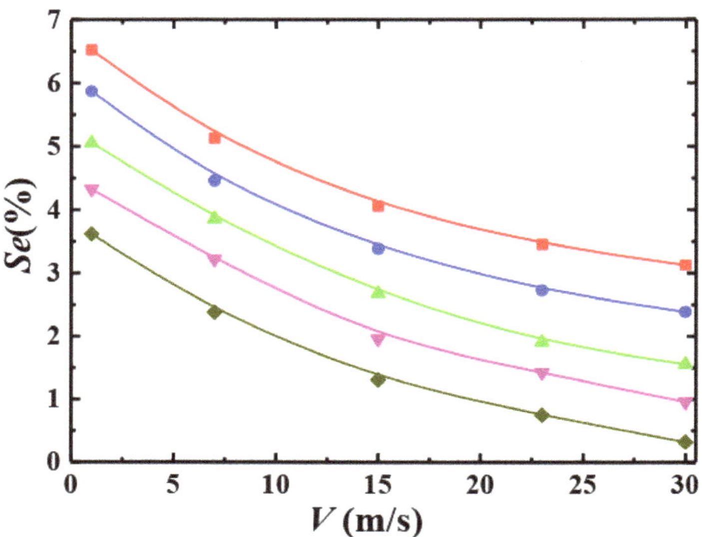

Figure 7. Relationship between *Se* and *V* for different concentrations (d_p = 100 μm, m_s = 15 t/h). α_s: ■: 1%; •: 5%; ▲: 10%; ▼: 15%; ♦: 20%.

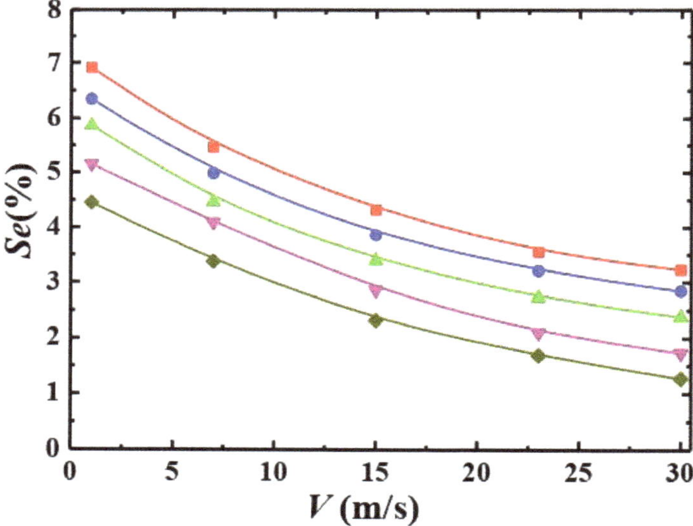

Figure 8. Relationship between *Se* and *V* for different particle mass flow (d_p = 100 μm, α_s = 5%). m_s: ■: 5 t/h; •: 10 t/h; ▲: 15 t/h; ▼: 20 t/h; ♦: 25 t/h.

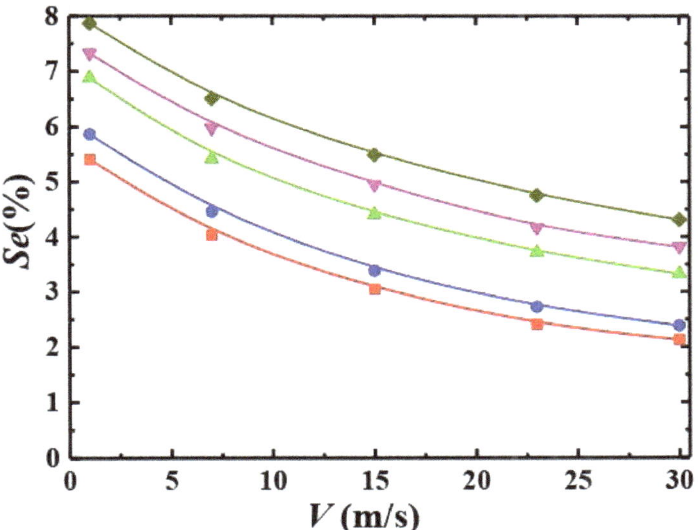

Figure 9. Relationship between *Se* and *V* for different particle diameters (α_s = 5%, m_s = 15 t/h). d_p: ■: 50 μm; ●: 100 μm; ▲: 500 μm; ▼: 750 μm; ◆: 1000 μm.

4.5. Relationship between the Pressure Drop and Mixture Inlet Velocity

4.5.1. Effect of Particle Volume Concentration

The relationship between the pressure drop per unit length p/L and mixture inlet velocity V for different particle volume concentrations is shown in Figure 10, where the values of p/L increase as the V increases for different volume concentrations, which is in accordance with the law that the pressure drop is directly proportional to the velocity in the Hagen–Poiseuille flow. In the figure, the values of p/L also increase as the particle volume concentration increases for the different inlet velocities. Since the particle density is larger than that of the gas density, the high particle concentration per unit volume means that a larger pressure drop is required to transport the mixture over the same distance.

4.5.2. Effect of Particle Mass Flow

Figure 11 shows the relationship between the pressure drop per unit length p/L and mixture inlet velocity V for different particle mass flows. For a given inlet velocity, the values of p/L increase as the particle mass flow increases because the particle mass flow is directly proportional to the particle volume concentration.

4.5.3. Effect of Particle Diameter

The relationship between the pressure drop per unit length p/L and mixture inlet velocity V for different particle diameters is shown in Figure 12, where we can see that the values of p/L decrease as the particle diameter increases. The reason for this is that under conditions where the particle volume concentration is constant, the smaller the particle, the more particles there are, and the stronger the effect of particle gas interaction. The stronger particle and gas interactions makes the required pressure drop larger due to the drag effect of the gas on the particles. It is obvious that the effect of particle diameter on pressure drop is less significant than that of the particle volume concentration and mass flow.

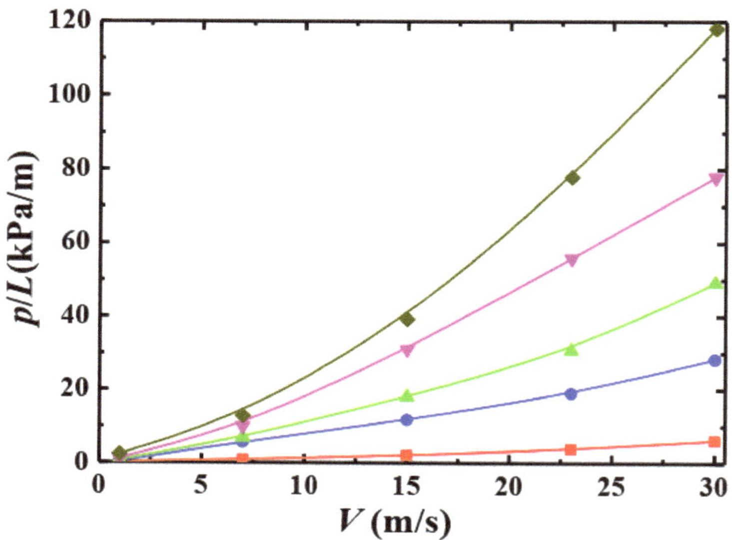

Figure 10. Relationship between p/L and V for different concentrations ($d_p = 100$ μm, $m_s = 15$ t/h). α_s: ■: 1%; ●: 5%; ▲: 10%; ▼: 15%; ◆: 20%.

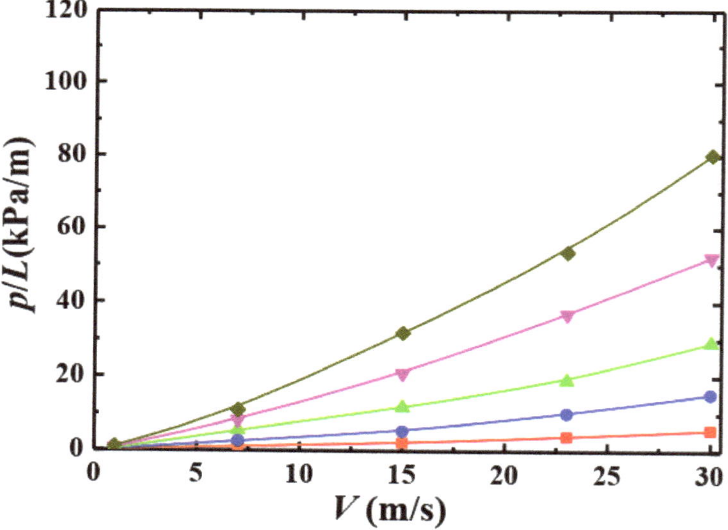

Figure 11. Relationship between p/L and V for different particle mass flow ($d_p = 100$ μm, $\alpha_s = 5$%). m_s: ■: 5 t/h; ●: 10 t/h; ▲: 15 t/h; ▼: 20 t/h; ◆: 25 t/h.

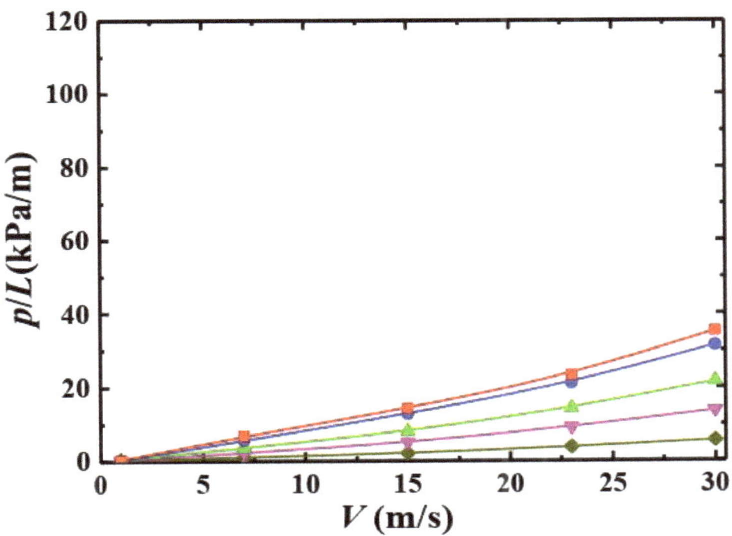

Figure 12. Relationship between p/L and V for different particle diameters ($\alpha_s = 5\%$, $m_s = 15$ t/h). d_p: ■: 50 μm; ●: 100 μm; ▲: 500 μm; ▼: 750 μm; ◆: 1000 μm.

4.6. Relationship of Settlement Index, Pressure Drop and Related Parameters

It is necessary to build a relationship between the settlement index, pressure drop per unit length, and related parameters in order to effectively characterize the gas–solid two-phase flow in a pipe. As shown in Figures 7–9, the settlement index Se is inversely proportional to the inlet velocity V, particle volume concentrations α_s, and particle mass flow m_s, while it is also directly proportional to the particle diameter d_p. As shown in Figures 10–12, the pressure drop per unit length p/L is proportional to the inlet velocity V, particle volume concentrations α_s, and particle mass flow m_s, while it is inversely proportional to the particle diameter d_p. As such, we can combine V, α_s, m_s, and d_p into a synthetic parameter:

$$\eta = \frac{d_p}{V\alpha_s m_s}, \qquad \zeta = \frac{V\alpha_s m_s}{d_p}. \tag{9}$$

Based on the above numerical data and expression (9), we can establish the following settlement index Se and pressure drop per unit length p/L formula:

$$Se = 0.69854 + 2.68062 \log \eta - 0.15859 (\log \eta)^2, \tag{10}$$

$$\frac{p}{L} = 119.33207 \exp\left(\frac{\zeta}{1.35994}\right) - 117.66952. \tag{11}$$

The settlement index and pressure drop per unit length as a function of related synthetic parameter are shown in Figures 13 and 14, where each solid dot represents different numerical data under different η and ζ, which are composed of different V, α_s, m_s, and d_p.

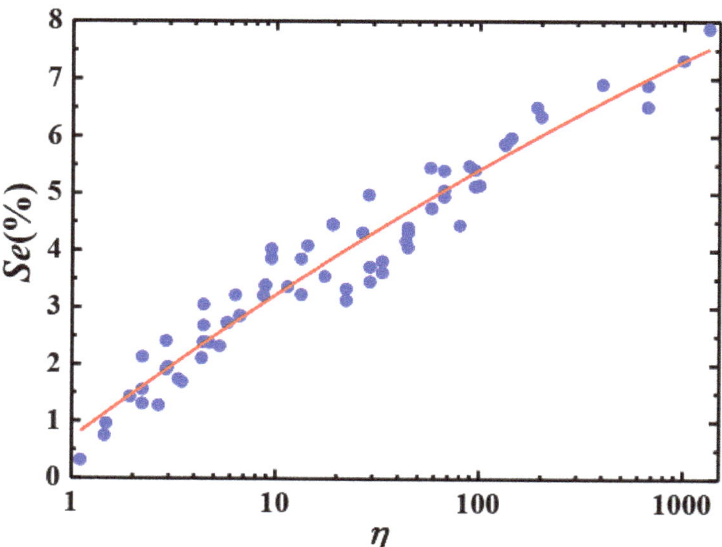

Figure 13. Relationship between *Se* and η. •: numerical data; ——: Formula (10).

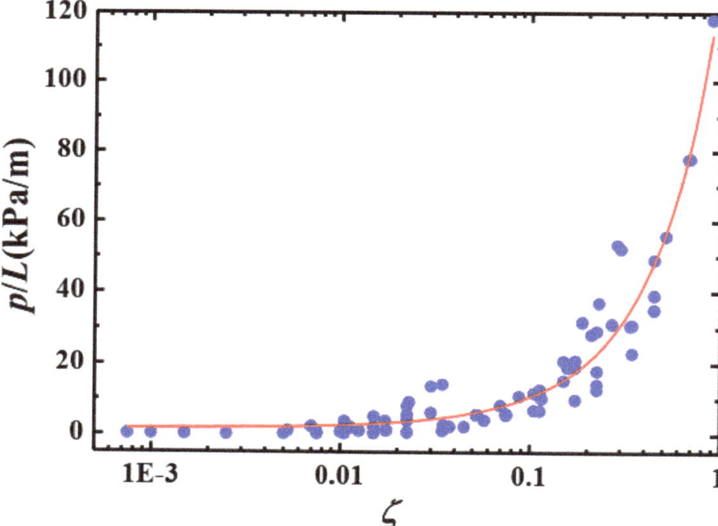

Figure 14. Relationship between *Se* and ζ. •: numerical data; ——: Formula (11).

5. Conclusions

In order to clarify the effect of inlet velocity, particle volume concentration, particle mass flow, and particle diameter on the sedimentation degree of particle and pressure drop in gas–solid two-phase flow in a pipe with a circular cross-section, the continuity equation, momentum equation, and state equation in the range of mixture inlet velocities ranging from 1 m/s to 30 m/s, particle volume concentrations ranging from 1% to 20%, particle mass flows ranging from 5 t/h to 25 t/h, and particle diameters ranging from 50 μm to 1000 μm were solved numerically based on a two-fluid model. Some results were validated by comparing the experimental results. The main conclusions can be summarized as follows:

(1) The gas and particle velocity distributions are asymmetrical around the center of the pipe and as the maximum velocity point moves up. The distance between the radial position of the maximum velocity and the center line for the gas is larger than that for the particles. The particle motions lags behind that of the gas flow.

(2) As the flow develops downstream, the particle volume concentration increases and decreases gradually at the bottom and the upper part of the pipe, respectively, showing obvious particle sedimentation. The particle settlement phenomenon is more serious, and the particle distribution on the cross-section is more inhomogeneous with the decrease in the mixture inlet velocity, particle volume concentration, and particle mass flow as well as with the increase in the particle diameter.

(3) The pressure at the inlet is the maximum, and it then decreases gradually to the atmospheric pressure at the outlet. It can be divided into three areas according to the pressure changes, i.e., inlet area, transition area, and fully developed area. The distinction between the three areas is more obvious as the particle volume concentration increases. The pressure drop per unit length increases as the mixture inlet velocity, particle volume concentration, and particle mass flow increase and as the particle diameter decreases.

(4) Finally, the expressions of settlement index and pressure drop per unit length functions of the mixture inlet velocity, particle volume concentration, particle mass flow, and particle diameter are derived based on numerical data in order for the settlement index and pressure drop to be calculated conveniently.

Author Contributions: Conceptualization, Y.W. and W.L.; methodology, W.L. and L.L.; software, W.L. and L.L.; validation, L.L. and W.L.; writing, W.L. and L.L.; resources, W.L. and Y.W.; review, Y.W. All authors have read and agreed to the published version of the manuscript.

Funding: This work was supported by the National Natural Science Foundation of China (Grant no. 12132015).

Conflicts of Interest: There are no conflicts of interest regarding the publication of this paper.

References

1. Sergeev, V.; Vatin, N.; Kotov, E.; Nemova, D.; Khorobrov, S. Slug regime transitions in a two-phase flow in horizontal round pipe. CFD simulations. *Appl. Sci.* **2020**, *23*, 8739. [CrossRef]
2. Nie, D.M.; Lin, J.Z. A LB-DF/FD Method for particle suspensions. *Commun. Comput. Phys.* **2010**, *7*, 544–563.
3. Jin, Y.; Lu, H.; Guo, X.; Gong, X. Flow patterns classification of dense-phase pneumatic conveying of pulverized coal in the industrial vertical pipeline. *Adv. Powder Technol.* **2019**, *30*, 1277–1289. [CrossRef]
4. Lin, J.Z.; Qian, L.J.; Xiong, H.B. Effects of operating conditions on the droplet deposition onto surface in the atomization impinging spray with an impinging plate. *Surf. Coat. Technol.* **2009**, *203*, 1733–1740. [CrossRef]
5. Tong, Z.H.; Liu, H.T.; Chang, J.Z.; An, K. Direct simulation of melting solid particles sedimentation in a Newtonian fluid. *Acta Phys. Sin.* **2012**, *61*, 024401. [CrossRef]
6. Balakin, B.; Hoffmann, A.C.; Kosinski, P.; Rhyne, L.D. Eulerian-Eulerian CFD model for the sedimentation of spherical particles in suspension with high particle concentrations. *Eng. Appl. Comput. Fluid Mech.* **2010**, *4*, 116–126. [CrossRef]
7. Tao, S.; Guo, Z.L.; Wang, L. P Numerical study on the sedimentation of single and multiple slippery particles in a Newtonian fluid. *Powder Technol.* **2017**, *315*, 126–138. [CrossRef]
8. Chiodi, F.; Claudin, P.; Andreotti, B. A two-phase flow model of sediment transport: Transition from bedload to suspended load. *J. Fluid Mech.* **2014**, *755*, 561–581. [CrossRef]
9. Senapati, S.K.; Dash, S.K. Computation of pressure drop and heat transfer in gas-solid suspension with small sized particles in a horizontal pipe. *Part. Sci. Technol.* **2019**, *38*, 985–998. [CrossRef]
10. Naveh, R.; Tripathi, N.M.; Kalman, H. Experimental pressure drop analysis for horizontal dilute phase particle- fluid flows. *Powder Technol.* **2017**, *321*, 355–368. [CrossRef]
11. Ariyaratne, W.; Ratnayake, C.; Melaaen, M. CFD modeling of dilute phase pneumatic conveying in a horizontal pipe using Euler-Euler approach. *Part. Sci. Technol.* **2019**, *37*, 1011–1019. [CrossRef]
12. Narimatsu, C.; Ferreira, M. Vertical pneumatic conveying in dilute and dense-phase flows: Experimental study of the influence of particle density and diameter on fluid dynamic behavior. *Braz. J. Chem. Eng.* **2001**, *18*, 221–232. [CrossRef]
13. Herbreteau, C.; Bouard, R. Experimental study of parameters which influence the energy minimum in horizontal gas-solid conveying. *Powder Technol.* **2000**, *112*, 213–220. [CrossRef]

14. Levy, A. Two-fluid approach for plug flow simulations in horizontal pneumatic conveying. *Powder Technol.* **2000**, *112*, 263–272. [CrossRef]
15. Levy, A.; Mooney, T.; Marjanovic, P.; Mason, D.J. A comparison of analytical and numerical models for gas-solid flow through straight pipe of different inclinations with experimental data. *Powder Technol.* **1997**, *93*, 253–260. [CrossRef]
16. Benyahia, S.; Arastoopour, H.; Knowlton, T.M.; Massah, H. Simulation of particles and gas flow behavior in the riser section of a circulating fluidized bed using the kinetic theory approach for the particulate phase. *Powder Technol.* **2000**, *112*, 24–33. [CrossRef]
17. Tsuji, Y.; Morlkawa, Y.; Tanaka, T.; Nakatsukasa, N.; Nakatani, M. Numerical simulation of gas-solid two phase flow in a two-dimensional horizontal channel. *Int. J. Multiph. Flow* **1987**, *13*, 671–692. [CrossRef]

Review

Heat Transfer Enhancement of Nanofluids with Non-Spherical Nanoparticles: A Review

Xiaoyin Li [1,2], Fangyang Yuan [1,2,*], Wenma Tian [1,2], Chenlong Dai [1,2], Xinjun Yang [1,2], Dongxiang Wang [1,2], Jiyun Du [1,2], Wei Yu [1,2] and Huixin Yuan [3]

[1] Jiangsu Key Laboratory of Advanced Food Manufacturing Equipment and Technology, Jiangnan University, Wuxi 214122, China; 6200809017@stu.jiangnan.edu.cn (X.L.); 6210810102@stu.jiangnan.edu.cn (W.T.); 6210810042@stu.jiangnan.edu.cn (C.D.); xinjun_yang@jiangnan.edu.cn (X.Y.); dxwang@jiangnan.edu.cn (D.W.); jiyundu@jiangnan.edu.cn (J.D.); yuwei0301@jiangnan.edu.cn (W.Y.)
[2] School of Mechanical Engineering, Jiangnan University, Wuxi 214122, China
[3] Department of Mechanical Engineering, Taihu University of Wuxi, Wuxi 214063, China; yhx@cczu.edu.cn
* Correspondence: fyyuan@jiangnan.edu.cn

Abstract: This article reviews the heat transfer enhancement of nanofluids with non-spherical nanoparticles. We divided the non-spherical nanoparticles suspended in nanofluids into three categories based on the dimension of geometric particle structure. Based on the measured data in experimental studies, we then evaluated the shape effect of non-spherical nanoparticles on thermal conductivity and convective heat transfer enhancement of nanofluids. Recent studies explored the numerical predictions and related heat transfer mechanisms. Due to large aspect ratios, thermal conductivity is abnormally enhanced only for nanofluids with carbon nanotubes/nanofibers/nanowires. The approximate enhancement effect exerted by three types of non-spherical nanoparticles on thermal conductivity was 4.5:2.5:1. Thermal conductivity enhancement per concentration was larger for nanorods/ellipsoids with small aspect ratios. The convective heat transfer coefficient was increased by suspending non-spherical nanoparticles in the base fluid. Consequently, no significant thermo-hydraulic performance was discovered for convective heat transfer of non-spherical nanoparticle nanofluid flow, specifically for turbulent flows, due to increased pumping power. However, the temperature and particle concentration effect on convective heat transfer remains unclear. In addition, no perfect model for predicting the thermal conductivity and convective heat transfer of non-spherical nanoparticle nanofluids has been reported.

Keywords: nanofluids; non-spherical nanoparticles; heat transfer enhancement; thermal conductivity; convective heat transfer

Citation: Li, X.; Yuan, F.; Tian, W.; Dai, C.; Yang, X.; Wang, D.; Du, J.; Yu, W.; Yuan, H. Heat Transfer Enhancement of Nanofluids with Non-Spherical Nanoparticles: A Review. *Appl. Sci.* **2022**, *12*, 4767. https://doi.org/10.3390/app12094767

Academic Editor: Luis Lugo

Received: 21 April 2022
Accepted: 6 May 2022
Published: 9 May 2022

Publisher's Note: MDPI stays neutral with regard to jurisdictional claims in published maps and institutional affiliations.

1. Introduction

Studies on heat transfer enhancement of nanofluids have largely matured over the past decade. Since Choi and Eastman [1] introduced the concept of "nanofluids," which are fluids with suspended nanoparticles, scholars have reported significant heat transfer enhancement of nanofluids with low particle loadings. In addition, the suspension is stable and induces a small amount of pumping power compared to the base fluid [2]. Therefore, nanofluids are considered the next generation of a heat transfer medium that will be extensively applied in advanced heating or cooling technology.

Due to the complexity of the nanofluid flow transport, the mechanism underlying the excellent heat transfer performance of nanofluids is poorly understood. The bulk medium shows rheological behavior after the nanoparticles are dispersed in the base fluid [3,4]. Murshed and Estellé reviewed the viscosity of nanofluids with different types of nanoparticles or base fluids, particle concentration, shear rate, etc. [5]. However, they discovered scattered and inconsistent literature data from different researchers. Moreover, the conventional and proposed empirical models could not effectively predict the viscosity of nanofluids containing non-spherical nanoparticles. Similar scenarios have been reported in heat transfer characteristics of nanofluids. First, there is a substantial variance in the thermal conductivity of nanofluids measured in the literature [6,7].

On the other hand, the convective heat transfer coefficient or Nusselt number provided in literature for nanofluid flow is different and inconsistent [8,9]. The contributing factors for nanofluids' heat transfer characteristics multiply, resulting in nonlinear correlations. Therefore, reviewing the results from previous studies is essential to identify research gaps.

Heat transfer enhancement of nanofluids is influenced by several factors, including particle material, size, shape, concentration, type of base fluid, the temperature of bulk fluid, etc. For convective heat transfer (CHT), the flow parameters and thermal boundary conditions promote nanofluids flow. Most of the previous studies focused on the importance of fluid type and particle concentration. Based on the effective medium theory, the enhancement of nanofluids heat transfer increases with the concentration and the thermal conductivity of the particle material. Nonetheless, the effect of particle shape and size distribution was partially reported and considered a constant in experiments or theoretical studies. The nanoparticles prepared for experiments in laboratories or applications in industries are polydisperse. The shape and size of particles vary around the nominal value given by nanomaterial producers.

Moreover, most studies on nanofluids' heat transfer enhancement are based on bulk fluid with spherical nanoparticles. With nanotechnology, more nanoparticles with different shapes can be industrially developed. In recent years, several experimental, theoretical, and numerical studies reported that particle shape modulates the CHT characteristic of nanofluids [10,11]. Nanoparticles with shapes such as cylinders, bricks, blades, and platelets have been discussed (Figure 1). Furthermore, a theoretical and numerical investigation of heat transfer enhancement of nanofluids containing non-spherical nanoparticles (NSN nanofluids) has recently gained a premium [12,13]. Therefore, it is essential to review the existing research on the importance of the particle shape effect on the nanofluid application in heat transfer enhancement.

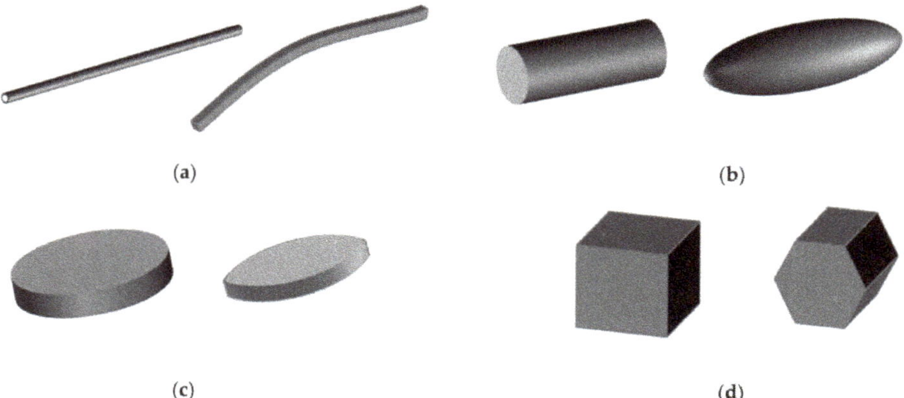

Figure 1. Shapes of non-spherical nanoparticles used in nanofluids. (**a**) CNTs/nanofibers/nanowires; (**b**) rods/cylinder/ellipsoids; (**c**) platelets/blades; (**d**) bricks/diamonds/polygons.

This article reviews research findings and the development of the heat transfer enhancement of NSN nanofluids. We collect and analyze thermal conductivity enhancement (TCE) measured in experiments based on NSN nanofluids. This work also summarizes the classical and recently proposed thermal conductivity models for NSN nanofluids and the related mechanisms. Further, we evaluate the experimental data in studies on CHT of NSN nanofluids. Finally, we present conclusions on the basic theory and numerical predictions for NSN nanofluids fluid with CHT.

2. Thermal Conductivity of NSN Nanofluids

Thermal energy transfer occurs through conduction, convection, or radiation [14]. Considering that radiative energy transport is quite distinct from the first two mechanisms because it does not require a material medium, we primarily focus on conduction and convection behaviors. This section deals with the thermal conductivity of NSN nanofluids, whereas heat transfer via convection will be discussed in the next sections.

2.1. Experimental Data Evaluation

Thermal conductivity is an essential physical property of nanofluid conduction. Several studies have been performed to enhance nanofluids' thermal conductivity. For NSN nanofluids, Table 1 summarizes experimental studies on the thermal conductivity enhancement of NSN nanofluids. The experimental conditions vary in the nanofluid type, particle shape, size, volume fraction, and temperature. Distilled water (DW) was commonly used for aqueous nanofluids, and oil was used as the base fluid. Most of the experiments were performed by transient hotwire technology in the lab. The insulation treatment of the sensor and control of surfactant is significantly essential [15]. As shown in the table, all of the experimental results showed the thermal conductivities of nanofluids were enhanced after nanoparticles were suspended in the base fluid. Results showed that the thermal conductivity of nanofluids increases as the particle loading grows. However, not all data demonstrated the abnormal thermal conductivity capacity of nanofluids with non-spherical nanoparticles. Figure 2 presents the experimental data in Table 1 to compare the TCEs of different NSN nanofluids at room temperature. Considering the continuous variation in TCE with temperature, data were obtained by interpolation within the temperature range.

The shapes of non-spherical nanoparticles used in studies can be divided into three categories based on the dimensionality of particle geometry [13,16]. Carbon nanotubes (CNTs), nanofibers, and nanowires are approximated as one-dimensional elongated particles with a large aspect ratio (AR, ratio of length to diameter of particles). Their cross-section size is in the nanometer range. However, the length is several microns or even longer. In addition, their bending states differ due to different materials.

Nevertheless, these particles with large aspect ratios are easily intertwined, inducing a network effect [17]. Their rheological characteristics are significantly apparent. Rod-like and ellipsoidal particles are categorized as two-dimensional nanomaterials with a moderate aspect ratio of 1 to 10. If the length is much less than the cross-sectional diameter, the particle usually appears as a disk shaped like a platelet or a blade, as shown in Figure 1c. Additional types of particles with arbitrary shapes such as bricks, diamonds, and other polygonal shapes are three-dimensional classes. From the average slope of the three zones, the approximate enhancement effect by three types of non-spherical nanoparticles on thermal conductivity is 4.5:2.5:1. The thermal conductivity characteristics of three types of NSN nanofluids are discussed.

2.1.1. CNTs/Nanofibers/Nanowires

CNTs are the most popular suspension medium for nanofluids since they display an average thermal conductivity of 4000 W/(m·K), which is higher than that of other nanoparticles [18]. Many articles and reviews [19–21] focused on nanofluids with CNTs, and only representative work is listed in Table 1. The type of nanofluid with elongated nanoparticles shows excellent performance in TCE due to the large size and aspect ratio of CNTs, which are hundreds of nanometers in diameter and at least tens of microns in length [15,22]. Nevertheless, the addition of large-aspect-ratio particles into a base fluid could significantly increase viscosity compared to the continuous phase [23]. Moreover, CNTs, another nanofibrous polymer [15], and nanowires [24] entangle with each other, which could cause a complex particle morphology and heat transfer properties in different experiments. Ali et al. [21] recently reviewed the thermal conductivity of commonly used particles and base fluids for fabricating nanofluids and showed that carbon-based nanofluids hold superior thermal features to those prepared by metal oxides and metals.

Figure 2 displays a number of points showing the enhancement of heat conduction in varying ranges. Maheshwary et al. [25,26] reported doubled thermal conductivities after suspending 2.5 wt.% metal oxide nanoparticles. They compared three nanofluids with cubic, nanorod, and spherical nanoparticles; they concluded that cubic particles displayed the best performance. Their abnormal results are significantly more excellent than others represented in Figure 2a. Thus, they are not plotted in the figure. The TCE shows two distinct trends that the black dotted line can distinguish in the figure in a wide range of volume fractions. Several studies reported abnormal TCE within 1% particle loading. Xie et al. [27,28] prepared nanowires with high aspect ratios (25 for Ag and approximately 82 for CuO nanowires) and measured an intriguingly high thermal conductivity increment at low volume fractions.

In contrast, the TCE for nanofluid containing CuO nanospheres remains low. Therefore, thermal conductivities for NSN nanofluids can be much higher than those of nanofluids containing spherical nanoparticles. The study also showed that the TCE linearly increases with the volume fraction when the nanowire volume fraction is lower than 1%, and the authors discovered that their data effectively conforms to the Hamilton–Crosser (H-C) model. Intriguingly, Carbajal-Valdéz et al. [29] reported a TCE of 20.8% by suspending only 0.0174% Ag nanowires, which shows a performance approximately 20 times better than the results of Gu et al. [24]. Overall, nanofluids with CNTs/nanofibers/nanowires demonstrate the best performance in different types of nanofluids. Specifically, nanofluids prepared with Ag nanowires at low concentrations show abnormal TCE.

2.1.2. Nanorods/Ellipsoids

Nanofluids containing cylindrical nanoparticles are another type of suspension commonly used in research [2,10,30,31]. Notably, nanoparticles in cylindrical shape are referred to as nanorods with stiffness and finite length. These nanomaterials are synthesized from metals or semiconducting materials and cannot bend. The cross-section of particles is circular and nanosized, with a moderate aspect ratio range of around 5 [32]. Yang and Han [31] documented that nanofluids containing cylindrical nanoparticles with such an aspect ratio could show different behaviors.

In Figure 2, the findings reported by Murshed et al. [2] and Zhu et al. [33] are quite similar when particle loading ranges from 2% to 5%. The aspect ratios of used nanorods are approximately 4 and 6.25, and the materials include TiO_2 and CuO, respectively. Timofeeva et al. suspended aluminum oxide (Al_2O_3) nanoparticles of four different shapes [34] in DW and EG mixed 50/50 by volume to assess the particle shape effect on thermal conductivity of nanofluids. The nanoparticles supported by a company have the shapes of rods, bricks, platelets, and blades, with different sizes and aspect ratios. The data measured in experiments illustrated that nanofluids containing cylindrical nanoparticles exhibit the best heat conductivity performance. They found that particle shape and interfacial layer contribute to the particle volume fraction thermal conductivity of nanoparticle suspensions. The predictions of the classical H-C model are higher than the measured TCE for particles with blade and platelet shapes.

Other studies [10,31,35] measured similar values of TCE, which are approximately half of the TCE reported by Murshed et al. [2] and Zhu et al. [33]. Chen et al. [3] prepared aqueous nanofluids containing CNTs with an aspect ratio of 10, closer to rod-like. Nithiyanantham et al. [36] suspended rod-like Al_2O_3 nanoparticles into molten salt to prepare nanofluids and discovered approximately 10% TCE in the liquid state. The particle shapes discussed above have an aspect ratio larger than 1. As shown in Figure 1, the nanofluid TCE is positively related to the particle concentration. To eliminate the effect of particle concentration to examine the shape effect, we defined the enhancement per concentration as the ratio of TCE and particle volume fraction. Figure 3 shows the enhancement per concentration as a function of aspect ratio at room temperature. Only a handful of studies have provided particle aspect ratios. Ag nanowire/CNT-based nanofluids made by Gu et al. [24] and Carbajal-Valdéz et al. [29] were not plotted due to the out-of-range values.

Nanoparticles agglomerate and form aggregates with a small aspect ratio; this explains why many studies have found enhanced heat transfer except for the concentration increment. With increasing AR, the enhancement per concentration increases; this implies that a non-spherical shape helps TCE. The reported data are near the diagonal (enhancement per concentration/AR = 1). Interestingly, the increase induced by the aspect ratio appears to be more apparent in the small-aspect-ratio region (AR < 10), which represents rod-like particles. TCE per concentration no longer increased with increasing AR for a tubular/wire-shaped dispersed phase with a large aspect ratio. This means that the enhancement of the network effect on heat transfer is limited. Jiang et al. [37] discovered that the effect of particle AR on TCE was more apparent for small particles.

2.1.3. Platelets/Blades/Bricks/Diamonds/Polygons

Platelet/blade-shaped particles have a large section area. The data plotted in Figure 2 reveal a relatively small TCE of this nanofluid type. Singh et al. [38] measured a TCE of approximately 29.51% at a high volume fraction of SiC–water nanofluid of 7%. Timofeeva et al. [34] compared the effects of the particle shapes of platelets, blades, and cylinders on TCE by eliminating the material and agglomeration effect. They discovered that although the sphericities of blades and platelets are larger than those of cylinders, the measured TCE of blades and platelets is smaller than that of cylinders. The classical H-C model considers the sphericity of non-spherical particles and cannot estimate the shape effect on the TCE of nanofluids. Similar results were obtained by Kim et al. [39] in a comparison of platelet-, brick-, and blade-shaped particles.

Torii and Yang [40] and Xie et al. [41] investigated nanofluids with diamond-like particle shapes; however, these particles are treated as spheres. Their findings showed that TCE linearly increases with particle volume fraction. Ferrouillat et al. [42] tested nanofluids with polygonal nanoparticles and discovered a slight difference between nanofluids and base fluid. Notably, particle sizes differ among these studies, which could also influence the TCE. Enhancement per concentration as a function of particle size at room temperature is illustrated in Figure 4. Experimental data reported in Table 1 are plotted, except for those of Maheshwary et al. [25,26], whose findings were two orders of magnitude higher than other results. As shown in Figure 4, most of the enhancement per concentration is smaller than 10, indicating a relatively weak shape effect of these particles on TCE. From the data of diamond and platelet particles, the enhancement per concentration increases with increasing particle size.

Nonetheless, the materials of nanoparticles as additives dispersed in the nanofluids are different, and studies demonstrated a different behavior in particle size effect [43]. Tahmooressi et al. [44] recently argued that there is insufficient evidence that smaller nanoparticles increase ETC more than larger nanoparticles. Heat conductivities of nanofluids with blade- or brick-shaped nanoparticles measured by Kim et al. [39] and Timofeeva et al. [34] are close and lower than those of other shapes due to the sphericity of bricks being close to 1.

Table 1. Summary of experiments data for heat conductivity of NSN nanofluids.

Authors	Nanofluid Type	Particle Shape and Size (nm as Default)	Volume Fraction ϕ (Vol. as Default)	Temperature	Maximum TCE
Xie et al. [30]	SiC–water/EG	Cylindrical 600 (d)	<4.2%	4 °C	22.9%
Xie et al. [22]	CNTs–DE/EG/DW	Nanotube 15 (d) × 30 mm (l)	1%	–	19.6% in DE, 12.7% in EG, 7.0% in DW
Assael et al. [45]	CNTs–water	Nanotube, 30 to 250 (d), $l > 70{,}000$	0.6%	Room	38%
Murshed et al. [2]	TiO$_2$–water	Nanorod 10 (d) × 40 (l)	<5%	Room	33%
Yang and Han [31]	Bi$_2$Te$_3$–perfluoro–n–hexane	Nanorod 20 (d) × 170 (l)	0.8%	3–50 °C	7.7% at 3 °C, 6.3% at 50 °C
Yang and Han [31]	Bi$_2$Te$_3$–hexadecane oil	Nanorod 20 (d) × 170 (l)	0.8%	20–50 °C	6.1% at 20 °C, 3.9% at 50 °C

Table 1. *Cont.*

Authors	Nanofluid Type	Particle Shape and Size (nm as Default)	Volume Fraction ϕ (Vol. as Default)	Temperature	Maximum TCE
Zhang et al. [15]	CNTs–water	Nanofiber 150 (d) × 10,000 (l)	0.1–0.89%	23 °C	40%
Zhu et al. [33]	CuO–water	Nanorod 30–50 (d) × 200–300 (l)	0.1–10%	Room	18% at ϕ = 1%, 28% at ϕ = 3%, 31% at ϕ = 5%
Chen et al. [3]	TiO$_2$–water	Nanorod 10 (d) × 100 (l)	0.12, 0.24, and 0.60%	20–40 °C	5.38%
Singh et al. [38]	SiC–water	Platelet 170 (d)	<4%	Room	~29.51%
Timofeeva et al. [34]	Al$_2$O$_3$–EG and water (50/50)	Platelet 16 (d) × 3 (l)	<7%	21 °C	18% at ϕ = 7%
Timofeeva et al. [34]	Al$_2$O$_3$–EG and water (50/50)	Blade36 (d) × 6 (l)	<7%	21 °C	18% at ϕ = 7%
Timofeeva et al. [34]	Al$_2$O$_3$–EG and water (50/50)	Cylinder 8 (d) × 64 (l)	<8.5%	21 °C	35% at ϕ = 8.5%
Timofeeva et al. [34]	Al$_2$O$_3$–EG and water (50/50)	Brick 54 (l)	<7%	21 °C	25% at ϕ = 7%
Torii and Yang [40]	nanodiamonds–water	Diamond 10 (d)	<5%	-	16%
Xie et al. [41]	nanodiamonds–water/EG	Diamond 30–50 (d)	<2%	10–60 °C	18%
Yu et al. [10]	Al$_2$O$_3$–PAO	Nanorod 7 (d) ×85 (l)	<1.3%	25 °C	12% at ϕ = 1.3%
Nasiri et al. [46]	SWNT/SWNT/FWNT/MWNT–water	-	0.25 wt.%	15–40 °C	13%, 16%, 21%
Gu et al. [24]	CNTs–water	Nanofiber 10–15 (d) × 10–20 µm (l)	0.2%	25 °C	3.7%
Gu et al. [24]	Ag–water	Nanowire 60 (d) × 20,000–30,000 (l)	0.2%	25 °C	12.1%
Gu et al. [24]	Cu–water	Nanowire 100–200 (d) × 800–6000 (l)	0.2%	25 °C	2.8%
Ferrouillat et al. [42]	SiO$_2$–water	Banana-like	0.82%	20–70 °C	2% at 70 °C
Ferrouillat et al. [42]	ZnO–water	Nanorod	0.93%	20–70 °C	1% at 70 °C
Fang et al. [47]	Ag–EG	Nanowire 100 (d) × 50,000 (l) Platelet, 300–400 (d) × 30–40 (l)	0.1%	10–30 °C	15.6% 5.3%
Jeong et al. [48]	ZnO–water	Nanorod, 150–370 (d) Platelets,15 (d) × 5 (l)	0.5–5%	Room	19.8% 23%
Kim et al. [39]	Al$_2$O$_3$–water	Blades, 15 (l) × 8 (w) × 5 (h) Bricks, 40 (d) × 40 (l) × 20 (l)	0.3–7%	20–80 °C	16% 28%
Farbod et al. [49]	CuO–engine oil	Nanorod	<6 wt.%	25 °C	8.3%
8.3%	TiO$_2$–water	Cubic, 87.21 (d) Nanorod, 8.27 (d) × 92.47 (l)	<2.5 wt.%	27–87 °C	169% 96%
Zhang et al. [28]	Ag–EG	Nanowire 40 (d) × 1000 (l)	0.46%	25 °C	13.42%
Zhu et al. [27]	CuO–dimethicone	Nanowire 30–80 (d) × 3500–5500 (l)	0.15% 0.3% 0.45% 0.6% 0.75%	25 °C	13.42% 23.15% 36.98% 47.67% 60.78%
Shah et al. [50]	CuO–EG and DW (70/30)	Cube, 68.4 (l) Brick, AR = 1.07 Polygonal, AR = 1.57 Nanorod, AR = 5.84	0.3%	30–80 °C	16.98% 22.30% 29.50% 33.17%
Carbajal et al. [29]	Ag–water	Nanowire 96 (d) × 40,000 (l)	0.0174%	Room	20.8%
Maheshwary et al. [25]	CuO–water	Cubic, Nanorod	2.5 wt.%	30 °C	72.49% 48.81%
Maheshwary et al. [25]	MgO–water	Cubic, Nanorod	2.5 wt.%	30 °C	110.96% 72.57%
Maheshwary et al. [25]	TiO$_2$–water	Cubic Nanorod	2.5 wt.%	30 °C	148.46% 115.55%
Maheshwary et al. [25]	ZrO$_2$–water	Cubic, Nanorod	2.5 wt.%	30 °C	164.01% 135.36%
Maheshwary et al. [25]	Al$_2$O$_3$–water	Cubic, Nanorod	2.5 wt.%	30 °C	209.70% 173.31%
Nithiyanantham et al. [36]	Al$_2$O$_3$–molten salt	Nanorod, 3–7 (d) × 30–70 (l)	1 wt.%	50–200 °C	10.08%

Table 1. *Cont.*

Authors	Nanofluid Type	Particle Shape and Size (nm as Default)	Volume Fraction ϕ (Vol. as Default)	Temperature	Maximum TCE
Cui et al. [35]	TiO$_2$–water	Ellipsoidal, 20 (d) × 30 (l) Nanorod, 15 (d) × 35 (l) Sheet, 5 (w) × 70 (l) × 70 (h)	0.5–4%	20–60 °C	20.58% 20.63% 23.43%
Ni et al. [51]	Cu$_2$O–water	Nanowire, 2–3 (d)	-	30–80 °C	66.8%

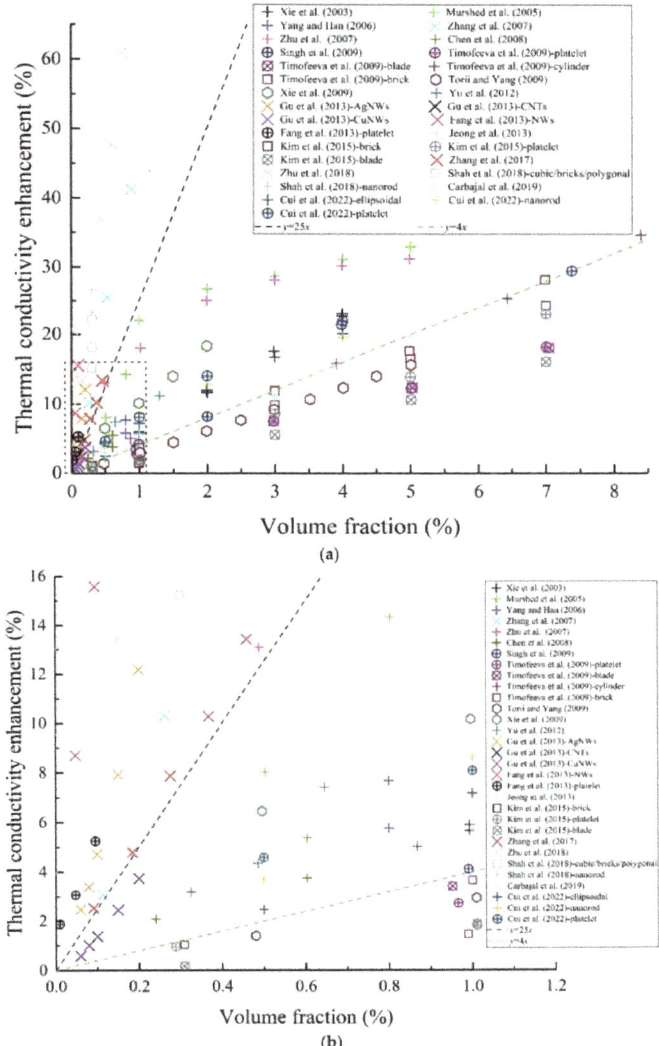

Figure 2. Collection of experimental data for TCE of NSN nanofluids at room temperature (×: CNTs/nanofibers/nanowires; +: nanorods/cylinders/ellipsoids; $\oplus$: platelets; $\otimes$: blades; □: bricks; ⬡: diamonds). (**a**) Full range. (**b**) Enlarged low-volume-fraction region (volume fraction < 1.2%, TCE < 16%) [2,3,10,15,22,24,27–29,31,33–35,38–41,47,48,50].

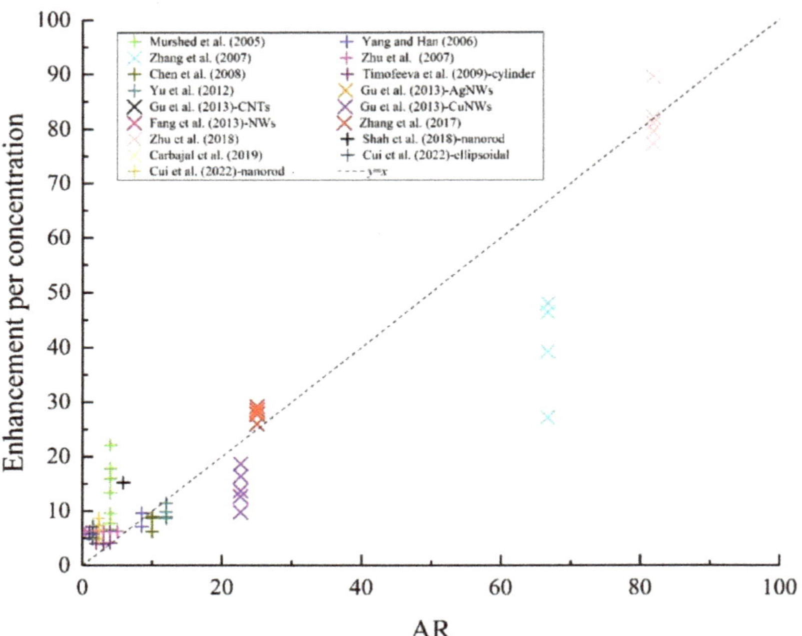

Figure 3. Enhancement per concentration as a function of aspect ratio at room temperature [2,3,10,15,24,27–29,31,33–35,47,50].

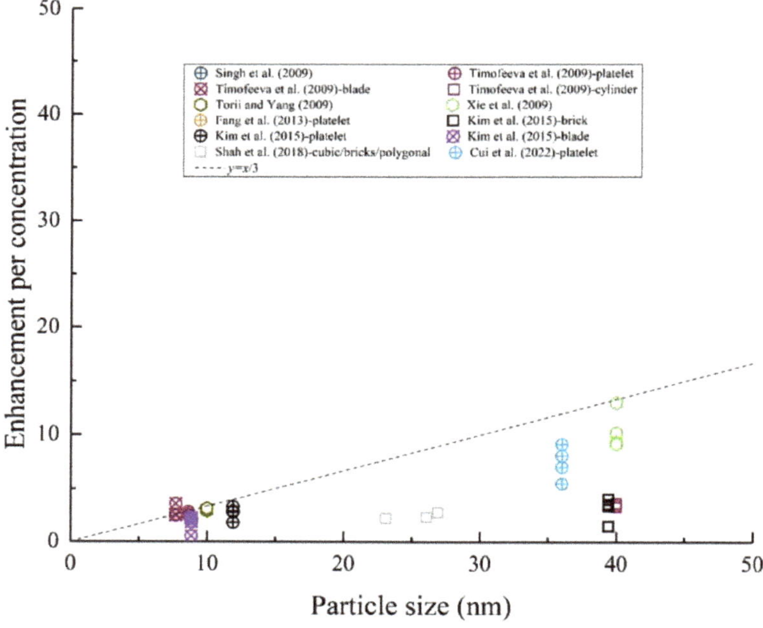

Figure 4. Enhancement per concentration as a function of particle size at room temperature [34,35,38–41,47,50].

2.2. Numerical Predictions and Mechanism Discussion

Effective heat conductivity (EHC) k is often used to describe the bulk ability of thermal conductivity. For suspensions with spherical particles, Maxwell [52] first presented the classical EHC model:

$$k_{nf} = k_f \left[\frac{(k_p + 2k_f) + 2\phi\left(k_f - k_p\right)}{(k_p + 2k_f) - \phi\left(k_f - k_p\right)} \right] \tag{1}$$

The formula is derived from spherical particles, but recent studies have found that it is also effective for diluting Newtonian nanofluids [17]. Based on the Maxwell model, Hamilton and Crosser [53] presented the model for suspensions with non-spherical particles:

$$k_{nf} = k_f \left[\frac{k_p + (n-1)k_f - (n-1)(k_p - k_f)\phi}{k_p + (n-1)k_f + \left(k_p - k_f\right)\phi} \right] \tag{2}$$

where n is the shape factor, and $n = 3/s_i$. s_i is the sphericity, which equals 3 for spherical particles. The data listed in Table 1 indicate that the EHC for nanofluids is influenced by particle shape and materials, particle loading, and pH. Wang et al. [54] established a model for nanoparticle aggregates by combining the effective medium approximation and the fractal theory. Nonetheless, the fractal dimension or shape factor index could not provide particle shape characteristics and the interaction with base fluids. Therefore, there is no perfect model to predict the thermal conductivity of various nanofluids accurately. Table 2 lists several popular models and numerical studies for EHC of NSN nanofluids. Nanofluids with tube/wire/cylinder-shaped nanoparticles showed superior TCE. Thus, the models in the literature are primarily established to focus on this type of particle. Most of these models are based on the classical H-C model and modified based on the experimental data or by combining the characteristics of nanofluids.

2.2.1. Interfacial Layer Theory

Nanofluids are composites with particle additives [55]. The liquid atoms of the base fluid near a nanoparticle will be absorbed into the solid surface of the nanoparticle and form an absorption layer [56]. The interfacial layer between particles and base fluid has a remarkable effect on thermal conductivity. For non-spherical particles, the surface area of the interfacial layer is much larger than that of spherical particles, which can trigger a larger heat flux. Nan et al. [57] presented a model for CNT nanofluids considering the interfacial thermal barrier resistance and found a significant interface effect on TCE. Many models [58–60] were built by considering the interfacial layer effect. The benefit of this theory is that it considers the effect of particle morphology from the microscopic point of view. Chandrasekar et al. [61] proposed a model considering the interfacial layer thickness, particle shape, and Brownian motion. They attributed the anomalous TCE to the particle shape.

Timofeeva et al. [34] believed that TCE for NSN nanofluids depends on the competition between surface contact area (enhancement) and Kapitza resistance (weakening). The model predicted that TCE would be negative when sphericity is smaller than 0.6 for Al_2O_3–EG/water (50/50) nanofluids. Yang et al. [62–64] developed several EHC models based on the anisotropy analysis of cylindrical nanoparticles. They summed axial and radial direction heat transfer flux of cylindrical nanoparticles whose orientation distribution is uniform. These models are built exquisitely and are challenging to use. The shape of nanoparticles was first incorporated into an AI-based model for thermal conductivity by Cui et al. [35]. The results of the developed CFFNN model revealed that the cylindrical shape of nanoparticles with a large aspect ratio could trigger a rapid heat flow along longer thermally conducting pathways without the need to cross an interparticle boundary or junction point; this is beneficial to the thermal energy transfer in the nanofluids.

2.2.2. Nanoparticle Aggregation

The aggregation of nanoparticles significantly affects the thermal conductivity of nanofluid [65]. Studies based on nanofluid with spherical nanoparticles revealed that high TCE could be caused by particle aggregation [66]. Primary nanoparticles appear to aggregate to form aggregates or clusters which are non-spherical, particularly with increasing concentration. Wang et al. [67] evaluated the nanofluid thermal conductivity by molecular dynamics (MD) simulation and found that the aggregates can be divided into compact aggregation and loose aggregation. The atoms in the nanolayer are mobilized and dynamically balanced, which could be the mechanism for the TCE of the nanofluid. Due to the significant computational workload, only six nanoparticles were involved. Then, they proposed a hybrid method of multi-particle collision dynamics (MPCD) and MD to increase nanoparticles in calculations [68,69]. The simulations involving 32 nanoparticles showed that the EHC of nanofluid linearly increases with the decrease in the fractal dimension of the nanoparticle aggregates. Lee et al. [70] compared the classical density functional theory (DFT) to Poisson–Boltzmann theory and found a good agreement with experiments on heat transfer for nanofluids.

2.2.3. Network Effect

Sastry et al. [71] constructed a model based on the thermal resistance network by considering the random CNT orientation and CNT–CNT interaction. Their model effectively agreed with experimental data by assuming that a CNT contacts only two neighboring CNTs. Subsequently, Koo et al. [72] improved the model by considering the excluded volume of cylindrical particles. The revised model describes the effect of particle diameter and aspect ratio of CNTs and CNFs on TCE. The alignment of CNTs and CNFs due to the long-range repulsion force decreases the excluded volume, nonlinearly increasing the convexity and concavity and linearly increasing the thermal conductivity with particle concentration. Tahmooressi et al. [44] recently simulated the TCE of nanofluid using the lattice Boltzmann method and discovered that the network effect promotes the enhancement of heat transfer. Their algorithm prevents nanoparticles from forming aggregations by defining a minimum proximity distance.

2.2.4. Rotational Diffusion and Micro Convection

Xue [73] presented the equivalent field factor for CNTs distributed randomly in the base fluid and constructed a model for CNT nanofluids based on the Maxwell theory. They took the CNT as a rotational elliptical particle with a large aspect ratio. Ebrahimi et al. [74,75] built a model by neglecting the micro convection at the surface of cylindrical particles because the Brownian motion is slow. In addition, the collision model for non-spherical particles is difficult to construct. Models with the Brownian effect are based on spherical particles [76,77]. Cui et al. [78] found that cylindrical nanoparticles have a larger surface area and more energetic atoms than spherical nanoparticles, resulting in a larger TCE. Moreover, the high-speed rotation of cylindrical nanoparticles accelerates micro convection in the base fluid due to the stirring effect.

Table 2. Typical models for TCE of NSN nanofluids.

Authors	Particle Shape	Models (k_{nf}/k_f as Default)	Remarks
Hamilton and Crosser [53]	Arbitrary	$\dfrac{k_p+(n-1)k_f-(n-1)(k_p-k_f)\phi}{k_p+(n-1)k_f+(k_p-k_f)\phi}$	Reduce to Maxwell model when $n = 3$
Yamada and Ota [79]	Cylinder	$\dfrac{k_p/k_f+K-K\phi(1-k_p/k_f)}{k_p/k_f+K+\phi(1-k_p/k_f)}$	Unit-cell model Consider the shape factor $K = 2\phi^{0.2}$ ($2\,l/d$) for cylindrical particles
Wang et al. [54]	Aggregates	$k_{eff} = (1 - \Phi) + 3\Phi \int_0^\infty \dfrac{\frac{k_{cl}(r)n(r)}{k_{cl}(r)+2k_f}dr}{(1-\Phi)+3\Phi \int_0^\infty \frac{k_f n(r)}{k_{cl}(r)+2k_f}dr}$	Combine the effective medium approximation and the fractal theory

Table 2. *Cont.*

Authors	Particle Shape	Models (k_{nf}/k_f as Default)	Remarks
Nan et al. [57]	CNTs	$\dfrac{3+\left(\frac{2(k_{11}^c-k_f)}{k_{11}^c+k_f}+\frac{k_{33}^c}{k_f}-1\right)\Phi}{3-\frac{2(k_{11}^c-k_f)}{k_{11}^c+k_f}\Phi}$	Incorporating the interface thermal resistance
Xue [73]	CNTs	$\dfrac{1-\Phi+2\Phi\frac{k_p}{k_p-k_f}\ln\frac{k_p+k_f}{2k_f}}{1-\Phi+2\Phi\frac{k_f}{k_p-k_f}\ln\frac{k_p+k_f}{2k_f}}$	Based on Maxwell theory and considering the random CNT orientation distribution
Zhou and Gao [58]	Ellipsoid	Complicated	Differential effective medium theory
Ebrahimi et al. [74,75]	Cylinders/CNTs	$1-\phi(1+M')+\phi k_f\left(k_p+k_{layer}M'\right)+\phi(1+M')$ $\dfrac{a_f}{\mathrm{Pr}_f(2a_p+\delta)}\left(0.35+0.56\mathrm{Re}_f^{0.52}\right)\mathrm{Pr}_f^{0.3}$	Interfacial layer theory Brownian motion is neglected
Sastry et al. [71]	CNTs	$k_{eff}=\dfrac{X}{A}\left(\sum\limits_{i=1}^{N}\dfrac{1}{\frac{k_{Fluid}A}{dx_i}+\frac{M}{\frac{L_i}{\pi k_{CNT}d^2}+\frac{2}{Gd^2}}}\right)^{-1}$	Assuming CNT contacts only two neighboring CNTs
Koo et al. [72]	CNTs/CNFs	Based on model proposed by [71]	Excluded volume concept Monte Carlo simulation
Murshed et al. [59]	Cylinder	$k_{eff}=((k_p-k_{lr})\Phi_p k_{lr}[2\gamma_1^3-\gamma^3+1]$ $+(k_p+2k_{lr})\times\gamma_1^3[\Phi_p\gamma^3(k_{lr}-k_f)$ $+k_f])(\gamma_1^3(k_p+2k_{lr})-$ $(k_p-k_{lr})\Phi_p[\gamma_1^3+\gamma^3-1])^{-1}$	Deduced in cylindrical coordinates
Timofeeva et al. [34]	Rods/bricks/ platelets/blades	$1+(C_k^{shape}+C_k^{surface})\Phi$	Consider particle shape and interfacial contributions
Chandrasekar et al. [61]	Arbitrary	$\dfrac{k_s+(n-1)k+(n-1)(1+\beta)^3\Phi(k_s-k)}{k_s+(n-1)k-(1+\beta)^3\Phi(k_s-k)}+c\dfrac{\Phi(T-T_0)}{\mu k a^4}$	Consider interfacial layer, particle shape, and Brownian motion 14.8% enhancement
Cui et al. [78]	Cylinder	$k=\dfrac{1}{3Vk_BT^2}\int_0^\infty\langle J(0)J(\mathrm{t})\rangle dt$	MD simulation based on the Green–Kubo formula
Jiang et al. [60]	CNTs	$\dfrac{k_pR(1+t/R-k_f/k_p)\ln(1+t/R)}{tk_f\ln\left[(1+t/R)k_p/k_f\right]}\beta_1=1+t/R$	Interfacial layer theory
Yang et al. [64]	Cylinder	$k_{eff}=\dfrac{1}{\pi}\int\limits_{0}^{\pi}(k_z^2,\sin^2\varphi+k_x^2,\cos^2\varphi)^{1/2}d\varphi$ $k_{eff}=k_{eff2}\dfrac{2\pi rH}{2\pi r^2+2\pi rH}+k_{eff2}\dfrac{R_x}{R_z}\dfrac{2\pi r^2}{2\pi r^2+2\pi rH}$ $k_{eff2}=\dfrac{(k_p-k_{lr})\phi k_{lr}(\beta_1^2-\beta^2+1)+(k_p+k_{lr})\beta_1^2[\phi\beta^2(k_{lr}-k_f)+k_f]}{\beta_1^2(k_p+k_{lr})-(k_p-k_{lr})\phi_p(\beta_1^2+\beta^2-1)}$	Interfacial layer theory Consider end effect of cylinder
Yang et al. [62]	Cylinder	$k_{eff}=\dfrac{(H+2t)k_{eff\_x}+(R+t)k_{eff\_z}}{H+R+3t}$	Interfacial layer theory Anisotropy analysis
Yang and Xu [63]	Cylinder	$\dfrac{\overline{k_{pe}}+k_{bf}(n-1)+(n+1)(\overline{k_{pe}}-k_{bf})(1+C)\phi}{\overline{k_{pe}}+k_{bf}(n-1)-(\overline{k_{pe}}-k_{bf})(1+C)\phi}$	Based on Hamilton–Crosser model Interfacial layer theory Anisotropy analysis
Wang et al. [67]	Aggregates (2–6 spheres)	Increases linearly with decrease in fractal dimension of aggregations	MD simulation Interfacial layer effect
Du et al. [69]	Aggregates (6–32 spheres)	Increases linearly with decrease in fractal dimension of aggregations	MPCD-MD simulation Interfacial layer effect
Tahmooressi et al. [44]	Cylinder	$k_{eff}=\dfrac{L\int q dA}{\Delta T\int dA}$	Lattice Boltzmann method
Cui et al. [35]	Arbitrary	-	CFFNN model Artificial intelligence estimation

3. Convective Heat Transfer of NSN Nanofluids

Convective heat transport occurs when the bulk motion of nanofluids transports energy. The migration of suspended nanoparticles is induced by fluid hydrodynamics and thermodynamics. Furthermore, the relative motion between particles and a fluid affects the hydrodynamics and thermodynamics of the fluid. The complex interaction between discrete and continuous phases shows differences under different particle morphologies and surface treatments, flow structures, and heat transfer conditions. In this section, the experimental and numerical studies of NSN nanofluids are reviewed. The pool boiling heat transfer studies are not discussed since they have been exhaustively covered in the literature [8,80–82]. In addition, CHT based on hybrid nanofluids is not included; the related studies have been reviewed by Vallejo et al. [83]. Several recent studies have shown that hybrid nanofluids have significant potential as a coolant in solar cells [84,85].

3.1. Experimental Data Evaluation

The Nusselt number is used to evaluate the ratio of CHT across the boundary. A more significant Nusselt number corresponds to more active convection. The dimensionless local Nusselt number in the channel is defined as:

$$\mathrm{Nu} = \frac{h_{nf}D}{k_{nf}} \tag{3}$$

where the CHT coefficient is:

$$h_{nf} = \frac{q}{T_w - T_b} \tag{4}$$

where T_w is the wall temperature, T_b is the bulk temperature, and q is the heat flux. Flow loop experiments measure the parameters in Equation (4). A test section is set in a fully developed region with a straight or curved pipe/microchannel and a square or circular cross-section. In addition, it includes boundary layer flow, cavity flow [86,87], impinging jets, peristaltic flow, and flow in heat exchangers [12]. It can be divided into forced convection heat transfer or natural convection heat transfer. Based on the Reynolds number (Re = $u_0\,L/v_{nf}$), the flow state is laminar, turbulent, or transitional flow [88]. Ghasemiasl et al. [89] analyzed the studies on the forced convection of nanofluids in circular and non-circular channels in terms of geometry, particles, methodology, and regime. Researchers evaluated the CHT features of nanofluids affected by different types of parameters and flow conditions. Table 3 presents the experimental and numerical studies for CHT of NSN nanofluids. The nanofluid type, particle shape and size, particle loading, and flow state are listed with CHT characteristics. Notably, all of the variations of the CHT coefficient or Nusselt number are typically nonlinear.

3.1.1. Different Analysis Parameters and Values

Research findings on nanofluid CHT document controversial arguments. The first is whether the CHT, not just the factor of TCE, is enhanced by suspending nanoparticles in the base fluid. The second is whether the thermohydraulic performance of nanofluids is better than that of the base fluid, relating to the efficacy of nanofluids for practical cooling applications. The different views could be caused by different analysis parameters. Studies perform the standard dimensionless analysis of CHT based on the Nusselt number and Reynolds number.

Nonetheless, researchers believe that the constant Reynolds number basis can be misleading since the net result for the constant Reynolds number comparison combines the nanofluid property effect and the flow velocity effect [90]. In the interpretation of nanofluid CHT, Buschmann et al. [17] argued that no anomalous phenomena are involved in the forced convection heat transfer of nanofluids. Their results show that heat transfer enhancement provided by nanofluids equals the increase in thermal conductivity of nanofluids compared to the base fluid. The CHT coefficient rather than the Nusselt number is more suitable to evaluate the intensity of the CHT of nanofluids. A notable exception was the experiments performed with non-spherical particles showing CHT enhancement of NSN nanofluids. Therefore, it is necessary to discuss the CHT of NSN nanofluids.

The magnitude of parameters selected for study is another point of view in nanofluid research. For experimental studies, the values are practical. However, for some numerical studies, the range of parameters could be beyond the scope of practical applications. Buongiorno [91] first evaluated different mechanisms in the convective transport in nanofluids. Myers et al. [92] claimed that the use of parameter values should represent an actual physical situation. Therefore, the experimental and numerical studies are discussed separately in the next section.

3.1.2. Thermohydraulic Performance Evaluation

Thermohydraulic performance is evaluated via a different criterion. As a heat transfer medium, a nanofluid should meet the appropriate guidelines before it can be applied. Yu et al. [93] evaluated their experimental data by different forms of figures of merit (FOMs) as follows:

- The ratio of CHT coefficient, $\text{FOM}_h = h_{nf}/h_b$;
- The ratio of the maximum overall temperature difference, $\text{FOM}_T = (T_{w,o} - T_{in})_{nf}/(T_{w,o} - T_{in})_b$;
- Cooling with minimum pumping power, $\text{FOM}_P = (c_p h/P)_{nf}/(c_p h/P)_b$;
- The relative ratio of heat transfer rate and pumping power, $\text{FOM}_Q = (q/P)_{nf}/(q/P)_b$.

The following criteria should be met: $\text{FOM}_h > 1$, $\text{FOM}_T < 1$, $\text{FOM}_P > 1$, and $\text{FOM}_Q > 1$. Research [94,95] has shown that the criteria for nanofluids with spherical particles are hardly met in tests. We sampled the CHT data of NSN nanofluids reported in the literature (Table 3). Ji et al. [96] used the relative thermal resistance to estimate the CHT performance of the nanofluid in an oscillating heat pipe; hence, the data are not shown. Nelson et al. [97] reported about 110 times viscosity of nanofluid with EG of 0.6% by weight in PAO, leading to a quite small FOM_P compared to others, which was excluded. The pumping power for other studies can be estimated based on Mansour et al. [98] for laminar and turbulent flows.

Most of the studies found an enhancement of the CHT coefficient if the FOM_h or FOM_T were used to evaluate the CHT varying with the Reynolds number. Nevertheless, suppose other performance evaluation criteria (PEC) are used. In that case, it can be found from the experimental data in Figure 5 that CHT was not far beyond the base fluid, with the majority of thermohydraulic FOM values being between 0.8 and 1.2. This is because the FOM_P and FOM_Q criteria were employed in most research, which combines heat transfer enhancement with an increase in pumping power. The heat capacity of nanofluids with low particle loading is close to that of the base fluid. The FOM_P for CNT nanofluids at Re = 1200 was a maximum of 1.536, which possibly meant that the data collection location was not fully developed. Ali et al. [99,100] tested the hydrodynamic performance of graphene nanoplatelet (GNP) nanofluids and discovered that the pumping power of nanofluids (caused by increased viscosity) was over twice that of the base fluid. Consequently, their results had the lowest FOM_P and FOM_Q values. Yu et al. [93] also found that different FOMs presented similar PEC for the same nanofluid.

Mikkola et al. [101] investigated the particle properties of CHT of nanofluids in the turbulent regime. Their experimental results based on oval-shaped Al_2O_3 nanoparticles demonstrated an increase of less than 5% in Nusselt number. Additionally, the CHT coefficient of nanofluids was roughly equal to that of base fluid when the volume concentration was lower than 1%. They used near-spherical particles. Furthermore, Ferrouillat et al. [42] and Wu et al. [102] investigated the CHT performance of nanofluids in turbulent regimes, and the PEC values were smaller than 1. Although the increased pumping power in turbulent flow is less than that of laminar flow, the thermohydraulic performance for NSN nanofluid in turbulent regimes is uneconomical. This also confirms why most recent studies are based on the laminar flow [89].

Yang et al. [23] and Contreras et al. [103] measured CHT coefficients of several types of nanofluids containing GNPs at different temperatures. The effect of operating temperature on CHT was unclear. In contrast, nanoparticle additives have a more significant impact on PEC. Table 3 shows that most tests are performed based on CNT or GNP nanofluids. These materials are easily accessible and commercially used in flow loop experiments. They have more significant thermal conductivity and specific surface area than those spherical particles. Bai et al. [104] also prepared GNP nanofluids with different particle loadings. The reported results revealed an increase in PEC with particle volume fraction.

Nonetheless, no similar findings were reported in other studies [93,101,102]. Similarly, no significant effect of shape factors on CHT was found, as shown in Figure 5. Additional data should be collected to confirm the CHT pattern of nanofluids under multiple factors.

Table 3. Experimental studies for CHT of NSN nanofluids.

Authors	Nanofluid	Particle Shape and Size (nm)	Particle Loading	Flow State	CHT Enhancement
Yang et al. [23]	Graphite–ATF graphite–oils	Plate-like, 1–2 μm (d) × 20–40 (l)	2, 2.5 wt.%	Laminar, 5 < Re < 110	Re↑, h↑ ϕ↑, h↑ T↑, h↓
Ding et al. [105]	CNTs–water	-	<1 wt.%	Laminar, 800 < Re < 1200	ϕ↑, h↑ (significantly) x/D↑, h↓, $\Delta h/h$ ↗ ↘ pH↑, h↓
Chen et al. [3]	Titanate NTs–water	Nanotube 10 (d) × 100 (l)	0.5, 1.0 and 2.5 wt.%	Laminar, 1100 < Re < 2300	ϕ↑, h↑ x/D↑, h↓ Re↑, h↑
Nelson et al. [97]	Graphite–PAO	Plate-like, 20 μm (d) × 100 (l)	0.3 and 0.6 wt.%	Laminar, 72 < Re < 365	ϕ↑, h↑
Ji et al. [96]	Al$_2$O$_3$–EG and water (50/50)	Platelet, 9 (l) Blade, 60 (l) Cylinder, 80 (l)Brick, 40 (l)	0.3, 1, 3, and 5 vol.%	Oscillating heat pipe with input power 25–250 W	Heat transfer was enhanced significantly, nanofluids with cylindrical nanoparticles achieve the best performance
Yu et al. [10]	Al$_2$O$_3$–PAO	Nanorod 7 (d) × 85 (l)	0.65, 1.3 vol.%	Laminar, 150 < Re < 450	Re↑, h↑ ϕ↑, h↑ x/D↑, h↓
Ferrouillat et al. [42]	SiO$_2$–water	Banana-like (nanorod)	2.28 vol.%	200 < Re < 15,000	Larger Nu for particles in banana shape than sphere in turbulent regime
Ferrouillat et al. [42]	ZnO–water	Polygonal/nanorod	0.82, 0.9 vol.%	200 < Re < 15,000	8% and 3% increase in Nu, respectively
Paul et al. [95]	Al$_2$O$_3$–NEILs	Whisker	0.18, 0.36, 0.9 vol.%	-	Degradation of natural convection
Wu et al. [102]	CNTs–water	Nanotube 9.5 (d) × 1500 (l)	<1 wt.%	-	Has no CHT enhancement
Arshad and Ali [100]	Graphene–water	Platelet, 5000–10,000 (d)	10 vol.%	300 < Re < 1000	Re↑, h↑ Pumping power increases as well
Mikkola et al. [101]	Al$_2$O$_3$–water	Ellipsoid, 10 (d)	0.5, 1 vol.%	1000 < Re < 11,000	Re↑, h↑, Nu↑ Φ/k↑, h = enhancement < 5%
Contreras et al. [103]	Graphene–EG and water (50/50)	Platelet	0.01, 0.05, 1 vol.%		Thermohydraulic performance coefficient ≈ 1
Bai et al. [104]	Graphene oxide–DI	Platelet, 0.8–1.2 (h) × 500–5000 (d)	0.02, 0.05, 0.075, 0.1 vol.%	150–800	ϕ↑, Nu ratio↑ Re↑, Nu ratio↑

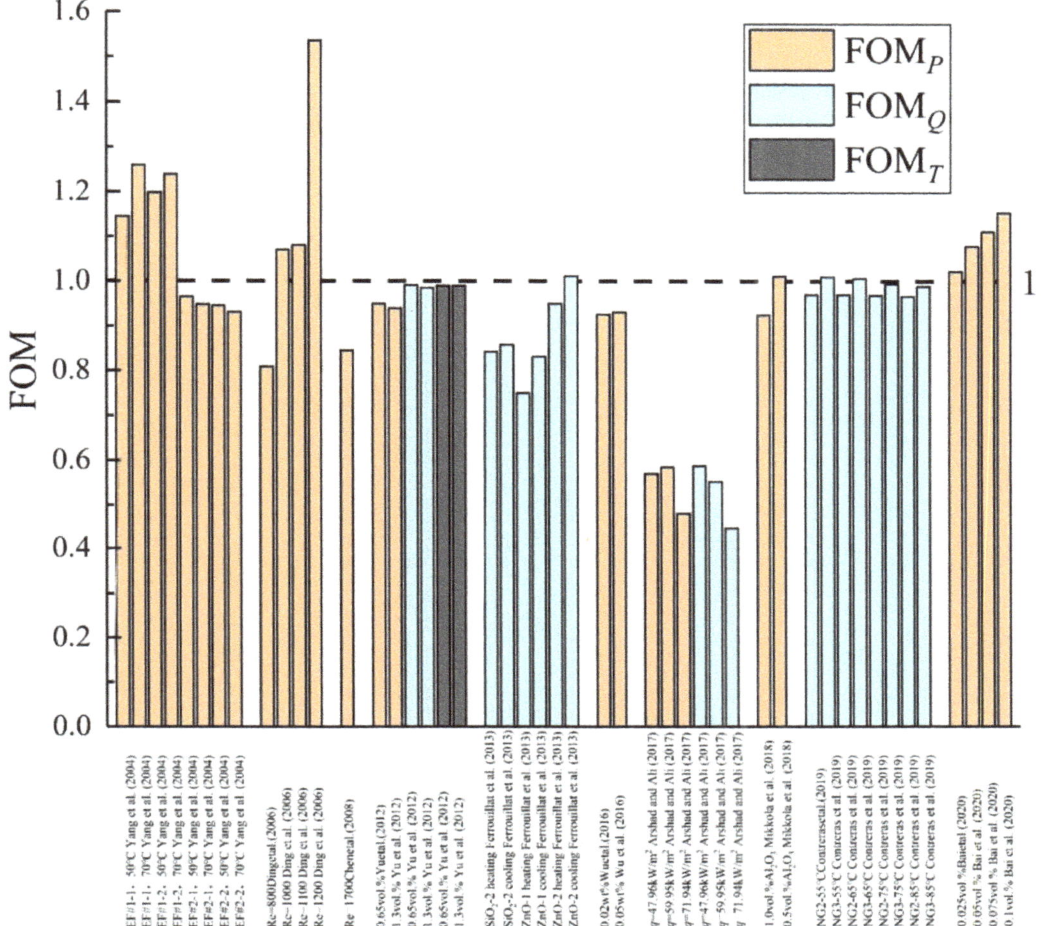

Figure 5. Thermohydraulic performance evaluation in the literature [3,10,23,42,100,101,103–105].

3.2. Numerical Predictions and Mechanism Discussion

Zahmatkesh et al. [12] recently reviewed nanoparticle shape effects in different flow regimes. They listed approximately 60 relevant publications and found no uniform conclusion on the effect of nanoparticle shape on CHT. The platelet-shaped nanoparticles caused the best CHT performance in the natural and forced convection regimes. Nonetheless, most of the works reported the optimum CHT for the blade-shaped nanoparticles in the mixed convection regime. More attention has been channeled to numerical predictions [89], and only one of these studies is based on experiments [95]. Some typical numerical studies for CHT of NSN nanofluids are listed chronologically in Table 4. Minea et al. [106] recently performed a benchmark study on nanofluid simulations. The main difference between thermal conductivity and CHT is the state of particle additives. Driven by the hydrodynamics and the inhomogeneous temperature field, the movement and distribution of particles will be inhomogeneous.

3.2.1. Particle Concentration Distribution and Interaction

Sonication promotes the uniform dispersion of nanoparticles in the base fluid during preparation. Nonetheless, there is no uniform standard for optimal ultrasonication duration for different types of nanofluids [13]. In addition, the uniform distribution of nanoparticles is overlooked by researchers. Lin et al. [107] simulated the particle number concentration in a straight pipe using the method of moments. The results revealed the non-uniformity of the cylindrical nanoparticle volume concentration across the section. Yuan et al. [108] modeled the Poiseuille flow and CHT of nanofluids in a circular minichannel and found that the nanorod volume fraction distribution is non-uniform near the boundary.

In contrast, the particles are more uniform when their aspect ratio is larger. The thermal resistance and temperature gradient are largest near the wall and are sensitive to particle concentration. Lin et al. [109–111] investigated the distribution and deposition of cylindrical nanoparticles in turbulent straight and curved pipes. The coupled model considered the effect of turbulent diffusivity on particle concentration distribution and interaction. The results revealed that the distribution of the particle concentration in the cross-section becomes non-uniform along the flow direction. In the curved duct, the extent of non-uniformity of the distribution of the particle number concentration increases with increasing Stokes number, Dean number, Reynolds number, and particle AR. They showed that particle transport and deposition in curved tubes are important; however, limited studies have considered the effect. Their numerical results demonstrated that the penetration efficiency increases as the Dean number, Reynolds number, and particle aspect ratio decrease. The penetration efficiency is highest when the Stokes number is approximately 0.02.

3.2.2. Particle Rotational Diffusion and Orientation Distribution

The morphology and orientation of the dispersed solids are complex in particle suspensions. Yu et al. [10] suggested four possible particle configurations in nanofluids, including the parallel series, Hashin–Shtrikman (or H-S), and EMT configurations. Researchers assume the H-S configuration when the TCE is estimated [64,72]. Nevertheless, the alignment of non-spherical nanoparticles is apparent in internal flows, specifically near the wall. Researchers give less consideration to the orientation distribution of nanoparticles. Elias et al. [112,113] found the highest overall heat transfer coefficient when nanofluids with cylindrical shapes were used for nanofluid flow in a shell and tube heat exchanger.

Moreover, non-spherical nanoparticles rotate, which delays and disturbs the thermal boundary layer [102]. The rotational diffusion coefficient of nanoparticles has recently attracted research attention. Lin et al. [109–111] and Yuan et al. [108] analyzed the turbulent and laminar NSN nanofluid flows in straight or turbulent pipes by considering the Brownian rotational diffusion and orientation distribution. They found that the orientation distribution of cylindrical nanoparticles was less concentrated as the Reynolds number increased in the turbulent regime. Particle orientation components at the cross-section are nearly 1/3, implying that the nanorod orientation is nearly random in space at the channel center. The nanorod is more likely to align with the flow direction with the increasing shear near the wall. A nanorod with a higher aspect ratio is likely to be rotating towards the flow direction.

Table 4. Typical numerical studies for CHT of NSN nanofluids.

Authors	Nanofluid	Particle Shape and Size (nm)	Particle Loading	Flow State	CHT Enhancement
Elias et al. [112,113]	γ-AlOOH–EG and water (50/50)	Cylinder, AR = 1:8 Brick, AR = 1:1:1 Blade, AR = 1:6:1/12 Platelet, AR = 1:1/8	<1 vol.%	In shell and tube heat exchanger	Cylinder >brick > blade > platelet > sphere, for h, entropy generation, and heat transfer rate of nanofluid
Amin et al. [114]	Al_2O_3–water/Ethylene glycol	Platelets, AR = 0.125 Blades, 1:6:1.12 Cylinders, AR = 8 Bricks, 1:1:1	1 vol.%	Flat-plate solar collector tube 12,000 < Re < 25,000	Brick-shape particles have the highest Nusselt number
Ooi and Popov [115]	Cu–water	Oblate spheroid, Prolate spheroid	<20 vol.%	Natural convection in a square cavity	Increases the CHT as well as flow resistance
Lin et al. [116]	Cu–water	Cube, rod, lamina, tetrahedron	<6 vol.%	Marangoni boundary layer flow	Sphere nanoparticles have the best CHT enhancement
Lin et al. [107]	Al_2O_3–PAO	Cylinder AR = 6, 12, 18	0.65, 1.3, 2.5 vol.%	Laminar, 100 < Re < 2000	Nusselt number increases with ϕ, derived Nu formula based on the numerical data
Yuan et al. [117]	ZnO–water	Cylinder AR = 8, 12, 16	0.4, 0.93, 1.3 vol.%	Turbulent, 2500 < Re < 15,000	Nu_{nf}/Nu_f increases when Reynolds number, AR and ϕ grow
Trodi and Benhamza [118]	Al_2O_3–water	Oblate spheroid, $d_p = 1$ Prolate spheroid, $d_p = 2, 5, 7.5$ and 10	5, 10 vol.%	Flow in differentially heated square enclosures, $10^3 < Ra < 10^6$	Heat transfer increases with Ra and ϕ, oblate spheroid has the best performance
Liu et al. [119]	Al_2O_3–water	Platelet, 78.6 (d) $\times$ 9.8 (l) Blade, 85 (l) $\times$ 14.15 (w) $\times$1.18 (h) Cylinder, 19.6 (d) $\times$ 157 (l) Brick, 36.6 (l)	0.5, 1, 1.5, 2 vol.%	Curved square duct laminar flow	Eulerian–Lagrangian two-phase approach
Sheikhzadeh and Aghaei [120]	Al_2O_3/SiO_2–water	Platelets, AR = 0.125 Blades, 1:6:1.12 Cylinders, AR = 8 Bricks, 1:1:1	2–4 vol.%	Square cavity flow, $10^5 < Ra < 10^7$	Platelets and cylindrical nanoparticles are more effective
Lin et al. [121]	ZnO–water	Cylinder AR = 2, 6, 10, 14	<5 vol.%	Curved pipe flow, $5000 \leq Re \leq 30,000$	Nanofluid PEC is higher than base fluid PEC

4. Conclusions

Research on heat transfer enhancement of nanofluids is a long-term global initiative, and the unified understanding of this issue continues. Herein, we reviewed the heat transfer enhancement of nanofluids containing non-spherical nanoparticles. Non-spherical nanoparticles suspended in nanofluids were divided into three categories based on the dimension of the geometric particle structure. We collected and analyzed data on thermal conductivity and convective heat transfer enhancement of nanofluids measured in experiments. Recent studies investigated the numerical predictions and related heat transfer mechanisms. The main conclusions for NSN nanofluids are as follows:

Due to large aspect ratios, thermal conductivity is enhanced abnormally only for nanofluids containing carbon nanotubes/nanofibers/nanowires. On the other hand, thermal conductivity enhancement per concentration is larger for nanorods/ellipsoids with small aspect ratios. The enhancement of the network effect on heat transfer is limited. Polygonal particles enhanced the thermal conductivity least due to the sphericity being close to 1. The approximate enhancement effect by three types of non-spherical nanoparticles on thermal conductivity is 4.5:2.5:1. However, the particle size effect on nanofluids' thermal conductivity is unclear.

The convective heat transfer coefficient is increased by suspending non-spherical nanoparticles in the base fluid. Due to the increase in pumping power, no significant thermohydraulic performance was found for convective heat transfer of NSN nanofluid flow. NSN nanofluid is uneconomical for turbulent flows, and the temperature and particle concentration effect on convective heat transfer remains unclear. In addition, there is no perfect model to precisely predict the thermal conductivity and convective heat transfer of NSN nanofluids.

Author Contributions: Conceptualization, X.L. and F.Y.; investigation, D.W.; resources, X.Y.; data curation, W.T.; writing—original draft preparation, C.D.; writing—review and editing, X.L.; visualization, J.D.; supervision, W.Y.; project administration, H.Y.; funding acquisition, F.Y. All authors have read and agreed to the published version of the manuscript.

Funding: This research was funded by the National Natural Science Foundation of China (No. 12172152, 11802105).

Institutional Review Board Statement: Not applicable.

Informed Consent Statement: Not applicable.

Data Availability Statement: Not applicable.

Conflicts of Interest: The authors declare no conflict of interest.

Abbreviations

NSN nanofluid	Nanofluid containing non-spherical nanoparticles
TCE	Thermal conductivity enhancement
CHT	Convective heat transfer
DW	Distilled water
CNTs	Carbon nanotubes
GNPs	Graphene nanoplatelets
AR	Aspect ratio
EG	Ethylene glycol
EHC	Effective heat conductivity
MD	Molecular dynamics
FOM	Figure of merit
PEC	Performance evaluation criteria
PAO	Polyalphaolefin
DFT	Density functional theory

Nomenclature

k	Thermal conductivity (W/(m·K))
Re	Reynolds number
Nu	Nusselt number
h	Convective heat transfer coefficient (W/(m^2·K))
ϕ	Particle volume fraction
d	Particle diameter (nm)
l	Particle length (nm)
h	Particle length (nm)
P	Pumping power
Q	Flow rate
q	Heat flux (kW/m^2)
c_p	Specific heat capacity
ρ	Density (kg/m^3)
Ts_i	Temperature (K)sphericity

Subscripts

f	Base fluid
nfb	NanofluidBulk

References

1. Choi, S.; Eastman, J. Enhancing thermal conductivity of fluids with nanoparticles. In Proceedings of the ASME International Mechanical Engineering Congress & Exposition, San Franscisco, CA, USA, 12–17 November 1995; pp. 99–106.
2. Murshed, S.M.S.; Leong, K.C.; Yang, C. Enhanced thermal conductivity of TiO$_2$—water based nanofluids. *Int. J. Therm. Sci.* **2005**, *44*, 367–373. [CrossRef]

3. Chen, H.; Yang, W.; He, Y.; Ding, Y.; Zhang, L.; Tan, C.; Lapkin, A.A.; Bavykin, D.V. Heat transfer and flow behaviour of aqueous suspensions of titanate nanotubes (nanofluids). *Powder Technol.* **2008**, *183*, 63–72. [CrossRef]

4. Chen, H.; Ding, Y.; Lapkin, A. Rheological behaviour of nanofluids containing tube/rod-like nanoparticles. *Powder Technol.* **2009**, *194*, 132–141. [CrossRef]

5. Murshed, S.M.S.; Estellé, P. A state of the art review on viscosity of nanofluids. Renew. *Sustain. Energy Rev.* **2017**, *76*, 1134–1152. [CrossRef]

6. Yu, W.; France, D.M.; Routbort, J.L.; Choi, S.U.S. Review and Comparison of Nanofluid Thermal Conductivity and Heat Transfer Enhancements. *Heat Transf. Eng.* **2008**, *29*, 432–460. [CrossRef]

7. Aybar, H.; Sharifpur, M.; Azizian, M.R.; Mehrabi, M.; Meyer, J.P. A Review of Thermal Conductivity Models for Nanofluids. *Heat Transf. Eng.* **2015**, *36*, 1085–1110. [CrossRef]

8. Murshed, S.S.; de Castro, C.N.; Lourenço, M.; Lopes, M.; Santos, F. A review of boiling and convective heat transfer with nanofluids. *Renew. Sustain. Energy Rev.* **2011**, *15*, 2342–2354. [CrossRef]

9. Hussein, A.M.; Sharma, K.; Bakar, R.; Kadirgama, K. A review of forced convection heat transfer enhancement and hydrodynamic characteristics of a nanofluid. *Renew. Sustain. Energy Rev.* **2014**, *29*, 734–743. [CrossRef]

10. Yu, L.; Liu, D.; Botz, F. Laminar Convective Heat Transfer of Alumina-Polyalphaolefin Nanofluids Containing Spherical and Non-Spherical Nanoparticles. In Proceedings of the International Electronic Packaging Technical Conference and Exhibition, Portland, OR, USA, 6–8 July 2011; Volume 44625, pp. 343–355. [CrossRef]

11. Yang, L.; Chen, X.; Xu, M.; Du, K. Roles of surfactants and particle shape in the enhanced thermal conductivity of TiO2 nanofluids. *AIP Adv.* **2016**, *6*, 95104. [CrossRef]

12. Zahmatkesh, I.; Sheremet, M.; Yang, L.; Heris, S.Z.; Sharifpur, M.; Meyer, J.P.; Ghalambaz, M.; Wongwises, S.; Jing, D.; Mahian, O. Effect of nanoparticle shape on the performance of thermal systems utilizing nanofluids: A critical review. *J. Mol. Liq.* **2020**, *321*, 114430. [CrossRef]

13. Qiu, L.; Zhu, N.; Feng, Y.; Michaelides, E.E.; Żyła, G.; Jing, D.; Zhang, X.; Norris, P.M.; Markides, C.N.; Mahian, O. A review of recent advances in thermophysical properties at the nanoscale: From solid state to colloids. *Phys. Rep.* **2019**, *843*, 1–81. [CrossRef]

14. Bird, R.B.; Stewart, W.E.; Lightfoot, E.N. *Transport Phenomena*; JohnWiley & Sons: New York, NY, USA, 2002.

15. Zhang, X.; Gu, H.; Fujii, M. Effective thermal conductivity and thermal diffusivity of nanofluids containing spherical and cylindrical nanoparticles. *Exp. Therm. Fluid Sci.* **2007**, *31*, 593–599. [CrossRef]

16. Cao, G.; Wang, Y. *Nanostructures and Nanomaterials: Synthesis, Properties and Applications*; World Scientific: London, UK, 2011.

17. Buschmann, M.; Azizian, R.; Kempe, T.; Juliá, J.E.; Martínez-Cuenca, R.; Sundén, B.; Wu, Z.; Seppälä, A.; Ala-Nissila, T. Correct interpretation of nanofluid convective heat transfer. *Int. J. Therm. Sci.* **2018**, *129*, 504–531. [CrossRef]

18. Mahian, O.; Kolsi, L.; Amani, M.; Estellé, P.; Ahmadi, G.; Kleinstreuer, C.; Marshall, J.S.; Siavashi, M.; Taylor, R.A.; Niazmand, H.; et al. Recent advances in modeling and simulation of nanofluid flows-Part I: Fundamentals and theory. *Phys. Rep.* **2018**, *790*, 1–48. [CrossRef]

19. Murshed, S.S.; de Castro, C.A.N. Superior thermal features of carbon nanotubes-based nanofluids—A review. *Renew. Sustain. Energy Rev.* **2014**, *37*, 155–167. [CrossRef]

20. Yazid, M.N.A.W.M.; Sidik, N.A.C.; Yahya, W.J. Heat and mass transfer characteristics of carbon nanotube nanofluids: A review. *Renew. Sustain. Energy Rev.* **2017**, *80*, 914–941. [CrossRef]

21. Ali, N.; Bahman, A.; Aljuwayhel, N.; Ebrahim, S.; Mukherjee, S.; Alsayegh, A. Carbon-Based Nanofluids and Their Advances towards Heat Transfer Applications—A Review. *Nanomaterials* **2021**, *11*, 1628. [CrossRef]

22. Xie, H.; Lee, H.; Youn, W.; Choi, M. Nanofluids containing multiwalled carbon nanotubes and their enhanced thermal conductivities. *J. Appl. Phys.* **2003**, *94*, 4967. [CrossRef]

23. Yang, Y.; Zhang, Z.G.; Grulke, E.A.; Anderson, W.B.; Wu, G. Heat transfer properties of nanoparticle-in-fluid dispersions (nanofluids) in laminar flow. *Int. J. Heat Mass Transf.* **2005**, *48*, 1107–1116. [CrossRef]

24. Gu, B.; Hou, B.; Lu, Z.; Wang, Z.; Chen, S. Thermal conductivity of nanofluids containing high aspect ratio fillers. *Int. J. Heat Mass Transf.* **2013**, *64*, 108–114. [CrossRef]

25. Maheshwary, P.; Handa, C.; Nemade, K.; Chaudhary, S. Role of nanoparticle shape in enhancing the thermal conductivity of nanofluids. *Mater. Today Proc.* **2020**, *28*, 873–878. [CrossRef]

26. Maheshwary, P.; Handa, C.; Nemade, K. A comprehensive study of effect of concentration, particle size and particle shape on thermal conductivity of titania/water based nanofluid. *Appl. Therm. Eng.* **2017**, *119*, 79–88. [CrossRef]

27. Zhu, D.; Wang, L.; Yu, W.; Xie, H. Intriguingly high thermal conductivity increment for CuO nanowires contained nanofluids with low viscosity. *Sci. Rep.* **2018**, *8*, 5282. [CrossRef]

28. Zhang, L.; Yu, W.; Zhu, D.; Xie, H.; Huang, G. Enhanced Thermal Conductivity for Nanofluids Containing Silver Nanowires with Different Shapes. *J. Nanomater.* **2017**, *2017*, 1–6. [CrossRef]

29. Carbajal-Valdez, R.; Rodríguez-Juárez, A.; Jiménez-Pérez, J.; Sánchez-Ramírez, J.; Cruz-Orea, A.; Correa-Pacheco, Z.; Macias, M.; Luna-Sánchez, J. Experimental investigation on thermal properties of Ag nanowire nanofluids at low concentrations. *Thermochim. Acta* **2018**, *671*, 83–88. [CrossRef]

30. Xie, H.; Wang, J.; Xi, T.; Liu, Y. Thermal Conductivity of Suspensions Containing Nanosized SiC Particles. *Int. J. Thermophys.* **2002**, *23*, 571–580. [CrossRef]

31. Yang, B.; Han, Z.H. Temperature-dependent thermal conductivity of nanorod-based nanofluids. *Appl. Phys. Lett.* **2006**, *89*, 83111. [CrossRef]
32. Becker, J.; Trügler, A.; Jakab, A.; Hohenester, U.; Sönnichsen, C. The Optimal Aspect Ratio of Gold Nanorods for Plasmonic Bio-sensing. *Plasmonics* **2010**, *5*, 161–167. [CrossRef]
33. Zhu, H.T.; Zhang, C.Y.; Tang, A.Y.M.; Wang, J.X. Novel Synthesis and Thermal Conductivity of CuO Nanofluid. *J. Phys. Chem. C* **2007**, *111*, 1646–1650. [CrossRef]
34. Timofeeva, E.V.; Routbort, J.L.; Singh, D. Particle shape effects on thermophysical properties of alumina nanofluids. *J. Appl. Phys.* **2009**, *106*, 14304. [CrossRef]
35. Cui, W.; Cao, Z.; Li, X.; Lu, L.; Ma, T.; Wang, Q. Experimental investigation and artificial intelligent estimation of thermal conductivity of nanofluids with different nanoparticles shapes. *Powder Technol.* **2021**, *398*, 117078. [CrossRef]
36. Nithiyanantham, U.; González-Fernández, L.; Grosu, Y.; Zaki, A.; Igartua, J.M.; Faik, A. Shape effect of Al2O3 nanoparticles on the thermophysical properties and viscosity of molten salt nanofluids for TES application at CSP plants. *Appl. Therm. Eng.* **2020**, *169*, 114942. [CrossRef]
37. Jiang, W.; Ding, G.; Peng, H. Measurement and model on thermal conductivities of carbon nanotube nanorefrigerants. *Int. J. Therm. Sci.* **2009**, *48*, 1108–1115. [CrossRef]
38. Singh, D.J.; Timofeeva, E.V.; Yu, W.; Routbort, J.L.; France, D.M.; Smith, D.Y.; Lopez-Cepero, J.M. An investigation of silicon carbide-water nanofluid for heat transfer applications. *J. Appl. Phys.* **2009**, *105*, 64306. [CrossRef]
39. Kim, H.J.; Lee, S.-H.; Lee, J.-H.; Jang, S.P. Effect of particle shape on suspension stability and thermal conductivities of water-based bohemite alumina nanofluids. *Energy* **2015**, *90*, 1290–1297. [CrossRef]
40. Torii, S.; Yang, W.-J. Heat Transfer Augmentation of Aqueous Suspensions of Nanodiamonds in Turbulent Pipe Flow. *J. Heat Transf.* **2009**, *131*, 43203. [CrossRef]
41. Xie, H.; Yu, W.; Li, Y. Thermal performance enhancement in nanofluids containing diamond nanoparticles. *J. Phys. D: Appl. Phys.* **2009**, *42*, 95413. [CrossRef]
42. Ferrouillat, S.; Bontemps, A.; Poncelet, O.; Soriano, O.; Gruss, J.-A. Influence of nanoparticle shape factor on convective heat transfer and energetic performance of water-based SiO2 and ZnO nanofluids. *Appl. Therm. Eng.* **2013**, *51*, 839–851. [CrossRef]
43. Yang, L.; Ji, W.; Huang, J.-N.; Xu, G. An updated review on the influential parameters on thermal conductivity of nano-fluids. *J. Mol. Liq.* **2019**, *296*, 111780. [CrossRef]
44. Tahmooressi, H.; Kasaeian, A.; Yavarinasab, A.; Tarokh, A.; Ghazi, M.; Hoorfar, M. Numerical simulation of nanoparticles size/aspect ratio effect on thermal conductivity of nanofluids using lattice Boltzmann method. *Int. Commun. Heat Mass Transf.* **2020**, *120*, 105033. [CrossRef]
45. Assael, M.J.; Chen, C.-F.; Metaxa, I.; Wakeham, W.A. Thermal Conductivity of Suspensions of Carbon Nanotubes in Water. *Int. J. Thermophys.* **2004**, *25*, 971–985. [CrossRef]
46. Nasiri, A.; Shariaty-Niasar, M.; Rashidi, A.; Khodafarin, R. Effect of CNT structures on thermal conductivity and stability of nanofluid. *Int. J. Heat Mass Transf.* **2012**, *55*, 1529–1535. [CrossRef]
47. Fang, X.; Ding, Q.; Fan, L.-W.; Yu, Z.-T.; Xu, X.; Cheng, G.-H.; Hu, Y.-C.; Cen, K.-F. Thermal Conductivity Enhancement of Ethylene Glycol-Based Suspensions in the Presence of Silver Nanoparticles of Various Shapes. *J. Heat Transf.* **2013**, *136*, 34501. [CrossRef]
48. Jeong, J.; Li, C.; Kwon, Y.; Lee, J.; Kim, S.H.; Yun, R. Particle shape effect on the viscosity and thermal conductivity of ZnO nanofluids. *Int. J. Refrig.* **2013**, *36*, 2233–2241. [CrossRef]
49. Farbod, M.; Asl, R.K.; Abadi, A.R.N. Morphology dependence of thermal and rheological properties of oil-based nanofluids of CuO nanostructures. *Colloids Surfaces A Physicochem. Eng. Asp.* **2015**, *474*, 71–75. [CrossRef]
50. Shah, J.; Kumar, S.; Ranjan, M.; Sonvane, Y.; Thareja, P.; Gupta, S.K. The effect of filler geometry on thermo-optical and rheological properties of CuO nanofluid. *J. Mol. Liq.* **2018**, *272*, 668–675. [CrossRef]
51. Ni, Z.; Cao, X.; Wang, X.; Zhou, S.; Zhang, C.; Xu, B.; Ni, Y. Facile Synthesis of Copper(I) Oxide Nanochains and the Photo-Thermal Conversion Performance of Its Nanofluids. *Coatings* **2021**, *11*, 749. [CrossRef]
52. Maxwell, J.C. *A Treatise on Electricity and Magnetism*; Clarendon Press: London, UK, 1881; Volume 1.
53. Hamilton, R.L.; Crosser, O.K. Thermal Conductivity of Heterogeneous Two-Component Systems. *Ind. Eng. Chem. Fundam.* **1962**, *1*, 187–191. [CrossRef]
54. Wang, B.-X.; Zhou, L.-P.; Peng, X.-F. A fractal model for predicting the effective thermal conductivity of liquid with suspension of nanoparticles. *Int. J. Heat Mass Transf.* **2003**, *46*, 2665–2672. [CrossRef]
55. Hasselman, D.; Johnson, L.F. Effective Thermal Conductivity of Composites with Interfacial Thermal Barrier Resistance. *J. Compos. Mater.* **1987**, *21*, 508–515. [CrossRef]
56. Xue, L.; Keblinski, P.; Phillpot, S.; Choi, S.-S.; Eastman, J. Effect of liquid layering at the liquid–solid interface on thermal transport. *Int. J. Heat Mass Transf.* **2004**, *47*, 4277–4284. [CrossRef]
57. Nan, C.-W.; Liu, G.; Lin, Y.; Li, M. Interface effect on thermal conductivity of carbon nanotube composites. *Appl. Phys. Lett.* **2004**, *85*, 3549–3551. [CrossRef]
58. Zhou, X.F.; Gao, L. Effective thermal conductivity in nanofluids of nonspherical particles with interfacial thermal resistance: Differential effective medium theory. *J. Appl. Phys.* **2006**, *100*, 24913. [CrossRef]

59. Murshed, S.M.S.; Leong, K.; Yang, C. Investigations of thermal conductivity and viscosity of nanofluids. *Int. J. Therm. Sci.* **2008**, *47*, 560–568. [CrossRef]
60. Jiang, H.; Xu, Q.; Huang, C.; Shi, L. The role of interfacial nanolayer in the enhanced thermal conductivity of carbon nanotube-based nanofluids. *Appl. Phys. A* **2014**, *118*, 197–205. [CrossRef]
61. Chandrasekar, M.; Suresh, S.; Srinivasan, R.; Bose, A.C. New Analytical Models to Investigate Thermal Conductivity of Nanofluids. *J. Nanosci. Nanotechnol.* **2009**, *9*, 533–538. [CrossRef]
62. Yang, L.; Xu, X.; Jiang, W.; Du, K. A new thermal conductivity model for nanorod-based nanofluids. *Appl. Therm. Eng.* **2017**, *114*, 287–299. [CrossRef]
63. Yang, L.; Xu, X. A renovated Hamilton–Crosser model for the effective thermal conductivity of CNTs nanofluids. *Int. Commun. Heat Mass Transf.* **2016**, *81*, 42–50. [CrossRef]
64. Yang, L.; Du, K.; Zhang, X. A theoretical investigation of thermal conductivity of nanofluids with particles in cylindrical shape by anisotropy analysis. *Powder Technol.* **2016**, *314*, 328–338. [CrossRef]
65. Khalifeh, A.; Vaferi, B. Intelligent assessment of effect of aggregation on thermal conductivity of nanofluids—Comparison by experimental data and empirical correlations. *Thermochim. Acta* **2019**, *681*, 178377. [CrossRef]
66. Alawi, O.A.; Sidik, N.A.C.; Xian, H.W.; Kean, T.H.; Kazi, S. Thermal conductivity and viscosity models of metallic oxides nanofluids. *Int. J. Heat Mass Transf.* **2018**, *116*, 1314–1325. [CrossRef]
67. Wang, R.; Qian, S.; Zhang, Z. Investigation of the aggregation morphology of nanoparticle on the thermal conductivity of nanofluid by molecular dynamics simulations. *Int. J. Heat Mass Transf.* **2018**, *127*, 1138–1146. [CrossRef]
68. Chen, R.; Zhang, T.; Guo, Y.; Wang, J.; Wei, J.; Yu, Q. Recent advances in simultaneous removal of SO2 and NOx from exhaust gases: Removal process, mechanism and kinetics. *Chem. Eng. J.* **2020**, *420*, 127588. [CrossRef]
69. Du, J.; Su, Q.; Li, L.; Wang, R.; Zhu, Z. Evaluation of the influence of aggregation morphology on thermal conductivity of nanofluid by a new MPCD-MD hybrid method. *Int. Commun. Heat Mass Transf.* **2021**, *127*, 105501. [CrossRef]
70. Lee, J.W.; Nilson, R.H.; Templeton, J.A.; Griffiths, S.K.; Kung, A.; Wong, B.M. Comparison of Molecular Dynamics with Classical Density Functional and Poisson–Boltzmann Theories of the Electric Double Layer in Nanochannels. *J. Chem. Theory Comput.* **2012**, *8*, 2012–2022. [CrossRef]
71. Sastry, N.N.V.; Bhunia, A.; Sundararajan, T.; Das, S.K. Predicting the effective thermal conductivity of carbon nanotube based nanofluids. *Nanotechnology* **2008**, *19*, 55704. [CrossRef]
72. Koo, J.; Kang, Y.; Kleinstreuer, C. A nonlinear effective thermal conductivity model for carbon nanotube and nanofiber suspensions. *Nanotechnology* **2008**, *19*, 375705. [CrossRef]
73. Xue, Q.Z. Model for thermal conductivity of carbon nanotube-based composites. *Phys. B Condens. Matter* **2005**, *368*, 302–307. [CrossRef]
74. Sabbaghzadeh, J.; Ebrahimi, S. Effective Thermal Conductivity of Nanofluids Containing Cylindrical Nanoparticles. *Int. J. Nanosci.* **2007**, *6*, 45–49. [CrossRef]
75. Ebrahimi, S.; Sabbaghzadeh, J.; Lajevardi, M.; Hadi, I. Cooling performance of a microchannel heat sink with nanofluids containing cylindrical nanoparticles (carbon nanotubes). *Heat Mass Transf.* **2010**, *46*, 549–553. [CrossRef]
76. Yang, B. Thermal Conductivity Equations Based on Brownian Motion in Suspensions of Nanoparticles (Nanofluids). *J. Heat Transf.* **2008**, *130*, 42408. [CrossRef]
77. Koo, J.; Kleinstreuer, C. Impact analysis of nanoparticle motion mechanisms on the thermal conductivity of nanofluids. *Int. Commun. Heat Mass Transf.* **2005**, *32*, 1111–1118. [CrossRef]
78. Cui, W.; Bai, M.; Lv, J.; Li, G.; Li, X. On the Influencing Factors and Strengthening Mechanism for Thermal Conductivity of Nanofluids by Molecular Dynamics Simulation. *Ind. Eng. Chem. Res.* **2011**, *50*, 13568–13575. [CrossRef]
79. Yamada, E.; Ota, T. Effective thermal conductivity of dispersed materials. *Wärme-Und Stoffübertragung* **1980**, *13*, 27–37. [CrossRef]
80. Liang, G.; Mudawar, I. Review of pool boiling enhancement with additives and nanofluids. *Int. J. Heat Mass Transf.* **2018**, *124*, 423–453. [CrossRef]
81. Kamel, M.S.; Lezsovits, F. Boiling heat transfer of nanofluids: A review of recent studies. *Therm. Sci.* **2019**, *23*, 109–124. [CrossRef]
82. Barber, J.; Brutin, D.; Tadrist, L. A review on boiling heat transfer enhancement with nanofluids. *Nanoscale Res. Lett.* **2011**, *6*, 280. [CrossRef]
83. Vallejo, J.P.; Prado, J.I.; Lugo, L. Hybrid or mono nanofluids for convective heat transfer applications. A critical review of experimental research. *Appl. Therm. Eng.* **2021**, *203*, 117926. [CrossRef]
84. Al-Hossainy, A.; Eid, M.R. Structure, DFT calculations and heat transfer enhancement in [ZnO/PG + H2O]C hybrid nanofluid flow as a potential solar cell coolant application in a double-tube. *J. Mater. Sci. Mater. Electron.* **2020**, *31*, 15243–15257. [CrossRef]
85. Alam, M.; Hussain, S.; Souayeh, B.; Khan, M.; Farhan, M. Numerical Simulation of Homogeneous–Heterogeneous Reactions through a Hybrid Nanofluid Flowing over a Rotating Disc for Solar Heating Applications. *Sustainability* **2021**, *13*, 8289. [CrossRef]
86. Hussain, S.; Pour, M.; Jamal, M.; Armaghani, T. MHD Mixed Convection and Entropy Analysis of Non-Newtonian Hybrid Nanofluid in a Novel Wavy Elbow-Shaped Cavity with a Quarter Circle Hot Block and a Rotating Cylinder. *Exp. Technol.* **2022**, *46*, 1–20. [CrossRef]
87. Khodabandeh, E.; Akbari, O.A.; Toghraie, D.; Pour, M.S.; Jönsson, P.G.; Ersson, M. Numerical investigation of thermal performance augmentation of nanofluid flow in microchannel heat sinks by using of novel nozzle structure: Sinusoidal cavities and rectangular ribs. *J. Braz. Soc. Mech. Sci. Eng.* **2019**, *41*, 443. [CrossRef]

88. Souayeh, B.; Bhattacharyya, S.; Hdhiri, N.; Alam, M.W.; Yasin, E.; Aamir, M. Investigation on inlet obstruction in transitional flow regime: Heat transfer augmentation and pressure drop analysis. *Case Stud. Therm. Eng.* **2022**, *34*, 102016. [CrossRef]

89. Ghasemiasl, R.; Hashemi, S.; Armaghani, T.; Tayebi, T.; Pour, M.S. Recent Studies on the Forced Convection of Nano-Fluids in Channels and Tubes: A Comprehensive Review. *Exp. Technol.* **2022**, *46*, 1–35. [CrossRef]

90. Wu, Z.; Wang, L.; Sundén, B. Pressure drop and convective heat transfer of water and nanofluids in a double-pipe helical heat exchanger. *Appl. Therm. Eng.* **2013**, *60*, 266–274. [CrossRef]

91. Buongiorno, J. Convective Transport in Nanofluids. *J. Heat Transfer.* **2006**, *128*, 240–250. [CrossRef]

92. Myers, T.G.; Ribera, H.; Cregan, V. Does mathematics contribute to the nanofluid debate? *Int. J. Heat Mass Transf.* **2017**, *111*, 279–288. [CrossRef]

93. Yu, L.; Liu, N. Study of the Thermal Effectiveness of Laminar Forced Convection of Nanofluids for Liquid Cooling Applications. *IEEE Trans. Compon. Packag. Manuf. Technol.* **2013**, *3*, 1693–1704. [CrossRef]

94. Alkasmoul, F.S.; Al-Asadi, M.; Myers, T.; Thompson, H.; Wilson, M. A practical evaluation of the performance of Al_2O_3-water, TiO_2-water and CuO-water nanofluids for convective cooling. *Int. J. Heat Mass Transf.* **2018**, *126*, 639–651. [CrossRef]

95. Paul, T.C.; Morshed, A.; Fox, E.; Khan, J.A. Experimental investigation of natural convection heat transfer of Al2O3 Nanoparticle Enhanced Ionic Liquids (NEILs). *Int. J. Heat Mass Transf.* **2015**, *83*, 753–761. [CrossRef]

96. Ji, Y.; Wilson, C.; Chen, H.-H.; Ma, H. Particle shape effect on heat transfer performance in an oscillating heat pipe. *Nanoscale Res. Lett.* **2011**, *6*, 296. [CrossRef] [PubMed]

97. Nelson, I.C.; Banerjee, D.; Ponnappan, R. Flow Loop Experiments Using Polyalphaolefin Nanofluids. *J. Thermophys. Heat Transf.* **2009**, *23*, 752–761. [CrossRef]

98. Ben Mansour, R.; Galanis, N.; Nguyen, C.T. Effect of uncertainties in physical properties on forced convection heat transfer with nanofluids. *Appl. Therm. Eng.* **2007**, *27*, 240–249. [CrossRef]

99. Ali, H.M.; Arshad, W. Effect of channel angle of pin-fin heat sink on heat transfer performance using water based graphene nanoplatelets nanofluids. *Int. J. Heat Mass Transf.* **2017**, *106*, 465–472. [CrossRef]

100. Arshad, W.; Ali, H.M. Graphene nanoplatelets nanofluids thermal and hydrodynamic performance on integral fin heat sink. *Int. J. Heat Mass Transf.* **2017**, *107*, 995–1001. [CrossRef]

101. Mikkola, V.; Puupponen, S.; Granbohm, H.; Saari, K.; Ala-Nissila, T.; Seppälä, A. Influence of particle properties on convective heat transfer of nanofluids. *Int. J. Therm. Sci.* **2018**, *124*, 187–195. [CrossRef]

102. Wu, Z.; Wang, L.; Sundén, B.; Wadsö, L. Aqueous carbon nanotube nanofluids and their thermal performance in a helical heat exchanger. *Appl. Therm. Eng.* **2016**, *96*, 364–371. [CrossRef]

103. Contreras, E.M.C.; Oliveira, G.A.; Filho, E.B. Experimental analysis of the thermohydraulic performance of graphene and silver nanofluids in automotive cooling systems. *Int. J. Heat Mass Transf.* **2019**, *132*, 375–387. [CrossRef]

104. Bai, M.-J.; Liu, J.-L.; He, J.; Li, W.-J.; Wei, J.-J.; Chen, L.-X.; Miao, J.-Y.; Li, C.-M. Heat transfer and mechanical friction reduction properties of graphene oxide nanofluids. *Diam. Relat. Mater.* **2020**, *108*, 107982. [CrossRef]

105. Ding, Y.; Alias, H.; Wen, D.; Williams, R.A. Heat transfer of aqueous suspensions of carbon nanotubes (CNT nanofluids). *Int. J. Heat Mass Transf.* **2006**, *49*, 240–250. [CrossRef]

106. Minea, A.A.; Buonomo, B.; Burggraf, J.; Ercole, D.; Karpaiya, K.R.; Di Pasqua, A.; Sekrani, G.; Steffens, J.; Tibaut, J.; Wichmann, N.; et al. NanoRound: A benchmark study on the numerical approach in nanofluids' simulation. *Int. Commun. Heat Mass Transf.* **2019**, *108*, 104292. [CrossRef]

107. Lin, J.; Xia, Y.; Ku, X. Friction factor and heat transfer of nanofluids containing cylindrical nanoparticles in laminar pipe flow. *J. Appl. Phys.* **2014**, *116*, 133513. [CrossRef]

108. Yuan, F.; Yu, W.; Lin, J. Numerical study of the effects of nanorod aspect ratio on Poiseuille flow and convective heat transfer in a circular minichannel. *Microfluid. Nanofluidics* **2020**, *24*, 1–15. [CrossRef]

109. Lin, J.; Shi, R.; Yuan, F.; Yu, M. Distribution and penetration efficiency of cylindrical nanoparticles in turbulent flows through a curved tube. *Aerosol Sci. Technol.* **2020**, *54*, 1255–1269. [CrossRef]

110. Lin, W.; Shi, R.; Lin, J. Distribution and Deposition of Cylindrical Nanoparticles in a Turbulent Pipe Flow. *Appl. Sci.* **2021**, *11*, 962. [CrossRef]

111. Lin, J.-Z.; Xia, Y.; Ku, X.-K. Flow and heat transfer characteristics of nanofluids containing rod-like particles in a turbulent pipe flow. *Int. J. Heat Mass Transf.* **2016**, *93*, 57–66. [CrossRef]

112. Elias, M.; Miqdad, M.; Mahbubul, I.; Saidur, R.; Kamalisarvestani, M.; Sohel, M.; Hepbasli, A.; Rahim, N.; Amalina, M. Effect of nanoparticle shape on the heat transfer and thermodynamic performance of a shell and tube heat exchanger. *Int. Commun. Heat Mass Transf.* **2013**, *44*, 93–99. [CrossRef]

113. Elias, M.; Shahrul, I.; Mahbubul, I.; Saidur, R.; Rahim, N. Effect of different nanoparticle shapes on shell and tube heat exchanger using different baffle angles and operated with nanofluid. *Int. J. Heat Mass Transf.* **2014**, *70*, 289–297. [CrossRef]

114. Amin, T.E.; Roghayeh, G.; Fatemeh, R.; Fatollah, P. Evaluation of Nanoparticle Shape Effect on a Nanofluid Based Flat-Plate Solar Collector Efficiency. *Energy Explor. Exploit.* **2015**, *33*, 659–676. [CrossRef]

115. Ooi, E.H.; Popov, V. Numerical study of influence of nanoparticle shape on the natural convection in Cu-water nanofluid. *Int. J. Therm. Sci.* **2013**, *65*, 178–188. [CrossRef]

116. Lin, Y.; Li, B.; Zheng, L.; Chen, G. Particle shape and radiation effects on Marangoni boundary layer flow and heat transfer of copper-water nanofluid driven by an exponential temperature. *Powder Technol.* **2016**, *301*, 379–386. [CrossRef]

117. Yuan, F.; Lin, J.; Ku, X. Convective Heat Transfer and Resistance Characteristics of Nanofluids with Cylindrical Particles. *Heat Transf. Eng.* **2017**, *39*, 526–535. [CrossRef]
118. Trodi, A.; Benhamza, M.E.H. Particle Shape and Aspect Ratio Effect of Al2O3–Water Nanofluid on Natural Convective Heat Transfer Enhancement in Differentially Heated Square Enclosures. *Chem. Eng. Commun.* **2016**, *204*, 158–167. [CrossRef]
119. Liu, F.; Cai, Y.; Wang, L.; Zhao, J. Effects of nanoparticle shapes on laminar forced convective heat transfer in curved ducts using two-phase model. *Int. J. Heat Mass Transf.* **2017**, *116*, 292–305. [CrossRef]
120. Sheikhzadeh, G.A.; Aghaei, A.; Soleimani, S. Effect of nanoparticle shape on natural convection heat transfer in a square cavity with partitions using water-SiO$_2$ nanofluid. *Chall. Nano Micro Scale Sci. Technol.* **2018**, *6*, 27–38. [CrossRef]
121. Lin, W.; Shi, R.; Lin, J. Heat Transfer and Pressure Drop of Nanofluid with Rod-like Particles in Turbulent Flows through a Curved Pipe. *Entropy* **2022**, *24*, 416. [CrossRef]

 *applied sciences*

Article

Research on the Influence of Inlet Velocity on Micron Particles Aggregation during Membrane Filtration

Peifeng Lin [1,*], Qing Wang [1], Xiaojie Xu [1], Zuchao Zhu [1], Qiangmin Ding [2] and Biaohua Cai [3]

[1] Key Laboratory of Fluid Transmission Technology of Zhejiang Province, Zhejiang Sci-Tech University, Hangzhou 310018, China
[2] Hefei General Machinery Research Institute, Hefei 230032, China
[3] Wuhan Second Ship Design and Research Institute, Wuhan 430064, China
* Correspondence: linpf@zstu.edu.cn

Abstract: Membrane filtration is an efficient wastewater treatment technology. However, sludge particles will easily aggregate and deposit upon the membrane surface, which will decrease the water productivity of membrane filaments. Focusing on the influence of velocity on particle behavior, experimental and numerical research was carried out. The $k - \varepsilon$ turbulent model, porous media model and DPM model were adopted in the simulation. The flow characteristics including pressure, velocity and particle concentration contour are discussed using different inlet velocities of 0.6, 0.8, 1 m/s. The effects of gravity were also investigated. The final evaluation suggests the best working conditions in three scenarios, which could help to suppress membrane pollution. The results indicate that when the inlet velocity is about 1 m/s, particle deposition is weakest, resulting in better water productivity.

Keywords: membrane filtration; membrane fouling; numerical simulation; DPM; water productivity

Citation: Lin, P.; Wang, Q.; Xu, X.; Zhu, Z.; Ding, Q.; Cai, B. Research on the Influence of Inlet Velocity on Micron Particles Aggregation during Membrane Filtration. *Appl. Sci.* **2022**, *12*, 7869. https://doi.org/10.3390/app12157869

Academic Editors: Dino Musmarra and Roberto Camussi

Received: 24 March 2022
Accepted: 29 July 2022
Published: 5 August 2022

Publisher's Note: MDPI stays neutral with regard to jurisdictional claims in published maps and institutional affiliations.

1. Introduction

Membrane filtration is widely used in water treatment, liquid–solid separation and in other fields of application. However, during the membrane filtration process, due to the influence of dynamics and chemical factors, the sludge particles will deposit, or be adsorbed, onto the membrane surface. This leads to membrane filament fouling, reducing both filtration efficiency and the membrane lifetime. With the development of computer technology, Computational Fluid Dynamics (CFD) simulation can effectively help us understand the influence of various factors in the particle aggregation process.

The factors affecting the water productivity of membrane bioreactors have been numerically and experimentally investigated by many scholars, for decades. Ling, Q et al. [1] studied the effects of modified fly ash and powdered activated carbon on sludge mixture characteristics and the operation cycle in a membrane bioreactor (MBR). The results showed that the addition of powdered activated carbon is beneficial in delaying membrane fouling and improves filtration efficiency due to the longer operation cycle of powdered activated carbon. Ou yang, K et al. [2] studied the effect of adding powdered activated carbon on the characteristics of the sludge mixture and membrane fouling in a long−running membrane bioreactor, and analyzed the mechanism of its effect on membrane fouling. The results showed that adding powdered activated carbon increases the average particle size of the flocs and decreases the viscosity of the sludge, but the effect on the sludge content is not obvious. Feng, Q et al. [3] studied the effect of flow shear force on the settling characteristics of activated sludge through the sequencing batch reactor activated sludge process (SBR) reactor model, compared the degree of change in the activated sludge floc morphology of different water flow shear forces, and analyzed the effect of flow shear force on activated sludge flocs. The results showed that the flow shear force changed the sedimentation characteristics of the activated sludge in the SBR reactor to a certain extent due to the shear force affecting the microbial ecosystem of activated sludge, thereby changing the structure of the flocs. Karimi, H et al. [4] synthesized a reverse osmosis polyamide membrane by designing a thermal curing method in a temperature-controlled steam and water environment, which enhanced the hydrophilicity of the membrane surface and increased the permeation flux. Chang, Q et al. [5] used nano−titanium dioxide coatings to improve the hydrophilic properties of commercial ceramic microfiltration membranes. Wei, P et al. [6] periodically introduced large bubbles to reduce the pollution of the membrane surface by using the method of VOF, which effectively increased membrane water productivity. Radu, A.I. et al. [7] studied the effect of the geometry, position and cross flow velocity of the separators between the particles on particle deposition patterns to reduce the pollution on the surface of membrane filaments, which increased the water productivity of the membrane surface. Xie, F et al. [8] used Fourier transform infrared spectroscopy, scanning electron microscopy and other methods to study the effect of microporous corrugated microchannel turbulence promoters (MCTP−MPs) on the pollution characteristics of underwater flat-membrane bioreactors. The results showed that the SMBR filter cake layer thickness using MCTP−MPs is smaller, the content of organic and inorganic contaminants is lower, and the filter cake layer is more easily removed by hydraulic conditions, thus reducing membrane fouling. Liu, X et al. [9] used the method of CFD to simulate and study the influence of fixed and moving membrane filaments on the flux of membrane filaments. An increase in the pressure drop on the luminal side leads to an increase in transmembrane pressure and membrane flux. Yu, W et al. [10] discussed the impact of aluminium polychlorid (PAC) on membrane fouling and found that the addition of low-dose (PAC) could decrease membrane fouling, which is more conducive to the removal of dissolved organic matter. Yu, W et al. [11] studied the effect of Fe/Mn oxidation on the fouling of the filter cake layer and membrane pores to decrease membrane fouling. The results showed that Fe/Mn reduced the amount of two types of fouling substances in the filter cake layer and membrane pores, and increased the membrane runtime. Qaisrani, T.M. et al. [12] explored the effect of air bubbles and backwashing in decreasing membrane fouling and improving membrane cleaning efficiency through experimental methods. Bai, H et al. [13] used the thermally induced phase separation method of polyvinylidene fluoride to compare and analyze the membrane performance of different effective membrane filament lengths under different operating parameters, and found that the shorter the effective lengths of membrane filaments, the less likely that membrane fouling occurred and the higher the membrane water productivity. Han, X et al. [14] prepared a BUT−172 modified polyamide composite forward osmosis membrane to improve the fouling resistance of the membrane filament and increase the membrane water productivity. Vera, L et al. [15] investigated the effect of flushing conditions on membrane fouling and showed that gas jet−assisted backwashing improved membrane cleaning efficiency. Lu, X et al. [16] studied the effect of colloidal particles and soluble polymers on membrane fouling, and the results showed that the decrease in particle size and the increase in the adhesion of gel-like flocs, due to the secretion of hydrophobic protein biopolymers, accelerated the fouling. Deposition and cake layer formation resulted in a better mitigation of membrane fouling. Bouhabila, E.H. et al. [17] used aluminum chloride to prepare ultrafiltration nanocomposite membranes to increase the pores on the membrane surface, which increased the membrane of water productivity. Tay, J.H. et al. [18] studied the effect of shear stress generated by upstream aeration on aerobic granulation, and the results showed that appropriate shear stress is beneficial in the generation of a stable particle structure. Hong, S.H. et al. [19] studied the effect of sequencing changes in dissolved oxygen (DO) concentration on membrane permeability of underwater membrane bioreactors (MBR), and the results show that the rate of increase in transmembrane pressure (TMP) in the anoxic phase is always steeper than that in the aerobic phase, indicating that the rate of fouling in the anoxic phase is higher than that in the aerobic phase. Lin, W et al. [20] used the computational fluid dynamics coupling method and the response surface method to compare the differences in the hydraulic performance of the full−effect membrane flow channel and the traditional inlet flow channel, and discussed the influence of the geometric parameters of the inlet flow channel and the inlet velocity on the hydraulic performance. The results showed that, compared with the traditional membrane flow channel, the pressure drop difference between the inlet and outlet, the average velocity, and the shear force, was greatly improved, and the concentration polarization efficiency and membrane fouling rate was effectively reduced. Momenifar, M et al. [21], by using the method of simulation, explored the influence of the Taylor Reynolds number and Froude number on the gravitational acceleration of particles, and found that gravity drastically decreased the clustering of bidisperse particles, whereas it could increase the clustering of monodisperse particles. Ouellette, N et al. [22] studied the influence of tracer particles on the diffusion rate in strongly turbulent water flow in the laboratory, and also compared measurements of this turbulent-relative dispersion with the longstanding work of Richardson and Batchelor, finding excellent agreement with Batchelor's predictions. Biferale, L et al. [23] compared the experimental measurement and simulation data of the Lagrangian velocity structure function in turbulent flow, and resolved an apparent disagreement between observed experimental and numerical scaling in order to generate interest and awareness amongst other researchers so that they could consider these phenomena in their studies as well.

In this paper, a simplified membrane bioreactor model is established and then simulated. The influence of different inlet velocities on particle distribution, velocity and pressure, are studied in the flow. The results of flow evaluation and particle concentration under different conditions could help develop new strategies to control membrane fouling and thus improve water productivity.

2. Materials and Methods

2.1. Geometric Model

A simplified membrane cell with a circular tube was built, with reference to the experimental model. The structure of each zone is displayed in Figure 1. The entire flow domain was divided into three zones: external flow zone with inlet and outlet nozzles, porous media zone and internal flow zone. The raw water with particles flowed into the pipe at the inlet nozzle of the external zone, partly permeating across the semipermeable membrane (modeled as porous media) because of the negative pressure at outlet1 and outlet2 of internal flow zone, and the remaining water flowed out through the outlet nozzle. The overall length of the entire pipeline was set to 500 mm, the innermost suction pipe radius was set to 2 mm, the thickness of the porous media semipermeable membrane is set to 2 mm, the thickness of the outermost outlet pipe is set to 16 mm, and the length and radius of the inlet and outlet nozzles were set to 10 mm and 2 mm, respectively.

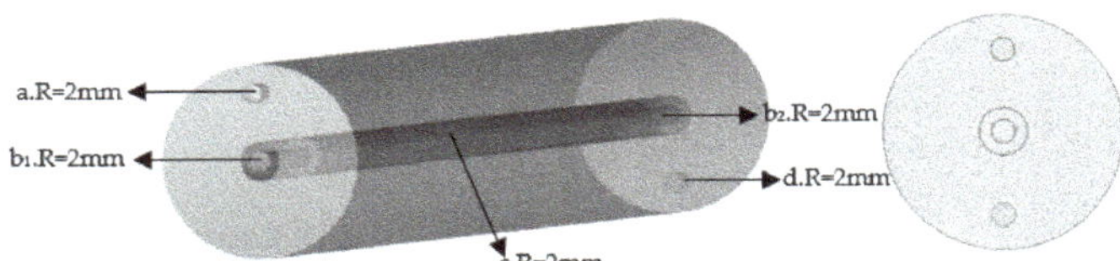

Figure 1. The structure diagram of each zone of the flow channel of the membrane pool, a: inlet; b1: outlet1; b2: outlet2 c: porous media semipermeable membrane; d: outlet.

2.2. Governing Equations and Parameters

2.2.1. Governing Equation

The flow was controlled by the continuity equation and momentum equation:

$$\frac{\partial \rho}{\partial t} + \frac{\partial}{\partial x_i}(\rho u_i) = 0 \tag{1}$$

$$\frac{\partial}{\partial t}(\rho u_i) + \frac{\partial}{\partial x_j}(\rho u_i u_j) = -\frac{\partial p}{\partial x_i} + \frac{\partial}{\partial x_j}\left[\mu\left(\frac{\partial u_i}{\partial x_j} + \frac{\partial u_j}{\partial x_j}\right)\right] + \frac{\partial}{\partial x_j}\left(-\rho\overline{u_i'u_j'}\right) + S_i \tag{2}$$

where S_i is the addition of a momentum source term.

The turbulent k-ε model was used to take turbulence into account.

$$\rho\frac{dk}{dt} = \frac{\partial}{\partial x_i}\left[\left(\mu + \frac{\mu_t}{\sigma_k}\right)\frac{\partial k}{\partial x_i}\right] + G_k + G_b - \rho\varepsilon - Y_M \tag{3}$$

$$\rho\frac{d\varepsilon}{dt} = \frac{\partial}{\partial x_i}\left[\left(\mu + \frac{\mu_t}{\sigma_k}\right)\frac{\partial \varepsilon}{\partial x_i}\right] + C_{1\varepsilon}\frac{\varepsilon}{k}(G_k + C_{3\varepsilon}G_b) - C_{2\varepsilon}\rho\frac{\varepsilon^2}{k} \tag{4}$$

where μ is dynamic viscosity, μ_t is the turbulent viscosity coefficient, G_k is the turbulent kinetic energy generation due to the mean velocity gradient, G_b is the turbulent kinetic energy generation with floating effects, e is the turbulent dissipation rate, k is the turbulent kinetic energy, Y_M is the influence of compressible turbulent pulsating expansion on total dissipation rate, and $C_{1\varepsilon}$, $C_{2\varepsilon}$, $C_{3\varepsilon}$ are model parameters.

The standard wall function, based on Launder, B.E. and Spalding, D.B. [24], was used in this numerical calculation. Furthermore, by setting the boundary layer close to the wall, the mesh near the wall was refined, and the y+ of the first layer near the wall was set to about 30.

The particle's motion is controlled by the equation:

$$\frac{d\vec{u}_p}{dt} = \frac{\vec{u} - \vec{u}_p}{\tau_r} + \frac{\vec{g}(\rho_p - \rho)}{\rho_p} + \vec{F} \tag{5}$$

$$\tau_r = \frac{\rho_p d_p}{18\mu}\frac{24}{C_d Re} \tag{6}$$

$$Re \equiv \frac{\rho d_p \left|\vec{u}_p - \vec{u}\right|}{\mu} \tag{7}$$

here τ_r is the particle relaxation time, $\vec{u}$ is the fluid phase velocity, $\vec{u}_p$ is the particle velocity, μ is the molecular viscosity of the fluid, ρ is the fluid density, ρ_p is the density of the particle, d_p is the particle diameter, Re is the relative Reynolds number, and $\vec{F}$ is the virtual quality force.

Darcy's law describes the linear relationship between the seepage velocity and hydraulic gradient of water in saturated soil, also known as the linear seepage law. Porous media were modeled by the addition of a momentum source term to the standard fluid flow equations. The source term is composed of two parts: a viscous loss term and an inertial loss term.

$$\nabla p = -\frac{\mu}{\alpha}\vec{v} \tag{8}$$

$$\nabla p = -\sum_{j=1}^{3} C_{2_{ij}}\left(\frac{1}{2}\rho v_j |v|\right) \tag{9}$$

where C_2 is the inertia resistance coefficient, and $\frac{1}{\alpha}$ is the viscous resistance coefficient. The parameters $\frac{1}{\alpha}$ and C_2 are determined by experimental results, as shown later.

2.2.2. Parameters

The coefficient of viscous resistance and the coefficient of inertial resistance of the porous media was obtained by water productivity experiments at different pressures. The experimental equipment included a tube membrane battery, membrane wire, a pressure gauge, a fixed membrane plug, a 250 mL beaker and a circulating water pump, as shown in Figure 2. After fixing the membrane filament with a perforated cover plate, the membrane filament was placed into the circular tube membrane pool, the membrane pool was filled 90% with water so that all the membrane filaments are submerged in water, and the various pressure gauges were adjusted to show pressures of 0.04, 0.05, 0.06, 0.07, 0.08, 0.09, 0.10, and

0.11 MPa. The membrane filament produced water productivity at the different pressures. To minimize errors, the experiment was repeated. The averaged experimental results are shown in Table 1.

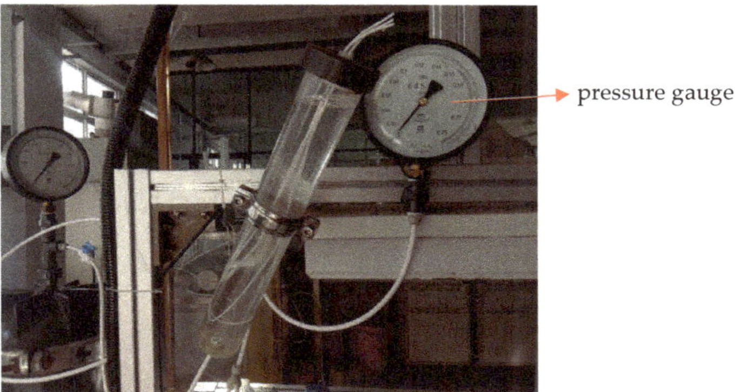

Figure 2. Illustration of experimental setup.

Table 1. Experimental water productivity and velocity at different pressures.

P/MPa	Q/(mL/min)	v/(m/s)
0.04	78.5	0.11
0.05	87.9	0.14
0.06	100.9	0.17
0.07	111.2	0.21
0.08	129.3	0.24
0.09	150.5	0.29
0.10	168.1	0.32
0.11	175.3	0.41

Finally, as shown in Figure 3 the viscous resistance coefficient and the inertial resistance coefficient were obtained using the fitting calculation, and were found to be 2.05×10^5 and 332, respectively.

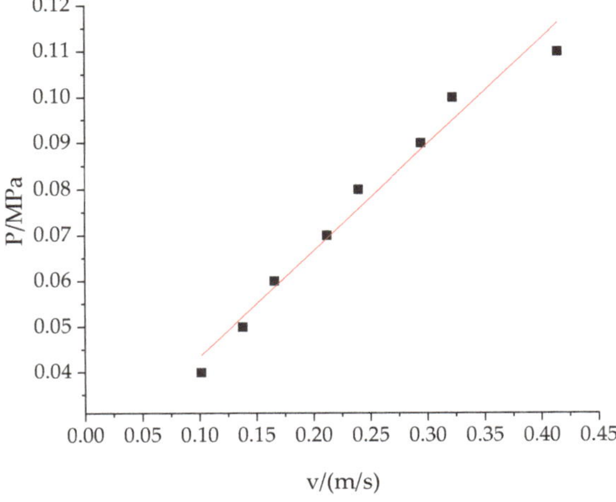

Figure 3. Fitting Curve of experimental value.

2.3. Numerical Methods and Boundary Conditions

Each zone is divided into a structured grid to improve the quality of the grid. As shown in Figure 4, the grids of the porous media zone and the boundary layer zone are respectively encrypted, in order to improve the calculation accuracy of the core zone. The overall grid number is about 500,000; the grid quality is about 0.8. The skewness of the mesh is between approximately 0.3 and 0.4. A boundary layer is added near each wall of the porous media, and the y + = 30.

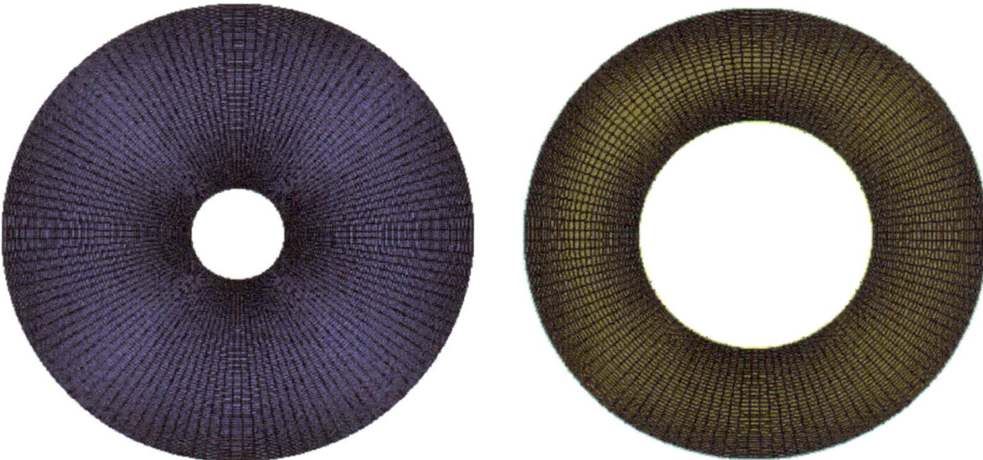

Figure 4. Schematic diagram of boundary layer and porous media zone mesh refinement.

ANSYS FLUENT was used for numerical simulation, and a pressure−based solver was used. The convection term of the equation adopts the second-order upwind discrete format, and the other terms of the equation adopt the central difference format. The SIMPLE algorithm was used to separate and iteratively solve the velocity and pressure. Turbulence intensity was set to 5%. If the relative residual value of each variable was less than 10^{-5}, it was considered that the results had converged.

The inlet velocity condition at which the particle aggregation effects were to be investigated, was set. The outlet pressures at outlet1 and outlet2 were both set as −5 Pa. The walls were all set as non−slip walls.

In the discrete phase setup, the particles were set to be injected at the inlet surface with mass flow rates for the three operating conditions of 0.013188 kg/s, 0.017584 kg/s and 0.02198 kg/s, respectively. The particle boundary conditions were the escape conditions of the inlet and outlet. The surface of the porous media was set as the trap condition.

2.4. The Influence of the Grid on the Calculation Results

Three simulation results based on grids of 300,000, 500,000, and 800,000 were compared, in order to verify the independence of the grid. Figure 5 shows the curve of water productivity rising with time. It can be seen from the curve that water productivity was basically the same under these three grids. Therefore, grid independence was verified. In this study, 500,000 grids were used for simulation.

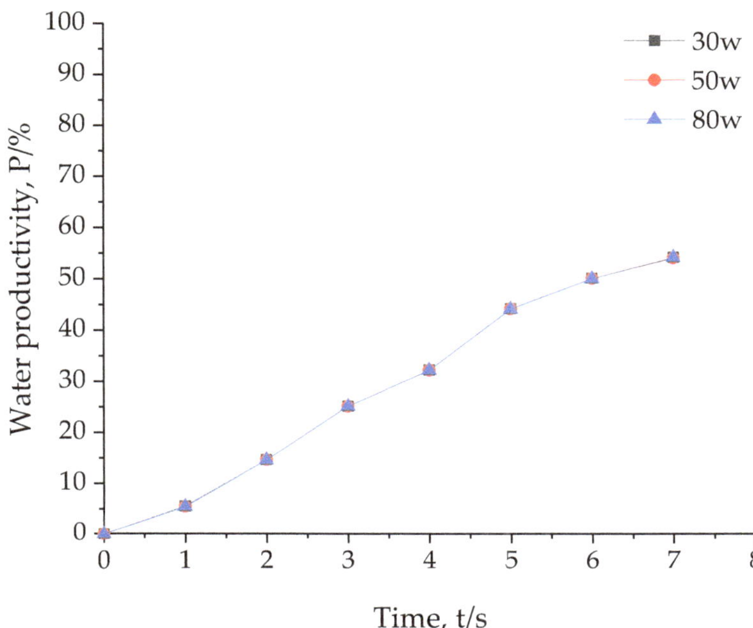

Figure 5. Curve of water productivity rising with time under different grid numbers.

3. Results

3.1. Simulation Results and Analysis

3.1.1. Pressure Contour Analysis

The pressure contour of section $X = 0$, when the inlet velocity is 0.6 m/s (Re = 19,000), is shown in Figure 6a. It can be seen from the figure that the pressure in the entire flow channel gradually increases stepwise from the inlet to the outlet boundary, the pressure increment is about 20 Pa, and the average pressure of the entire flow channel is about 80 Pa.

The pressure contour of section $X = 0$, when the inlet velocity was 0.6 m/s without gravity, is shown in Figure 6b. It can be seen from the figure that the pressure in the entire flow channel was evenly distributed from the inlet to the outlet boundary, the pressure increment was basically 0, and the average pressure of the entire flow channel was about 100 Pa.

The pressure contour of section $X = 0$, when the inlet velocity is 0.8 m/s (Re = 25,000), is shown in Figure 6c. It can be seen from the figure that the pressure was distributed in steps in the entire flow channel, and gradually increased from the inlet to the outlet boundary. The pressure increment was about 22 Pa, and the average pressure of the entire flow channel was about 180 Pa.

The pressure contour of the section $X = 0$, when the inlet velocity is 1 m/s (Re = 31,000), is shown in Figure 6d. As can be seen from the figure, compared to the first three working conditions, the pressure of the entire flow channel reached the maximum value, the pressure increment was basically 0, and the average pressure was about 200 Pa.

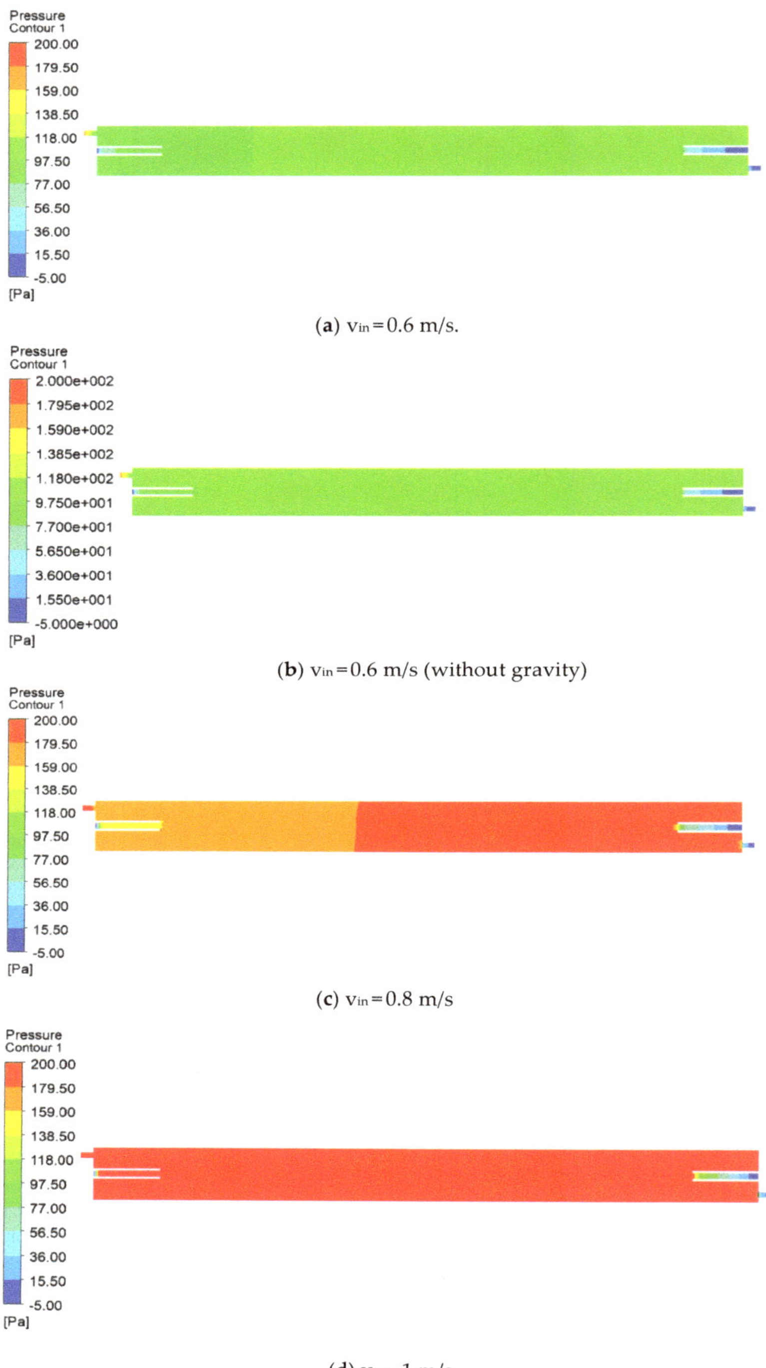

(**a**) $v_{in}=0.6$ m/s.

(**b**) $v_{in}=0.6$ m/s (without gravity)

(**c**) $v_{in}=0.8$ m/s

(**d**) $v_{in}=1$ m/s

Figure 6. Pressure contour on $X=0$ section.

3.1.2. Velocity Contour Analysis

The velocity contour of the section $X = 0$, when the inlet velocity is 0.6 m/s, is shown in Figure 7a. It can be seen from the figure that the flow velocity of the entire flow channel presented a gradually decreasing step-like distribution from the inlet to the outlet boundary. The closer to the middle porous media zone, the smaller the flow velocity, which was due to the fact that the surface of the porous media is a tangential, no−slip boundary, the tangential velocity was 0 and the resulting normal penetration velocity. This indicates that the porous media zone can effectively reduce the tangential flow velocity.

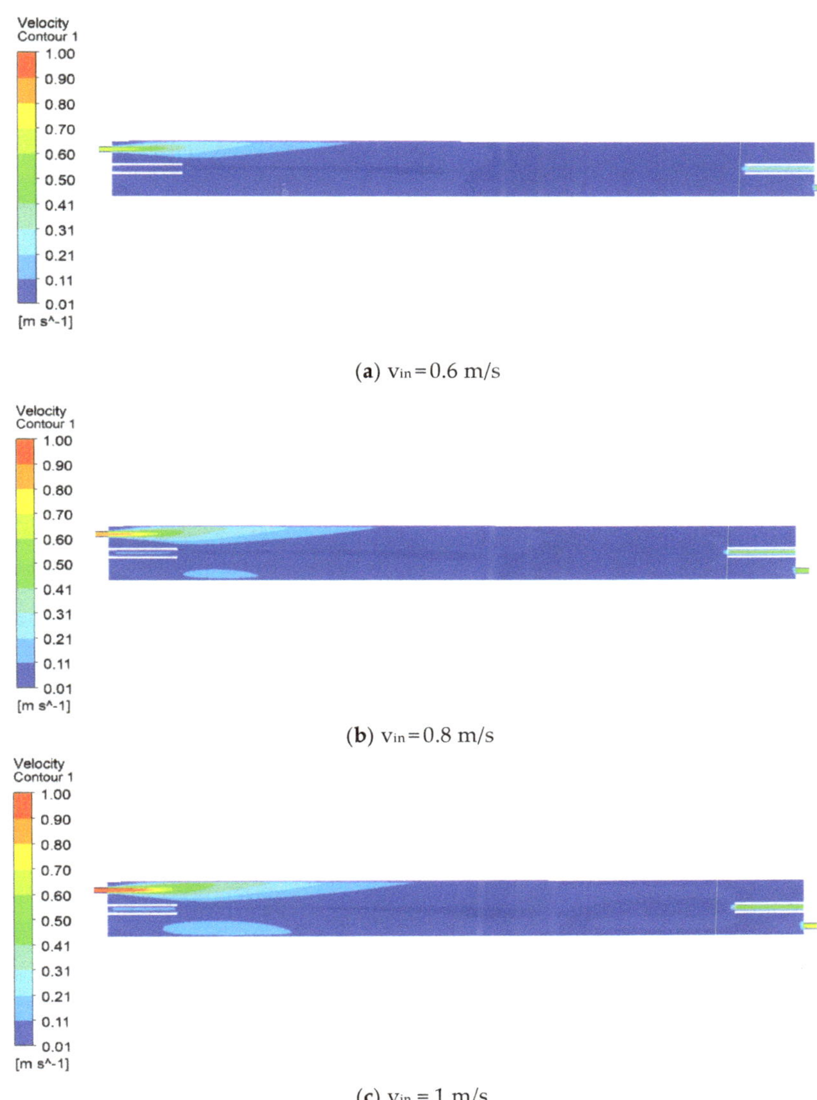

(**a**) $v_{in} = 0.6$ m/s

(**b**) $v_{in} = 0.8$ m/s

(**c**) $v_{in} = 1$ m/s

Figure 7. Velocity contour on $X = 0$ section.

The velocity contour of the section $X = 0$, when the inlet velocity was 0.8 m/s, is shown in Figure 7b. It can be seen from the figure that the flow velocity of the entire flow channel still presented a gradually decreasing step—like distribution from the inlet to the outlet boundary. The closer to the middle of the porous media zone, the smaller the flow velocity. Compared to the working condition at 0.6 m/s, the permeation range of the porous media zone becomes wider due to the increase in the flow velocity, which is more conducive to the increase in membrane flux.

The velocity contour of the section $X = 0$, when the inlet velocity was 1 m/s, is shown in Figure 7c. It can be seen from the figure that compared with the first two working conditions, as the flow velocity gradually increases, the permeation velocity range in the porous media zone reaches the widest range, which is beneficial to the effective improvement of membrane Flux.

3.1.3. Particle Concentration Contour Analysis

The particle concentration contour when the inlet velocity is 0.6 m/s, is shown in Figure 8a. It can be clearly seen from the figure that the particle concentration in the inlet zone and the upper wall surface is the highest, reaching about 0.005 mg/um^3. As the distance from the inlet increases, the particle concentration gradually decreases. When the particle concentration is close to the middle zone of the porous media surface, the particle concentration is the lowest, about 0.001 mg/um^3. The distribution is relatively uniform, while the particle concentration is higher in the porous media surface near the inlet zone, due to the suction pressure, which makes it easy to produce a large amount of accumulation.

The particle concentration contour, when the inlet velocity is 0.8 m/s, is shown in Figure 8b. It can be seen from the figure that the particle concentration in the inlet zone and the upper wall is the highest, reaching about 0.005 mg/um^3. With the increase in the distance from the inlet, the particle concentration gradually decreases. When approaching the middle zone of the porous media surface, the particle concentration is the lowest. Compared with the working condition of 0.6 m/s, when the flow velocity is 0.8 m/s, the particle distribution range is wider.

The particle concentration contour, when the inlet velocity is 1 m/s, is shown in Figure 8c. It can be seen from the figure that with the increase in flow velocity, the distribution range of the particle concentration reaches the widest, and the particles gradually decrease from the pipe wall to the middle of the flow channel. Compared to the first two working conditions, the particle concentration distribution is more uniform, about 0.001 mg/um^3. When the flow velocity is 1 m/s, the transmembrane pressure difference is the largest, as shown in Figure 6d, which is more conducive to the improvement in membrane water productivity.

Figure 9 shows the average particle concentration in the local zone near the wall at 0.6 m/s, 0.8 m/s, and 1 m/s, respectively. Comparing the three working conditions, it can be seen that the overall particle concentration of 0.6 m/s and 0.8 m/s varies greatly, and the difference between the lowest concentration and the highest concentration is 0.0014 mg/um^3. However, when the flow velocity is 1 m/s, the variation range of particle concentration is relatively uniform, and the difference between the lowest concentration and the highest concentration is only 0.0005 mg/um^3, due to the relatively high scour velocity near the surface of the porous media zone.

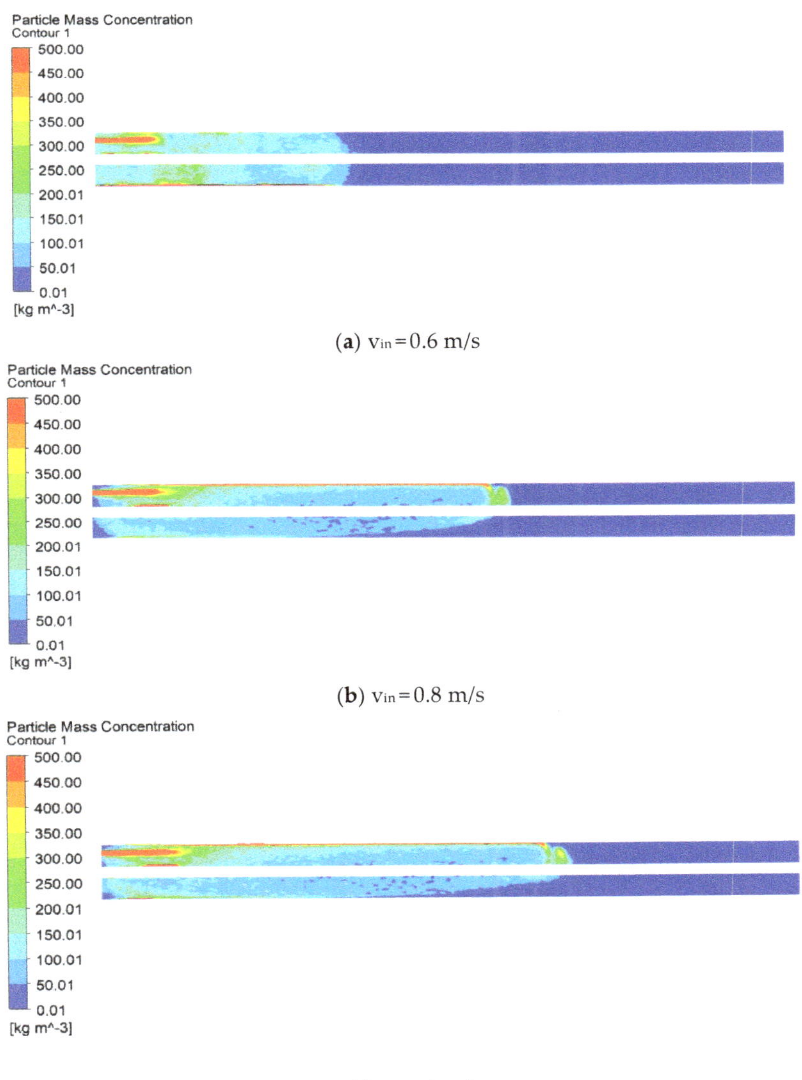

(**a**) $v_{in} = 0.6$ m/s

(**b**) $v_{in} = 0.8$ m/s

(**c**) $v_{in} = 1$ m/s

Figure 8. Contour of particle concentration in $X = 0$ section.

As shown in Figure 10 $v_{in} = 0.6$ m/s, when the flow velocity is 0.6 m/s, comparing the particle concentration distribution under the two working conditions with gravity and without gravity, it can be seen that when the influence of gravity is present, most of the high−concentration particles are concentrated in the lower wall zone, and only a small amount diffuses near the surface of the porous media zone. This is due to the particle's own gravity, which can generate a radial velocity. However, when there is no gravity, most particles follow the fluid along the upper wall, which is due to a radial velocity of 0 from the particle's own gravity.

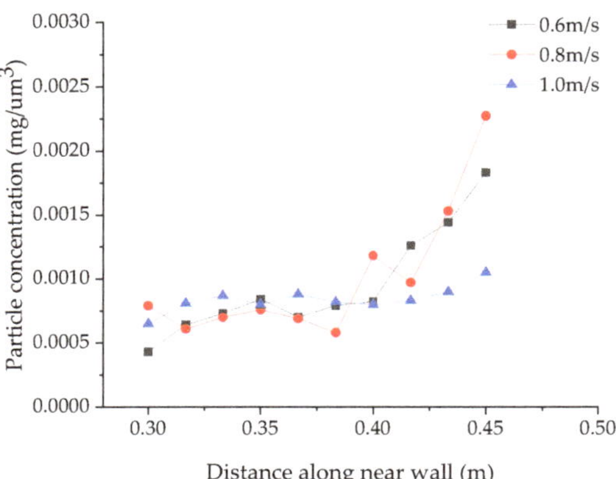

Figure 9. Average particle concentration near the wall.

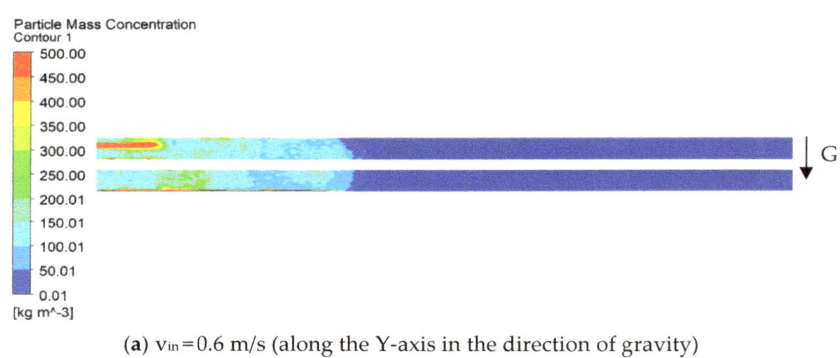

(**a**) $v_{in} = 0.6$ m/s (along the Y-axis in the direction of gravity)

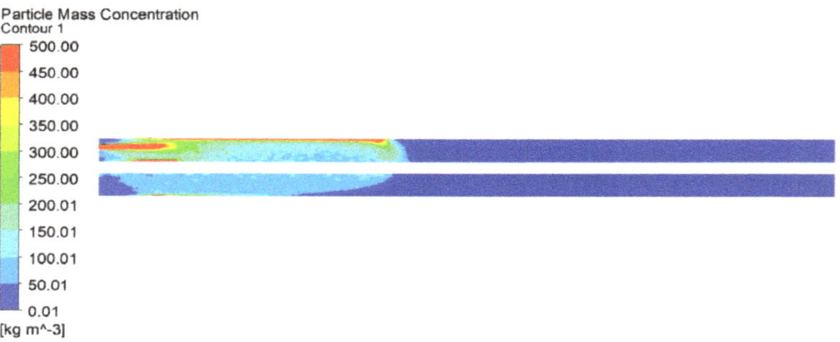

(**b**) $v_{in} = 0.6$ m/s (without gravity)

Figure 10. Particle concentration contours.

The water productivity of different inlet velocities is shown in Figure 11. The results show that when the inlet velocity is 0.6 m/s, the water productivity is 45.2%; when the inlet velocity is 0.8 m/s, the water productivity is 46.1%; when the inlet velocity is 1 m/s, the water productivity is 48.5%; water productivity gradually increases with an increase in inlet velocity.

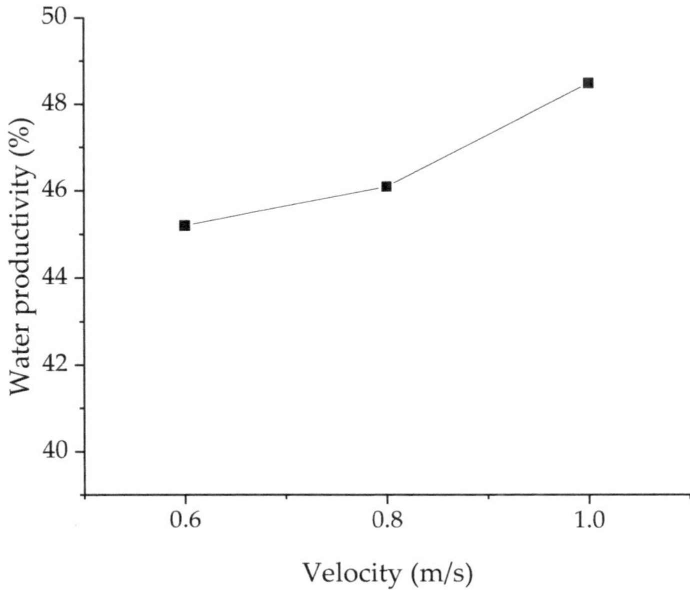

Figure 11. Water productivity with different inlet velocities.

4. Conclusions

In this paper, the micron particle aggregation during the membrane filtration process was simulated under different inlet velocities. The influence of inlet velocity on particle aggregation and water productivity was studied. The following conclusions were obtained:

(1) The porous media model can be used to simulate the flow across the semipermeable membrane, as long as accurate values for the coefficient of viscous resistance and the coefficient of inertial resistance are obtained, via experimental technology.

(2) The particle concentration distribution was affected by different Reynolds numbers. When the Reynolds number is 19,000, the particle concentration near the surface of the porous media zone was higher, and the highest particle concentration reached 0.005 mg/um^3. With an increasing Reynolds number, the particle concentration near the surface of the porous media zone, gradually decreased. When the Reynolds number increased to 31,000, the particle concentration near the surface of the porous media zone was about 0.001 mg/um^3, which was due to the increased scour velocity near the surface. Particle deposition near the surface of the porous media zone was closely related to the Reynolds number. The larger the Reynolds number, the less particles were deposited on the surface of the porous media zone.

(3) The motion of particles in a flow field is susceptible to gravity. When there is gravity, because the particle's own gravity can generate a velocity along the direction of gravity, the particle is easy to deposit and not easy to diffuse. When there is no gravity, particles are more likely to follow the fluid motion and diffuse more freely.

(4) Comparing the three working conditions, when the Reynolds number reached 31,000, the flow velocity near the porous media zone was larger, resulting in a larger trans-membrane pressure difference, which can promote higher water productivity.

This topic only discusses the effect of particle deposition on water productivity at three velocities, and the conclusions obtained have certain limitations. It is hoped that there will be more extensive discussions in the future.

Author Contributions: Conceptualization, P.L., Z.Z., Q.D. and B.C.; methodology, P.L.; software, X.X.; validation, X.X. and Q.W.; formal analysis, P.L., X.X. and Q.W.; investigation, X.X. and Q.W.; resources, P.L.; data curation, X.X.; writing—original draft preparation, X.X.; writing—review and editing, X.X., Q.W. and P.L.; visualization, X.X.; supervision, P.L.; project administration, P.L.; funding acquisition, P.L. All authors have read and agreed to the published version of the manuscript.

Funding: The present work is financially supported by the Key R&D Program of Zhejiang Province (Grant No. 2020C03081), the Joint Funds of the National Natural Science Foundation of China (Grant No. U2006221), the National Natural Science Foundation of China (Grant No. 51676173), and 521 Talents Fostering Program Funding of Zhejiang Sci-Tech University of China. The supports are gratefully acknowledged.

Data Availability Statement: The data that support the findings of this study are available from the corresponding author upon reasonable request.

Conflicts of Interest: The authors declare no conflict of interest.

References

1. Ling, Q.; Zhang, X.; Wu, C.; Ma, Y.; Qu, J. Comparison of the influence of adding modified fly ash and PAC on the operation effect of MBR. *Water Wastewater China* **2015**, *31*, 93–96.
2. Ou Yang, K.; Xie, S. Effect of PAC dosing on sludge characteristics and membrane fouling of membrane bioreactor. *Water Treat. Technol.* **2011**, *37*, 120–122.
3. Feng, Q.; Xue, Z.; Wang, H.; Chen, L. Experimental study on the influence of water flow shear force on the characteristics of activated sludge. *J. Hohai Univ.* **2006**, *34*, 374–377.
4. Karimi, H.; Bajestani, M.; Mousavi, S.; Garakani, R. Polyamide membrane surface and bulk modification using humid environment as a new heat curing medium. *J. Membr. Sci.* **2016**, *7338*, 31733–31734. [CrossRef]
5. Chang, Q.; Zhou, J.; Wang, Y.; Liang, J.; Zhang, X.; Cerneaux, S.; Wang, X.; Zhu, Z.; Dong, Y. Application of ceramic microfiltration membrane modified by nano-TiO$_2$ coating in separation of a stable oil-in-water emulsion. *J. Membr. Sci.* **2014**, *456*, 128–133. [CrossRef]
6. Wei, P.; Zhang, K.; Gao, W.; Kong, L.; Field, R. CFD modeling of hydrodynamic characteristics of slug bubble flow in a flat sheet membrane bioreactor. *J. Membr. Sci.* **2013**, *445*, 15–24. [CrossRef]
7. Radu, A.I.; van Steen, M.S.H.; Vrouwenvelder, J.S.; van Loosdrecht, M.C.M.; Picioreanu, C. Spacer geometry and particle deposition in spiral wound membrane feed channels. *Water Res.* **2014**, *64*, 160–176. [CrossRef]
8. Xie, F.; Chen, W.; Wang, J.; Liu, J. Fouling characteristics and enhancement mechanisms in a submerged flat-sheet membrane bioreactor equipped with micro-channel turbulence promoters with micro-pores. *J. Membr. Sci.* **2015**, *7388*, 30151–30154. [CrossRef]
9. Liu, X.; Wang, Y.; Waite, T.D.; Leslie, G. Fluid structure interaction analysis of lateral fiber movement in submerged membrane reactors. *J. Membr. Sci.* **2015**, *7388*, 30401–30405.
10. Yu, W.; Xu, L.; Qu, J.; Graham, N. Investigation of pre-coagulation and powder activate carbon adsorption on ultrafiltration membrane fouling. *J. Membr. Sci.* **2014**, *459*, 157–168. [CrossRef]
11. Yu, W.; Graham, N. Application of Fe (II)/K2MnO4 as a pre-treatment for controlling UF membrane fouling in drinking water treatment. *J. Membr. Sci.* **2015**, *473*, 283–291. [CrossRef]
12. Qaisrani, T.M.; Sam Haber, W.M. Impact of gas bubbling and backflushing on fouling control and membrane cleaning. *Desalination* **2011**, *266*, 154–161. [CrossRef]
13. Bai, H.; Lin, Y.; Li, N.; Hu, Y.; Jin, Y.; Zhang, J.; Zheng, X.; Ye, J.; Zhang, Y. Research on design and operation parameter optimization of pressure ultrafiltration membrane modules for advanced municipal wastewater treatment. *Membr. Sci. Technol.* **2021**, *62*, 1–12.
14. Han, X.; Wang, D.; Wang, M. Preparation of In-MOF modified polyamide composite forward osmosis membrane and its pollution resistance performance. *Membr. Sci. Technol.* **2021**, *41*, 71–80.
15. Vera, L.; González, E.; Ruigómez, I.; Gómez, J.; Delgado, S. Analysis of backwashing efficiency in dead-end hollow-fiber ultrafiltration of anaerobic suspensions. *Environ. Sci. Pollut. Res.* **2015**, *22*, 16600–16609. [CrossRef]
16. Lu, X.; Zheng, C.; Zhen, G.; Tan, Y.; Zhou, Y.; Zhang, Z.; Niu, C.; Li, W.; Kudisi, D.; Wang, Y.; et al. Roles of colloidal particles and soluble biopolymers in long-term performance and fouling behaviors of submerged anaerobic membrane bioreactor treating methanolic wastewater. *J. Clean. Prod.* **2021**, *290*, 125816. [CrossRef]
17. Bouhabila, E.H.; Aim, R.B.; Buisson, H. Fouling characterization in membrane bioreactors. *Sep. Purif. Technol.* **2001**, *22*, 123–132. [CrossRef]
18. Tay, J.H.; Liu, Q.S.; Liu, Y. The effects of shear force on the formation, structure and metabolism of aerobic granules. *Appl. Microbiol. Biotechnol.* **2001**, *57*, 227–233.
19. Hong, S.H.; Lee, W.N.; Oh, H.S.; Yeon, K.M.; Hwang, B.K.; Lee, C.H.; Chang, I.S.; Lee, S. The Effects of Intermittent Aeration on the Characteristics of Bio-Cake Layers in a Membrane Bioreactor. *Environ. Sci. Technol.* **2007**, *41*, 6270–6276. [CrossRef]

20. Lin, W.; Shao, R.; Wang, Q.; Lei, J.; Wang, X.; Huang, X. Research on optimization of inlet channel of full-effect membrane element based on CFD and RSM. *Membr. Sci. Technol.* **2020**, *40*, 89–94.
21. Momenifar, M.; Dhariwal, R.D.; Bragg, A. Influence of Reynolds number on the motion of settling, bidisperse inertial particles in turbulence. *Phys. Rev. Fluids* **2019**, *4*, 054301. [CrossRef]
22. Ouellette, N.; Xu, H.; Bourgoin, M.; Bodenschatz, E. An experimental study of turbulent relative dispersion models. *New J. Phys.* **2006**, *109*, 1367–2630. [CrossRef]
23. Biferale, L.; Bodenschatz, E.; Cencini, M.; Lanotte, A.S.; Ouellette, N.T.; Toschi, F.; Xu, H. Lagrangian structure functions in turbulence: A quantitative comparison between experiment and direct numerical simulation. *Phys. Fluids* **2008**, *20*, 65103. [CrossRef]
24. Launder, B.E.; Spalding, D.B. The Numerical Computation of Turbulent Flows. *Comput. Methods Appl. Mech. Eng.* **1974**, *3*, 269–289. [CrossRef]

MDPI
St. Alban-Anlage 66
4052 Basel
Switzerland
Tel. +41 61 683 77 34
Fax +41 61 302 89 18
www.mdpi.com

Applied Sciences Editorial Office
E-mail: applsci@mdpi.com
www.mdpi.com/journal/applsci